1–2 CHRONICLES

ABINGDON OLD TESTAMENT COMMENTARIES

1–2
CHRONICLES

STEVEN L. McKENZIE

Abingdon Press
Nashville

ABINGDON OLD TESTAMENT COMMENTARIES
1–2 CHRONICLES

Copyright © 2004 by Abingdon Press

This book is printed on recycled, acid-free, elemental-chlorine–free paper.

Library of Congress Cataloging-in-Publication Data

McKenzie, Steven L., 1953-
   1-2 Chronicles / Steven L. McKenzie.
     p. cm. — (Abingdon Old Testament commentaries)
   Includes bibliographical references and index.
   ISBN 0-687-00750-X (binding: paper, adhesive : alk. paper)
   1. Bible. O.T. Chronicles—Commentaries. I. Title: First through second Chronicles. II. Title. III. Series.

   BS1345.53.M37 2004
   222'.607—dc22

2004005398

All scripture quotations, unless otherwise noted, are taken from *The New Revised Standard Version of the Bible,* copyright © 1989, Division of Christian Education of the National Council of the Churches of Christ in the United States of America. Used by permission. All rights reserved.

The author has on occasion rendered the divine name "Yahweh" rather than "the LORD" as in the NRSV.

The Hebraica® and Graeca® fonts used to print this work are available from Linguist's Software, Inc., PO Box 580, Edmonds, WA 98020-0580 tel (206) 775-1130.

04 05 06 07 08 09 10 11 12 13—10 9 8 7 6 5 4 3 2 1

MANUFACTURED IN THE UNITED STATES OF AMERICA

FOR AIMEE

CONTENTS

FOREWORD

The *Abingdon Old Testament Commentaries* are offered to the reader in hopes that they will aid in the study of Scripture and provoke a deeper understanding of the Bible in all its many facets. The texts of the Old Testament come out of a time, a language, and socio-historical and religious circumstances far different from the present. Yet Jewish and Christian communities have held to them as a sacred canon, significant for faith and life in each new time. Only as one engages these books in depth and with all the critical and intellectual faculties available to us, can the contemporary communities of faith and other interested readers continue to find them meaningful and instructive.

These volumes are designed and written to provide compact, critical commentaries on the books of the Old Testament for the use of theological students and pastors. It is hoped that they may be of service also to upper-level college or university students and to those responsible for teaching in congregational settings. In addition to providing basic information and insights into the Old Testament writings, these commentaries exemplify the tasks and procedures of careful interpretation.

The writers of the commentaries in this series come from a broad range of ecclesiastical affiliations, confessional stances, and educational backgrounds. They have experience as teachers and, in some instances, as pastors and preachers. In most cases, the authors are persons who have done significant research on the book that is their assignment. They take full account of the most important current scholarship and secondary literature, while not attempting to summarize that literature or to engage in technical academic debate. The fundamental concern of each volume is analysis and discussion of the literary, socio-historical, theological, and ethical dimensions of the biblical texts themselves.

The New Revised Standard Version of the Bible is the principal translation of reference for the series, though authors may draw upon other interpretations in their discussion. Each writer is attentive to the original Hebrew text in preparing the commentary. But the authors do not presuppose any knowledge of the biblical languages on the part of the reader. When some awareness of a grammatical, syntactical, or philological issue is necessary for an adequate understanding of a particular text, the issue is explained simply and concisely.

Each volume consists of four parts. An *introduction* looks at the book as a whole to identify *key issues* in the book, its *literary genre* and *structure*, the *occasion and situational context* of the book (including both social and historical contexts), and the *theological and ethical* significance of the book.

The *commentary* proper organizes the text by literary units and, insofar as is possible, divides the comment into three parts. The *literary analysis* serves to introduce the passage with particular attention to identification of the genre of speech or literature and the structure or outline of the literary unit under discussion. Here also, the author takes up significant stylistic features to help the reader understand the mode of communication and its impact on comprehension and reception of the text. The largest part of the comment is usually found in the *exegetical analysis*, which considers the leading concepts of the unit, the language of expression, and problematical words, phrases, and ideas in order to get at the aim or intent of the literary unit, as far as that can be uncovered. Attention is given here to particular historical and social situations of the writer(s) and reader(s) where that is discernible and relevant as well as to wider cultural (including religious) contexts. The analysis does not proceed phrase by phrase or verse by verse but deals with the various particulars in a way that keeps in view the overall structure and central focus of the passage and its relationship to the general line of thought or rhetorical argument of the book as a whole. The final section, *theological and ethical analysis* seeks to identify and clarify the theological and ethical matters with which the unit deals or to which it points. Though not aimed primarily at contemporary issues of faith and life, this section should provide readers a basis for reflection on them.

Each volume also contains a select bibliography of works cited in the commentary as well as major commentaries and other important works available in English.

The fundamental aim of this series will have been attained if readers are assisted not only to understand more about the origins, character, and meaning of the Old Testament writings, but also to enter into their own informed and critical engagement with the texts themselves.

Patrick D. Miller
General Editor

ABBREVIATIONS

AB	Anchor Bible
ABD	David Noel Freedman (ed.), *The Anchor Bible Dictionary* (New York: Doubleday, 1992)
ANEP	J. B. Pritchard (ed.), *The Ancient Near East in Pictures Relating to the Old Testament* (Princeton: Princeton University Press, 1954)
ANET	J. B. Pritchard (ed.), *Ancient Near Eastern Texts Relating to the Old Testament* (Princeton: Princeton University Press, 3rd edition, 1969)
BEATAJ	Beiträge zur Erforschung des Alten Testaments und des antiken Judentums
B.C.E.	Before the Common Era (= BC)
BZAW	Beiträge zur Zeitschrift für die alttestamentliche Wissenschaft
CBQ	*Catholic Biblical Quarterly*
C.E.	The Common Era (= AD)
FOTL	The Forms of the Old Testament Literature
FRLANT	Forschungen zur Religion und Literatur des Alten und Neuen Testaments
FTS	Freiburger theologische Studien
HAT	Handbuch zum Alten Testament
HSM	Harvard Semitic Monographs
HTR	*Harvard Theological Review*
ICC	International Critical Commentary
IEJ	*Israel Exploration Journal*
Interp	*Interpretation*
JBL	*Journal of Biblical Literature*

JSOT	*Journal for the Study of the Old Testament*
JSOTSup	Journal for the Study of the Old Testament: Supplement Series
KAT	Kommentar zum Alten Testament
LXX	Septuagint (the Greek translation of the Old Testament)
MT	Masoretic Text
NCB	New Century Bible
NRSV	New Revised Standard Version
OTL	Old Testament Library
RevQ	*Revue de Qumran*
RSR	*Recherches de science religieuse*
SBLDS	Society of Biblical Literature Dissertation Series
SBLMS	Society of Biblical Literature Monograph Series
SBLSCS	Society of Biblical Literature Septuagint and Cognate Studies
VT	*Vetus Testamentum*
VTSup	Vetus Testamentum: Supplements
WBC	Word Biblical Commentary
WMANT	Wissenschaftliche Monographien zum Alten und Neuen Testament
//	is parallel to
<	is borrowed from

INTRODUCTION

There has never been a better time to embark on a study of Chronicles. Nor is there a better example of the vitality of biblical scholarship than that on Chronicles. Biblical scholarship has had a long tradition of tending to ignore this part of the canon. Its repetition of much of Samuel and Kings, together with its pietism and lateness, led scholars to regard it as unhistorical and uninteresting. But the work of Sara Japhet and Hugh Williamson in the 1960s and 1970s sparked an explosion of interest in the so-called "Chronicler's History" (1–2 Chronicles + Ezra–Nehemiah). Their independent reevaluations of the widely assumed common authorship of these books headed a reappraisal of other features of Chronicles—its historical value, its interpretive strategies, its theology, and, more recently, its literary sophistication. While the history of the academic study of Chronicles cautions against overconfidence in one's conclusions at any given stage, it also illustrates the capacity of biblical scholarship to correct itself and to grow in appreciation and perhaps understanding of its object of study.

OUTLINE AND CONTENTS

Originally a single work, the book of Chronicles may be outlined as follows:

Genealogies (1 Chr 1–9)

The united monarchy (1 Chr 10–2 Chr 9)

The reign of David (1 Chr 10–21)

Transition (1 Chr 22–29)

The reign of Solomon (2 Chr 1–9)

The divided kingdom (2 Chr 10–36)

As the outline indicates, there are three large sections to the book: the collection of genealogies in 1 Chr 1–9 and the accounts of the united and divided kingdoms, respectively, in the remainder of the book. The reigns of David and Solomon, while distinct, are presented as a single era—Israel's "golden age," when it achieved its peak geographically, financially, internationally, and religiously. David is the founder of the nation and its institutions; Solomon brings them to their apex by completing what David had begun. Indeed, the accounts of their two reigns may be perceived as having matching components: David becomes king (1 Chr 10–12), establishes the worship of Yahweh in Jerusalem (1 Chr 13–17), and fights wars that will ensure the tranquility needed to build the temple (1 Chr 18–21). Likewise, Solomon is confirmed as king (2 Chr 1), builds and dedicates the temple (2 Chr 2–7), and reaps the fiscal and administrative benefits of his loyalty to Yahweh (2 Chr 8–9). The two reigns are separated by the transition and preparation for the temple in 1 Chr 22–29.

The outline of 1 Chronicles given above is based on genre (genealogy, narrative, lists) and on the fact that the central section (chs. 10–21) is essentially drawn from the book of 2 Samuel. However, other considerations suggest that the author of Chronicles (commonly called "the Chronicler") may have structured his (the Chronicler was almost certainly a male) account in different ways and at different levels. For instance, the reference to Yahweh handing the kingdom over to David in 10:14 serves with the summary of his reign in 29:26-29 as a literary frame around the account of his reign. In addition, in terms of content, chapters 17–29 might be seen as a unit focusing on the preparations for building the temple. Chapter 17 relates David's intent to build a temple and Yahweh's postponement of it. Chapters 18–20 describe David's wars that would ultimately bring the peace necessary for Solomon to complete the project. Other structuring devices that have been noted by scholars are discussed below under "speeches and prayers." The point is not to try to choose one structural scheme over another or to limit the Chronicler to one. It is rather to point out the sophistication and variety of structural activity represented in the book of Chronicles.

A word about chapter and verse divisions is in order at this point. The current system of division into chapters and verses was invented long after the Bible was written—not until the thirteenth century C.E. and then revised in the sixteenth century. Because it was introduced into the Hebrew text and the versions (e.g., Greek, Latin, English) at different times, the divisions sometimes vary slightly. The first instance of this kind of variation is in 1 Chronicles 6. In this commentary, the English divisions will be followed for the sake of convenience to the reader, with Hebrew numbers in brackets.

NAME

Like all Ancient Near Eastern writings, the book of Chronicles originally bore no title. In rabbinic tradition it came to be called "the matters of the days," typically translated "annals," as in the designation "the Book of the Annals of the Kings" (1 Kgs 14:19, 29; Esth 2:23; 10:2; Neh 12:23; 1 Chr 27:24). The assumption behind this title, then, is that the book of Chronicles was written as or purports to be an official work of historiography in the nature of annals. In fact, this title does not accurately represent the original genre of the work (on which see below). The name "Chronicles" originated with Jerome (in the fourth century C.E.), who referred to it in the prologue to his translation of Samuel and Kings as "Chronicle of the Entire Divine History." Jerome's use of the term "Chronicle" referred to a type of literary work in his day that summarized a broad sweep of history (Knoppers and Harvey 2002). The title was appropriate for Chronicles since its account of history ranged from Adam to the end of the Babylonian exile. Martin Luther (sixteenth century), who was heavily influenced by Jerome, borrowed the title "the Chronicle" for his German translation, which in turn led to its adoption as "Chronicles" in most English Bibles. Thus, while the sense intended by Jerome was lost, the term has come to be the modern title of the book. Jerome's Latin translation of the book itself, however, retained the Septuagint's title, *Paraleipomena,* meaning "things omitted" and implying a parallel, at least in scope, with Genesis–Kings. The title is unfortunate to the extent that it suggests inferiority: "things omitted," that is, things deemed unworthy of inclusion in the earlier corpus.

PLACE IN CANON

English Bibles also inherit their placement of Chronicles from the Septuagint, which first divided the book in two and grouped it together with the other historical books, after Samuel–Kings (1–4 Kingdoms) and before Ezra–Nehemiah (1–2 Esdras). Hebrew Bibles treated Chronicles as a single book until the fifteenth century C.E. and placed it either at the head or the end of the Writings, the third division of the Hebrew canon. Modern printed editions of the Hebrew Bible consistently include 1–2 Chronicles as the final book. The notations by the Masoretic editors identifying the middle (1 Chr 27:25) and end points (at the end of 2 Chronicles, but not 1 Chronicles) show that the two are still considered a single book. The book's location at the end of the Writings should not be understood as a sign that its canonicity was questioned or of its late acceptance into the canon, as is sometimes alleged. In fact, there does not appear to have been much debate about Chronicles' canonicity, perhaps because so much of the book repeats material from other canonical works. The placement and firm acceptance of the book within the canon are further indicated by allusions to it in the first-century works of Josephus (*Against Apion* 1.40) and the New Testament. Josephus's tally of books included in the Bible evidently includes Chronicles. In Matt 23:35 and Luke 11:47-51, Jesus refers to the martyrs in the Old Testament from the first, Abel, to the last, Zechariah. The story of the latter is found in 2 Chr 24:20-22, indicating that Chronicles was at or near the end of what was considered the Hebrew canon.

AUTHORSHIP

Relationship to Ezra–Nehemiah

According to the Talmud (*Baba Bathra* 15*a*), Chronicles and Ezra–Nehemiah were written by Ezra. This understanding of authorship was reversed in 1832 by Leopold Zunz, who contended that it was the anonymous author of Chronicles who had also composed Ezra–Nehemiah. Zunz's conclusion was influential, and the existence of a unified "Chronicler's History" encompassing Chronicles and Ezra–Nehemiah was widely accepted until it came under fire by Japhet (1968, 1997) and Williamson (1977), who have effectively reversed the consensus.

As is often observed, the case for the unity of Chronicles and Ezra–Nehemiah rests on four pillars: (1) the repetition of the Cyrus edict in parallel versions in 2 Chr 36:22-23 and Ezra 1:1-3*a*; (2) the book of 1 Esdras, which contains material parallel to 2 Chr 35–36 and Ezra 1–10; Neh 8 in a single book; (3) linguistic and stylistic similarities between Chronicles and Ezra–Nehemiah; and (4) commonality of theology and outlook among the works. Each of these pillars has been scrutinized in detail over the past four decades. What follows is an attempt to compile and summarize the primary observations that have emerged in the many studies that comprise that scrutiny.

1. Ezra begins where Chronicles ends: the last two verses of Chronicles (2 Chr 36:22-23) and the first two and one-half verses of Ezra (1:1-3*a*) both relate the edict of Cyrus allowing the people of Judah to return home. This overlap clearly implies some kind of relationship between the two books. But what kind of relationship was it? Traditionally, the doublet was taken as a sign of common authorship; the same author took up his work in Ezra–Nehemiah where he had left it off with Chronicles and signaled this by repeating the final paragraph of the earlier work. He even left the ending of Chronicles in midsentence ("let him go up") and concluded the thought at the start of Ezra ("let him go up to Jerusalem, which is in Judah, and rebuild the temple of Yahweh the God of Israel"). But it is just as likely that the doublet was added secondarily to one of the works in order to connect it with the other one, particularly since the canonical order does not match the sequence of events that they relate.

In fact, there are some hints that the version of the edict in Chronicles is by a different writer from the author of preceding material: The introduction to the edict (2 Chr 36:22) uses a different verb for "fulfill" *(kālāh)* from that found in the verse just before it *(mālēʾ)*, and the edict represents the only place in all of Chronicles where Yahweh is called "the God of heaven" (a designation otherwise common in texts from the Persian period). The evidence of the Cyrus edict doublet, therefore, is inconclusive; its interpretation depends on the other indications of common or separate authorship.

2. The "apocryphal" or "deuterocanonical" book of 1 Esdras is a work in Greek translation that dates in its present form to the second century B.C.E. It contains a continuous narrative of material paralleling 2 Chr 35:1–36:23, the book of Ezra (with the addition of 1 Esdr 1:23-24 [Hebrew 1: 21-22] and 3:1–5:6), and Neh 7:73–8:12, ending abruptly with the statement "and they came together" (1 Esdr 9:55). The following chart illustrates the parallels.

1 Esdras	Chronicles–Ezra–Nehemiah
1 Esdras 1 (Josiah's Passover to the exile)	2 Chr 35–36
2:1-15 [Heb. 1-14] (Return under Cyrus with inventory of temple vessels)	Ezra 1
2:16-30 [Heb. 15-25] Letter of complaint from people of the land	Ezra 4:6-24
3:1–5:6 Story of the three youths	No parallel
5:7-70 List of returnees, building of altar, temple building interrupted	Ezra 2:1–4:5
1 Esdras 6–7 temple building resumed, temple finished and dedicated	Ezra 5–6
8:1–9:36 Ezra's mission in Jerusalem	Ezra 7–10
9:37-55 Ezra reads the law	Neh 7:73–8:12

The significance of 1 Esdras for the matter of the authorship of Chronicles revolves around its nature, and the two stances typically taken by scholars regard it, respectively, as a fragment or a compilation. As the fragment of an older, longer work (Cross 1975, 1998:151-72; Howorth 1893; Mowinckel 1964; Pohlmann 1969; Torrey 1910; 1945), 1 Esdras might show that Chronicles and Ezra–Nehemiah were once united as the product of either an author or an editor (on editorial theories see below under "Date and Setting"). The strongest considerations in favor of this position are the abrupt beginning and ending of 1 Esdras and the lack of a clear rationale for its composition. These considerations have come under attack, however, by recent scholarship.

Van der Kooij's re-examination of the grammar and syntax of the Greek at both the beginning and end of 1 Esdras (van der Kooij 1991a; 1991b) has led him to contend that both are deliberate and not the result of accidental fragmentation. Even more significant are recent literary analyses of 1 Esdras that show its dependence on Ezra and indicate that it has ben built around the story of the three youths in 3:1–5:6 (McKenzie 1999:72-78, Talshir 1999:3-109, Williamson 1996). As such, the story in 3:1–5:6 was not a later addition to 1 Esdras, but is the book's centerpiece and perhaps the very reason for its existence. If so, then 1 Esdras does not attest an earlier united version of Chronicles–Ezra–Nehemiah, nor is it merely a compilation. It is best understood as a composition in its own right—one that made use of the materials in Chronicles and Ezra–Nehemiah and revised them for the purpose of including the story of Zerubbabel's wisdom. The most that can be gleaned from 1 Esdras in regard to our present topic is that it may indicate that at the time of its writing (likely the second century B.C.E.) Chronicles and Ezra–Nehemiah were read together as a sequential history that may or may not have reflected original unity. Hence, the evidence from 1 Esdras is also inconclusive.

3. Japhet (1968) first challenged the consensus viewpoint about the linguistic unity of Chronicles and Ezra–Nehemiah, demonstrating the existence of variations in spelling, language, and style, which she regarded as irreconcilably opposed to one another. She concluded that these differences precluded common authorship and indicated that Chronicles was written later than Ezra–Nehemiah. Her position was reinforced by Williamson (1977:37-59), who examined a list of 140 similarities between the works that had been accumulated by previous scholars. Williamson was able to eliminate all but six items as irrelevant or tending to favor diversity of authorship. Polzin (1976) challenged this conclusion, arguing that both Chronicles and Ezra–Nehemiah, except for the Nehemiah memoir in Neh 1:1–7:5; 12:27–13:31, exemplified late biblical Hebrew and thus

favored common authorship. Throntveit (1982) and Talshir (1988) subsequently reviewed these analyses, the former pointing out that "while Japhet and Williamson have provided strong arguments against the ability of linguistic analysis to prove common authorship, they have not shown separate authorship on these grounds" (1982:215) and that Polzin had not demonstrated the common authorship of Chronicles and Ezra–Nehemiah but only that the two works shared characteristics of late biblical Hebrew. Talshir (1988) questioned the claim of linguistic opposition between the two, showing that Chronicles shared more features with Ezra–Nehemiah (minus the Nehemiah memoir) than with Esther or the Nehemiah memoir, thus reopening the linguistic case for single authorship. As with the previous two pillars, therefore, the evidence from linguistic analysis appears to be inconclusive.

A subcategory of linguistic and stylistic analysis—that of compositional style or technique—is more promising. Both Chronicles and Ezra–Nehemiah incorporate genealogies and other lists as well as accounts of cultic occasions. Both also make use of chronological techniques involving dual (i.e., theological and historical) chronologies and the narration of events out of chronological order (Knoppers 2004). But Chronicles typically uses exaggerated numbers, especially in reference to national victories, which is not the case in Ezra–Nehemiah, and while Ezra–Nehemiah cites sources by name, Chronicles typically integrates them without notice of their origin. Knoppers (2004), following Williamson, further contends that the series of challenges in Ezra–Nehemiah, each followed by opposition and then ultimate success, represents a typological structure that distinguishes it from Chronicles. However, he does not consider the degree to which this difference may be determined by the subject matter of the two works and by Chronicles' dependence on its Samuel–Kings source.

4. Traditionally, scholars found the same ideological perspective operating in Chronicles as in Ezra–Nehemiah in such

matters as the centrality of Jerusalem and the temple, details about the temple cult and personnel, and genealogical lists. Again, however, the older consensus has come under strong attack in recent years following the impulse of Japhet and Williamson. The latter pointed out that the Chronicler's stress on "all Israel" (see under "Theology" below) contrasted with the narrow idea in Ezra–Nehemiah of Israel as essentially the Judean and Benjaminite returnees (Williamson 1977). Other key doctrines or themes in Chronicles that scholars have pointed to as represented quite differently or not at all in Ezra–Nehemiah include immediate retribution, the Davidic covenant, the importance of Jacob (consistently called "Israel"), and the role of prophets (Braun 1979, Williamson 1977:60-70). In addition, foreign marriages (especially Solomon's, cf. Neh 13:26), which are strongly condemned in Ezra–Nehemiah, are condoned in Chronicles. Some also argue that the exodus is important to Ezra–Nehemiah but downplayed in Chronicles. Not all such observations of difference in ideology carry equal weight. But the different attitude toward the north and toward mixed marriages, as well as the complete absence from Ezra–Nehemiah of some of the themes of greatest importance to the Chronicler, are difficult to explain under the assumption of a single author. As with compositional technique, then, considerations of ideology seem to tip the scales in favor of a theory of separate authorship.

Some scholars have sought to explain the inconclusiveness or ambiguity of much of the evidence by means of theories that would account for both the distinctiveness of the works and the features they hold in common. For instance, Welten (1973:199) and Willi (1972:179-84) suggest that a single author wrote both Chronicles and Ezra–Nehemiah but as separate books. A more complex reconstruction is that of Cross (1975, 1998:151-72), who posits three editions:

(1) Chr$_1$ = "a genealogical introduction [i.e., the original form of 1 Chr 1–9] + much of 1 Chr 10:1–2 Chr 36:21 + the

continuing Hebrew material in Ezra 1:1–3:13 (= 1 Esdr 2:1-15; 5:1-62);

(2) Chr_2 = 1 Chronicles 10–2 Chronicles 34 + the Hebrew version of all of 1 Esdras;

(3) Chr_3 =1–2 Chr and Ezra–Nehemiah as we have them.

This reconstruction depends upon 1 Esdras being a fragment of an older version of "the Chronicler's History," the case for which is based partly on the perception that the order of materials in 1 Esdras is superior to that of Ezra. But if 1 Esdras actually presupposes Ezra and its materials have been composed around the story in 3:1–5:6, as I have suggested, then Cross's reconstruction cannot be valid. It may still be that some editorial activity bridged Chronicles and Ezra–Nehemiah, especially in Ezra 1–3 where scholars have noted the strongest similarities to and continuity with Chronicles. But such activity has so far not been demonstrated, and the case for it will have to be made on grounds other than the content of 1 Esdras.

INTEGRITY

Besides Cross's reconstruction, there are a number of theories about redactional layers in Chronicles. These theories have tended to follow the models of composition adopted for other sections of the canon. Thus, in the 1920s–1930s under the influence of the Documentary Hypothesis, Rothstein and Hänel (1927) posited a basic narrative in line with the Priestly source in the Pentateuch that received a Deuteronomistic overlay. Then, Welch (1939) went the opposite way, asserting that the original layer, written before the end of the exile showed Deuteronomy's influence and that more Priestly texts were secondary. Von Rad (1930) also emphasized the importance of Deuteronomy for Chronicles but still argued for secondary editing in certain passages about priests and Levites.

A second trend in the 1940s–1950s, represented by Noth (1943) and Rudolph (1955) seems to reflect the influence of the

Deuteronomistic History as Noth understood it. Just as Noth postulated the existence of a comprehensive history of Israel— the "Deuteronomistic History"—by a single author in the books of Deuteronomy, Joshua, Judges, 1–2 Samuel, and 1–2 Kings, so Chronicles was viewed as essentially the work of a single author but with many later additions that could not be ascribed to a single redaction.

More recent decades have witnessed a trend, at least in North American biblical scholarship, toward trying to read Chronicles essentially as a unit by an author who made use of both Priestly and Deuteronomistic materials. Instances of secondary additions are limited, by and large, to three sections of 1 Chronicles: chapters 1–9, 15–16, and 23:3–27:34. Williamson's influential reconstruction, for instance, assigns a scattering of verses within 1 Chr 15–16 and then the bulk of chapters 23–27 to a secondary, Priestly redactor from the same school as the editor who linked Chronicles with Ezra–Nehemiah with the addition of Ezra 1–3 (Williamson 1979a). Other scholars (cf. esp. Japhet 1993; Knoppers 2004) question the identification of all of these verses as secondary and/or ask whether the connections between texts identified as secondary are strong enough as to indicate systematic redaction.

Based on the scholarly treatment of Chronicles' authorship just summarized and in anticipation of the discussion below about the nature and genre of Chronicles and its themes, we may pause here to draw the following portrait of the Chronicler. Chronicles appears to be predominately the work of a single individual. One may occasionally find additions from a later hand. There may even have been a light redaction along the lines proposed by Williamson. But, there is no compelling reason to deny all or most of 1 Chr 1–9; 15–16; 23–27 to the Chronicler. The genealogies and lists of cultic personnel in these chapters are best understood as integral to his work. The Chronicler was most likely male, to judge from what we know of education in Israel and from the book's interest in the exclusively male clergy. His intimate acquaintance with the operational systems of the temple and its personnel, especially the Levites, suggests that he came from those circles. He probably lived in Jerusalem, the cultic and political center of postexilic Judah, now known as the Persian province of Yehud. Jerusalem was also the cultural and literary center of Yehud, and the Chronicler was well read in its literature. In addition to the citations from Samuel and Kings, we will find frequent allusions to other parts of the Hebrew canon, especially the Torah or Pentateuch. The Chronicler did not make such allusions casually or haphazardly; he was a skillful editor and exegete. Above all, he was a sophisticated theologian who used Israel's past to convey powerful, if sometimes subtle, religious messages to his contemporaries.

DATE AND SETTING

The date one assigns to Chronicles is closely related to the view of authorship that one adopts. For instance, if one determines that a single author is responsible for Chronicles and Ezra–Nehemiah, then the entire work must obviously be dated after the missions of Ezra and Nehemiah, 398 B.C.E. according to the late date for Ezra. A theory of separate authorship allows for a wider range of possibilities and makes the date of Chronicles harder to pinpoint. Still, there is an absolute range. The reference to the kingdom of Persia in 2 Chr 36:20 sets the earliest possible date at 539 B.C.E. Then, Chronicles is cited or alluded to in a number of second-century B.C.E. works. Among the most important of these are the Jewish historian Eupolemus (about 158 B.C.E.), the apocryphal or deuterocanonical books of Sirach (about 180 B.C.E.) and 1 Maccabees (about 90 B.C.E.), the biblical book of Daniel (about 165 B.C.E.), and certain of the Dead Sea Scrolls that perhaps date as early as 200 B.C.E. Scholars often contend that the purported lack of Greek influence in Chronicles requires that it be dated earlier than Alexander the Great's conquest of Palestine in 332 B.C.E. But Knoppers (2004) has rightly pointed out the artificiality of this argument, noting that contacts between Greece and Palestine, especially in the literary arena, were broader and earlier than Alexander's conquest in 332. He has also observed that a number of features of the Chronicler's use of genealogies, in particular, can be explained by analogy to Greek historiography (Knoppers 2004).

Within the period beginning with 539 and moving into the second century B.C.E. a variety of proposed settings for Chronicles have been put forward:

1. Freedman (1961) advocated the reconstruction of the temple (completed in 515 B.C.E.) as the most fitting context for the Chronicler's interests in the temple and the dynasty of David. Cross adapted Freedman's view when he dated the original version of Chronicles between 520 and 515 B.C.E. and subsequent editions at around 450 and 400 B.C.E., as described earlier.

2. Williamson suggested a mid-fourth-century date (i.e., around 350 B.C.E.) with a pro-priestly reviser who added a few brief texts about a generation later. Japhet (1993:23-28) also dated Chronicles toward the end of the fourth century, citing, among other considerations, the need for distance from the final forms of the Pentateuch and Deuteronomistic History, as well as Zechariah and Lamentations.

3. A third-century date has been advocated by several German scholars, who initially proposed this date because they took Chronicles as a response to the schism with the Samaritans (e.g., Noth 1987:83-87). But that schism is now dated later. Some scholars continue to advocate this date on other grounds. For instance, Welten (1973:196-98) argues (probably incorrectly) that the battle machines in 2 Chr 26:14-15 were catapults, which were first used in the third century.

The earliest and latest dates are unlikely based on general considerations. Regarding the early date (520–515 B.C.E.), it should be observed that interest in restoring the temple and monarchy to the condition imagined under David and Solomon was not limited to any period in Israel and continued for centuries after the rebuilding of the temple in 515. At the other extreme, the late-third-century date is difficult in view of the allusions to Chronicles in second century literature as described above. Such allusions presuppose the passage of a certain amount of time. Chronicles would have to be completed and have become accepted as authoritative. In some case, it would also have to have been transported to Egypt, translated into Greek, and the translation accepted. Also, while Knoppers's reservations about the claims of the absence of Greek influence are well taken, the complete lack of Greek vocabulary from Chronicles might also caution against too late a date in the third century.

Internal indicators of date may also help to narrow the range:

1. The Davidic genealogy in 1 Chr 3:17-24 extends either nine or fourteen generations beyond Jeconiah, depending on the interpretation of the genealogy. This yields a date between 416 and 336 B.C.E. for the composition of the genealogy, assuming that the author followed it down to his own day. A late-sixth-century date for Chronicles would then be impossible, unless this genealogy is secondary or has been secondarily extended.

2. The reference to darics in 1 Chr 29:7 also precludes a sixth-century date, since they were not minted before 515 B.C.E. and the passage of some time would be required before they came into common usage. However, Mosis (1973:105-06) and Throntveit (1987:97-107) believe that the passage in which this reference occurs is secondary.

3. Second Chronicles 16:9 appears to borrow from Zech 4:10 and 2 Chr 30:6-9 from Zech 1:2-4. Since Zechariah prophesied around 520–518 B.C.E., and some time would be needed for his oracles to be recorded and disseminated, these citations again render a late-sixth-century date for Chronicles unlikely. Citations and allusions to other biblical materials push the date of Chronicles well past 400 B.C.E. These include: the allusions to Malachi in 2 Chr 30:6-9, the influence of Lamentations on 2 Chr 30, and the borrowing of Ezra 1:1-3*a* in 2 Chr 36:22-23

and of Neh 11:3-19 in 2 Chr 36:22-23 and 1 Chr 9:2-17, respectively (Japhet 1993:27). These observations must be tempered, however, by the recognition that 2 Chr 36:22-23 is probably a secondary addition to Chronicles and that the direction of dependence of 1 Chr 9:2-27 and Neh 11:3-19 is not certain.

4. Finally, Japhet (1993:26-27) observes that the view of the clergy in Chronicles, where the singers are regarded as an independent class and the gatekeepers are integrated as Levites, seems more advanced than in Ezra–Nehemiah. This observation assumes that the passages concerning the clergy, especially 1 Chr 23–27, are original to the Chronicler's work and not later additions.

In sum, the narrowest range for the date of composition of Chronicles that the evidence allows is around 400–250 B.C.E., with the second half of the fourth century (350–300 B.C.E.) being perhaps the most likely period within that range. Unfortunately, it is impossible to be more precise. It is also impossible to set the book with any certainty in the context of any historical event or set of events that have been proposed by scholars as its setting.

Discerning the social setting of Chronicles is more promising. Some scholars have focused on attempting to sketch the makeup of the Chronicler's postexilic society. Weinberg (1992), in particular, describes it as a "citizen-temple community" in which the temple served as the center of life for the community of free citizens in Jerusalem in the post-exilic period. Certainly, this is the idealized portrait of Israel that the Chronicler wishes to promote. In addition to being a free citizen, the Chronicler was a member of an elite class in Jerusalem. We have already seen that he may have been a Levite. He was also likely a scribe. He was certainly well educated and very familiar with the literary works that had been produced by the literate elite in Jerusalem. Recognition of this social setting also speaks to the matter of the Chronicler's audience. He would not have been interested so much in addressing the general population of Yehud. After all, many, if not most, of them could not read, and scrolls were not published or widely available. Rather, his primary interest was in the other members of the elite, the political and religious leadership at the core of Jerusalem's society. That was the Chronicler's world.

GENRE AND PURPOSE

Since the purpose of Chronicles cannot be related clearly to any specific historical event, it is perhaps to be sought in the nature of the work itself. A number of different proposals have been offered in this regard, including midrash, exegesis, propaganda, and theology. But each of these seems too limited in scope and none of them by itself fully accounts for all of Chronicles' features. Two recent proposals are somewhat more satisfactory. One of these views Chronicles as a "rewritten Bible." This is a term coined for a kind of early Jewish literature found at Qumran (the site of the Dead Sea Scrolls) and in the work of writers such as Josephus (cf. Knoppers 2004). Basically, such works retell some portion of biblical literature while at the same time interpreting it through paraphrase, elaboration, allusion to other texts, expansion, conflation, rearrangement, and other such techniques, which would be further developed in later Judaism (Kalimi 1995). Understanding Chronicles as "rewritten Bible" (especially a "rewriting" of the books of Samuel and Kings) accounts for many of its features. But it still does not explain the extensive genealogical introduction in 1 Chr 1–9, which, as a whole, is quite different from what one finds in any of Chronicles' biblical predecessors.

The other genre frequently associated with Chronicles at present is that of history writing (Hoglund 1997, Kalimi 1997). What is meant by this literary genre is not an attempt to recount the past "as it actually happened" as the task of modern historiography is popularly conceived, but an effort to "render an account of the past" that leads to or explains the present (Van Seters 1983). The distinction between history and theology is foreign to this genre. Ancient Greek histories also frequently incorporate extensive lists of genealogies. Other items that Chronicles has in common with these histories include the use of speeches composed by the author and source citations as literary devices, the use of specific, albeit exaggerated, numbers to lend authenticity to the work, and the borrowing of earlier narratives without attribution. Like Chronicles, the Greek histories also use stories about prophets as structuring devices and to focus the reader's attention on the author's main themes. But again, the genre of history writing does not explain all the features of Chronicles. Intriguingly, where Chronicles differs from the Greek histories, as well as from the works of the Pentateuchal writers and the Deuteronomistic History is precisely where it resembles the "rewritten Bible" genre—namely in its primary, if not exclusive, reliance on previous biblical works for its historical narrative rather than on a variety of gathered sources (see below under "Sources and Historicity").

Despite its affiliations with these genres, then, Chronicles appears to be a unique work. Van Seters (1997:300) calls it revisionist historiography, and he notes its function as legitimation for the contemporary Jerusalem community and its institutions. Chronicles presents past and present in a complex interrelationship (cf. Japhet 1997:516). The past is idealized—history as it should have been. It is, therefore, not history for history's sake but history interpreted theologically. Israel is not so much a nation as a religious community. The past is treated as authoritative, foundational, and paradigmatic, so that the institutions of the present find their justification in the "golden age" of the past. Perhaps the closest we can come to capturing the essence of Chronicles in a single phrase is to call it a theological rewriting of Bible history for instructional purposes.

TEXT

There are two principal witnesses to the text of Chronicles: the received Hebrew or Masoretic Text (abbreviated MT) and the Greek translation or Septuagint (abbreviated LXX). Unlike the case with other biblical books (especially Samuel), the MT and LXX are generally very similar to each other in Chronicles and do not contain many significant variant readings. Only one fragment of Chronicles containing about a dozen complete words from 2 Chr 28:27–29:3 was found among the Dead Sea Scrolls (Trebolle 1992). For the final two chapters of 2 Chronicles, the book of 1 Esdras is also an important textual witness. Detailed analysis of Chronicles's text is available in the works of Allen (1974a, 1974b) and Klein (1966), and systematic evaluation of the text of 1 Chronicles has been carried out by Knoppers (2004).

SOURCES AND HISTORICITY

The Chronicler's sources may be divided into two large categories: canonical and non-canonical. The former refers to the other biblical books quoted or alluded to in Chronicles. The books of Samuel and Kings are the Chronicler's main source and the basis for his "rewritten Bible." Therefore, our discussion of these sources will focus on how the Chronicler used them. As for noncanonical sources, the questions here have to do with their existence and nature: Did the Chronicler in fact make use of any non-canonical sources, acknowledged or not, and if so, what were they?

Canonical Sources

In addition to Samuel–Kings, the book of Chronicles also attests familiarity with a wide variety of other canonical materials. For the genealogies the Chronicler draws from Genesis as well as Exodus, Numbers, Joshua, Samuel, and perhaps Ruth. His work throughout shows familiarity with the laws in

Exodus, Leviticus, Numbers, and Deuteronomy. He cites from the Psalms, especially in 1 Chr 16, which borrows from Pss 96, 105, and 106. The Cyrus edict and the list of residents of Jerusalem (1 Chr 9:2-17a // Neh 11:3-19) are borrowed from Ezra–Nehemiah, though the former was probably not the Chronicler's work, and the direction of dependence for the latter is disputed. There are also allusions to the prophets—Isaiah (2 Chr 28:16-22), Jeremiah (2 Chr 36:21), Zechariah (2 Chr 36:9), and Malachi (2 Chr 30:6-9), at least.

The Chronicler's use of Samuel–Kings in particular affords a unique opportunity to study the use that a biblical author makes of his source, since we possess both the source and its "rewriting." Chronicles must be read in close comparison with Samuel–Kings but also as a work of literature in its own right. The first approach highlights the overarching themes of Chronicles; the latter shows the sometimes minute changes that the Chronicler made in his Samuel–Kings source in order to bring his themes into relief. In the remainder of this section, we will focus on the former issue—Chronicles in comparison with Samuel–Kings—and the special problems this involves. In the following section we will survey the main doctrines and themes of Chronicles.

The Chronicler clearly anticipates his audience's familiarity with the content of Samuel–Kings in a passage such as 1 Chr 10:13-14, which alludes to episodes of the Saul story that Chronicles does not include. However, the Chronicler probably did not expect his audience to make the kinds of detailed comparisons of his work with Samuel and Kings that modern scholars make. For one thing, copies of those books were not readily available as they are today. At most, the readers of Chronicles were likely generally familiar with the stories he borrowed. It was that general familiarity that allowed the Chronicler to reshape the stories for his own purposes. The larger changes that the Chronicler made in his Samuel–Kings source are obvious and may be placed into the following categories: omissions, rearrangements, additions, and changes.

Omissions

In the first place, the Chronicler is selective, omitting material that does not fit his agenda. Thus, he begins his narrative with David, leaving out all of the material about Saul and the period before the monarchy. He also leaves out the stories of the Bathsheba affair (most of 2 Sam 11–12) and Absalom's revolt (2 Sam 13–20) because of their negative depiction of David, as well as the negative material about Solomon (1 Kgs 11). He omits material about the north, except where it overlaps with Judah, which, as the place of the temple and the Davidic dynasty, is the Chronicler's primary concern.

Rearrangements

The Chronicler also rearranges the material in Samuel–Kings, again for ideological purposes. The best example of such rearrangement is his transfer of the lists and stories of David's "mighty men" from the end of the account of David in Samuel (2 Sam 23:8-39) to the setting of David's coronation in Chronicles (1 Chr 11:10-47) in order to stress the active involvement of "all Israel" in making David king, conquering Jerusalem, and bringing up the ark.

Additions

The Chronicler has added a great deal of material to the Samuel–Kings narrative. All of 1 Chr 1–9 and 23–29 is additional in Chronicles and attests the Chronicler's interests in all Israel, the temple, and the Davidic–Solomonic monarchy, even if some of the material in these chapters is secondary.

Changes

This catch-all term is particularly applicable to the narratives about individual kings in 2 Chronicles, where the Chronicler's evaluation of a king based on the account of his reign may be the opposite of that of Kings or may divide the reign into distinct periods of good and evil. The reason is again ideological, as it illustrates the Chronicler's doctrine of immediate retribution.

In addition to these larger, more obvious changes, there are numerous differences in detail between the narrative of Chronicles and that of Samuel–Kings in the passages they have in common. These have to do with word choice, word order, phrasing, additions and omissions on a smaller scale, and a host of other differences. Until the discovery of the Dead Sea Scrolls, the basic assumption was that all such differences were due to intentional change on the part of the Chronicler, and ideological reasons were often sought as motivations. While deliberate change for ideological purposes remains a possibility, scholarship in recent decades has highlighted two other factors that are of considerable importance for understanding the Chronicler's relationship to his Samuel–Kings forerunner.

The first of these is the matter of the text of Samuel and Kings that the Chronicler had in front of him. Before the discovery of the Dead Sea Scrolls, a common assumption was that the Chronicler's text of these books was essentially what we have in the MT. The LXX of Samuel and Kings was typically ignored or dismissed as interpretive when it disagreed with the MT. But the Dead Sea Scroll fragments of Samuel (4QSam[a]) frequently agree with readings shared by 1 Chronicles and the LXX of Samuel against the MT of Samuel. This set of agreements indicates that the Chronicler's text of Samuel was not the same as the MT but was closer to the version of Samuel translated by the LXX. This in turn means that some differences between Chronicles and the MT of Samuel are actually due to the Chronicler following his Samuel source closely, and this may be the case even in instances where no Dead Sea Scroll fragment exists (Lemke 1963, 1965). This is less of an issue for 2 Chronicles and its parallels in 1–2 Kings, because the text of Kings used by the Chronicler was of the same type as the MT (McKenzie 1985:119-58).

The evidence for a variant textual tradition is one factor that has led some scholars to suggest that the Chronicler's version of Samuel–Kings was actually an earlier edition (not just a variant copy) than the one we now have. One scholar (Auld 1994) has gone so far as to reconstruct a common source (he names it the "Book of the Two Houses") used by both the Deuteronomistic Historian and the Chronicler (cf. McKenzie 1999:80-87 and Auld 1999:91-99). However, the majority of scholars continue to view most of the differences between Chronicles and Samuel–Kings as the Chronicler's doing, though for reasons not always understood, rather than assigning them to his source.

The second factor refining our understanding of the Chronicler's use of Samuel–Kings is the development of a fuller appreciation of the authorial and interpretive methods and techniques used by the Chronicler. The similarity of later Jewish works, which display a further evolution of these methods and techniques, with Chronicles has only recently begun to be explored in depth but has yielded compelling results. Kalimi (1995), in particular, has compiled a host of examples of such exegetical techniques in operation in Chronicles, most of which are not driven by ideology. These include: structuring devices such as narrative resumption and chiasm, allusions to other biblical texts, moving from general to specific or the reverse, catchwords, measure-for-measure comparisons, updating of terminology or style, and the like. Kalimi thus demonstrates that the variations in Chronicles in relation to Samuel–Kings should not be attributed automatically to theological motives but reflect a broad range of literary creativity and expression.

In short, the Chronicler's use of his primary biblical source, Samuel–Kings, was a sophisticated process, textually, literarily, and theologically. The Chronicler borrowed, sometimes verbatim, from his biblical source, which, in the case of Samuel, was a different textual version from that of the MT. At the same time, the Chronicler was not hesitant to revise his source. He made significant changes for theological or ideological reasons. He also reshaped and reinterpreted Samuel–Kings, not just revising it slightly but writing an entirely new literary work. His use of canonical sources, therefore, was not wooden but creative.

Noncanonical Sources

Consideration of non-canonical sources used by the Chronicler involves two questions: whether the source citations in Chronicles refer to actual documents and whether the Chronicler used sources that he did not acknowledge. Both questions, but especially the latter one, touch on the matter of the historical reliability of Chronicles, the assumption being that if the Chronicler used genuine sources, then the reports he drew from them were more likely based on historical events.

The *source citations* refer basically to two kinds of documents—royal or official works of some sort (e.g., "the book of the kings of Judah and Israel") and prophetic works. There are good reasons for believing that both are allusions to Samuel–Kings rather than extra-canonical works (cf. Klein 1992:996-97):

1. The source citations in Chronicles occur at the same places in the narrative as they do in Kings even when they are not at the exact end of the Chronicles account of the king's reign (2 Chr 16:11; 20:34; 25:26), and they are absent where there are none in Kings.

2. Chronicles never refers to "the book of the kings of Judah" and only once, in reference to Jehoshaphat (2 Chr 20:34), to "the book of the kings of Israel." All other cases refer either to Judah and Israel or Israel and Judah, betraying an interest on the part of the Chronicler in including Judah as part of all Israel. Most scholars believe that these titles are interchangeable and refer to the same work, namely the book

of Kings. The variation may be due to the fact that Kings had no set title at the time. But it may also reflect a deliberate effort to make it appear as though the Chronicler had consulted many different sources. The midrash of the book of kings in 2 Chr 24:27 is probably yet another one of the variant titles and a rephrasing of the source citation in 2 Kgs 12:20.

3. Except for 2 Chr 20:34; 32:32 the references to official works do not occur together with those to prophetic sources. This fact leads to the suspicion that the latter are also new titles for sources mentioned in Samuel–Kings. This suspicion is supported by cases such as that of Solomon's reign, where 2 Chr 9:29 refers to three prophetic records instead of "the book of the acts of Solomon" as in 1 Kgs 11:41, even though all of the materials about Solomon in 2 Chr 19 appear to be drawn from 1 Kgs 1–11 with no evidence of other sources.

4. Knoppers (2004) has observed further that the references to prophetic sources in Chronicles usually occur for kings who are viewed positively, indicating that these source citations are part of the Chronicler's larger compositional strategy.

These observations, therefore, indicate that the source citations in Chronicles function as a literary device upholding the authenticity of its account.

If the Chronicler's source citations are all veiled references to Samuel–Kings, it is nearly certain that the Chronicler made use of other sources without attribution. As noted previously, this was a common feature of Greek historiography as well. But the exact nature of the Chronicler's sources is impossible to reconstruct. The content of certain materials, such as genealogies, census records (7:1-5, 6-27, 30-40), and lists of temple personnel suggests their derivation from external sources. The reference to Hezekiah's tunnel (2 Chr 32:30) may have come from oral traditions surrounding the tunnel in the Chronicler's day and need not have been written. Similarly, 2 Chr 35:20 corrects 2 Kgs 23:29, which claimed that Pharaoh Neco went to fight against the king of Assyria. As Assyrian records have shown,

Neco was actually going to the aid of the Assyrians against Babylon. The Chronicler could not have derived this from an exegesis of Kings, so that the postulation of some other source is required. But was that source written or oral, an official document or popular lore?

It is generally agreed that the genealogies in 1 Chr 1–9 come from different sources, as this would explain such features as the variety of genealogical forms included in these chapters, the different amounts and specificity of genealogical material included for different tribes, and the references to events not recounted elsewhere in the Old Testament. But this conclusion says nothing about the nature of these sources—whether they were written or oral, their age, even in some cases the tribe or family group to which they originally belonged. The same might be true for other lists, especially those that are military in orientation. The names may be genuine, but everything else about such lists is the Chronicler's doing. The numbers typically are exaggerated for ideological reasons (Klein 1997), and the settings are likely anachronistic. The Chronicler may have inherited some such lists from preexilic records, but most appear to be records of the postexilic community. The Chronicler has removed them from their original context and placed them in a setting conducive to his purposes. Many scholars, for instance, think that the list of Rehoboam's fortifications in 2 Chr 11:5-10 was actually taken from Hezekiah's reign.

As regards possible unacknowledged narrative sources, scholars have become increasingly sceptical of their existence because of the obvious fit of passages alleged to derive from source material in the Chronicler's program. Such matters as building projects and military victories are typical rewards for faithful kings in Chronicles. It is possible to maintain, as do such distinguished scholars as Japhet and Williamson, that the Chronicler's reports of such items are not wholesale inventions but preserve a kernel of historical authenticity. But such claims are ultimately fruitless.

Any sources the Chronicler did have for these episodes could well have come from a quite different setting and time period. Moreover, the Chronicler likely rewrote his sources, as he did Samuel–Kings. In some cases, his hand was so obviously pervasive that any underlying historical source is impossible to recover.

In sum, the Chronicler's citations of sources all seem to be creative ways of referring to Samuel–Kings; they serve to add a sense of authenticity to his work. To judge from the nature of some materials that he included in his work, the Chronicler may well have had access to sources outside of Samuel–Kings that he did not explicitly acknowledge. Little can be ascertained about the nature of these putative sources precisely because the Chronicler has removed them from their original settings and exploited them for his own purposes.

GENRES IN CHRONICLES

The book of Chronicles employs four basic genres: narrative, speeches (including prayers), lists, and genealogies. (For more detailed categories see De Vries 1989; Kegler and Augustin 1984:26-46.) Most of what has just been discussed regarding the Chronicler's use of sources applies to narrative, so that it need not be treated separately here. The other three genres, though, do merit special attention. Of particular interest in the following survey will be the way in which the Chronicler uses speeches, lists, and genealogies to advance his theological agenda.

Speeches and Prayers

Like other ancient historians, the Chronicler uses the technique of inserting speeches into the mouths of his characters. Thus, except for speeches such as Nathan's oracle in 1 Chr 17 and Solomon's prayer in 2 Chr 6, which are effectively taken from the Deuteronomistic History, the speeches and prayers in Chronicles are the Chronicler's own composition and convey his theological ideas. The speech of Abijah in 2 Chr 13:4-12 is a particularly good example of this practice. This speech is the clearest expression of the Chronicler's view of the northern kingdom and the "all Israel" ideal. A particularly intriguing kind of speech in Chronicles is that of warnings. These are usually given by prophets, but not always. They can appear even in the mouth of an enemy, as the well-known story of Josiah's death at the hands of Pharaoh Neco shows (2 Chr 35:21-22). They function to offer fair warning of impending punishment and one last chance to repent. In that sense, they illustrate the great reach of the patience and mercy of the Chronicler's God.

Von Rad (1966:267-80) found another common genre of speech in Chronicles, an exhortation based on scripture that he called the "Levitical sermon." But this identification has largely been abandoned by scholars, who have pointed out that the designation "sermon" is decidedly Christian and anachronistic and that there is no real evidence that exhortation was a particular activity of the Levites. Von Rad's observation of the way in which speeches in Chronicles appeal to scriptural texts for authority remains valid. Speeches, thus, are one of the means through which the Chronicler offers interpretation of scripture, especially the law of Moses.

Throntveit (1987) analyzed the royal speeches and prayers in Chronicles, identifying several genres of the former that he designated edicts (1 Chr 15:12-13; 22:5; 29:20; 2 Chr 29:31; 35:3-5), rationales (1 Chr 15:2; 22:1; 2 Chr 8:11; 23:25-32; 28:23), and orations with historical retrospects (1 Chr 13:2-3; 29:1-5; 2 Chr 2:2-9; 13:4-12; 14:6; 29:3-11; 30:4-9). Throntveit also observed that the speeches in Chronicles serve various structuring functions. David's three speeches in 1 Chronicles (22:16, 18-19; 28:2-8, 9-10, 20-21; and 29:1-5) and his prayer in 29:10-19 link him with Solomon and highlight the idea of the temple as the project of both kings together with all Israel. David's preparations for the temple are bracketed by his prayers in 17:16-27; 29:10-19. Moreover, Williamson (1982:185-86) has shown that the latter prayer matches the psalm included by the Chronicler in 1 Chronicles 16:8-36 segment for segment. Together, they provide a further framework for the temple preparations in chapters 17–29. In 2 Chronicles, much of the history of the divided kingdom is enclosed in speeches by Abijah (2 Chr 13:4-12) and Hezekiah (2 Chr 30:6-9) that call for repentance and display an openness toward the residents of the north.

Lists

Lists are common in Chronicles, especially in 1 Chronicles where they dominate chapters 1–9 (genealogies), 11–12 (military personnel), and 23–28 (cultic personnel and artifacts). The following sample of lists found in Chronicles is based on that compiled by Japhet (1993:40), exclusive of the genealogies. Within 1 Chr 1–9 are lists of the kings of Judah (1:43-51; 3:10-14), David's sons (3:1-9), cities (4:28-33), census lists (7:1-5, 6-11), and inhabitants of cities (9:3-17, 35-38). Other lists occurring outside of these chapters are those of warriors (1 Chr 12:3-8, 10-14), officials (1 Chr 18:15-17; 27:25-34), building materials (1 Chr 22:3-4; 29:2-5, 7-8), clerical orders (1 Chr 24:7-18; 26:1-11, and others), military divisions (1 Chr 27:1-15), tribal leaders (1 Chr 27:16-22), temple vessels and furnishings (1 Chr 28:14-18; 2 Chr 4:12-22), cities (2 Chr 11:6-10), and Rehoboam's wives and sons (2 Chr 11:19-21).

Such lists play an important literary role in the Chronicler's overall presentation, as they provide his account with an aura of facticity and thus bolster the perception of the historical reliability of his account. They can also serve an ideological purpose, comparable to that of genealogies, by connecting families and even individuals of the Chronicler's own day with specific roles in the temple cult. Some of the lists are drawn from canonical writings. As discussed above under "Sources and Historicity," some are likely derived from external sources. However, there are indications, to be explored in the commentary, that the Chronicler has removed some such lists from their original settings and placed them in entirely new and different contexts. Since the lists serve a literary function, it is also not impossible that the Chronicler has invented some lists on his own.

Genealogies

Chronicles begins with the most extensive collection of genealogies in the Bible (1 Chr 1–9), and other genealogies occur elsewhere, especially in 1 Chr 23–27. The definitive study of genealogies as a biblical genre is that of Wilson (1977), who points out that genealogies were rarely fixed lists of names but were "living" documents with religious, political, or social functions. They were used, as Ezra 2:59-63 indicates, to determine the legitimacy or status of individuals or families within a community (e.g., Israel or one of its tribes) or guild (e.g., priests). As such, kinship terms might reflect some other kind of relationship. Clans or tribes that had established a treaty could appear as brothers in a genealogy. The founder of a village or trade might be referred to as the "father" of the community or guild.

A linear genealogy, one that traced a single line of descent, sought to legitimate the last-named individual by demonstrating direct descent from an established, prominent ancestor. A segmented genealogy, one that gave different branches of a family, expressed relationships between those branches, whether they were political, social, or familial in nature. Genealogies, therefore, were fluid rather than static; they reflected social and political changes. The addition or deletion of a name likely reflected the gain or loss of status on the part of a tribe or clan. The same is true for a change in the order of names in a genealogical list.

Genealogies could also have an ideological purpose. The listing of many progeny might be understood as a tangible sign of Yahweh's blessing. They could also have a more specific ideological goal. The genealogy of David in 1 Chr 2:10-15, for instance, seeks to connect him to Judah through Ram and Salma and thus to crystallize his Judahite heritage. First Chronicles 6:16-30 [Heb. 1-15] contains an effort to identify Samuel as a Levite because of the priestly functions that he exercises in the narratives about him.

THEOLOGY

It is easy for modern readers to get lost in the repetitiveness of Chronicles's lists and genealogies and fail to appreciate its theological nature. But Chronicles is, above all, a theological work. The interest in presenting a theological interpretation of history somewhat different from that already available in the Deuteronomistic History is what drove the Chronicler to write this work in the first place. There are four widely recognized theological emphases in Chronicles. They are: Davidic-Solomonic kingship, the temple, "all Israel," and divine retribution and reward.

Davidic-Solomonic Kingship

There is disagreement among scholars about the role of the Davidic kingship in Chronicles. Some (cf. Kelly 1996) see it as the grounds for the Chronicler's eschatological hope for the restoration of Israel to its former splendor, while others (cf. Riley 1993) argue that it functions only or primarily to legitimate the postexilic temple cult. In the latter view, David and Solomon are subordinated to the temple. They are important only for their role in establishing and then, along with subsequent kings, providing for the temple worship.

While a case can be made for both of these positions, the nod should probably be given to the former. Chronicles is quite clear that kingship and the kingdom in Israel ultimately belong to God (1 Chr 10:14; 17:14; 29:23; 2 Chr 9:8; 13:8). God chose to exercise kingship over Israel through David and his line. Thus, he turned the kingdom over to David (1 Chr 10:14) and placed Solomon on his (God's) throne (1 Chr 29:23; 2 Chr 9:8). The covenant with David (2 Sam 7) is interpreted in Chronicles as a unilateral promise (2 Chr 13:7; 21:5). It is a theological declaration that David's dynasty is the only legitimate ruling house over Israel. That is why the north's rebellion against the house of David is apostasy against God (2 Chr 13:5-7). Since kingship is grounded in God, however, there is no question that it will continue beyond the exile.

That having been said, it is also the case that the reigns and deeds of David and Solomon revolve around the temple in Chronicles. The three great events of David's reign are the transfer of the ark to Jerusalem, the founding of the dynasty, and the preparation for building the temple. David establishes the music and orders of musicians and other cultic personnel for the worship in the temple. The account of Solomon's reign is focused on his building of the temple. But to claim that their sole function is to serve the temple and legitimate its cult probably does not do justice to the full treatment of kingship in Chronicles. After all, one of David's great deeds was the establishment of the dynasty. David and Solomon are the founders of Israel's ruling dynasty as well as the founders, in many ways, of its faith. It is also striking in this regard how little attention the Chronicler devotes to the high priest, something that is difficult to explain if the Davidic king is subordinated to the temple in the Chronicler's theology.

The Chronicler presents the reigns of David and Solomon together as a kind of "golden age" for Israel. Hence, it is appropriate to speak of the "Davidic-Solomonic kingship" as a single era in Israel's history in Chronicles. The Chronicler idealizes both kings, omitting all of the negative material about Solomon and most of it about David. He presents the two of them as equal in importance, though for different reasons: David established the dynasty and brought about the peace necessary for the temple's construction; Solomon built the temple and enhanced Israel's international prestige and prosperity. All of these accomplishments were divine gifts in response to their faithfulness.

Temple

While David and Solomon do not function in Chronicles merely to serve the temple, it is fair to say that the temple, its personnel, and the activities that take place there represent the Chronicler's dominant concern. The Chronicler wishes to demonstrate the centrality of Israel's religious life, with its heart in the temple, to its existence as a people. Writing after the reconstruction of the temple, he may also be advocating a restoration of temple worship to the place it held during the period of Israel's grandeur.

In 1 Chr 1–9, the genealogy of the Levites, the temple personnel, is one of the longest in 1 Chr 1–9 and is the centerpiece of that collection. As we have seen, David's career as king in Chronicles revolves around the temple. He brings the ark up to Jerusalem in 1 Chr 13–16 and prepares for the construction of the temple in chapters 22–29, which also list the divisions of temple personnel. The very blueprint of the temple is delivered by God to David (1 Chr 28:19). The Chronicler even risks tarnishing David's reputation somewhat by including the story in 1 Chr 21 in order to explain how the location of the temple altar was divinely ordained. Solomon is chosen as David's successor for the express purpose of building the temple, and that is the focus of the account of his reign. The north's abandonment of the temple in Jerusalem and the appointment of a rival priesthood constitute rejection of Yahweh and apostasy; the temple is what signals Yahweh's presence with Judah (2 Chr 13:8-12).

The remaining kings of Judah are evaluated primarily on their faithfulness in maintaining the proper worship of Yahweh at the temple. Hezekiah, in particular, is cast as a model in his own right, albeit in the tradition of David and Solomon, when he restores the temple worship and celebrates the Passover (2 Chr 29–30). Hezekiah's story is also important for showing that the Chronicler's emphasis on adherence to proper ritual and practice was not rigid. Hezekiah prays for those whose hearts were set on seeking Yahweh but who were not ritually clean for Passover observance as prescribed, and his prayer is heard (2 Chr 30:18-20). For all of the importance that he attaches to rules and liturgy, the Chronicler recognizes that it is not these but the attitude of the worshiper that forms the essence of religion that is pleasing to God.

All Israel

Chronicles does not recount the history of the northern kingdom except when it overlaps with that of Judah. It used to be widely thought that this was because the Chronicler shared the perspective of Ezra–Nehemiah that the northerners were, in essence, foreigners and no longer part of the chosen people. But in his breakthrough study on *Israel in the Books of Chronicles,* Williamson showed that the Chronicler's attitude toward the north was much more nuanced than was commonly allowed. For the Chronicler, the northern kingdom is politically and religiously illegitimate and therefore does not merit a separate record. But the citizens of the north are not entirely omitted from Chronicles, nor are they regarded as no longer having a heritage in Israel. To the contrary, the vision of "all Israel" united under the Davidic king is part of the Chronicler's ideal for restoration.

To begin with, the genealogy that opens Chronicles and characterizes the ideal extent of Israel includes the northern tribes. The patriarch Jacob is always called Israel in Chronicles, suggesting that the nation is composed of all his descendants, north and south. The enthronements of both David and Solomon are celebrations in which "all Israel" takes part (1 Chr 11:1; 28:1). All Israel is also involved in the conquest of Jerusalem (1 Chr 11:4), the transfer of the ark (1 Chr 13:2), and the building and dedication of the temple (2 Chr 1:2; 7:8). The division of the kingdom is an act of rebellion against the Davidic line and, in a sense, against Yahweh, who awarded the kingship to David. But it was an act perpetrated by Jeroboam and "certain worthless scoundrels," not by all northerners, and the rebellion succeeded because of Rehoboam's youth and inexperience (2 Chr 13:5-7). Some kings of Judah are described as extending their dominion, quite properly, into northern territory (e.g., 2 Chr 15:8; 17:2). Jeroboam led the Israelites into apostasy (2 Chr 13:8-9). But the Chronicler shows that the division of the kingdom did not remove the north from Israel. They are still the people of Yahweh and the brothers and sisters of Judah (2 Chr 13:12). True Israel is those descendants of Jacob who remain faithful to the God of Israel and the institutions in Jerusalem that he established (2 Chr 13:10-11). Even though the Israelites have abandoned Yahweh, they can still repent and return, just as the people of Judah forsake God but then repent at several points in their history. Thus, the Chronicler invites the northerners to return not only through the speech of Abijah in 2 Chr 13 but also through accounts of their participation in the reforms of other kings of Judah, especially Hezekiah (2 Chr 34:6, 9, 21), who is the first king since Solomon to restore worship on the part of united Israel in Jerusalem (2 Chr 30:1, 25-26; 31:1).

Retribution, Reward, Responsibility, and Repentance

Scholars often speak of the principle of "immediate retribution" in Chronicles. The principle is articulated in David's address to Solomon in 1 Chr 28:9: "If you seek him, he will be found by you; but if you forsake him, he will abandon you forever." Since the principle has a positive component as well as a negative one, it is more appropriately called the principle of immediate reward or retribution. The principle surfaces first with Saul in 1 Chr 10:13-14: "So Saul died for his unfaithfulness. . . . Therefore Yahweh put him to death and turned the kingdom over to David. . . . " But it is most apparent in the Chronicler's treatment of kings in 2 Chronicles. It is "immediate" because the reward or punishment takes place in the king's lifetime. This principle, then, coincides with that of individual responsibility. When the people of Judah are punished or rewarded, it is because they choose to follow the lead of their king. Each person and each generation is responsible for his or her own behavior.

The principle of immediate retribution is one of the tools used by the Chronicler to interpret his Deuteronomistic source, especially in Kings. While he generally follows the Deuteronomist's evaluation of the kings of Judah, the Chronicler sometimes sees disasters that befall certain kings according to the book of Kings as divine retribution for sin. The reigns of several kings are even divided into a period of faithfulness followed by reward, and unfaithfulness followed by punishment (e.g., Asa, 2 Chr 14–16; Jehoram, 2 Chr 21; Joash, 2 Chr 24; Amaziah, 2 Chr 25; Uzziah, 2 Chr 26), or vice versa (esp. Manasseh, 2 Chr 33). The rewards that become characteristic of the Chronicler's account of history include "rest" and "quiet," building activity, military strength, a large family, wealth, international reputation, and respect from subjects. The Chronicler typically uses the verb "to succeed, prosper" to express the reward for righteous behavior (1 Chr 22:11, 13; 29:23; 2 Chr 7:11; 14:6; 20:20; 26:5; 31:21; 32:20). While punishment follows evildoing, the process is not mechanical. There is always a chance for repentance and typically a prophetic warning, which makes the reading audience aware of the availability of forgiveness for repentance.

SUPPORTING THEMES

In addition to the major theological emphases just outlined, a number of themes appear in Chronicles that appear to reflect special interests on the part of its author. These themes serve to support and enhance the major theological tenets of the book.

Prophets

Prophets are accorded an exalted role in Chronicles. Kings are rebuked on account of the prophets and ordered not to harm them (1 Chr 16:22). The special significance attached to them by the Chronicler is indicated in 2 Chr 20:20: "Believe in Yahweh your God and you will be established; believe his prophets." One's receptivity toward Yahweh's prophets is equated with receptivity toward Yahweh himself.

References to prophets in Chronicles are of four kinds: prophets mentioned in source citations, prophetic stories borrowed from Samuel–Kings (Nathan, Gad, Shemaiah, Micaiah, and Huldah), prophetic stories without parallel in Samuel–Kings but about prophets mentioned therein (Shemaiah, Hanani, Jehu, Elijah, Jeremiah), and stories about prophets not mentioned in Samuel–Kings (Azariah, Jehaziel, Eliezer, Zechariah, Oded, and an anonymous man of God). The oracles of the prophets in the last two categories are most likely compositions of the Chronicler and fit the warning and judgment functions that he typically assigns to prophetic speeches. As Yahweh's mouthpieces, the prophets warn of impending retribution in order to effect repentance. They also assign responsibility for misdeeds and announce impending retribution and reward.

Levites

The Levites are a particularly significant component of the daily operation of the temple in Chronicles. The book contains a variety of materials pertaining to the Levites, including: a list of high priests (1 Chr 5:27-41 [Eng. 6:1-15]), genealogies for Gershom, Kohath, and Merari with Samuel's genealogy inserted into that of the Kohathites (1 Chr 6:1-15 [Eng. 6:16-30]), a genealogy for Kohath, Gershom, and Merari ending with the singers, Heman, Asaph, and Ethan (1 Chr 6:16-32 [Eng. 6:31-47]), and a list of Levitical cities (1 Chr 6:39-66 [Eng. 6:54-81]).

Chronicles also ascribes a wide variety of tasks to the Levites, especially in 1 Chr 23–26. These include teaching, maintenance of objects in the temple, gatekeepers and bakers (1 Chr 9:31), serving as judges in Jerusalem (1 Chr 19:8-11), scribal activity, and singing and praise. Presumably, these were the roles of the

Levites in the Chronicler's day, and he traces them back to the time and authority of David. This presentation suggests that there were tensions in the postexilic period concerning the role of the Levites and that the Chronicler seeks to legitimate his organizational scheme by appealing to Davidic authority.

Of particular interest is the place of the Levitical singers in Chronicles. Uniquely in Chronicles, a prophetic role is ascribed to the Levitical singers (1 Chr 25; 2 Chr 20; 29; 34:30; 35:15). Petersen's 1977 study of this matter concluded that the Levites did not adopt this role in the monarchic period but that these texts reflected the Chronicler's effort to support the singers' claim to cultic authority in his day. Other scholars have noted significant differences in the various lists and references to the Levitical singers in Chronicles and Ezra–Nehemiah. For instance, the list of returnees from exile (Ezra 2:41 // Neh 7:44) calls the singers the "sons of Asaph" and does not seem to reckon them as Levites. But other texts (1 Chr 9:2, 14-16 and Neh 11:3, 15-18) do reckon them as Levites and divide them into two groups, the sons of Asaph and the sons of Jeduthun. Other lists mention three groups—the sons of Asaph, Heman, and Jeduthun (1 Chr 16:37-42; 2 Chr 5:12; 29:13-14; 35:15). Still others have Ethan in place of Jeduthun, and Heman seems to be the most prominent (1 Chr 6:31-48 [Heb. 16-33]; 15:16-21). These differences may represent developmental stages, as some scholars have argued (Gese 1963). In any case, they probably reflect sociological changes over time as well as different writers (either sources used by the Chronicler or later additions to his work) in their composition. Hence, the organizational scheme of temple personnel was in flux before the Chronicler's time and perhaps afterwards, and he may not have been the last writer to try to legitimate the practice of his day by grounding it in the time of David.

Scripture

An intriguing feature of Chronicles is the increasing extent to which the word of God derives not from inspired individuals but from codified, written tradition. There are appeals to the law of Moses (1 Chr 15:15; 2 Chr 35:6), which was in written form, as demonstrated by the Josiah's discovery of the book of the law (2 Chr 34:21). But the Chronicler also makes reference to books written by prophets, as we have seen (e.g., 1 Chr 29:29; 2 Chr 36:22). If we are correct in concluding that these actually refer to material in Samuel–Kings, the Chronicler may already be working with the tradition that identified these books as "Former Prophets." Even the design of the temple is given in writing to David (1 Chr 28:19). In short, Chronicles seems to represent a crucial stage in the development of scripture, wherein the locus of authority is seen increasingly to be in the written word. This stage is comparable to the identification of the Levitical singers as prophets. In both instances, authoritative leadership is transferred from a charismatic figure to tradition (law, songs, etc.) recorded in writing. In this development, the Chronicler again reflects his time.

Personal Attitudes

Despite the Chronicler's emphasis on proper ritual and obedience to prescription, it would be a grave error to conceive of him as a rigid legalist. We have already seen the allowance made for those at Hezekiah's celebration of the Passover whose heart was in the right place even though they were ritually unclean (2 Chr 30:18-20). In the same vein, the Chronicler consistently emphasizes the attitude of those involved in cultic celebration. Joy is a regular feature of the cultic celebrations described in Chronicles— at David's coronation (1 Chr 12:39-40 [Heb. 40-41]), in preparing to build the temple (1 Chr 29:9, 17, 22), at the dedication of the temple (2 Chr 7:10), and at the celebration of the Passover (2 Chr 30:25). These occasions also showcase the generosity and voluntary spirit of both king and people. The best instance of these displays is in the account of David's preparations for temple building (1 Chr 28–29). David instructs Solomon to serve Yahweh with a whole heart and willing spirit (28:9), and the people indeed follow their king, contributing voluntarily with great joy and generosity to the project of building the temple (1 Chr 29, esp. vv. 9, 17, 22). But on other occasions as well, the king's generosity in supporting an occasion of cultic and popular celebration is highlighted. Hezekiah (2 Chr 29:20-24, 31-35; 20:24-25) and Josiah (2 Chr 35:7-9), in particular, follow Solomon's example (2 Chr 7:5) in such generous provisioning. In other cases, it is the people who display remarkable generosity. In 1 Chr 12:40 [Heb. 41] it is people from northern tribes who come with generous provisions to share with their brothers and sisters; in 2 Chr 31:4-10 it is the citizens of Judah who willingly bring their tithes and generous contributions to the celebration.

Vocabulary

One of the clearest ways in which the Chronicler articulates themes and theology that are important to him is by the repetition of words and expressions that he invests with particular significance. Some of the Chronicler's characteristic vocabulary, such as "success," "rest" and quiet, "willingness," and a "complete heart," have already been touched on above. A handful of others merit attention.

The verb "to be unfaithful, rebellious" is the Chronicler's typical way of expressing disobedience or unfaithfulness to Yahweh. It is the reason for Saul's rejection (1 Chr 10:13), apparently involving "seeking" (see below) help from a medium rather than from Yahweh. But Saul is not alone. "Unfaithfulness" or "rebellion" is committed by kings when they become well established and prosperous (2 Chr 12:2; 26:16, 18). "Faithlessness" is characteristic of the reign of Ahaz, the worst king of Judah according to Chronicles (2 Chr 28:19, 22; 29:6). It is the term used to account for the apostasy of the north leading to the demise of the nation (1 Chr 5:25; 2 Chr 30:7) and for that of Judah bringing on the exile (2 Chr 36:14).

Unfaithfulness does not mean that disaster is inevitable. It may be averted, or further punishment avoided by "humbling oneself." That is the force of Yahweh's response to Solomon's prayer at the dedication of the temple (2 Chr 7:14). Thus,

Rehoboam's punishment at the hands of Shishak is diminished because he humbled himself (2 Chr 12:6-12). Hezekiah pleads with the northerners to humble themselves and return to Yahweh represented by the institutions in Jerusalem (2 Chr 30:6-11). Hezekiah's own humility helps him avoid Yahweh's wrath (2 Chr 32:26). It also leads to Manasseh's return from captivity (2 Chr 33:12-14) and might have saved Josiah (2 Chr 34:27) had he not ignored Neco's warning. The Chronicler's use of this expression suggests that for him the basic cause of sin is arrogance or pride.

In addition to humbling themselves, 2 Chr 7:14 calls for the penitent to pray and to seek Yahweh. Prayer is effective in rescuing Hezekiah from Sennacherib (2 Chr 32:20) and in extending his life (2 Chr 32:24). It also contributes to Manasseh's restoration (2 Chr 33:13). Seeking Yahweh is perhaps the Chronicler's favorite expression for personal devotion to God. There are two verbs for "seek" in Hebrew (*dāraš* and *biqqēš*), and while the former often has the nuance of "seek information, divine," as in the reference to Saul in 1 Chr 10:13, the Chronicler appears to use them more or less synonymously (cf. 1 Chr 16:11). Even in Saul's case, the verb seems to have broader implications concerning his entire life rather than being limited to the incident with the medium. The idiom occurs throughout 2 Chronicles but is especially frequent in the account of Asa's reign. In that context, the prophet Azariah articulates the principle that Yahweh will be found by those who seek him but will abandon those who abandon him (15:2, cf. v. 15). A sense of the profundity of meaning that the Chronicler attaches to the word is seen in 15:12-15, where Asa's subjects enter into covenant to "seek" Yahweh* with all their heart, soul, and desire, and those who do not seek him are executed. The latter usage implies a specifically cultic nuance, but in the broader context it is clear that the Chronicler has in mind a deep, personal devotion to God of which cultic activity is only a superficial manifestation.

Finally, the common word *ḥesed* ("loyalty, loving-kindness, steadfast love") occurs repeatedly in Chronicles in the refrain "his steadfast love endures forever" (1 Chr 16:34, 41; 2 Chr 5:13; 7:3, 6; 20:21). Its repetition is a constant reminder of Yahweh's love and mercy to those who remain loyal to him. Indeed, if one were constrained to sum up the Chronicler's theology in a single word it would have to be this one. The temple is a constant symbol of Yahweh's *steadfast love* and *loyalty* toward Israel and is also a reward for the *loyalty* of David and Solomon, who model it for all Israel for all time. Yahweh desires that his people remain *steadfast* in their *love* and devotion to him. When they do so, he rewards them. When they go astray into acts of unfaithfulness, he punishes them. But Yahweh never removes his *steadfast love* for Israel; that remains constant.

*All translations are from the NRSV, unless otherwise noted, except that here the divine name is rendered "Yahweh" rather than "the LORD," as in the NRSV.

COMMENTARY: 1 CHRONICLES

ALL ISRAEL UNITED UNDER KING DAVID
(1 CHRONICLES 1–9)

The first nine chapters of 1 Chronicles obviously constitute the book's first major section. These chapters are, in
effect, one large genealogy—the most extensive genealogy in the Bible. As a whole, this genealogy is segmented rather
than linear. That is, it traces the descendants of all the sons of
Israel (Jacob) rather than following a single line through one
individual of each generation.

Understandably, modern readers find ancient genealogies—
especially one of this length and detail—difficult to appreciate
and often skip over them. After all, we do not have any personal or family stake in them, so that the names, many of
which seem unpronounceable, are meaningless. But a genealogy can be a powerful literary and theological tool, both in the
"big picture" that it provides about the group of people who,
as a whole, are its subject, and in the specific details.

An example from the New Testament may help to illustrate.
The Gospels give two distinct genealogies for Jesus—one in
Matt 1:1-17 and another in Luke 3:23-38. At least part of the
reason for the differences between them is the fact that the
function of the genealogy in Matthew is primarily theological.
Matthew writes for a Jewish or Jewish-Christian audience. He
thus begins the genealogy with Abraham, showing that Jesus,
like his audience, was ethnically Jewish. Luke, in contrast,
traces Jesus' roots all the way back to Adam, making the point

that Jesus' ministry was aimed at all people. This is because Luke's audience was primarily Gentile. Matthew's genealogy draws on stories from the Old Testament, with which his audience would have been familiar. He emphasizes that Jesus was not only descended from Abraham, but also from David. In fact, Matthew's genealogy consists largely of the list of kings of Judah. This is crucial for Matthew, who wishes to show that Jesus was the "Messiah" or "anointed one" in the line of David. No Jew of Jesus' day could have had a more prestigious genealogy. Yet, when one examines stories about the history of Judah in the Old Testament, it becomes evident that this illustrious genealogy was full of sinful individuals. Perhaps part of Matthew's point in the genealogy, therefore, is to suggest not only that Jesus had the right pedigree to be the Messiah, but that his role was to redeem sinful humanity among whom he was born.

Like the genealogy in Matthew, 1 Chr 1–9 introduces the Chronicler's history. It provides a historical, theological, and literary background to the narrative that follows. It then provides a literary link between the list of Saul's heirs (9:35-44 // 8:29-38) and the narrative about his death in chapter 10. Chapter 9, especially, is transitional. If its mention of the exile (v. 1*b*) is original, it makes the point that the postexilic community is continuous with preexilic Israel. In any case, the genealogy of Saul prepares for the narrative about his removal and replacement by David in chapter 10.

Substituting for a narrative synopsis of Israel's history, the genealogy relates who Israel is and then what happened to it. The genealogy gives the reader the sense that God is guiding Israel toward its divinely ordained destiny. It depicts the continuity of Israel by showing how the current constituency of Israel beyond the exile derives from the past. This would have been particularly important for the Chronicler's principal audience—people in the postexilic, Persian period whose connection with their past had been interrupted by the exile. The specifics of the genealogy legitimize the make-up and institutions of the postexilic community and even the place of particular individuals within families or guilds.

As a whole, the genealogy highlights the unity of Israel by including all of the tribes, thereby introducing the theme of "all Israel" that is one of the Chronicler's major theological emphases. The Chronicler's use of the term "Israel" in these genealogies is significant. Israel is in effect Judah. The Chronicler regards the northern kingdom as illegitimate and does not relate its history except where it overlaps with that of Judah. Hence, the fact that he includes the genealogies of the northern tribes in chapters 1–9 is remarkable and indicates that he still considers them a part of Israel, albeit one that is apostate. It is true that there are no genealogies for either Dan or Zebulun. But their absence is probably due to accidental omission or simply because the Chronicler had no real sources of information about the far northern tribes of Asher, Dan, Zebulun, and Naphtali. (See commentary on 7:12, 30-40.) Both Dan and Zebulun are included in the list of the sons of Israel in 2:1-2 and must be considered parts of "all Israel."

First Chronicles 1–9 is actually a collection of shorter, independent genealogies, many of which are borrowed from elsewhere in the Old Testament, especially Genesis 46 and Numbers 26. The mixture of forms (e.g., descending: "the sons of X: Y his son, Z his son, and so on" or "X begat Y, who begat Z"; ascending: "Z son of Y son X, and so on") indicates that this is a collection rather than a single genealogy. In some cases the Chronicler composed a genealogy drawing on the narrative material in Genesis. The genealogical collection consists of three main parts: chapter 1 begins with Adam and extends to Israel (Jacob); chapters 2–8 cover the tribes of Israel; then chapter 9 lists the residents of Jerusalem and the genealogy of Saul. The most extensive genealogies occur for the tribes of Judah, Levi, and Benjamin. As the three tribes that made up Judah, they were the most important and familiar to the Chronicler and his contemporaries. He built the genealogy in chapters 1–9 around these three tribes. Hence, the very make-up of the genealogy betrays two of the Chronicler's theological emphases, since Judah is the tribe of David and Levi is the tribe of the priests.

FROM ADAM TO ABRAHAM (1 CHRONICLES 1:1-27)

The Chronicler begins at the beginning, with Adam. He thus paints the background for his focus on Abraham's descendants, especially the Israelites. These verses well illustrate the nature of the Chronicler's work as a "chronicle" (see the introduction) or epitome of biblical history, since they basically summarize in genealogical form all of Gen 1–11.

Literary Analysis

The first twenty-seven verses of 1 Chronicles move from Adam to Abraham and are closely based on Gen 1–11, especially chapters 5 and 10. Verses 1-4a, 24-27 are linear while the intervening verses are a segmented genealogy with anecdotes. The change in form suggests that verses 4b-23 are either an interpolation or come from a different source than verses 1-4a.

Exegetical Analysis

Verses 1-4 simply reproduce the names from Gen 5 without any narrative information about the characters. The genealogy is selective; there is no mention, for instance, of Cain. The reader must be familiar with Genesis in order to understand that this list is a linear genealogy and each name represents a succeeding generation. In verse 4 the form unexpectedly changes, since Shem, Ham, and Japheth are all Noah's sons rather than his son, grandson, and great grandson, respectively. But again, one must know the story in Genesis in order to recognize this. The LXX reads "sons of Noah" before the three names, a reading that was either accidentally lost from the MT or was added to the LXX (or its underlying Hebrew text) in order to smooth the abrupt change in form.

The change to a segmented genealogy (see introduction under genealogies) with the naming of Noah's sons in verse 4b may begin an addition that extends through verse 23. Not only do verses 4b-23 differ in form from the surrounding ones, but verses 24-27 seem to be the continuation of verses 1-4a. Just as verses 1-4a list ten generations from Adam to Noah, so verses 24-27 list ten generations following Noah up to Abraham. Also, verses 11-16, 17b-24 are lacking in the LXX. While verses 17b-24 may have been lost accidentally, a scribe's eye skipping from Arpachshad in verse 17 to the same name in verse 24, there is no apparent reason for the loss of verses 11-16. Still, the genealogy in verses 17-23 does not fit well with that in verses 24-27; the former does not extend beyond the sons of Joktan, while the latter does not mention Joktan. Therefore, verses 4b-23 were probably originally distinct from verses 1-4a, 24-27. Whether verses 4b-23 were incorporated by the Chronicler or were added later to his work is impossible to tell.

Verses 4b-23 are drawn from the "table of nations" in Genesis 10, which describes how the 70 peoples of the world descended from Noah and his three sons. A glance at a map shows that the "descendants" are all place names. Gomer, Tubal, and Meshech (v. 5) are in Anatolia (Turkey); Javan is Greece; Elishah is Cyprus; Kittim is Caphtor or Crete; and Rodanim is Rhodes (v. 6). Thus, the Japhethites inhabit Anatolia and the western Mediterranean. Cush is Nubia (Ethiopia), and Put is Libya; Egypt and Canaan are transparent (v. 8), so that the Hamites represent Egypt's political sphere. Elam is Persia; Asshur, and Arpachshad are in Mesopotamia; Aram is Syria (v. 17), indicating that the Shemites are those east and northeast of Palestine. These three regions are somewhat artificial, as the text does not follow them consistently. Thus, Kittim (Capthor) is a "descendant" of Japheth (v. 7) but Caphtorim is a descendant of Ham (v. 12), and Nimrod, which is transparently Nimrud in Mesopotamia (cf. Gen 10:8-14), is described as the son of Cush (1 Chr 1:10).

The author in Chronicles has retained the same basic structure and language of Gen 10 while also abbreviating it, as in the account of Nimrod. Even the misplaced reading "and Caphtorim" (v. 12; cf. the correction in the NRSV) and the play on the name Peleg ("divide," v. 19) are retained from Gen 10:14, 25 and are marks of how closely the author in Chronicles has followed Genesis. Differences between the two texts are minor and are typically matters of spelling or minor errors occurring in transmission. In verse 17, for instance, the Hebrew word "sons of" has evidently been lost (cf. Gen 10:22-23) with the result that the names following Aram appear as his brothers rather than his sons. The order of names of Noah's sons is reversed in comparison to verse 4, as is also the case in Gen 10, according to the common pattern of placing the most important last. Shem thus receives pride of place as the ancestor of the Hebrews (the gentilic of Eber) and of Abraham and Israel (vv. 17-23 // Gen 10:22-29).

Theological Analysis

The same themes that were described earlier as present in the genealogies of Matthew and Luke may be perceived in the Chronicler's opening genealogy. Like Matthew's genealogy 1 Chr 1:1-27 highlights national identity by tracing a line more or less directly from Adam to Abraham. This emphasis on being children of Abraham would have been especially meaningful for the members of the postexilic community, who struggled with the issue of national self-identity in the wake of the destruction of the kingdom of Judah and subsequent exile to Babylon. But as with Luke's genealogy, Abraham and his heirs are one component of humanity as a whole. Here, the Chronicler's message is even more powerful. The exile and its aftermath raised questions about Yahweh's supremacy and Israel's place in the world. By beginning with creation, the

Chronicler affirms that Israel's God is the sovereign lord of the earth and all its peoples. Implicit in this doctrine is that of election. While Yahweh controls all nations and peoples, Israel is his unique people and the special focus of his love and attention. The message is one of reassurance. Yahweh has a will and a plan for the future of his people, one that cannot fail.

FROM ABRAHAM TO ISRAEL (1 CHRONICLES 1:28-54)

The next genealogical segment moves from Abraham to his grandson, Jacob, who is always called Israel in Chronicles. Somewhat surprisingly, however, this segment is not at all focused on Isaac but contains a full account of other descendants of Abraham, especially Ishmaelites and Edomites.

Literary Analysis

These verses are basically a segmented genealogy (see introduction under genealogies) leading up to the extended genealogy of Israel beginning in chapter 2. As in the first half of the chapter, all of these materials come from Genesis with occasional adaptation. There are three smaller sections that may seem foreign to the main interest of this genealogy and have been considered secondary additions. These are the descendants of Keturah in verses 32-34, the descendants of Seir in verses 38-42, and especially the list of Edomite kings and chiefs in verses 43-54.

Exegetical Analysis

Verse 27 is transitional. It closes the previous unit; Abraham, the father of the chosen people, is the goal. At the same time, with Abraham the author begins to focus in on the people of Israel, who are the real objective in chapters 1–11. The gloss on Abram's name draws upon Gen 17, and the genealogies in verses 28-54 are also taken from Genesis, as indicated below. The brief genealogy for Abraham (v. 28) is composed on the basis of the Genesis narratives. Isaac is mentioned first in this verse, but the genealogy for him follows the one for Ishmael. Both are signs of the author's primary interest in Isaac. Ishmael's genealogy in verses 29-31 borrows from Gen 25:12-16. The line of Keturah (vv. 32-33) is from Gen 25:1-4. Verse 32 conflates two introductions to Keturah's line—one that follows the pattern in this chapter of Chronicles ("the sons of Keturah") and the other perhaps drawn from Genesis ("[Keturah] bore"), although the form of the verb differs. The reference to Keturah as Abraham's concubine is understandable in the light of Gen 25:6, which refers to Abraham's concubines.

The genealogy for Isaac in verse 34, like the one for Abraham in verse 28, is based on the Genesis stories, and this time the order of the sons, Esau and Israel, follows that of Genesis. The genealogy of Esau in verses 35-37 abridges Gen 36:1-13, revising it to the extent that Timna is referred to as Eliphaz's son rather than his concubine. The line of Seir (vv. 38-42) summarizes Gen 36:20-28. The absence of a genealogical link between Esau and Seir is striking, but it is again a result of the author in Chronicles following Genesis. The list of Edomite kings and chiefs in verses 43-54 adapts Gen 36:31-43. The heading in verse 43 indicates that the author envisions the cessation of Edomite kingship with the beginning of the Israelite monarchy. Hence, the chiefs in verses 51b-54 (NRSV translates "clans") are apparently seen as replacing the kings.

Theological Analysis

Chapter 1, in effect, summarizes the book of Genesis. The non-Israelite genealogies and lists in this half of the chapter have often been seen as the work of an interpolator who evidently wanted to fill out the text with other materials from Genesis, and so they may be. However, they can be seen as quite appropriate to the Chronicler's theological concerns. This second half of the chapter continues to set Israel in the context of the peoples of the earth and hence to recognize Yahweh's universal control as creator. The detailed acknowledgment of the other heirs of Abraham enhances Abraham's importance and suggests that Yahweh may be concerned with peoples outside of Israel. At the same time, the net effect of the genealogy in chapter 1 is also to focus the reader's attention on Israel as the primary object of Yahweh's interest.

JUDAH (1 CHRONICLES 2:1–4:23)

With chapter 2 the Chronicler begins his detailed genealogies of the individual tribes of Israel. Judah's preeminence in the Chronicler's outlook is indicated by its primacy of place in the genealogies, a point made explicit in 1 Chr 5:2.

Literary Analysis

The list of the twelve sons or tribes of Israel in 2:1-2 is transitional. It provides the goal and hence the conclusion of the genealogies in chapter 1. Its placement accords with the pattern in chapter 1 of placing the genealogy of the favored individual or group last, since Israel's genealogy follows Esau's. At the same time, it serves as a heading of sorts for the extended genealogies in chapters 2–9.

Following the list in 2:1-2, the Chronicler launches into detailed genealogies of the individual tribes, beginning with Judah, in 2:3–4:23. The unique order of tribes in chapters 2–8 has occasioned a good deal of discussion among scholars, but it remains unexplained. The one thing that seems clear is that three tribes—Judah, Levi, and Benjamin—provide the framework around which the other tribes are listed. These three tribes claim the most extensive genealogies in chapters 1–9. As constituents of postexilic Judah, they were the three tribes that remained loyal to the temple and the Davidic king, at least in the Chronicler's view. The primary listing of Judah for ideological reasons is a reversal of the practice in chapter 1 where the favored individual or group was treated last.

Sandwiched between two genealogies for Judah in 2:3-55 and 4:1-23 is the genealogy of David, specifically, the royal line of Judah. This simple scheme belies a more complex structure to this material that helps to explain its repetitive and disjointed nature. Williamson (1979b) has discerned here the following chiastic arrangement.

A genealogy of Judah (2:3-8)
    B genealogy of Ram up to David (2:10-17)
        C genealogy of Caleb (2:18-24)
            D genealogy of Jerahmeel (2:25-33)
            D' more descendants of Jerahmeel (2:34-41)
        C' more descendants of Caleb (2:42-55)
    B' line of David, Ram's descendant (3:1-24)
A' genealogy of Judah (4:1-23), ending with Judah's oldest surviving son, Shelah

Williamson finds four sources used by the Chronicler to construct this unit: (1) biblical texts (2:3-8, 10-17, 20; 3:1-16), though differences in detail indicate that the Chronicler knew a variant textual tradition from that of the MT; (2) the genealogy of Jerahmeel and Caleb in 2:25-33, 42-50*a*, recognizable as an original unit by their similar opening and closing formulae; (3) the genealogy of Caleb in 2:18-19, 24, 50*b*-52; 4:2-4, 5-7, which had already been supplemented with 2:53-55 + 4:1 before it reached the Chronicler; and (4) miscellaneous fragments, notably 2:21-23, 34-41; 3:19-24; 4:8-23. The key to the formation of the entire unit is 2:9, which is the Chronicler's own composition, in which he combined for the first time the genealogy of Ram with those of Jerahmeel and Caleb. The Chronicler, therefore, is the editor responsible for fashioning the unit as it now stands. This reconstruction is reasonable and compelling for the order it perceives behind what initially appears to be a chaotic conglomeration. However, some problems remain, as we shall see below, and it is still possible that this unit was formed at least in part by individuals or groups supplementing the Chronicler's work in an effort to attach themselves to David or Judah.

Exegetical Analysis

The order of names in 2:1-2 is unique when compared with other such lists (Gen 35:22b-26; 46:8-27). The problem is the placement of Dan. Otherwise the order is by mother (cf. Gen 29:31–30:24) in agreement with Gen 35:22b-26: Leah—Reuben, Simeon, Levi, Judah, Issachar, Zebulun; Rachel—Joseph, Benjamin; Bilhah—[Dan], Naphtali; Zilpah—Gad, Asher. Dan's genealogy, as well as Zebulun's, is also lacking in chapters 2–9, though the two problems do not seem to be related. Dan's (mis)placement in 2:1-2 may have been accidental; no other explanation is evident.

In 2:3-8 the Chronicler draws on a series of canonical texts. Verses 3-4 condense the story in Gen 38. The specific details of the story that the Chronicler has chosen to reiterate are suggestive. By noting the Canaanite origin of Judah's wife he openly acknowledges the indigenous roots of the tribe and nation of Judah. The wickedness and death of Er reflect the doctrine of immediate retribution. It is less clear why he mentions Judah's fathering children through his daughter-in-law, though some scholars have found here an allusion to divine mercy despite human frailty. Just as curious is the omission of God's having killed Onan, and this could be the result of an inadvertent scribal error (Rudolph 1955:10). Verse 5 comes from Gen 46:12. Verse 7 draws on Josh 7, although the names are different: Zimri occurs as Zabdi in Joshua and Achar as Achan. But the Greek text of Joshua attests both of the Chronicles variants, and Achar is reminiscent of, if not a contributing factor in the etiology in Josh 7:24-25. The Hebrew root of Zimri's name (*zimmēr*) means "to make music," and the names of his brothers in verse 6 occur elsewhere for Levitical musicians (1 Chr 6:33-48; Ps 88:1; 89:1). The Chronicler has borrowed this list beginning with Ethan from 1 Kgs 4:31 (Heb 5:11), apparently because of the occurrence of the name Ethan and the similarity, which is greater in Hebrew than in English, of the name Zerah and the gentilic "Ezrahite." It is striking that no genealogy is given for Hamul, Hezron's brother (v. 5). This has been cited as an indication that the Chronicler did not invent genealogies out of whole cloth when he did not have them. On the other hand, the list of the sons of Zerah in verse 5 shows that he did create new genealogies by borrowing names from other sources.

With the genealogy of Hezron through Ram beginning in verse 9 the author reaches his main focus—David's line. That verse 9 is the Chronicler's work is indicated by the expression "that were born to him," which is a characteristic introduction of the genealogies that he constructs. The order of Hezron's sons here is problematic because of the way it differs from the subsequent genealogies. Since Ram is treated first (vv. 10-17), one expects his name to be either first or last in the series in verse 9. Ram's occurrence between his brothers is one of the reasons that some scholars continue to see different hands in the formation of this unit. It makes sense if the Chronicler is using verse 9 to combine the genealogies of Jerahmeel and Caleb, as suggested by Williamson. Another possible explanation for the unusual order is text-critical (Curtis 1910:82): If Ram's name once occurred last in the series, it could have been lost accidentally because of the "and Ram" at the beginning of verse 10 and then inserted out of order as a later correction. However, there is no support for this explanation from textual witnesses, so it remains conjectural.

A second anomaly of this verse is the name Chelubai. It seems clear from the genealogy as a whole that Chelubai is understood as a variant of Caleb, but it does not occur anywhere else in the Bible outside of Chronicles. This raises a series of questions: What is the name's origin? That is, did the Chronicler find it in one of his genealogical sources? Did the name originally refer to Caleb or to a completely different individual? Why did the Chronicler borrow or retain this name? Why did he not replace it with "Caleb"? It is another feature of this unit that remains unexplained and that some adduce as evidence of later additions to the Chronicler's work.

The genealogy for Ram in verses 10-17 is different in form from the ones for Jerahmeel and Caleb that follow, and this fact strongly suggests that Ram's was once independent of the other two, as Williamson theorized. The genealogy of Ram is linear (see introduction under genealogies) up to and including Jesse in verse 12. Then Jesse's family, in other words, David with his brothers and sisters, are named in verses 13-17. The genealogy finds a parallel in Ruth 4:18-22. While complete certainty is impossible, a number of considerations suggest that the genealogy originated with Chronicles. It has often been seen as an appendix to the book of Ruth but is integral to its context in Chronicles. Moreover, the genealogy's manufacture resembles the Chronicler's work elsewhere. It has been artificially constructed in order to provide a clear chain from Judah to David—something that does not exist elsewhere in the Bible. This has been accomplished through Ram and Salma, both of whom are unknown outside of this genealogy (and the one in Ruth). Ram, who is otherwise the son of Jerahmeel (vv. 25, 27), here bridges Hezron and Amminadab (v. 10). The reference to Amminadab and his son Nahshon, "the prince of the sons of Judah," is borrowed from Num 2:3. Then, Salma (the father of Bethlehem in 1 Chr 2:51) is used to connect Nahshon to Boaz (v. 11).

The list of David's siblings in verses 13-17 is unique to

Chronicles. The first three brothers, Eliab, Abinadab, and Shimea are mentioned in 1 Samuel 16, although there is disagreement about the spelling of Shimea (Shammah). The other three are not named elsewhere, and 1 Sam 16:10-11 indicates that David was the eighth son rather than the seventh as in Chronicles. Similar discrepancies exist regarding David's sisters. The "sons of Zeruiah" are well known in 1 and 2 Sam, and 2 Sam 17:25 calls Zeruiah Joab's mother. However, 1 Chr 2:16 alone identifies her as David's sister. The same verse in Samuel names Abigail's father as Nahash, rather than Jesse, and her husband as Ithra. Jether and Ithra are essentially different spellings of the same name in Hebrew, and "Nahash" in 2 Sam 17:25 may be due to the misplacement of the name that occurs two verses later.

According to Williamson's scheme, two genealogies for Caleb, one in 2:18-19, 24, 50aβ-55; 4:1-7 and the other in 2:42-50aα, have been brought together with the genealogy of Jerahmeel (2:25-33) already attached to the latter. This Caleb, the son of Hezron, is apparently different from and earlier than the famous spy of Num 13, Caleb the son of Jephunneh, who has his own genealogy in 4:15 (but see below on 2:42-50aα). A further genealogy for Sheshan (2:34-41) has been bound with that of Jerahmeel, Sheshan himself being the link (2:31, 34-35). Even with this reconstruction, the genealogical data here are confused and incoherent. The reason for this confusion relates to the ethnological function of the genealogy as it attempts to account for the affiliation of once independent clans—Ephrathah, Hur, and Ashhur—with Caleb and their assimilation within Judah. The "children" of these clans are often names of cities or other geographical locations within the territory occupied or claimed by the clan.

The syntax of 2:18a is difficult. The Hebrew reads "Caleb the son of Hezron begat Azubah, a woman, and Jerioth." It is then unclear to whom the "her" of "her sons" in verse 18*b* refers. The NRSV understands both Azubah and Jerioth to be Caleb's wives, but it leaves the identity of the woman in verse 18*b* ambiguous. It may be preferable, therefore, to read with the versions: "Caleb ... begat Jerioth from Azubah his wife." The names in verse 18*b* would then be those of Caleb's grandsons from Jerioth. In any case, it seems clear from verse 19 that Azubah was Caleb's wife. This verse then links both Ephrath(ah) and Hur to Caleb. It also leads nicely into verse 50*a*β, which likely originally followed directly from it. The genealogy for Hur in verse 20, then, is interpolated, probably by the Chronicler. It borrows the reference to Hur the builder of the tabernacle from Exod 35:30 (cf. 2 Chr 2:5) apparently as a peg to the wilderness generation and perhaps as a tie between king (in the form of David's line) and cult.

Machir in verse 21 was a once independent clan east of the Jordan that was assimilated into the tribe of Manasseh (Gen 50:23; Num 32:39-40; Deut 3:14-15; Judg 5:14). Machir was the location of Gilead, which is mentioned next. This genealogy belongs to the tribe of Manasseh (1 Chr 7:14-17). Its purpose here is to claim portions of Gilead for Judah. Segub in verses 21-22 is otherwise unknown and may be an error for Argob, a region in Manasseh mentioned in Deuteronomy 3:14; 1 Kgs 4:13. Havvoth-jair (v. 23) probably refers to a group of settlements in the region of Jair ("havvoth" means "villages"). Jair was also in Manasseh, as indicated by Num 32:41 and Deut 3:14. The formula, "X the father of Y," in these verses associates an ethnic element (X) with a geographical location (Y). "Father" in this usage may have the sense of "founder."

Verse 24*a* (MT) is widely recognized as corrupt and is typically emended to read "Caleb went into Ephrathah." The next phrase is also likely corrupt and with slight emendation may be read, "the wife of his father," in apposition to Ephrathah. But this reading remains problematic, since Ephrath(ah) was

Caleb's wife according to verse 19, not Hezron's, and according to verse 50*a*β Hur, not Ashhur, was Ephrathah's firstborn. The entire phrase should probably be omitted as a misplaced gloss on verse 21 (Williamson 1979b:354-55). The emended verse then reads smoothly, "After the death of Hezron, Caleb went into Ephrathah and she bore him Ashhur the father of Tekoa."

The genealogies for Jerahmeel (vv. 25-33) and Sheshan (vv. 34-41) are unique to Chronicles. Little is known about the Jerahmeelites, except that they occupied the Negeb south of Judah (1 Sam 27:10; 30:29). Their genealogy here has a sociological function in addition to indicating their absorption within Judah. The report of sons dying childless reflects the disappearance or decline of certain branches of the clan, while the report of additional wives likely indicates the assimilation of other families. The excerpt about Sheshan in verses 34-35 is vaguely reminiscent of the story of Hagar in Genesis, but nothing more is known about him or any other members of his line.

The second genealogy for Caleb in verses 42-50*a* is defined by its opening and closing formulae referring to the "sons of Caleb." This passage causes a great deal of difficulty for sorting out the different Calebs for two reasons. First, most of the names here belong to cities in southern Judah. Hebron, in particular, was the Calebite capital. These cities were in the region occupied by the Kenizzites, the family of Caleb son of Jephunneh (Num 32:12; Josh 14:6, 14; 15:13-15), not Caleb the son of Hezron. Second, the mention of Caleb's daughter Achsah in verse 49*b* draws on Josh 15:16-19 and Judg 1:12-15, whose Caleb is the son of Jephunneh rather than the son of Hezron. It is evident, therefore, that the two Calebs, if indeed there were two, have become confused. Some scholars believe that the source of the confusion was the creation of Caleb the son of Hezron out of Caleb the son of Jephunneh in order to strengthen the genealogical tie between the Calebites and Judah.

In verses 50*aβ*-55 the genealogy returns to Hur. The three main branches are "fathers" of significant cities in Judah (v. 51). As noted earlier, verses 53-55 may be an interpolation interrupting the original continuation of the genealogy now in 4:2. Haroeh (v. 52) means "the seer" and is inappropriate as a personal name. It is probably a corruption of the name Reaiah in 4:2. The interpolated verses expand on the residents of Kiriathjearim. Their list of inhabitants clearly illustrates the ethnological and sociological function of the genealogies. The reference to scribes in verse 55 seems out of place and would perhaps fit better with the list of guilds in 4:21-22. For this reason, some scholars prefer to read the word as a gentilic, Siphrites (i.e., from Kiriath-sepher, literally, "town of Sepher"). Of note also in this verse are the Kenites and the Rechabites. The former were non-Israelites (Gen 15:19; Num 24:20-22; Judg 4:11, 17; 1 Sam 15:6; 30:29) who are evidently seen here as having been absorbed within Israel. The Rechabites are described in Jer 35 as an antiurban family renowned for their adherence to the nomadic lifestyle.

The line of David in chapter 3 follows naturally upon 2:17 and may once have been its direct continuation. In the present arrangement, this chapter picks up the genealogy of Ram following those of Caleb and Jerahmeel. The placement of David's line within that of Hur also connects him with Ephrathah and Bethlehem. The chapter falls into three parts: verses 1-9 list David's sons; verses 10-14 gives the kings of Judah down to Josiah in the form of a linear genealogy; and verses 15-24 are a segmented genealogy of the Davidic line from Josiah on.

In verses 1-9, the Chronicler has drawn from different places in 2 Samuel and placed a frame around the material in verses 1 ("these are the sons of David") and 9 ("all these were David's sons"). The list in verses 1-4*aα* comes from 2 Sam 3:2-5 with changes that are mostly textual or stylistic. The name of the second son is apparently corrupt in both Samuel and Chronicles (MT). Based on LXX witnesses for both books and on 4QSam[a]

(Dead Sea Scroll fragments of Samuel) the best reading seems to be *dlwyh*= Daluiah (McCarter 1984:101-02). Nothing more is known about this son, and it is generally assumed that he died in infancy. The Chronicler has omitted the reference to Abigail as the widow of Nabal, presumably because he did not include the story in 1 Sam 25. The Chronicler's hand is also evident in verse 4*a* in the expression "were born to him," which is a favorite of his in the genealogies and is a slight change from Samuel. The rest of verse 4 reworks 2 Sam 5:5. While mentioning the length of David's reign at Hebron, the Chronicler studiously avoids any indication that any part of David's reign was over anything less than all Israel. The origin and initial function of this list beyond Samuel are unknown. It is quite unlikely that these were all of David's sons born in Hebron, since each wife would hardly have been limited to one son. What is important here is to note the way that the Chronicler has adapted the list for his own purposes, giving the line of David as the focal point in his genealogy of Judah.

Verses 5-8 are based on 2 Sam 5:14-16, but there are some striking differences between the two texts. The differences between Shimea and Shammua, Ammiel and Eliam (2 Sam 11:3), and Elishama and Elishua are minor matters of spelling or textual corruption and need not detain us. The Chronicler's rendering of the name Bathshua instead of Bathsheba in Samuel may also be a variation in spelling but is seems to be a deliberate reminiscence of Judah's wife (Gen 38) in accord with a technique used elsewhere by the Chronicler. More striking is his ascription of the first four sons in the list, with Solomon as the fourth, to Bathshua, when Solomon is the first surviving son of David and Bathsheba according to 2 Sam 12:24. It may be that the Chronicler sought conformity with the pattern in verses 1-3 of naming the mothers. Since Bathsheba is the only Jerusalem mother mentioned in 2 Samuel and since Solomon was clearly her son, the Chronicler assigned the first four names in the list—that is, up to Solomon inclusive—to her. The names Eliphelet and Nogah may have been lost from Samuel by an inadvertent scribal error, though no feature of the text that might have occasioned such a loss is immediately apparent. It is more likely that they are accidental repetitions of Nepheg and the later Eliphelet. If so, the error(s) occurred before the list came to the Chronicler, since the total in verse 9 reflects them, and 1 Chr 14:5-6 also has both names.

Verses 10-14 trace the Davidic kingship over Judah through sixteen generations from Solomon to Josiah, inclusive. The Chronicler follows the order and spelling of the names in Kings, so that he gives the name Azariah (2 Kgs 15:1) instead of Uzziah (2 Chr 26). The only Judahite monarch missing from the list is Athaliah, who has been omitted intentionally because she was not a descendant of David.

The information about Josiah and his sons in verses 15-16 varies in several particulars from 2 Kgs 23–24. First, verse 15 names as Josiah's firstborn Johanan, who does not appear in Kings. He may have died in infancy or youth. Then, the order of sons differs. In Kings the order of reigns is Jehoahaz (= Shallum), Jehoiakim (= Eliakim), and Zedekiah (= Mattaniah), and the birth order that can be deduced from the narrative is Jehoiakim, Jehoahaz, Zedekiah. The order in Chronicles—apparently that of their births—is different from both of those in Kings. Chronicles has Johanan, Jehoiakim (also called Eliakim), Zedekiah, and Shallum. Moreover, 1 Chr 3:16 mentions a second Zedekiah, the son of Jehoiakim and brother of Jeconiah/Jehoiachin or the son of Jeconiah/Jehoiachin, and it is this second Zedekiah whom the author apparently describes as the last king of Judah (2 Chr 36:9-10) rather than the son of Josiah as in 2 Kgs 24:17 (Japhet 1993:98; contrast Knoppers 2004). This last difference betrays a disagreement in the tradition about the identity of Zedekiah that is reflected in the textual witnesses.

Verses 17-18 list the sons of Jeconiah (= Jehoiachin). The word translated "the captive" by the NRSV actually lacks the article in Hebrew and is taken as a proper name, Assir, by some. If it is a proper name, then Assir is Jeconiah's only son in the list (for the use of the plural "sons" when there is only one son see 2:31), and the subsequent names are Assir's sons. If it is a noun, then the following seven names are all Jeconiah's sons. Historical records from Babylon mention "Jehoiachin king of Judah" and his five sons (*ANET* 308), which would seem to indicate the latter reading. Scholars also debate whether Shenazzar (v. 18) is to be identified with Sheshbazzar (Ezra 1:8). Yet another problem is the fact that Zerubbabel is uniquely described in verse 19 as the son of Pedaiah, while he is known elsewhere as the son of Shealtiel (Hag 1:1; Ezra 3:2). The LXX reflects "Shealtiel," but this is likely a correction. Some have suggested that this may reflect the practice of levirate marriage whereby Shealtiel died childless and his brother Paltiel fathered Zerubbabel through the widow. The names of Zerubbabel's children in verses 19-20 are composed of Hebrew words with such meanings as "peace," "mercy," "blessing," and "loyalty," implying optimism and hope on the part of Zerubbabel and the returnees from exile whom he led.

Verse 21 presents a special problem. The NRSV adopts a common scholarly emendation based on the LXX, reading the plural for the first occurrence of "son" in the verse—"the sons of Hananiah"—and "his son" in all other instances in the verse where the Hebrew has "sons of." But does the genealogy cover six generations or only two? The difference in interpretation is important for dating this genealogy. If verse 21 covers two generations, the entire genealogy encompasses ten generations beginning with Jeconiah (Jehoiachin). If verse 21 has six generations, the entire genealogy is fourteen generations long. Setting Jeconiah's birth year at 616 and figuring twenty years per generation, the genealogy reflects a date of between 416 and 336 B.C.E. An even wider range is possible depending on further textual and interpretive matters. Assuming the genealogy was composed or incorporated by the Chronicler, this range then becomes one of the pieces of evidence for determining the date of the book.

The preservation of a record of the Davidic line deserves comment. Scholars interpret this in opposite ways. On the one hand, the lack of any explicit expression of hope in the present passage for the restoration of the Davidic dynasty has led some to question the extent to which the Chronicler endorsed such a "Messianic" expectation. On the other hand, the very fact that a detailed record of the royal line was kept into and beyond the exile suggests that the hope for a restoration of the monarchy remained alive and was embodied in certain candidates for the throne.

As we have seen, 4:1 summarizes Judah's genealogy down to Shobal in order to smooth the resumption of Hur's line that was broken off at 2:52 with the insertion of the Davidic genealogy (ch. 3) and subsequent interpolations (2:53-55). The naming of Carmi as Hur's father instead of Caleb or Chelubai (2:9, 19) is surprising and was Williamson's main reason for denying 4:1 to the Chronicler. Other scholars have asserted that Carmi is a simple error for Caleb. But there is no support among the textual witnesses for this explanation, and the Hebrew letters in question are not easily confused.

The remainder of chapter 4 is a collection of genealogical notices and anecdotes about different components of Judah. Many of the names that are known are place names. The notices generally seem unrelated to each other, and scholars struggle to find coherence in this chapter. The date and authorship (i.e., how much the Chronicler wrote or included) of these materials are uncertain. The diversity of the elements in the chapter suggests the importance of Judah in the post-exilic period and the efforts of various groups to affiliate themselves with it.

Verses 2-4 seem to continue the line of Hur, but there is no explicit link between Etam (v. 3) and the descendants of Hur in verse 2. Verses 5-8 then give the lineage of Ashhur through each of his two wives. Again, the line of Koz in verse 8 is disconnected with the genealogy that precedes it. Verses 9-10 relate an etymological etiology on the name Jabez, a character who is otherwise unknown, though 2:55 mentions a place named Jabez. Once more, the etiology is unrelated to both what precedes and what follows. Its content is unique and intriguing. Jabez's name is related to the word for "pain" (cf. Gen 3:16), although the last two consonants are reversed as if to avoid any consequences of the bad name. As a further measure, Jabez prays to God to keep him from pain. It is perhaps through God's answer to his prayer that Jabez is honored above his brothers (v. 9). The excerpt would have appealed to the Chronicler's emphasis on the effectiveness of prayer.

The genealogical form resumes in verse 11. Verses 11-15 contain several unconnected lists that are perhaps understood to share a Kenizzite affiliation. Like the Kenites, the Kenizzites are described as smiths or craftsmen (v. 14) who were originally non-Israelites (Gen 15:19). Genesis 36:11 gives Kenaz an Edomite heritage, suggesting that they inhabited the Arabah, the region south of the Dead Sea. "Chelub" in verse 11 may be another spelling of "Caleb," but nothing more is known about this brother of Shuhah and father of Mehir. Caleb the son of Jephunneh in verse 15 was the "faithful spy" whose heirs received the territory around Hebron (Josh 15:13-15).

Verses 16-20 represent several more unconnected genealogies. Of the sons of Jehallel (v. 16) only Ziph is otherwise known as a place name (1 Sam 23:14). Ziphah may be an inadvertent scribal duplication. As the text now stands, the line of Ezrah in verses 17-18 is unconnected with that of Jehallel. The anecdote about the marriage of Bithiah and Mered is remarkable. That an Egyptian princess would marry a Judahite commoner is historically unlikely. Moreover, the name Bithiah is Yahwistic! The excerpt indicates an Egyptian component within Judah. Eshtemoa, Gedor, Soco, and Zanoah are all cities mentioned in the list in Joshua 15:20-61. Several of these lay outside of postexilic Judah, suggesting that the list may derive from before the exile. It may also reflect the Chronicler's implicit claim on all of the promised land for Israel.

The genealogy for Judah closes in verses 21-23 with the line of Shelah, son of Judah (Gen 38:5). Most of the names are otherwise unknown. They have in common their listing here by trade. The list, therefore, seems to represent the founders of certain guilds and the locations where those trades were carried on. The reference in verse 22 to marrying into Moab indicates that some originally Moabite elements were assimilated into this line.

Theological Analysis

The theology of this section might be succinctly stated in the two words, *election* and *inclusiveness*. The occurrence of the two ideas together is paradoxical, because they are typically considered mutually exclusive: Election entails choosing one among several so that those not chosen are excluded. Yet 1 Chronicles offers a complex interplay between the two ideas. The list of the twelve sons of Israel in 2:1-2 and indeed the genealogies in chapters 2–9 as a whole testify to the Chronicler's interest in all Israel as God's chosen people. At the same time, Judah is clearly awarded favored status, both by the placement of its genealogy first among the tribes and by the length and detail of that genealogy. "All Israel is the kingdom of God, yet that kingdom is realized essentially in Judah" (Braun 1986:62). Then, within Judah the line of David receives special attention. Indeed, Judah's prominence among the tribes was due to the fact that it produced the divinely chosen ruler (5:2; cf. ch. 17).

But within this list of the elect tribe one finds the subtle but pervasive promotion of the idea of inclusiveness. At the very head of the genealogy the Chronicler reminds the reader of the Canaanite origins of the line of Judah. Then, throughout the genealogy for Judah, as we have seen, there are affiliations not only with other Israelite tribes but also with other Canaanites (e.g., Kenites, Kenizzites) and with Edomites, Moabites, Egyptians, and others. By including these elements within

Judah's genealogy, the Chronicler imputes a remarkable ethnic diversity to the tribe and nation, a diversity that stands in marked contrast to the exclusiveness promoted by Ezra–Nehemiah (Knoppers 2001). Indeed, this genealogy seems to attack directly one of the main premises of Ezra–Nehemiah. The latter insists upon Judahite men abandoning their "foreign" wives and children in order to preserve the ethnic purity of the tribe and nation. Chronicles indicates that Judah was ethnically diverse from its beginning and that mixed marriages contributed to Judah's expansion in land.

This tension between election and inclusiveness, though especially acute in the postexilic community period, is hardly limited to Chronicles and Ezra–Nehemiah. It pervades the Bible (cf. McKenzie 1997). It is present already in Genesis, which the genealogy in 1 Chronicles 1 epitomizes: Yahweh, who chose Israel as his special people, is interested in all human beings as their creator. Nowhere is this message clearer than in the book Jonah, where Yahweh's concern for the Ninevites contrasts with the bigotry and arrogance of his prophet. It is also an undercurrent in the book of Ruth, where David's great-grandmother, who models the Israelite virtue of "steadfast love," is a Moabite. One might well argue that the point of the election of Israel in the Old Testament was to provide a "light to the nations" whereby all peoples would come to revere Yahweh. This is the vision of Isa 2:2-4 // Mic 4:1-4, which envision the streaming of the peoples to Jerusalem to hear the word of Yahweh. The tension even lies behind the genealogies of Matthew and Luke that have been mentioned earlier. While Matthew emphasizes Jesus' status as one of the most elect—in the line of both Abraham and David—Luke traces his ancestry all the way back to Adam as a way of highlighting the relevance of his message to all humanity. The paradox of the gospel as presented in the New Testament is that election in Christ is available to persons of every race and ethnicity.

SIMEON AND THE TRANSJORDANIAN TRIBES
(1 CHRONICLES 4:24–5:26)

The next unit contains the genealogies of Simeon (4:24-43) and the tribes east of the Jordan—Reuben, Gad, and half of the tribe of Manasseh (5:1-26). They are really two distinct units but are treated here together for convenience, as they both lie between structuring genealogies of Judah and Levi. Reuben was the southernmost tribe east of the Jordan; Gad lay north of Reuben and half Manasseh north of Gad, so that the account moves from south to north geographically.

Literary Analysis

The genealogy of Simeon consists of three subunits: the line of Simeon through Shaul (4:24-27), their towns and villages (4:28-33), and their leaders and anecdotes about their expansion (4:34-43). This same three-part scheme of genealogies, settlements, and historical episodes occurs for other, especially less significant, tribes. Genealogies for Simeon also occur in Gen 46:10; Exod 6:15; and Num 26:12-13. The one in Numbers is by far the closest to 1 Chr 4:24.

Chapter 5 gives separate genealogies for the tribes of Reuben (5:1-10), Gad (5:11-17), and half of Manasseh (5:23-24), but treats them as a single entity in the anecdotes in 5:18-22, 25-26. The unity of this passage is also indicated formally. It opens, as was the case for Simeon, with the descendants of Reuben. But the treatments of Gad and half Manasseh both begin with notes about their settlements. The genealogy of Manasseh may have originally followed directly after Gad's, especially in view of the mention of all three in verse 18.

Exegetical Analysis

Descendants of Simeon

It is striking to find a genealogy for Simeon included in 1 Chr 1–9, since Simeon had disappeared as a geographic and political entity long before the Chronicler's time. Its absorption within Judah is already reflected in Josh 19:1-9 and Judg 1:3. The Chronicler's inclusion of Simeon, then, is part of his idealized portrait of "all Israel" rather than a realistic picture of the post-texilic makeup of Israel. Its relationship to Judah also makes its placement here immediately following Judah appropriate. Simeon typically comes second in such lists, but following Reuben rather than Judah, according to the "birth order" of the sons (Gen 29:31-35).

In 4:24 Chronicles uniquely lists Jarib instead of Jachin. The rest of the genealogy (4:25-28) is also unique to Chronicles. Verses 25-26 link Simeon's sons with the family of Shimei. It is not clear whether the genealogy in these two verses is linear and each name represents another generation or segmented such that Shallum, Mibsam, and Mishma are all Shaul's sons and Hammuel, Zaccur, and Shimei all Mishma's. The names Mishma and Shimei both pun on that of Simeon as all three are composed of the same Hebrew root. Verse 27 explains in genealogical terms why the tribe of Simeon decreased and was overshadowed by Judah.

All of the places in the list of Simeonite settlements in verses 28-33 that can be identified are in the area around Beer-Sheba. Some of the names also occur in the list of sites occupied by the returnees from exile in Neh 11:26-29. The present list, however, is taken from Josh 19:2-8 with some differences in details and a few editorial changes. Among the latter is the mention of David's kingship in verse 31b, by which the Chronicler makes a connection with the beginning point of his narrative in chapter 10. Thus, the genealogies in 1 Chr 1–9 purport to describe the tribes of Israel on the eve of David's reign. The Chronicler has also omitted the word "heritage, inheritance," which occurs repeatedly in Joshua. Japhet (1979; 1997:363-86) thinks that his change reflects the Chronicler's view that Israel was indigenous in the land rather than conquering and dividing it among the tribes (but see below on 5:25). In the present context, however, the change may have been motivated by the fact that Simeon had been assimilated within Judah and no longer possessed its "inheritance."

The final segment of this passage (4:34-43) recounts two expeditions of conquest by the Simeonites, the first (4:34-41) to Gedor, the second to Edom (4:42-43). Each episode is accompanied by a list of leaders who evidently led the conquest. The lists are not expressly related either to the preceding genealogy or to each other. The location of this Gedor is unknown; the word might refer to "pasture land" in general. Some scholars prefer to read Gerar with the LXX. The first episode is dated to the time of Hezekiah (4:41). Both explain conditions existing "to this day," which could refer either to the time of the Chronicler himself or to the date of his source. The ruthlessness of the Simeonites in verse 41 fits well with the characterization of the tribe and its ancestor in Genesis (34; 49:5-7).

The Transjordanian Tribes

Like Simeon, the Transjordanian tribes had largely disappeared as independent entities by the Chronicler's time, and their inclusion here reflects his emphasis on "all Israel." The genealogy of Reuben in 5:1*aα*, 3 is from Exod 6:14, but it has been interrupted in the rest of verse 1 and verse 2 with the information about Reuben's loss of status. This information has been inserted through the technique of resumptive repetition whereby the final portion of narrative immediately preceding the insertion is repeated when the narrative resumes. Here, the phrase "the sons of Reuben the firstborn of Israel" from the beginning of verse 1 is repeated at the start of verse 3. The inserted material probably derives from the Chronicler. Adapting and interpreting Gen 35:22 and 49:4, he provides a theological explanation for the decline of the tribe of Reuben and the prominence of the Joseph tribes, especially Ephraim, in the northern kingdom. Reuben's loss of his birthright was punishment for his sleeping with his father's concubine. The

Chronicler may even understand Joseph's representation in both Ephraim and Manasseh as the double portion accruing to the firstborn, as suggested by Jacob's adoption of the two in Gen 48:5. The NRSV translation of verse 1*b* ("so that he is not enrolled in the genealogy according to the birthright") seems to contradict the arrangement of the present genealogies in which Reuben precedes Ephraim and Manasseh. The conjunction that begins this clause may be concessive and refer to Joseph: "even though [Joseph] is not enrolled . . . ." Knoppers (2004) also contends that the Chronicler distinguishes between firstborn status, which Reuben retained, and the birthright, which went to Joseph. The Chronicler goes on to explain another facet of Reuben's demotion. Not only did he lose the birthright, but he also lost preeminence, which became Judah's by its production of the leadership over all Israel in the form of the line of David, as again articulated in Gen 49 (vv. 8-10).

The further descendants of Reuben in 5:4-8*a* are all traced through Joel, whose own descent from the patriarch is not given. Beerah and Jeiel, respectively, bear the titles "prince" and "the head," but their precise significance is unknown. Beerah is also set in a specific period—the invasion of Tiglath-Pileser (always Tilgath-Pilneser in Chronicles) presumably that of around 733–732 B.C.E. (2 Kgs 15:29).

As with the Simeonites, an account of the Reubenite settlements (vv. 8*b*-10) follows the tribe's genealogy. The sites of Aroer, Nebo, and Baal-meon are all listed in a ninth-century inscription of the Moabite king, Mesha. The Hagrites (v. 10) are mentioned several times in 1 Chronicles (5:19-20; 11:38; 27:30) but elsewhere only in 2 Sam 23:36 (reading "Hagri" for "the Gadite" as in 1 Chr 11:38, which it parallels) and in Ps 83:6 (Heb 7). Their eponymous ancestress was presumably Hagar (Gen 16, 21), although the biblical text never explicitly makes this connection.

The genealogy of Gad in 5:11-17 consists of several parts. Verses 11-13 list a total of eleven families of Gad by the names of their respective ancestors. A second genealogy in verses 14-15 is likely textually corrupt. It lists the ancestors of Abihail through eight generations, inclusive (v. 14), as a heading to one individual, Ahi (v. 15), who is not connected with Abihail. Verse 16 gives the Gadite settlements. Gilead was also inhabited by Reubenites (v. 9), and Bashan, which lay north of Gilead, was assigned to Manasseh in Josh 13:29-31. There is, thus, overlap in this list between the territorial holdings of all three of these tribes. Sharon was a town in the Transjordan that is also mentioned in the Mesha stele, rather than the more famous coastal plain of Sharon. The reigns of Jeroboam of Israel and Jotham of Judah, who are mentioned in the conclusion of verse 17, overlapped around 750–747 B.C.E.

The battle account in verses 18-22 contains some terminology that is unusual for the Chronicler, notably "expert in war" (v. 18) and "trust" (v. 20), but otherwise is typical of his style and theology. The idea that God "helped" those who relied upon him and "cried out" to him is a particular favorite of the Chronicler's. It appears, therefore, that the Chronicler has substantially elaborated an anecdote from one of his sources. Like the Hagrites, Jetur, Naphish, and Nodab were Arabian tribes. Nodab is unique to this passage, but the other two are mentioned in Genesis 25:15 as descendants of Ishmael. The exile in verse 22 is not the Babylonian exile but, in the light of verses 6 and 26, probably the Assyrian deportation of 734 B.C.E. (2 Kgs 15:29).

Verses 23-24 may have originally followed verse 17. Alternatively, Williamson (1982:66-67) thinks that 5:23-26 was once connected with the Manasseh material in 7:14-19. The names in this genealogy of Manasseh do not occur elsewhere. They are referred to as clan leaders and endowed with impressive titles—mighty warriors (which might also be translated "wealthy noblemen") and famous men—that are reminiscent of the Nephilim in Gen 6:4. Perhaps they are so designated because of their great proliferation and their possession of a large tract of land.

Verses 25-26 contrast deliberately with verses 18-22 to provide the flip-side of the theological principle of retribution, which is a major component of the Chronicler's theology. As the latter illustrates that victory results from obedience, the present passage shows that unfaithfulness brings defeat. There may also be a contrast with verses 23-24, showing that, as with the Nephilim of Gen 6:1-4, the mightiest and most renowned among humans are still subject to God's judgment. The Chronicler borrows terminology from both the Priestly writer of the Pentateuch ("they transgressed") and the Deuteronomistic Historian ("and prostituted themselves"). The transgressors (v. 25) are not just the Manassites but the two and one-half Transjordanian tribes as a whole. The last phrase of verse 25, "whom God had destroyed before them," alludes to the conquest of the land under Joshua and is a strong indication that, contrary to the claims of Japhet (1993), the Chronicler does not see Israel as a whole as indigenous to Canaan. Pul was another name for Tiglath-Pileser III, and the verbs that follow are in the singular, so that the latter here is intended further to identify the former. The Chronicler also seems to telescope the invasion of Tiglath-Pileser III in 734 with the destruction of Samaria by Shalmaneser in 721. The names of the places to which the exiles were taken are drawn from accounts relating to the latter in 2 Kgs 17:6; 18:11. The one exception is Hara, which is otherwise unknown and may be an accidental repetition of the word for "river" (*nāhār*) or an error for "mountain(s) of" (*hārê* or *harărê*).

Theological Analysis

The inclusion of these tribes, long defunct as independent entities, displays the Chronicler's interest in "all Israel." This is Israel according to its most inclusive definition. The Chronicler issues an invitation to all who consider themselves part of Israel to join in reestablishing the glorious past as he idealizes it. The Chronicler's definition of the land of Israel is also broad. Many scholars think these lists are preexilic in origin because the settlements in them lay mostly outside of Persian Yehud. Whatever their origin, the lists of settlements east of the Jordan implicitly claim that territory as Israel. The divine choice of David and his line surfaces in the explanation of Judah's preeminence in 5:2. Finally, the principle of retribution, which is especially common in 2 Chronicles, is well illustrated by the anecdotes in 5:18-22, 25-26. The former attributes the military success of the Transjordanians to their reliance upon Yahweh; the latter explains their later demise as the result of their rebellion against God.

LEVI (1 CHRONICLES 6 [HEBREW 5:27-41; 6:1-66])

The account of Levi in this chapter is second only to that of Judah in length and detail, thereby attesting the importance of the Levites for the Chronicler. This is also suggested by the placement of the genealogy of Levi at the center of the genealogies in chapters 1–9, perhaps influenced by Num 2, which describes the encampment of the tribes in a square around the Levites and the tabernacle. This arrangement highlights the centrality of the temple in the Chronicler's ideology. Moreover, this chapter is the first of many texts in 1 Chronicles that deal with the Levites: 9:10-34; 15:4-14; 16:4-43; chs. 23–26 (for a comparison of contents see De Vries 1989:69). It should be cautioned, however, that many scholars regard much of this material as secondary.

The verse numbers for this unit in most English Bibles differ from those in most Hebrew texts (see the introduction). For the sake of convenience, citations follow the English system with Hebrew numbers in brackets. The English division has the added advantage in this case of including all of the genealogical information for Levi in one chapter.

Literary Analysis

The present chapter falls into two main sections: the genealogies in 6:1-53 [5:27–6:38] and the record of their settlements in 6:54-81 [6:39-66]. The genealogies are further divided between those for the priests (6:1-15 [5:27-41]), the Levites (6:16-30 [6:1-15]), and the singers (6:31-48 [6:16-33]), with a note about the duties of the priests (6:49 [6:34]) and rehearsal of the line of Aaron to Ahimaaz (6:50-53 [6:35-38]). Thus, the genealogies of the priests in 6:1-15 [5:27-41] and 6:50-53 [6:35-38] enclose those of the Levites in 6:16-49 [6:1-34]. A major question regarding the chapter is whether the genealogies were all assembled and included by the Chronicler or grew by supplementation to his work. The correspondence in arrangement of material between the two main sections (cf. Williamson 1982:68-69) favors the first alternative.

The list in 6:1-15 [5:27-41] has been interpreted since at least Josephus as the high priestly line, the most extensive genealogy for that line (26 generations) in the Old Testament. But the absence of several high priests who are mentioned in Chronicles's narrative, most conspicuously Jehoiada (2 Chr 22:11–24:17), is one factor that has led Knoppers (2004) to suggest that it was not the high priestly genealogy but a document intended to legitimate a line of priests—some of whom were high priests—in Persian Yehud.

Exegetical Analysis

The first part of the list (6:1-3 [5:27-29]) is a segmented genealogy (see introduction under genealogies) from Levi to Aaron that has been composed based on various canonical texts (Gen 46:11; Exod 6:16-25; Num 3:17-20; 26:57-61). Verses 4-15 [5:30-41] then contain a linear genealogy from Eleazar to Jehozadak that is based on the genealogy for Ezra in Ezra 7:1-5. The version in Ezra is shorter, lacking the six names from Amariah through Azariah in 1 Chr 6:7-9 [5:33-35]. The difference is probably the result of supplementation (including inadvertent duplication?) in Chronicles, although inadvertent omission in Ezra is possible. The note in verse 10 about Azariah being the high priest at the time of Solomon is probably out of place and should apply to the Azariah in verse 9. This change would yield twelve generations or, figuring forty years per generation, 480 years, for the period from Kohath, the son of Levi and progenitor of the line to Zadok and twelve from Zadok to Jehozadak (compare 1 Kgs 6:1). In this scheme, the time of David, when Zadok lived, was the midpoint of Israel's history from the ancestors to the Babylonian exile (Knoppers 2004). The identification of Zadok as a Kohathite is unique to Chronicles, and the historical origins of Zadok and the Zadokites are debated among scholars. Chronicles also conflates the names Seraiah and Azariah (6:13-14 [5:39-40]), which resemble each other in Hebrew and appear as variants in other versions of this genealogy (1 Chr 9:11; Ezra 7:1; Neh 11:11).

Many scholars consider the entire genealogy in 6:1-15 [5:27-41] to be secondary because a briefer form of it from Aaron to Ahimaaz occurs in 6:50-53 [6:35-38]. However, it may be better to regard verses 50-53 as the secondary text in light of the correspondence of the two sections of the chapter. The genealogy in 6:1-15 resolves a problem raised by 2 Sam 8:17, which describes Zadok as the son of Ahitub, presumably the brother of Ichabod (1 Sam 14:3) and therefore the son of Eli (1 Sam 4), the very family that the Zadokites are supposed to have replaced as priests (1 Sam 2:27-36). The genealogy in Chronicles traces Zadok's descent through Ahitub but not through Eli.

The Levitical genealogies in 6:16-30 [6:1-15] are partitioned among the houses of the three sons of Levi, Gershom (always Gershon outside of Chronicles), Kohath, and Merari. Each of these Levitical branches was originally represented by a linear genealogy extending eight generations, that is, to the time of David, and this is still the case for Gershom and Merari. The genealogy of Kohath also originally encompassed eight generations, and it can be reconstructed with the help of Exodus 6:24

(Lefèvre 1950). In 6:22 [6:7] Kohath, Amminadab, and Korah represent three generations. Then, in 6:22-23 Assir, Elkanah, and Ebiasaph are all sons of Korah. The line of Assir is then traced in verse 24 through four generations: Tahath, Uriel, Uzziah, and Shaul. Two sons of Elkanah are named in verse 25. But the entire length of the genealogy from Kohath to Shaul is eight generations.

The genealogy of Korah has been further expanded in 6:25-30 by the genealogy of Samuel and the names of his sons from 1 Sam 1:1 and 8:2. The purpose of this addition was to provide Samuel a Levitical pedigree, since 1 Sam 1–15 depicts him as exercising priestly functions. It was facilitated by the occurrence of Elkanah, the name of Samuel's father, in the genealogy of Korah. The other remarkable feature of this genealogy is the occurrence in 6:22 [7] of Amminadab, who is otherwise unattested as Kohath's son and Korah's father. The name is often emended to Izhar (vv. 18, 38 [3, 23]), though Japhet (1993:155) argues for the emendation of Amminadab to Amram (see further below).

The list of Levitical musicians in 6:31-48 [16-33] begins with a heading (vv. 31-32 [16-17]) that ascribes the origin of the musical orders to David at a time when the ark had rested in Jerusalem so that the Levites were no longer needed to carry it (1 Chr 15–16). As with the Levitical genealogies in verses 16-30 [1-15], the present list betrays a pattern that has been disturbed by the addition of material relating to Samuel. As in the previous list, here also there are three families of musicians, each from one of the main Levitical branches: Heman from Kohath, Asaph from Gershom, and Ethan from Merari. Each family apparently traced its origin back to the second son of its forebear. Thus, Ethan is descended from Mushi, the second son of Merari (vv. 19, 47 [4, 32]). Asaph is from Shimei, the second son of Gershom (vv. 20, 43 [5, 28]). The name Jahath in verse 43 [28] is out of order and should either be transposed with Shimei or deleted; Jahath is properly the son of Libni,

Gershom's first son (v. 20 [5]). The lines of Ethan and Asaph then are represented, respectively, by thirteen and fourteen names—both by thirteen if Jahath is deleted. The line of Heman, on the other hand, contains twenty-one names from Heman to Kohath. Its length is due to the addition of the genealogy of Samuel from verses 25-28 (10-13) to that of Heman. (There are some slight differences in names due to textual transmission, and some brothers, such as Amasai and Ahimoth/Mahath, have become father and son.) Heman's line is traced from Izhar, who is Kohath's second son according to 6:2, 18 [5:28; 6:3], suggesting that Izhar should not be reconstructed for Amminadab in verse 22 [7]. The preeminence of Heman in the present passage is thus clear both from the length of the genealogy for him and from its placement first among the three groups of singers. The differences in the lists of singers likely reflect sociological changes over time. The list of singers closes with a conclusion in verse 48 [33] that matches the heading to the list in verses 31-32 [16-17] and distinguishes the work of the singers from that of the other Levites.

The note in verse 49 [33] also distinguishes the work of the priests from that of the Levites and makes clear that the orders of the former were established by Moses rather than David, who configured the Levites. The verse seems somewhat apologetic for the priests and may be a later addition. The line of priests that follows in verses 50-53 [35-38] is essentially the same in content as that of verses 1-15 [5:27-41]. It is of the same form as the genealogy of Levites in verses 16-31 [1-15] and the two may originally have gone together—perhaps even as the basic layer of the present chapter.

The list of Levitical settlements in the rest of chapter 6 is generally considered to be an abridgement and rearrangement of the similar list in Josh 21 according to the following correspondences: (1) 1 Chr 6:54-60 [39-45] < Josh 21:10-19, (2) 6:61-65 [46-50] < 21:5-9, and (3) 6:66-81 [51-66] < 21:20-40. The order in Chronicles follows the pattern Kohathites, Gershomites,

Merarites in verses 54-63 [39-48] and again in verses 65-81 [50-66], and this is the same pattern found in verses 1-49 [5:27–6:33]. The direction of borrowing is indicated by the verb "to give," which is used throughout the list in reference to the cities held by the Levites in each tribe, and which fits the setting of Joshua where the land is being apportioned among the tribes, much better than that of Chronicles, which merely reports the settlements of the Levites at the time of David. The rearrangement in Chronicles reflects some carelessness and has caused disruption to the order in Joshua. Joshua 21:4-8 provides an overview of the number of cities given to the Levites within the various tribes and then follows with detailed lists of cities (vv. 9-40). The Chronicles version reproduces the sequence of Josh 21:5-9 in 1 Chr 6:61-65 [46-50]. But while Josh 21:9 originally served as an introduction to the detailed lists, the new arrangement in Chronicles leaves the same verse (6:65 [50]) hanging out of place with no corresponding list following it. Thus, the verse calls for a list of "these cities which are mentioned by name," but no names follow. The original document seems to have assigned four cities within each tribe to the Levites, a dozen cities going to each of the four Levitical groups, and the text can be reconstructed in this way (Braun 1986:95-102). Some scholars have argued for the authenticity of the list from the period of the united monarchy, while others view it as late and utopian in nature.

The Chronicles version begins with the list of Aaronid cities in verses 54-60 [39-45]. All of these are in the tribes of Judah, Simeon, and Benjamin, although Simeon is not mentioned because of its early assimilation within Judah. The treatment of Hebron, already found in Joshua, combines its status as a city of refuge with its special possession by Caleb son of Jephunneh. The term translated "pasture land" in the NRSV occurs repeatedly in this section; it actually refers to an area of open or common land surrounding a city and was not strictly pasture. "Cities of refuge" were places where individuals guilty of involuntary manslaughter could seek asylum from family members of their victims. The names of two cities, Juttah and Gibeon, should be restored in verses 59-60 [44-45] in accord with the total number of thirteen in verse 60 [45] and with Josh 21:16. Hence, the Levites occupied nine cities in Judah and Simeon and four in Benjamin. Most of the cities in this list were not within the boundaries of Persian Yehud, a fact that would seem to support a date for it in the monarchy, unless the list is designed to present an idealistic portrait of Levitical holdings. The suggestion has been made that they served as provincial administrative centers (Mazar 1960).

Verses 61-65 [46-50] continue the overview of Levitical cities assigned to the rest of the Kohathites (v. 61 [46]), Gershomites (v. 62 [47]), and Merarites (v. 63 [48]). The omission of Ephraim and Dan from verse 61 [46] was accidental rather than deliberate (against e.g., Braun 1986:99-100), and they may be restored on the basis of Josh 21:5. Verse 64 [49] could be taken as the introduction of the detailed list of cities in verses 66-81 [51-66] (Japhet 1993:161). This is entirely different from the function of its parallel, Josh 21:8, which serves to conclude and summarize the overview of Israelite cities awarded to the Levites in that context. However, any introductory function that verse 64 [49] may have had is obscured by verse 65 [50], which we have seen is out of place due to the Chronicles writer having followed the order of Joshua.

The rest of the chapter details the cities occupied by the non-Aaronid Kohathites (vv. 66-70 [51-55]), the Gershomites (vv. 71-76 [56-61]), and the Merarites (vv. 77-81 [62-66]). The Kohathites, as noted in verse 61 [46], hold cities in Ephraim, Dan, and western Manasseh. The name of Dan and the two cities Elteke and Gibbethon are lacking in verses 68-69 [53-54], but there is good evidence to suspect that the omission was accidental and to restore them based on Josh 21:23. The Gershomites are allotted cities in eastern Manasseh, Issachar, and Asher, and the Merarites in Zebulun, Reuben, and Gad.

Theological Analysis

This chapter illustrates the importance of the priests and Levites in their respective rolls as officials of the cult of Yahweh. Israel is presented as a theocracy. The importance of Samuel in particular as a priest is also apparent in his incorporation within the genealogy of Heman. The fact that all twelve tribes were originally included in the list of Levitical cities depicts yet again the unity of the people of Israel under David. The distribution of the Levites among the tribes suggests that the author views them as integral to Israel's identity and make-up. The enumeration of the Levitical towns may also reflect the Chronicler's effort to defend or legitimate the Levites' right in the Persian period to a heritage in Israel consisting of certain towns and their "open lands."

The Northern Tribes (1 Chronicles 7)

Chapter 7 provides the genealogies for the remaining tribes in the following order: Issachar (vv. 1-5), Benjamin (vv. 6-11), Naphtali (vv. 11-12), Manasseh (vv. 14-18), Ephraim (vv. 20-29), and Asher (vv. 30-40). All of these tribes were located in the northern part of Palestine.

Literary Analysis

Similarities in form, length, and terminology among the genealogies of Issachar, Benjamin, and Asher indicate that they may once have stood together as part of a military census. Key idioms in these three genealogies—"to enroll" and "by their genealogies"—represent late biblical Hebrew and, in the latter instance, adopt the terminology of the Priestly writer in the Pentateuch. Given the Chronicler's interest in "all Israel," it is unusual not to find genealogies for Dan and Zebulun included among these northern tribes. Their absence is likely accidental, and many scholars restore a brief genealogy for Dan in v. 12 (see below).

Exegetical Analysis

Descendants of Issachar

The geneaology of Issachar (vv. 1-5) extends four generations beyond the patriarch. It is basically segmented in form (see introduction under genealogies), although it lists only one son of Uzzi's. The names of Issachar's sons in verse 1 are drawn from Gen 46:13 and Num 26:23-25, except for the different spelling of Puah in Chronicles. The notice about the judge Tola in Judg 10:1 is strikingly similar to the names of Issachar's sons (Tola, Puah, Jashub, Shimron): "After Abimelek there arose to save Israel Tola son of Puah, son of Dodo, a man of Issachar who lived [*yōšēb*] in Shamir in the highlands of Ephraim." The Chronicler apparently created a genealogy drawing from the Judges text. The military terms and titles in verses 2-4 are obvious. The setting of Issachar's grandsons at the time of David in verse 2 is chronologically erroneous. However, it reinforces the Chronicler's idealized portrait of the unity of "all Israel" in David's reign.

Descendants of Benjamin

It is surprising to find the genealogy of Benjamin next in verses 6-11. Typically in 1 Chronicles (2:1; 12:33-34; 27:18-19), as in Gen 46:13-14 and Num 26:23-27, Zebulun follows Issachar. Moreover, chapter 8 contains another, more extensive genealogy for Benjamin. The present genealogy for Benjamin begins abruptly with Benjamin's name in verse 6; the Hebrew text does not have the word "sons of," though it is certainly possible that this word was lost through accidental omission. The ending of the genealogy (v. 12) is also disturbed and many scholars restore a brief genealogy for Dan here, corresponding to the remarkably brief genealogy of Naphtali in verse 13. Taking all of these considerations into account, it is hard to resist the suspicion that the genealogy of Benjamin here has come in secondarily and perhaps displaced those of Dan and Zebulun and most of Naphtali's. Whether this happened as the result of editorial reworking or textual corruption is unclear. Some scholars (Curtis 1910:145-49) have even argued that the genealogy actually is Zebulun's rather than Benjamin's. Unfortunately, the present evidence admits little more than suspicion and speculation.

The structure of this genealogy is clear. The names of Benjamin's three sons are followed, each in turn, by the names of their sons and the total number of warriors in their lines. The source of the genealogy, then, or at least its names and numbers is a military census. Other genealogies for Benjamin occur in Gen 46:21; Num 26:38-41; and 1 Chr 8. However, the only name that all four have in common, besides that of Benjamin, is Bela, although 1 Chr 7:6 and Gen 46:21 both name Becher as one of Benjamin's sons. It may well be that the differences are due to sociological changes (e.g., the rise or decline of certain clans) that occurred within the tribe at various periods. With the exception of Anathoth and Alemeth (v. 8), which are place names, the names in the list all appear to be personal names.

Verse 12 clearly stands outside of the Benjaminite genealogy in verses 6-11. While it may simply be a fragmentary addition to that genealogy (Williamson 1973; 1982:78), most scholars reconstruct here a brief genealogy for Dan. The main reason for this is the similarity of verses 12-13 to the genealogies of Dan and Naphtali in Gen 46:23-25. The names of Naphtali's sons are the same except for minor spelling differences, and verse 13 refers to the "sons [plural] of Bilhah" as in Gen 46:25, where the sons are Dan and Naphtali. Perhaps more important is the occurrence of the name of Dan's son Hushim (Gen 46:23) in 1 Chr 7:12. A common reconstruction of the verse, therefore, begins by deleting Shuppim and Huppim as a misplaced gloss on verse 6 that draws on the names of Benjamin's sons in Gen 46:21; Num 26:39. Then, instead of "the sons of Ir, Hushim the sons of Aher" one reads, "the sons of Dan: Hushim, his one son." The major difficulty of this reconstruction is that the origin of the name "Ir" (which means "city" in Hebrew) and how it came to replace "Dan" remain unexplained.

Descendants of Manasseh

The genealogy for Manasseh in verses 14-19 is full of problems and requires frequent reconstruction. To begin, in other genealogies Manasseh has only one son, Machir. Asriel is mentioned in Num 26:31 as a son of Gilead and in Josh 17:1-3 as one of the clans descended from Manasseh and Machir. What is more, the following clause, "whom she bore," has no subject in Hebrew. It is common to regard the name Asriel as an erroneous scribal repetition of the clause ʾăšer yālĕdāh ("whom she bore") or vice versa. But this leaves either Asriel or the following clause in place and unaccounted for. Then, in verse 15 the names Huppim and Shuppim recur (cf. v. 12), yet they play no further role in the genealogy. As in verse 12, therefore, they are often deleted from verse 15 as a misplaced gloss on verse 6. Furthermore, in verse 15, Maacah is referred to as "his [apparently Machir's] sister," but in verse 16 as Machir's wife. Some scholars substitute the name of Hammolecheth, apparently Gilead's sister, from verse 18 for Maacah here. There is also an obscure reference to "the second, Zelophehad" with no indication how or to whom he was second. Attempts to reconstruct this verse differ, and there is no consensus solution. The problems continue in verses 16-17 where the list of Machir's sons concludes with the statement that these were the sons of Gilead, leading some scholars to replace Machir's name with Gilead's in verses 15-16 and to make Maacah Gilead's wife. Finally, there is the problem of Shemida in verse 19. While Shemida is mentioned in Num 26:32 as a son of Gilead, he does not appear previously in the present passage. Some have proposed adding Shemida's name to the list of Hammolecheth's sons in verse 18, but this still leaves his relationship to Gilead unclear.

Since a genealogy of the eastern half of Manasseh was given in 5:23-24, one might expect that the present genealogy would focus on the western half of the tribe, and the western half is indeed represented by Zelophehad (cf. Num 27:1-11; 36:1-12), as well as Abiezer, Mahlah, Shemida, Shechem, Likhi (= Helek?), and perhaps Asriel, all of which occur in other genealogies of western Manasseh (Num 26:28-34; Josh 17:1-3). Shechem, to be sure, is a well-known place west of the Jordan. Nevertheless, Manasseh's origins still seem to be eastern—through Machir and Gilead, each of which is a region or clan east of the Jordan—particularly if Asriel in verse 14 is an accidental repetition and not listed as Manasseh's firstborn son. The reference to the Aramaean concubine (v. 14) indicates ethnic ties between the Manassites and the Aramaeans. Similarly, Maacah is the name of a clan east of the Jordan associated with the Geshurites, who inhabited the Golan Heights (Deut 3:14), as well as the name of a Geshurite princess whom David married, probably as a treaty ratification, and who bore Absalom (2 Sam 3:3). The name Bedan (v. 17) occurs elsewhere only in 1 Sam 12:11, where it is problematic, referring to a judge who is not mentioned in the book of Judges.

Descendants of Ephraim

The genealogy of Ephraim in verses 20-29 actually consists of two genealogies (vv. 20-21a, 25-27) separated by an anecdote (vv. 21b-24) and followed by a list of settlements of Ephraim and Manasseh (vv. 28-29). The material here is similar in form to the genealogies for Simeon and the Transjordanian tribes in 4:24–5:22 and may once have been connected with them. The first genealogy for Ephraim in verses 20-21a presents one son (Shutelah) and eight grandsons of Ephraim, at least some of whom are killed by raiders from Gath (v. 22). This is probably not the Philistine Gath but rather the town of Gittaim (Mazar 1954). The names, however, are repetitive, with Shutelah being both the son and a grandson of

Ephraim, and there being two pairs of grandsons with the same names—Tahath and Elead(ah). Apparently, two genealogies have been combined here, and scholars have offered two explanations about how this took place. One view holds that the sons of Ephraim who were killed were Shutelah, Ezer, and Elead (vv. 20a + 21$a\beta$) and that another genealogy has been interpolated in between through the process of narrative resumption (see above on 5:1) with the name Shutelah. This explanation, however, does not really account for the repetition of Tahath. Another possibility is that two variant but parallel genealogies have been combined in verses 20-21a. This explanation accounts for the repetitions but not for the different form of presentation of the last two names, Ezer and Elead (v. 21a), that is, they are not followed by "his son." Shetulah is the only name in this list that also appears in the Ephraimite genealogy in Numbers 26:35-36, though the names Becher and Tahan, which appear there, are very similar to Bered and Tahath. A third, more recent reconstruction (Na'aman 1991) finds the core of this unit in the anecdote in verses 21$a\alpha\beta$-25$a\alpha$+ 31b-39 (see below) and sees the surrounding material in the rest of verses 20-21, 25-29 as the Chronicler's composition based on earlier biblical sources.

The narrative in verses 21-24 is primarily an etiology on the name Beriah that contains several interesting features. First of all, the story takes place with Ephraim, his brothers, and his children in the land of Canaan. This is in remarkable contrast to the story in Genesis and Exodus, according to which Ephraim was born in Egypt and evidently lived his entire life there in the course of the 400(+) years that the Israelites stayed in Egypt (Gen 15:13; Exod 12:40). The contradiction is difficult to explain. Japhet (1993:181-84) took it as evidence that the Chronicler saw the Israelites as indigenous to Canaan. But this seems unlikely in light of allusions elsewhere in Chronicles to the conquest of Canaan (see above on 4:34-43; 5:25) and of Chronicles's dependence on the Pentateuchal and Deuteronomistic traditions. Another possible explanation is that this etiology preserves a variant tradition of a much briefer stay in Egypt (Knoppers 2004:592). The etiology is reminiscent of the story of the prayer of Jabez in 4:9-10 in that both are based on popular etymologies. The narrative relates Beriah's name to the word for evil (rāʿāh), but this will only work if that word is prefixed with the preposition bĕ, "in" or "with." Even then it is not entirely clear how the name's meaning relates to the story. The journey of Ephraim's brothers "to comfort him" is reminiscent of the mission of Job's three friends (Job 2:11). Beriah's daughter, Sheerah, stands out as the only woman in the Bible credited with building cities (v. 24). While her namesake, Uzzen-sheerah, is otherwise unknown, Upper and Lower Beth-Horon are important towns in the Ephraimite highlands.

The goal of the second genealogy in verses 25-27 is Joshua, Moses' successor, although the Chronicler says nothing about Joshua's role as leader of the conquest. Joshua is the first of several Israelite leaders from Ephraim, including Samuel and Jeroboam, a fact that may explain the Chronicler's particular interest in Ephraim. Like the genealogy of David in 2:10-15, Joshua's genealogy may be artificially constructed. Joshua's father has been linked to Ephraim through Elishama son of Ammihud (Num 1:10). Tahan and Telah (= Shuthelah) are known from Num 26:35, and Ladan is very similar in Hebrew to "of Eran" in Num 26:36. Resheph may be an accidental repetition of part of the name Rephah that precedes it, since Resheph lacks the "his son" that typically follows a name in this genealogy. But both names may have been added to fill out ten generations between Ephraim and Joshua, inclusive.

Verses 28-29 conclude the section on the Joseph tribes (Manasseh and Ephraim) by listing their settlements. The Ephraimite list in verse 28 begins at Bethel then moves east (Naaran), west (Gezer), north (Shechem), and south (Ayyah). It therefore appears to detail the boundaries of the territory claimed by Ephraim. The list of Manasseh's towns in verse 29 is essentially taken from Judg 1:27-28 and Josh 17:11-13, both of which state that these towns were settled by Canaanites whom the Israelites were unable to drive out. The Chronicler omits this latter, his list of settlements implicitly claiming the promised land far beyond Persian Yehud for Israel.

Descendants of Asher

The genealogy of Asher in verses 30-40 consists of three parts: a list of the sons of Asher and of Beriah (vv. 30-31*a*), a mixed genealogy traced through Heber (vv. 31*b*-39), and a conclusion (v. 40). The Chronicler borrowed the first part from Gen 46:17 (cf. Num 26:44) and composed the conclusion. The second is unparalleled. Various inconcinnities in the list, especially the different forms of names—Shomer and Shemer, but also Hotham and Helem, whom some scholars would equate, as well as Shua and Ulla—indicate that this genealogy is a collection of loosely related notices dealing with the line of Heber. The conclusion makes use of military terminology and suggests that, like the genealogies for Issachar and Benjamin in this chapter, this one may be drawn at least in part from a military census. The total of warriors, 26,000, however, is small by comparison to the other two tribes. The Heberites were probably a southern branch of Asher that lived in the Ephraimite highlands rather than along the northern coast with the rest of the tribe (Edelman 1988; Na'aman 1991). The names of Helem's four sons (v. 36) correspond to the regions of Ephraim traversed by Saul in 1 Sam 9:4-5: Zophah = Zuph, Imna = (Ben)jamin, Shelesh = Shalishah, and Amal is an error for Shaalim. The Chronicler's inclusion of this genealogy suggests that he used whatever sources were at his disposal in an effort to include all of the tribes of Israel. It also suggests that he had little information about the northernmost tribes Asher, Dan, Zebulun, and Naphtali. A further intriguing feature of this genealogy is the presence of non-Israelite names: Shua is Canaanite (Gen 38:2); Aram is Aramaean; Harnepher is patently Egyptian. This may indicate the mixed heritage of the Heberites. These names lend further support to the idea that the Chronicler understands Israel's and Judah's make-up to be ethnically diverse.

Theological Analysis

The genealogies in this chapter reinforce two important points of the Chronicler's theology that have surfaced in earlier material. The first of these is the "all Israel" theme, which lies at the heart of chapters 1–9. The extremely brief genealogies of Naphtali and Dan (reconstructed) attest the Chronicler's desire to include all of the tribes in his portrait of Israel united under David. "All Israel" includes both people and land. The Chronicler's inclusions of the settlements of these tribes lays claim to the land promised to Israel, at least as an ideal. This ideal conception of the land of Israel includes much more than the territory of the Persian province of Yehud. Second, as in his presentation of Judah, the Chronicler has not shied away here from including non-Israelite elements in its ethnic make-up. While Japhet's contention that this chapter reflects the Chronicler's view of Israel as originating within the land rather than as a result of the exodus and conquest probably takes this point too far, it is quite striking that the Chronicler's idealized portrait of Israel is one that incorporates ethnic diversity within the unity of the tribes.

BENJAMIN (1 CHRONICLES 8)

Chapter 8 contains the second, more extensive genealogy for Benjamin (in addition to the one in 7:6-12). There is a certain geographical logic to the placement of this chapter in the arrangement of the tribal genealogies. The Chronicler begins with Judah, moves to the Transjordanian tribes, then to the Galilee and south to conclude with Benjamin. This arrangement is another indication that the present genealogy is original to the Chronicler's list while the one in chapter 7 is later. As the last of the tribal genealogies, this extensive genealogy for

Benjamin serves along with those for Judah and Levi as the basic structure around which chapters 1–9 are built. The multiple lists for Benjamin attest a special interest in the tribe in the post-exilic community because of its inclusion in Persian Yehud.

Literary Analysis

The genealogy for Benjamin divides into the following parts, each with a geographical reference: verses 1-7, the sons of Benjamin and Ehud at Geba; verses 8-14, the genealogy of Shaharaim in Moab; verses 15-28, Benjaminites in Jerusalem; verses 29-32, Benjaminites in Gibeon; verses 33-40, the genealogy of Saul. The primary genealogical form in the chapter is "X begat Y," but there is a mixture of other forms as well, indicating the collective nature of the genealogy. Several orga-nizing rubrics have been used to impose order on the diversity of independent, genealogical notices. These include: "[all] these were the sons of" (vv. 6*a*, 10*b*, 38*b*, 40*b*), "[these were] the heads of the fathers" (vv. 6*b*, 10*b*, 13*a*), and historical notices (vv. 6*b*, 12*b*, 13*b*).

Exegetical Analysis

Verses 1-2 match Num 26:38-39 in setting the number of Benjamin's sons at five, but the names are not identical. Both texts agree, along with Gen 46:21, in listing Bela first. The explicit reference to him as firstborn (*bkr*) in verse 1 may hide the name Becher, which also occurs in Gen 46:21. All three texts agree in naming Ashbel. Ahrah may be a corruption of Ahiram. Nohah and Rapha are otherwise unknown, though the latter name appears again in verse 37.

Among the sons of Bela in verses 3-5 Addar may be a variant of Ard (Gen 46:21; Num 26:40). The name Gera occurs twice, and this remains unexplained. Many scholars reconstruct Abihud as "the father of Ehud" (*ʾăbî ʾēhûd*), referring to the first Gera. The reconstruction provides a link between verses 3 and 6, without which there is no connection between Ehud

(v. 6) and the previous genealogy. The names Shephuphan and Huram continue the variation of Muppim/Huppim (Gen 46:21) and Shuppim/Huram (Num 26:39). Ehud (Abihud) does not appear in Gen 46:21 or Num 26:38-41 and was likely included here under the influence of the story about him in Judges. Manahath (v. 6) is customarily identified with a site just three miles southwest of Jerusalem, so that the reference to exile is unusual and may be used to connote emigration.

Shaharaim, whose family is the subject of verses 8-14, is not previously mentioned and may be a variant or error for one of the foregoing names that is similar—Huram or Ahrah (Ahiram?). Shaharaim is reported to have divorced his first two wives, one of whom, Hushim, is otherwise known as the only son of Dan (Gen 46:23). The settlements of her descendants are identified as Lod and Ono and Aijalon, all three Danite towns relatively far from Benjamin. This excerpt may indicate the absorption by Benjamin of originally Danite clans. Gath (v. 13) is probably Gittaim (see 7:21). In verse 14 Ahio could be a proper name or mean "his brother."

Verses 15-28 record the names of heirs in five families of Benjaminites who settled in Jerusalem. These five were already mentioned in verses 12-14: Beriah, Elpaal, Shemei (= Shema), Shashak, and Jeroham, who is probably to be identified with Jeremoth. The summary in verse 28 about the "heads of the fathers" living in Jerusalem is artificial and in some tension with what precedes. It seems to summarize the entire Benjaminite genealogy and, as such, contradicts previous references to Benjaminites living elsewhere (vv. 6, 8, 12, 13). It is nearly identical to 9:34 and may have been borrowed along with the passage in 9:35-44 (see below). Still, Jerusalem is described elsewhere as a part of Benjamin's allotment (Judg 1:21) in the same terms as of Judah's (Josh 15:63). The Chronicler may be trying to update that message for his time by showing that the Benjaminites were an essential part of Yehud and had equal claim with Judah to the institutions of Jerusalem.

The list of Benjaminites in Gibeon in verses 29-32 leads into the genealogy of Saul in verses 33-38. These verses are essentially repeated in 9:35-44, and it seems likely that they were borrowed from there into the present context. This would explain the awkward presence of 8:28, as we have seen. Also, the genealogy of Saul in 9:35-44 provides a transition into the narrative about him in chapter 10.

No explicit connection is given between Jeiel (restored in v. 29 from 9:35), founder of Gibeon, and Benjamin. Perhaps this reflects the tradition in Josh 9 that the Gibeonites were originally indigenous Hivites. It is surprising to find Saul's genealogy among the Benjaminites at Gibeon, since he was from Gibeah (1 Sam 10:26) and is accused of attempting to annihilate the Gibeonites (2 Sam 21:1-2). It may be that the two names—Gibeon and Gibeah—have been confused; they are similar in Hebrew, and their confusion is attested elsewhere. Gibeon was an important site in the postexilic community, so that it may have usurped Gibeah as Saul's home. However, this difference may also suggest that Saul's genealogy has been attached to that of the Gibeonite Benjaminites. Such an attachment would have been aided by the similarity of names, specifically that of Kish, Saul's father (vv. 31, 33). Zur (8:30) is also similar to Zeror, the name of Saul's great-grandfather in 1 Sam 9:1. However, Saul's grandfather in 1 Sam 9:1 is neither Ner nor Jeiel but Abiel. Some scholars believe that Saul was originally from Gibeon and that the Deuteronomistic Historian suppressed this information in favor of Gibeah (Blenkinsopp 1974; Edelman 2001:77). Others have suggested a literary/ideological explanation: that the Chronicler worsens Saul's attempt to annihilate the Gibeonites by making them his own flesh and blood.

The genealogy is the most extensive one for Saul in the Old Testament, encompassing fifteen generations from Ner to the sons of Azel. From Saul's grandson, Micah, on (vv. 35-38) the genealogy is unique in the Old Testament. Verse 33 (// 9:39) uniquely lists Saul's four sons—the three from chapter 10 and

Eshbaal. It is striking that Chronicles retains the –baal element of these names, including the name Baal in verse 30. In Samuel Eshbaal and Meribbaal appear as Ishbosheth and Mephibosheth. Most scholars believe that these names reflect a scribal substitution of the Hebrew word *bōšet* meaning "abomination" for the name of the Canaanite deity. The author(s) in Chronicles apparently borrowed the names from sources that had not yet been altered by scribes and did not change them. Indeed, the retention of the –baal element may be intended to reflect negatively on Saul and his line. The final two verses (vv. 39-40) are in a different form from the genealogy that precedes and are unattached to it in the sense that Eshek is not earlier mentioned as Azel's brother. These verses may originally have been independent and simply have been attached at the end, something that is not uncommon in genealogies.

Theological Analysis

The length of the genealogy for Benjamin and the fact that it is singled out from those of the other northern tribes illustrate the significance of Benjamin to the post-exilic community. Benjamin was one of the most important components, along with Judah and Levi, of Persian Yehud. The extensive genealogy for Saul (cf. also 9:35-44) may reflect the Chronicler's recognition of Benjamin's significance. These references to Saul, especially in 9:35-44 (see below) foreground the narrative about Saul in chapter 10. At the same time, the –baal names in Saul's line may hint at a negative orientation on the part of the Chronicler towards Saul in contrast to David.

THE RESIDENTS OF JERUSALEM AND GIBEON (1 CHRONICLES 9)

Chapter 9 has a dual function exhibited by its two main parts. The first part (vv. 1-34) serves as a conclusion to the genealogies in chapters 2–8 by listing the residents of Jerusalem who are at the heart of the people of Israel. Then, the genealogy of Saul in verses 35-44 provides a transition to the narrative about Saul's death in chapter 10.

Literary Analysis

The first part of the chapter (vv. 1-34) further divides the inhabitants of Jerusalem by groups (cf. v. 2): the laity of Israel (vv. 3-9), priests (vv. 10-13), Levites (vv. 14-16), gatekeepers and other Levites (vv. 17-34). This structure seems dependent on Neh 11 and is unique to these two texts, and most scholars believe that verses 3-17 have been adapted from Neh 11:3-19, albeit probably in an updated form or variant textual tradition. However, Knoppers (2004 and work cited there) has argued, largely on the basis of textual evidence, that the two lists represent independent development by their respective editors of a common list.

Exegetical Analysis

Residents of Jerusalem

Verses 1-2 have been interpreted in two ways, resulting in two very different settings for the subsequent lists. The more common interpretation sees these verses as turning to the post-exilic resettlement of Judah and especially Jerusalem. Such is clearly the case for the parallel in Neh 11:1-3, which characterizes the list that follows as a record of the "heads of the province" who lived in Jerusalem in order to help rebuild its walls. However, Japhet (1993:206-7) has argued that the Chronicler is really setting the passage in the time of David, as he did with chapters 2–8. The issue turns on verse 1*b*, which refers explicitly to the exile of Judah; Japhet thinks it is a secondary interpolation. She contends that the dichotomy of Israel and Judah and the severity of the exile are foreign to the Chronicler's perspective. She points out further that Chronicles lacks titles and designations such as "heads of the province" that are found in Nehemiah 11 and that betray a Persian setting for the lists. In addition, the expression *hayyôšĕbîm hāriʾšōnîm* may be understood as the first or former inhabitants and not "the first to live again," as in the NRSV (there is no "again" in the Hebrew). Japhet's proposal is appealing for the continuity in chronological setting that it discerns between chapter 9 and the texts on either side of it (chs. 2–8, 10). One consideration against the proposal is that the word "unfaithfulness" in verse 1*b* is typical of, though by no means unique to, the Chronicler.

The list of groups in verse 2*b* matches those in Neh 11:3, except that the Chronicler has left out the heirs of Solomon's servants to concentrate on the main groups. The verse is a kind of outline of the chapter. Verses 3 and 34 frame the enclosed lists as inhabitants of Jerusalem. The reference to Ephraim and Manasseh in verse 3 is an addition on the part of the Chronicler to the parallel in Neh 11:4; verses 4-9 do not include any Ephraimites or Manassites. These two tribes epitomize and stand for the northern kingdom and thus here attest the Chronicler's interest in all Israel as well as in Jerusalem as Israel's center.

The list of Judahites in verses 4-6 is drawn from Neh 11:4*b*-6, with some minor variations of names, such as Uthai (v. 4) for Athaiah (Neh 11:4). In both 1 Chr 9:5 and Neh 11:5, "Shelanite" should probably be read in place of Shilonite (i.e., from Shelah son of Judah; cf. 2:3; 4:21). Chronicles, therefore, lists representatives of the three main branches of Judahites (Perez, Zerah, and Shelah), while Neh 11 lists only two. Also in verse 5 Asaiah appears to be a variant of Maaseiah (Neh 11:5), unless the latter was lost from the text of Chronicles by inadvertent scribal omission. The reading "the firstborn and his sons" is unusual at this point and may be a corruption of "son of Baruch" in Nehemiah, since the word "firstborn" and the name "Baruch" have the same letters (but not in the same order) in Hebrew.

The list of Benjaminites in verses 7-9 is obviously related to the one in Neh 11:7-9. Both start with Sallu son of Meshullam, and Hodaviah son of Hassenuah is probably Judah son of Hassenuah in Neh 11:9. But otherwise, the lists are different. The Nehemiah reading with its unusually long pedigree for Sallu and its reference to his brothers seems corrupt. The summary statement in verse 9, "All these were heads of fathers' houses according to their fathers' houses," is the Chronicler's addition to the list, as it corresponds to his organizational rubrics elsewhere (e.g., 5:24; 7:40).

Scholars find the clearest evidence for the Chronicler's dependence in this chapter on Neh 11 in the list of priests in verses 10-13. As it stands, the list mentions six priestly families: Jedaiah, Jehoiarib, Jachin, Azariah, Adaiah, and Maasai. However, it seems odd that a lineage is provided for the last three but not for the first three. According to Ezra 2:37-38 and Neh 7:39-41, there were four priestly families who returned from Babylon: Jedaiah, Pashhur, Immer, and Harim. The post-exilic date of the present list is, therefore, obvious. The absence of Harim's line here is due either to textual corruption or to the decline of that family's importance. Some scholars (Rudolph 1955:84) reconstruct the names from Jedaiah through Ahitub as a single genealogy. While this reconstruction yields only three families—Jedaiah, Adaiah, and Maasai—it also makes the line of Jedaiah considerably longer than the other two. The line of Jedaiah might be longer if it is the high priestly line, as has been suggested on the basis of the title "prince of the house of God" in verse 11. But it remains uncertain that this title was ever used for the high priest. In verse 13, the Chronicler sums up the titles that are dispersed through the list in Nehemiah (11:12a, 13a, 14a), thus apparently abridging the latter. The Chronicler also uses what is typically a military title, "valiant men," to commend the priests' labors.

The list of other Levites in verses 14-16 actually contains two elements: Levites (vv. 14-15a, through Galal) and singers

(vv. 15*b*-16). The two parts are clearer in Neh 11:15-18; the text in Chronicles seems to have suffered corruption especially in the names Bakbakkar (< Bakbukiah in Neh 11:17), Heresh, and Galal (accidental repetition from v. 16?). Of the singers, the familiar houses of Asaph and Jeduthun are represented. The third representative, Berechiah, may reflect an early stage in the process of adding the family of Heman, where the name Elkanah occurs frequently (6:33-36 [Heb. 18-21]).

Verses 17-22 deal with the gatekeepers. Except for the names Akkub and Talmon in verse 17 (// Neh 11:19) the Chronicles account is independent. The office of gatekeeper emerges only in later portions of the Old Testament, although the origin of the office is ascribed to David (see below). Chronicles reflects a later understanding of the organization and affiliation of the gatekeepers than Ezra–Nehemiah. In the latter, the gatekeepers are not Levites (Ezra 2:42 = Neh 7:45; Ezra 10:45; Neh 11:19; 12:25), while their Levitical heritage is emphasized in this passage and elsewhere in 1 Chronicles (23:3-5; 26:1-11). Also, except for Shallum (also called Shelemiah, Meshullam, and Meshelemiah) the families of the gatekeepers change with new families emerging. In the present passage, Shallum is obviously the leading family; his name is listed first and he is called "the chief" (v. 17). This family is stationed at the "king's gate" on the eastern side of the temple (v. 18), which must have been the most prestigious post. The Levitical affiliation of the gatekeepers is explicitly affirmed (v. 18). Shallum's lineage is traced through Korah (v. 19). The Korahites at one time represented the Kohathites as one of the groups of singers (2 Chr 20:19; Pss 42, 44–49, 84–85, 87–88). They were apparently replaced by the family of Heman (6:33-38 [18-23]) and became gatekeepers. Even though 26:1 still lists them among the Asaphites (who were singers), the present passage describes them as gatekeepers (v. 19) and bakers (v. 31).

In addition to their Levitical heritage, the Chronicler appeals to the antiquity of the gatekeepers' office as a way of legitimizing their existence in the present. Phinehas, the grandson of Aaron, was their former or first leader (v. 20)—the Hebrew may be interpreted either way—hinting without explicitly claiming that the institution originated with Moses. Phinehas's execution of the Israelite man and Midianite woman in Num 25:6-8 made him an appropriate model for the combined cultic and marshal duties of the gatekeepers. But it was David and Samuel who "founded" the gatekeepers (v. 22), by which the Chronicler may have in mind David's organization of the gatekeepers into divisions (ch. 26). Throughout these verses the Chronicler alludes to the institutions of the wilderness period, especially the tabernacle: "the tent" and "the camp" (v. 19), "the tent of meeting" (v. 21), and even "the tent of the house" (v. 23). The Chronicler may be attempting here to harmonize variant traditions about the origins of the gatekeepers. But in this way he affirms both the antiquity and the continuity of their office and role.

The specific duties of the gatekeepers are laid out in summary form in verses 23-29. A more detailed description comes in chapter 26. Their tasks are basically three: opening and closing of the entrances on all four sides of the temple complex, standing guard over those gates, and maintaining the equipment and supplies used in the temple service. The set of tasks in verse 29 is comparable to the one in 1 Chr 23:29; only the mixing of spices is reserved for the priests (v. 30). This does deviate from other traditions (Num 4:16) that seem to reserve others of the duties in verse 29 for the priests. The reference in verse 31 to Mattithiah as Shallum's firstborn is at variance with verses 19 and 21, where that place seems to be held by Zechariah, explicitly so in 26:2. This variation illustrates the composite nature of the present list and reflects the changing nature of the gatekeepers over generations. Verse 33 mentions the singers and points out their exemption from the duties of the priests and other Levites. The verse seems somewhat out of place, and one wonders whether it may be a later addition patterned partly after the beginning of verse 34: "these are the singers/heads of the fathers' houses." Verse 34 then frames the passage, along with verse 3, making it clear that the list they enclose is of residents of Jerusalem.

Residents of Gibeon

Following the list of Jerusalem's residents, the author turns to Gibeon's residents and the genealogy of Saul. This provides a ready transition into the story of Saul's death in chapter 10. The juxtaposition of Jerusalem and Gibeon is also suggestive of the sequence of Saul and David, with Gibeon somehow standing in the place of Gibeah, Saul's capital, and Jerusalem being David's capital. The genealogy is the same as the one in 8:29-38 with a few minor differences. Ner may have been accidentally omitted from the version in chapter 8, although it is also possible that his name was added in 9:36 in order to link Saul's genealogy more closely to the Gibeonites.

Theological Analysis

In addition to the "all Israel" motif, which runs throughout chapters 1–9, the present chapter highlights the importance of Jerusalem as Israel's religious and political center. Both the Davidic king and the temple—the Chronicler's two major interests—are there. The genealogy for Saul at the end of the chapter, whether properly associated with Gibeah or Gibeon, reminds the reader that Saul's capital was not the divinely chosen city of Jerusalem. This is another indication of Saul's being out of favor with God.

An implicit point in chapters 1–9 as a whole is the continuity of the postexilic community with the preexilic era, especially the reigns of David and Solomon. It was then that Israel was united under a Davidic ruler with its capital in Jerusalem. That was Israel's "golden age," which the Chronicler presents idealistically in chapters 1–9 and with which he identifies the community of his own day. The presence of the Levites at Israel's center, both through their settlement in Jerusalem in the present chapter and through their placement in the center of the genealogies in chapters 1–9, illustrates the relationship of Israel with God and implies God's continuing direction of this people. Moreover, the

Chronicler presents the Levites and temple worship, either of his day or of David's—if not both!—as standing very much in continuity with the tabernacle and the institutions of Israel at its very beginnings in the wilderness. This continuity invests the institutions of the postexilic period with antiquity and tradition that stem from the very origins of Israel as a nation. It also leaves the reader with the sense that these cultic traditions, like the God they are intended to honor, are never changing in their true essence. Considering the background of chapter 1, the genealogies in chapters 1–9 present a global message about Israel's significance as the heart of God's plan for the world at large.

THE REIGN OF DAVID (1 CHRONICLES 10:1–22:1)

The account of David's reign in Chronicles is essentially a condensation of 1–2 Samuel. The narratives about Saul in 1 Samuel are all omitted, except for the account of his death in chapter 31. Also omitted are the stories about the affair with Bathsheba and Absalom's revolt in 2 Sam 10–20. What remains focuses on David's enthronement and transfer of the ark, the Davidic promise, and David's wars. The Chronicles story of David, therefore, is more than a simple repetition of what is in Samuel. As noted in the introduction, the Chronicler revised his Deuteronomistic source by omitting parts of it, adding to it, rearranging its episodes and making a variety of changes in wording, sentence structure, and the like. As a result, he created a new work, one that highlighted and enhanced the theological lessons from David's reign that the Chronicler perceived in Samuel. Thus, in omitting the Bathsheba story, for instance, the Chronicler did not necessarily intend to deny that it happened. It was simply not the part of the story and the aspect of David's character to which the Chronicler wished to draw attention as worthy of emulation.

Having both the Chronicler's finished product and his Samuel source provides the reader with a unique "laboratory" to examine how the Chronicler made use of his sources. No other portion of the Bible offers this opportunity. It also helps to place the Chronicler's own interests into clear relief. At the same time, we must try not to lose sight of the forest for the trees. Close comparison with Samuel is important, but Chronicles must also be appreciated in its own right as a work of literary creativity and theological sophistication.

A glance at the materials about David that the Chronicler retained suggests that of primary importance to him was David's preparation for the temple. David conquered Jerusalem and transferred the ark there, establishing, in the process, the musical orders for continued worship in the future temple. He also conquered Israel's enemies round about, creating an era of peace so that his successor could carry out the actual construction of the temple.

YAHWEH GIVES THE KINGDOM TO DAVID
(1 CHRONICLES 10:1-14)

This chapter is a report of the battle between the Israelites and the Philistines on Mount Gilboa. Its real concern, however, is not to recount the details of the battle but to report the deaths of Saul and his sons. While Saul's death may seem at first glance an odd starting point for a new history, the story plays an important transitional role in several respects. Generically, chapter 10 obviously begins a new section of Chronicles. It moves from genealogy of the first nine chapters to narrative. It has continuity through Saul with the Benjaminite genealogy in 9:35-44. It also introduces the narrative about the consolidation of David's kingdom and the bringing up of the ark in chapters 11–16. The chapter, thus, shifts the focus of the history from the house of Saul to that of David. Since the remainder of 1 Chronicles recounts David's reign, and 2 Chronicles then continues the history of Judah, which is synonymous with that of the Davidic royal line, 1 Chr 10 establishes the trajectory for the rest of the Chronicler's history and introduces one of the Chronicler's leading concepts—the central importance of the Davidic king and the model of kingship provided by David.

Literary Analysis

The narrative in the chapter divides easily into three parts. The first seven verses describe the death of Saul, his three sons, "and all his house" (v. 6) in battle. Verses 8-12 recount the burial of Saul and his sons by the men of Jabesh-gilead. Then verses 13-14 are an epitomizing conclusion explaining the reasons for and significance of Saul's death.

Recent scholars have discerned another theme present in this chapter that also helps to explain why the Chronicler begins here. That is the theme of the exile. Israel's situation following Saul's defeat is one that will be repeated in its history and with which the Chronicler's immediate audience in the postexilic period can well identify. The nation has been devastated and is now in the control of a foreign adversary; it is kingless and must feel abandoned by its God. David, by virtue of his relationship with God, is Israel's salvation.

The account in verses 1-12 closely parallels 1 Sam 31. From this point on, the books of Samuel and Kings will serve as the Chronicler's primary source. As for much of 1–2 Chronicles, the problems or challenges posed by this passage have to do with its variations from its source text in 1 Sam 31. The extent to which the Chronicler has introduced deliberate changes into his Samuel source is a matter of some disagreement among scholars (see below). Indeed, the issue of the Chronicler's use of Samuel has been the focus of scholarly research on this chapter. But, as indicated above, the chapter has a distinct function within the Chronicles narrative. Both issues—the relationship of Chronicles to Samuel and the overall structure and distinctiveness of the Chronicles narrative—are important, and they are really two sides of the same larger concern. Passages such as verses 13-14, which are the Chronicler's own words, are especially significant for both issues, as they illustrate the Chronicler's skill as author and editor and highlight his theological and ideological interests.

Exegetical Analysis

The reasons for the differences between Chronicles and Samuel are not always easy to pinpoint. But they often highlight the Chronicler's special interests or message, and their subtlety illustrates his sophistication as an author. Of particular note in this chapter is Chronicles' statement in 10:6 that Saul and "all his house" died together (contrast 1 Sam 31:6: "his armor-bearer and all his men"). The Chronicler is not interested in the deaths of Saul's armor-bearer or his men but only in the demise of his house, which is what led to David's accession. The fact that the genealogy in 1 Chr 9:35-44 has Saul's line continuing through his son Meribbaal seems contradictory. But the Chronicler's point is ideological and not dependent on historical details: God replaced Saul's line with David's.

There are other minor differences in the description of the fate of the corpses of Saul and his sons in verses 8-12. Chronicles lacks the mention of the Astartes, reading "their gods" instead (1 Chr 10:10). It also lacks the references to the corpses being displayed on the city wall of Beth-shan (1 Sam 31:10)—only Saul's head is displayed on the temple of Dagon (1 Chr 10:10)—and to the burning of the bodies of Saul and his sons (1 Sam 31:12). Chronicles also uses a later Hebrew word for "body" or "corpse" than does Samuel. Scholars have debated the reasons for these differences—whether they arose from textual transmission or deliberate change—without reaching consensus. For our purposes, they simply illustrate the kinds of variations that can occur between Chronicles and its Samuel source without affecting the sense of the passage in any meaningful way.

Verses 13-14 are undoubtedly the Chronicler's own composition. They are replete with vocabulary and ideas that are favorites of his, especially the Hebrew roots for "unfaithfulness" and "seek," each of which is used twice here. These verses are the key to understanding the Chronicler's aim in beginning his history, or the narrative portion of it, with the story of Saul's death. The reference to Saul not keeping Yahweh's command alludes to 1 Sam 13:8-15, where Samuel tells Saul "you did not keep the commandment of Yahweh your God which he commanded you" (v. 13) and probably to 1 Sam 15 as well, since Samuel later accuses Saul of failing to obey Yahweh on that occasion (1 Sam 28:18). In a broader sense, the statement characterizes Saul's reign as a whole as disobedient. The mention of Saul's consulting a medium refers more directly to 1 Sam 28 and involves a play on Saul's name with the verb *šāʾal* "to ask, consult." The Chronicler is obviously familiar with these stories and apparently assumes that his audience knows them as well. But he has chosen not to include any of the material relating to Saul because his primary interest is in David. These two verses, then, succinctly summarize what was important for the Chronicler about Saul. Because of his unfaithfulness, God killed Saul and removed his royal house in order to turn the kingdom over to David.

Theological Analysis

This brief story has far-reaching theological ramifications. First and foremost, the Chronicler emphasizes the sovereignty of God. Saul died in battle, but his death was not an accident of war. It was brought about by God. Yahweh, therefore, has power over life and death. Yahweh is also the one who directs the affairs of his people. Yahweh is also the sovereign of history. Historical outcomes do not run their own course in the Chronicler's view but are divinely determined. Thus, it was Yahweh who took the kingdom away from Saul and turned it over to David. The kingdom and the nation are not David's, much less Saul's, but belong to God (cf. 1 Chr 17:14).

While God is sovereign over human history and may be intimately involved in directing it, God is not a micromanager. This chapter indicates the importance to Israel of righteous human leadership albeit under Yahweh's aegis. Saul is judged not by his military or political successes and failures but by religious criteria. The human leader's first responsibility is to God, specifically trust in and reliance on God. Saul was unfaithful (v. 13), a key term for the Chronicler referring to a religious offense, especially committed by kings. He also failed to "seek" Yahweh—the Chronicler's expression for single-minded devotion to God coupled with right action. In both cases, the Chronicler seems to be characterizing Saul's entire reign rather than referring to a single event. Thus, the fact that the latter accusation stands in some tension with the story in 1 Samuel 28, where Saul consults a medium because of Yahweh's refusal to respond to his inquiries, is irrelevant. David is the model king because of his faithfulness and his inquiry of Yahweh (14:10, 14)—precisely the opposite of Saul.

The story of Saul illustrates the Chronicler's doctrine of divine (often immediate) retribution for sin. Unfaithfulness was typically punished, as here, by military defeat. Its consequences, therefore, are borne not only by the individual (Saul) but also by his family and by the entire nation. Saul's defeat was devastating for Israel. Under David Israel prospers. So the faithfulness or unfaithfulness of Israel's leaders has consequences for the nation as a whole. To the extent that Saul's situation is a metaphor for the exile, Israel's hope for restoration lies in faithfully seeking God and trusting in his intervention through a Davidic king.

David's Anointing by All Israel at Hebron (1 Chronicles 11:1–12:40 [Hebrew 41])

These two chapters together really function as a prelude to the account of David's transfer of the ark to Jerusalem in chapters 13–16. In effect, in chapters 11–16, three significant events— David's anointing, the conquest of Jerusalem, and the transfer of the ark—are combined into one enormous celebration involving all Israel. Our treatment of chapters 11–12 and 13–16 separately is done partly for purposes of manageability but is also warranted by structural features in the text (see below). English Bibles, following the LXX, render 1 Chr 12:4-5 of the Hebrew as one verse, so the Hebrew verse numbers from then on in that chapter are one later than the corresponding English ones. Our treatment follows the English numbers.

Literary Analysis

The unity and originality of these two chapters were widely doubted by scholars of previous generations, with most, if not all, of chapter 12 being attributed to later additions. But more recent scholarship has perceived evidence of overall unity here and has tended, therefore, to ascribe tensions and differences to underlying sources used by the Chronicler. (For a useful review of the arguments, see Knoppers 2004.) Thus these two chapters consist of several distinct, smaller units that have been organized in an artful and meaningful manner. These are best presented in table form:

11:1-3	report of David's anointing in Hebron, with a fulfillment notice in v. 3 (// 2 Sam 5:1-3)
11:4-9	battle report—the conquest of Jerusalem—plus a building report (v. 8) and an epitome or summary statement (v. 9) (// 2 Sam 5:6-10)
11:10-25	anecdotes about David's military heroes (// 2 Sam 23:8-23)
11:26-47	roster of leading warriors (vv. 26-41a // 2 Sam 23:24-39)
12:1-7	list of warriors who joined David at Ziklag
12:8-15	list of Gadites who joined David in the wilderness
12:16-18	anecdote about Benjaminites and Judahites who joined David in the wilderness
12:19-22	report about Manassites who joined David when he returned to Ziklag

12:23-37   tally of troops who came to David's anointing in
            Hebron
12:38-40   report of the festivities at Hebron

The extent of the unit is marked by a framework in 11:1-3
and 12:38-40. Both passages refer to the coming of all Israel to
Hebron to make David king. The unit contains three main kinds
of material—reports, anecdotes, and lists. The Chronicler has
employed two principal techniques in his arrangement of these
materials. One is what might be called "flashback"; the other is
chiasm. Thus the present unit begins at Hebron with anecdotes
and a roster of the warriors who supported David's enthronement (11:1-47). Then there is a flashback to the warriors who
joined David at Ziklag (12:1-7), followed by a flashback to
those who joined him even earlier in the wilderness (12:8-15).
This is the first half of the chiasm. The second half reverses the
order of the first, beginning with a flashback to the wilderness
(12:16-18), continuing with another flashback to Ziklag (12:19-
22), and ending where the unit began with another list of troops
who came to Hebron to celebrate David's anointing (12:23-40).

Further patterns operating in the arrangement of these materials have to do with the Chronicler's sources. The entire passage presupposes the chronological order and content of the
stories in 1 Samuel, where David, in flight from Saul, spends
time in the Judean wilderness (1 Sam 23–26) and then is given
the town of Ziklag (1 Sam 27). The mention of the Philistines'
dismissal of David from their army before the war on Mount
Gilboa (1 Chr 12:19) refers to 1 Sam 29, and the mention of
the band of raiders in 1 Chr 12:21 may allude to the Amalekite
band whom David pursued after their raid on Ziklag in 1 Sam
30. In addition, the first four units of the passage in Chronicles
—essentially chapter 11—are drawn from 2 Sam 5 and 23
(except for 1 Chr 11:41b-47). The rest of the materials—essentially chapter 12—come from sources not preserved in the Bible
or are the Chronicler's own compositions. The tally of troops

in 12:23-37 resembles musters in Num 1 and 26 and may have been composed with these texts as models but was not directly borrowed from them. The account progresses, therefore, from canonical (specifically Samuel) to non-canonical texts, though the latter presuppose and are based on canonical material.

Exegetical Analysis

The New King and His Army (1 Chr 11:1-46)

The Chronicler's emphasis on all Israel is affected both by what he has omitted from his rewriting of the Samuel story and by what he has included. Because of his omission of the material in 2 Sam 1–4 (David's accession to the throne of Judah, the subsequent civil war between Israel and Judah, and the assassinations of Ishbaal and Abner) the Chronicler is able to change entirely the meaning of the report of David's anointing over Israel that he has taken from 2 Sam 5:1-3. In 2 Sam 5:1 "all the tribes of Israel" refers to the northern tribes apart from Judah, for it is those tribes that had been at war with David and under the leadership of Ishbaal. But the Chronicler's narrative proceeds directly from the statement in 10:14 that Yahweh "turned the kingdom [as a unit] over to David son of Jesse" to the report that "all Israel gathered together to David at Hebron" (11:1). Thus in Chronicles, "all Israel" is "the kingdom" and includes Judah. The statement in 11:3 that the elders came "to the king" betrays its original context in Samuel where David is already king over Judah, but is premature in Chronicles where he becomes king over all Israel at once. What is more, David's anointing over united Israel in Chronicles is explicitly by divine ordination, in other words, "according to the word of Yahweh by Samuel" (1 Chr 11:3), a phrase lacking in Samuel and almost certainly added by the Chronicler. In short, the kingdom, which belongs to Yahweh and which he removed from Saul, was immediately turned over by God to David, whom all Israel anointed according to divine order.

The Chronicles version of David's anointing also lacks the summary statement for David's reign that occurs at this point in 2 Sam 5:4-5. These two verses are lacking in some of the textual witnesses to Samuel, leading some scholars to suggest that they were not in the text of Samuel copied by the Chronicler. This is possible, but the Chronicler would certainly have omitted these verses if they were in his Samuel text, since the distinction in 2 Sam 5:5 between David's reign over Judah alone and his reign over all Israel and Judah would undermine the Chronicler's "all Israel" theme. The Chronicler admits that David reigned seven or seven and a half years in Hebron and thirty-three years in Jerusalem (1 Chr 3:4; 29:27). But he never indicates that David's reign in Hebron was over Judah alone or anything less than all Israel. For the Chronicler it is only David's reign over united Israel that holds significance for his audience as the ideal of what Yahweh's people should be.

The story of the conquest of Jerusalem in 11:4-9 (// 2 Sam 5:6-10) is an irregularity in its present context. It is chronologically problematic. Why would the troops rally to Hebron if David had conquered Jerusalem and established it as his capital by moving there? It also interrupts the chiastic structure of this unit that was described earlier. The reason for this irregularity is that the Chronicler's point here is ideological rather than historical. He depicts the conquest of Jerusalem as David's first act as king not because it makes chronological sense but in order to show the primary importance of the temple for Israel. The author of Samuel did the same thing by placing David's conquest of Jerusalem immediately after his accession to the throne of Israel (2 Sam 5:1-10). By retaining the order of units in Samuel and then adding the rest of the material in chapters 11–12, the Chronicler reinforces and revises Samuel's message. Chronicles highlights not only the centrality of Jerusalem but also the involvement of all Israel in conquering it. Jerusalem is the heart not only of the Davidic dynasty but also of all Israel. Thus 1 Chr 11:4 says that "David and all Israel" (contrast 2

Sam 5:6: "the king and his men") marched to Jerusalem. The difference is significant. The king's men at this point in Samuel are his fellow Judahites who have been with him in the wilderness all the time he was fleeing from Saul. But in Chronicles Jerusalem is conquered by a united Israel. Moreover, the broader context in the rest of 1–2 Chronicles makes clear the reason for Jerusalem's primacy in a way that is not so immediately evident in Samuel–Kings. That reason is the temple. Indeed, from this point on, the rest of 1 Chronicles will really be focused on preparations for the temple.

Other changes in the Chronicles account of the conquest of Jerusalem in comparison to the version in Samuel appear to have been motivated by factors other than ideology. The Chronicler simplified the account by removing the confusing references to the blind and lame in Samuel. Chronicles also introduces Joab into this anecdote and uses it to explain how he came to be David's army commander. The brief note in 1 Chr 11:4 that Jerusalem is Jebus is borrowed from Judg 19:10 and attests the Chronicler's tendency to combine and interpret scripture with scripture. The "Millo" (v. 8) means "fill" and was apparently some structural feature of the city of Jerusalem. Its exact nature and location are uncertain, but some identify it with the "stepped stone structure" found by archaeologists on the eastern slope of the "city of David."

The introduction to the roster of leading warriors in 11:10 is the Chronicler's composition and shares his two principal concerns expressed in verses 1-3: the chiefs along with all Israel supported David's kingship, which took place "according to the word of Yahweh." The latter phrase is ambiguous. It could refer to a prophecy that was fulfilled in David's accession as in verse 3 or to a promise or a command, as in 10:13.

The roster of leading warriors in the remainder of chapter 11 falls into two sections. Verses 11-41*a* are drawn from 2 Sam 23, while the origin of verses 41*b*-47 is unknown. The first section consists of three parts: anecdotes about the "three" (vv. 11-14), anecdotes about other warriors (vv. 15-25), and the rest of the roster (vv. 26-47). The structure has become obscured because of two textual problems. The first was the accidental loss of most of 2 Sam 23:9-11 including the name of the third member of the "three." The result in Chronicles is that there are only two members of the "three" whose exploits are described in verses 11-14—Jashobeam and Eleazar. The correct reading is retained in 2 Sam 23:9-11, where one finds the name of the third member of the "three," Shammah. The second textual problem is the confusion throughout the chapter between the similar words "three" and "thirty." The common solution to this problem that is adopted here is that the "three" were Jashobeam, Eleazar, and Shammah, and that in verse 20, where Abishai is included among the "three," the word "thirty" should be read instead.

The anecdotes in verses 15-25 begin with a feat performed by three warriors. To judge from verse 15 ("three of the thirty") these warriors were not "the three" but three unnamed members of the larger honor guard known as the "thirty." However, it is clear from the placement of this anecdote as well as from verse 19 that the anecdote has come to be associated with "the three." The other anecdotes in this section concern Abishai (vv. 20-21) and Benaiah (vv. 22-25). The three warriors in verses 15-19 were honored by David's refusal to drink the water they had retrieved for him from Bethlehem, because he "poured it out to the LORD." David considered the water sacred because the men had risked their lives to acquire it. As such, it was not suitable for human consumption but could only be offered as a libation to God; only God was worthy of such a sacrifice. The description of the Egyptian whom Benaiah defeated in verse 23 resembles that of Goliath in 2 Sam 17. This is another example of the Chronicler combining references from earlier texts or interpreting one text through another.

The roster of warriors in verses 26-41a is drawn from 2 Sam 23:24-39, though several of the names have been altered in one version or the other in the process of textual transmission. The roster is explicitly identified in 2 Sam 23:24 as the "thirty," and the original list probably did consist of thirty names. (There are currently thirty-one, but there are several places where textual corruption could have resulted in the addition of an extra name.) However, Chronicles does not use the designation "the thirty" for the roster at all but instead calls it "the mighty men" (v. 26). This may be because the Chronicler has appended the additional roster in verses 41b-47, which increases the total number of warriors far beyond thirty.

Little can be said for certain about this additional roster. The place names that can be identified were all east of the Jordan, so that it appears to be a list of warriors who resided among the two and one-half tribes (Reuben, Gad, and half of Manasseh) in that region. It may even be another list of thirty, if this is the meaning of the thirty who were with Adina the Reubenite in verse 42. This verse may also have served as the heading of the original roster that has been appended. But the date and precise setting and nature of this list are uncertain.

Others Who Joined David (1 Chr 12)

Unlike chapter 11, 1 Chr 12 has no parallel in 1–2 Samuel. The chapter consists mainly of lists, but there is ample evidence of the Chronicler's hand. The theme of the chapter might be characterized as "coming to David," as various military contingents are described as joining David earlier in his career when he fled from Saul and in Hebron (see above on the literary analysis of the chapter). Thus, verses 1-22 fall into four sections, each beginning with a reference to some group of individuals who came to David (vv. 1, 8, 16, 19). The lists are not wooden but employ a striking variety of terms for weapons and for military units and offices. This variety, together with the thematic nature of the chapter, suggests that it is a literary composition rather than a collection of official documents. This is not to say that the Chronicler concocted the lists out of whole cloth. There are hints that sources of some kind underlie the lists. The small numbers in verses 1-22 suggest genuineness rather than invention. And while the numbers in verses 23-37 appear exaggerated, Judah's figures are relatively small—a fact that seems to run counter to the Chronicler's primary interest in Judah. The tribes are arranged not according to the traditional order of birth of their namesakes (Gen 29:31–30:24) but geographically, from south to north, first west of the Jordan, then east. But again, if the Chronicler did use source materials for these lists, we know nothing of their original setting. The distinction between priests and Levites as well as the prominence of the Zadokites in verses 27-28, if these verses are not an interpolation, indicate a post-exilic setting for the list in verses 23-37.

In the context of the lists in this chapter, the anecdote in verses 16-18 stands out. This is almost certainly the Chronicler's own composition; it accords well with his ideas and vocabulary, especially the repetition of the word "help." God's helping the king is an important subtheme, especially in 2 Chronicles. The story is anthological in the sense that it is made up to a large extent of excerpts from other biblical texts. The expression "although there is no wrong in my hands" (v. 17) is similar to Job 16:17; "may the God of our fathers see and rebuke you" is like Exod 5:21 with the epithet, "the God of our fathers," which is a favorite of the Chronicler's; and "the spirit came upon Amasai" resembles Judg 6:34 and 2 Chr 24:20. Amasai seems to be identified with Amasa—David's nephew and the commander of Absalom's army (2 Sam 17:25; 1 Chr 2:17), and his speech here may have been inspired by the report of David's reconciliation to the army of Judah through Amasa after the defeat of Absalom in 2 Sam 19:13-15. It also reverses the call to arms against Rehoboam and the Davidids in 2 Chr 10:16, and since the latter conflates 1 Kgs 12:16 and 2 Sam 20:1, it clearly served as the basis for the present passage rather than the other way around. David's speech and Amasai's response have four key words: peace (translated "friendship" in 12:17 NRSV), help, God, and David. Amasai and those with him assure David that they come in peace. As noted, this speech both is patterned after and counters the cry for secession from the Davidic house in 2 Chr 10:16. It is a pledge of loyalty to David motivated by the recognition that he is supported by God.

The first four lists of the chapter end with a summary statement in verse 22. The various military groups that came to David formed "a great army, like the army of God." The statement is ambivalent. It was an enormous army. It was also God's army because it served God's chosen king of God's chosen nation. Thus, David's coronation is a religious event as much as or more than a political one. The kingdom is also God's, and, just as in 10:14 God turned it over to David, so here the assembly's convening in order "to turn the kingdom of Saul over to [David]" is "according to the word of Yahweh" (v. 23). David is chosen by both God and the people. The numbers of soldiers reported in verses 24-37 are impossibly high. Scholars often explain them by resorting to the theory that the Hebrew word for "thousand" may refer to a military division of much fewer than a thousand men. However, the Chronicler is here depicting a celebration of enormous significance, and the exaggerated numbers are most likely part of this depiction (Klein 1997).

The final unit of the chapter (12:38-40) shows not only the unity with which all Israel anointed David king but also their enthusiasm. The latter point is evident in "with a whole heart" (translated "of a single mind" in NRSV) in verse 38 and the description of the occasion as one of celebration and joy. It is somewhat surprising at first glance that the celebration is entirely secular in character—without sermons, prayers, sacrifices, or any other explicitly religious element. This is understandable, however, once the nature of Hebron is considered. Hebron is not Jerusalem. It is the site of David's enthronement but not a sanctuary. But even Jerusalem at this time is not yet prepared for worship. The ark has not been brought there, and the temple has not been built. These matters will constitute the focus of the Chronicler's attention for the rest of David's reign.

Theological Analysis

The structure of the unit in chapters 11–12 hints at the aims and leading concepts that the Chronicler wished to communicate through it. His main point is that "all Israel" was united in anointing David as their king. This is in stark contrast to 1–2 Samuel, which recount David's flight and exile from Saul and then long civil war between the houses of Saul and David before David finally gains control. Even during his reign, tensions with the North and the Benjaminites remain. In Chronicles, David is unanimously celebrated as king immediately upon Saul's death. The various lists of military leaders, particularly in 12:23-37, show that by "all Israel" the Chronicler means that all of the tribes were represented—Saul's tribe, Benjamin, included. Indeed, the largest contingents come from the tribes at the northernmost reaches. The fact that the closing unit, 12:38-40, is the Chronicler's own composition reinforces the intentionality of the framework with 11:1-3 and the chiasm in the larger passage (chs. 11–12) and shows that the Chronicler is at pains to highlight the gathering of the troops representing all Israel in Hebron with the single purpose of making David king.

Thus, the three main ideological themes of 1 Chronicles—David, the temple, and all Israel—come together in a unique and forceful way in chapters 11–12. The tribes are united and enthusiastic in their support of David and in their conquest of Jerusalem. As just mentioned, the Chronicler's usual emphasis on ritual worship is lacking because Jerusalem has not yet become a sanctuary. But the Chronicler is obviously laying the groundwork for that eventuality, and the Levites are included among the tribes that endorse David.

Other theological points emerge particularly from the encounter of the Benjaminites and Judahites with David in

12:16-18. David is presented as someone who relies on divine guidance and help. The contrast with Saul, who failed to inquire of Yahweh (10:13-14), is implicit. David calls on God to judge, and Amasai notes that God helps David. It is this dependence upon God by David as Israel's leader and God's help in return that bring unity and peace to the people as a whole.

David Brings the Ark to Jerusalem
(1 Chronicles 13:1–16:43)

The next unit in 1 Chronicles comprises the subsequent four chapters, which are built around the account of David's bringing up the ark to Jerusalem. This account falls into three principal sections concerning David's first attempt to bring the ark to Jerusalem (ch. 13), David's other activities in Jerusalem (ch. 14), and David's second, successful transfer and installation of the ark (chs. 15–16).

Literary Analysis

Each of the three main sections of this unit mentioned above is composed of its own separate subunits and genres. The report of David's first, aborted attempt at bringing the ark to Jerusalem in chapter 13 also revolves around an etiology for the place name Perez-uzzah (v. 11). The report of David's other activities in Jerusalem in chapter 14 includes a brief report on the building of David's house (v. 1) and an epitome on Yahweh's establishment of David as king (v. 2), a list of David's sons born in Jerusalem (vv. 3-7), and two battle reports detailing David's victories over Philistines (vv. 8-12 and 13-17). The first battle report contains another etiology on a place name incorporating the Hebrew root *prṣ*; this time the name is Baal-perazim. The second battle report closes with another epitome for David, this one dealing with his fame and reputation among other nations. The report of David's successful transfer and installation of the ark in chapters 15–16 breaks down further into a report of David's instructions to the Levites (15:1-24), which in turn includes two rosters, one of the Levitical chiefs (vv. 5-10) and the other of Levitical musicians (vv. 16-24); a report of the installation proper of the ark in Jerusalem (15:25–16:3); and a report of David's ordering of the service before the ark (16:4-43). This final subunit further contains two rosters of Levitical musicians (vv. 4-6) and Levitical ministers (vv. 37-42) and Asaph's psalm of praise (vv. 8-36), which borrows portions of Pss 105, 96, and 106. The literary structure of this unit, then is quite sophisticated. An outline may help to clarify it.

I. Report of David's first attempt to bring up the ark (1 Chr 13)
II. Other activities in Jerusalem (1 Chr 14)
    A. David's palace and international fame (vv. 1-2)
    B. David's sons born in Jerusalem (vv. 3-7)
    C. Defeat of the Philistines at Baal-perazim (vv. 8-12)
    D. Defeat of the Philistines in the valley of Rephaim (vv. 13-17)
III. The successful installation of the ark (1 Chr 15–16)
    A. David's instructions to the Levites (15:1-24)
    B. Installation of the ark (15:25–16:3)
    C. Establishment of the Levitical orders of service for the ark (16:4-43)

Following his typical procedure, the Chronicler has made use of material in Samuel as the basic building blocks of his own account in this unit. But as usual, he has completely recast the Samuel narratives by altering their setting and order and by adding material from other sources and from his own hand. The result is a new, sophisticated literary creation with its own set of themes and ideological points. The following table showing the canonical parallels will aid our subsequent discussion.

1 Chr 13:1-4 no parallel
1 Chr 13:5-14 // 2 Sam 6:1-11
1 Chr 14:1-16 // 2 Sam 5:11-25
1 Chr 14:17 no parallel
1 Chr 15:1-24 no parallel
1 Chr 15:25–16:3 // 2 Sam 6:12*b*-19*a*
1 Chr 16:4-7 no parallel
1 Chr 16:8-22 // Ps 105:1-15
1 Chr 16:23-33 // Ps 96:1-13
1 Chr 16:34-36 // Ps 106:1, 47-48
1 Chr 16:37-42 no parallel
1 Chr 16:43 // 2 Sam 6:19*b*-20*a*

In effect, the Chronicler has taken the account of David's installation of the ark in Jerusalem from 2 Sam 6 and has divided it into three parts (vv. 1-11, 12*b*-19*a*, 19*b*-20) and used them as a framework. Then, he has inserted other materials between these three parts in order to build his own version of the event. The most striking alteration of the Samuel account in terms of historical setting is in the Chronicler's reversal of the passages in 2 Sam 6:1-11 and 5:11-25. The items in 2 Sam 5:11-25 all fall between the accounts of David's conquest of Jerusalem and his bringing up of the ark. This arrangement leaves the reader with the impression that a considerable amount of time passed between these two events—enough time for David to build his palace, father several children, and fight battles against the Philistines. By reversing 2 Sam 5:11-25 and 6:1-11, the Chronicler conveys the message that David's first official act following his anointment as king was to try to bring the ark to Jerusalem. The sequence of episodes in Chronicles is historically problematic in several respects—no interval of time is indicated between the events in 1 Chr 12 and those in 1 Chr 13; David could not have brought the ark to Jerusalem without encountering the Philistines; and the items now reported in 1 Chr 14 (// 2 Sam 5:11-25) would have taken much longer than the three-month interval between the first and second attempts to bring the ark to Jerusalem (1 Chr 13:14). But as we saw in the previous unit, it is the Chronicler's theological interest rather than any historical concern that determines the arrangement of episodes in his narrative.

The passages in Chronicles that are unparalleled in Samuel fall into three categories. Some (13:1-4; 14:17) are clearly the Chronicler's own compositions. Others (15:1-24; 16:4-7, 37-42) are likely based on sources that are no longer extant, though this does not necessarily mean that these sources originally had anything to do with the transfer of the ark or even dated from the time of David. Finally, in 16:8-36 the Chronicler pieced together portions of three psalms so as to create a new psalm fit for the occasion described in the narrative and in line with his theology. This compositional technique was not unique to the Chronicler but is also attested in the book of Psalms itself (compare Ps 57 and 60 with 108) and among the Qumran (Dead Sea Scroll) community. Of course, the Chronicler has also occasionally introduced minor but significant changes into the narrative of Samuel that he has borrowed.

The question of the authorship of chapters 15–16 has been debated intensely in the history of scholarship. Some have seen one or more of the lists as secondary. Others regard the references to the priests as the result of later editorial activity. Some have even considered the psalms to be secondary. As indicated above, chapters 13–16 evince an overall design that reflects a single hand. However, the design does preclude the possibility that some of chapters 15–16 were added secondarily.

Exegetical Analysis

The First Transfer of the Ark (1 Chr 13:1-14)

The first four verses of chapter 13 are the Chronicler's own composition and set the stage for his aims in the four chapters that comprise this unit. There is no chronological notice or break in the narrative in Chronicles to indicate a change of setting for the events described in chapter 13. Hence, the first attempt to bring the ark to Jerusalem in Chronicles follows immediately upon and indeed grows out of the enthronement of David in the previous chapter. Thus, the same interests that were present in 1 Chr 11–12 continue into this next unit. David has been established as the king over Israel, and as the model king, his first act is to ensure proper worship in Israel. He moves immediately to establish Jerusalem as the center of such worship. It is fair to say that the two institutions, Davidic kingship and cultic centrality of Jerusalem, go hand in hand in Chronicles. In the Chronicler's vision it is not possible to have one without the other. This will become even clearer in the account of Nathan's oracle to David about his proposal to build a temple (1 Chr 17), which could be seen as the capstone to this unit. The ideas of establishing and appointing are leading concepts in this unit. After David's establishment as king (14:2), he proceeds to establish (15:1, 3, 12; NRSV: "prepare") a place for the ark in Jerusalem. He then appoints the orders of the Levites for ministry to the ark, particularly the music associated with its service.

Of course, David does not act alone. He addresses his proposal to bring up the ark to all Israel who gathered for his enthronement according to chapter 12. Here they are called "the whole assembly of Israel," the term "assembly" being one that the Chronicler uses for liturgical gatherings. The Chronicler has David make his proposal to bring up the ark conditional upon two considerations: the approval both of the people ("if it seems good to you") and of God ("if it is the will of Yahweh our God"). The first condition really entails more than the approval of the people; it includes their active involvement. David comes up with the idea and takes the lead, but it is the people as a whole who carry it out. What is more, the people include not just those who are present but all the rest of the Israelites who were unable to attend David's anointing (v. 2).

The expression "our kindred who remain in all the land of Israel" inevitably brings to mind the remnant of the northern kingdom following the Assyrian destruction of 721 B.C.E. and the Babylonian captivity of 586 B.C.E. Evidently the Chronicler considered at least some of the people living in the former country of Israel in his day to be faithful to Yahweh, and they were among his target audience. The language of David's proposal, particularly the expression translated "let us send abroad" is unusual in its use of the verb *pāraṣ*, which usually means to "break forth." Its occurrence here anticipates one of the subthemes of the story in this chapter; the same root is found three times in the etiology in verse 11.

This entire setting is quite different from Samuel, where "David again gathered all the picked men of Israel" (2 Sam 6:1). There is no "again" in Chronicles, because the assembly from chapter 12 was never dispersed. While the "picked men" in Samuel are a military contingent, in Chronicles David adds to the already assembled people by summoning "all Israel from the Shihor of Egypt to Lebo-hamath" (13:6). These geographical designations are unusual and their exact references are uncertain. Shihor is Egyptian in origin and may refer, at least in the view of some biblical writers, to the Nile itself or a part of it (cf. Isa 23:3; Jer 2:18). But what is important is that these two places represent the northern and southernmost points, respectively, of the land settled by the people of Israel—even if other claims of the extent of David's empire exceeded these boundaries. It is all Israel—defined in the broadest terms possible—whom David invites and who have the power to approve or disapprove of the project. The Chronicles version is highly democratized in comparison to Samuel, where David's decision and actions are unilateral. The assembly is pleased by the proposal and instantly approves it (13:4). The Chronicler also gets in a reproach against Saul—the ark was ignored in his day despite the people's obvious enthusiasm for attending to it (13:3). As for David's second condition—if it is the will of

Yahweh—the narrative in Chronicles leaves the question open for the moment. It is this open condition that provides the narrative tension accounting for the placement of chapter 14.

The differences between the Chronicles version of the initial attempt to bring up the ark in 13:5-14 and its source in 2 Sam 6:1-11 seem to be due primarily to the Chronicler's use of a text of Samuel that was slightly different from and generally superior to the MT of Samuel. This is indicated in part by a comparison of the MT of Samuel and Chronicles with the Dead Sea Scroll fragments of Samuel (4QSam[a]). In cases where 4QSam[a] is not extant, it is often uncertain whether differences in Chronicles are intentional and if so the reasons for them. A case in point is the list of musical instruments in 1 Chr 13:8, which differs in its last two items ("cymbals and trumpets") from 2 Sam 6:5 ("sistrums and cymbals," and the Hebrew word for "cymbals" is different). In Chronicles, trumpets are priestly instruments (15:24; 16:6, 42), and cymbals, as well as lyres and harps, were associated with Levites (15:19-21; 16:5). But if the Chronicles reading is ideologically motivated, what is the reason behind it? Why would the Chronicler introduce these instruments, if he is trying to assert the need for Levitical and priestly involvement in the initial transport of the ark (so Knoppers 2004)? It may be that the Chronicler changed the list to reflect the presence of instruments that were more common in his day.

Aside from the nature of the Chronicler's text of Samuel, the main problem of this chapter is the death of Uzzah. Why did God "break forth" against him and what does that have to do with David and his effort to bring the ark to Jerusalem? On one hand, the answer to this question is easy. Uzzah died because he touched, and thereby desecrated, the most sacred object in Israel. How Uzzah's death related to David is more complex and sets up the narrative tension that holds this chapter and the following ones together. Uzzah's death showed divine disapproval. But for what? Was God unhappy with David? With the very attempt to move the ark? This is what lies behind David's question in verse 12, "How can I bring the ark of God into my care?" (NRSV). Hence, he leaves the ark with Obed-edom until he can determine the answer to this question. The fact that God blessed Obed-edom and his household (v. 14) shows that Uzzah's death was not occasioned by divine displeasure with the moving of the ark per se. The blessing is a sign from God— not an automatic benefit of the ark's presence. Incidentally, the Chronicler has turned Obed-edom into a Levite (1 Chr 26:4)— despite the fact that he is called a Gittite (v. 13), in other words, a person from the Philistine city of Gath—evidently because he hosted the ark for three months. In the next chapter, the Chronicler spells out the divine blessings upon David, indicating that God was not displeased with David either. In chapters 15–16, it becomes clear that Uzzah's death, though his own responsibility for desecrating the sacred ark, was brought on by the illegitimate process by which the ark was being moved.

Other Activities in Jerusalem (1 Chr 14:1-17)

As noted, this chapter is taken from 2 Sam 5:11-25 with the addition of verse 17. But the Chronicler has completely changed its meaning by placing it in a new setting. In its original setting in 2 Sam 5:11-25, this material followed directly on the accounts of David's anointing as king of Israel and of his conquest of Jerusalem and thus had as its overriding theme the transition of David's kingship from Hebron to Jerusalem. In Chronicles, as we have seen, the Hebron period is acknowledged but not stressed, since David rules over all Israel from the outset. Chapter 14 has a different function relating to the failed attempt at transferring the ark. One of the Chronicler's basic theological tenets, one that will surface more often in 2 Chronicles, is that of immediate, divine retribution for sin. Conversely, disaster and failure are typically explained by the Chronicler as punishment for sin. The story of Uzzah's death perfectly illustrated this doctrine. Uzzah was punished instantly for his violation of the sanctity of the ark. But David perceived that there was more behind this expression of divine displeasure than Uzzah's transgression. The blessings on Obed-edom showed that God was not unhappy with the simple transfer of the ark. David's own prosperity described in chapter 14 showed that he was still the recipient of divine favor. The problem would turn out to be the way in which the ark was transported.

The blessings on David in this chapter are of three kinds: political (vv. 1-2), familial (vv. 3-6), and military (vv. 7-16). Verses 1-2 well illustrate the Chronicler's subtle yet effective method of recasting the material. In 2 Sam 5:1-2 the building of David's palace takes place immediately after his conquest of Jerusalem and emphasizes God's establishment of David as king over Israel in his new capital. In the Chronicles arrangement of materials, as we have seen, David's first act is cultic—to bring up the ark—rather than to build his own house. The Chronicler also stresses God's establishment of David in Jerusalem, but there is an additional dimension. Hiram's contacting David is a sign to him that Yahweh has established him as king and therefore Uzzah's death was not the result of God's rejection of David. A very slight difference in Chronicles in regard to the reading of Samuel reinforces this point. Second Samuel 5:12 says, "David knew that Yahweh had established him as king over Israel *and that* his kingdom was highly exalted." First Chronicles 14:2 lacks the "and" and reads "David knew that Yahweh had established him as king over Israel *because* his kingdom was highly exalted." Whether this minor change was intentional or not, it alters the meaning of the verse in a way that fits with the Chronicler's point. David perceives that he has not lost favor with God because of the prestige he has in the view of rulers like Hiram, who is willing to build a palace for him.

The list of David's sons in 14:3-7 comes from 2 Sam 5:13-16. There is also a similar list in 1 Chr 3:5-8. While the three lists are very close, no two are identical. The differences are the result of textual transmission rather than any intentional change by the Chronicler. The introduction in 1 Chr 14:3 probably does reflect such a change, however. It lacks the references to concubines and to Hebron. No reason for the omission of "concubines" is immediately apparent; it could have been lost by accident, or it could be an addition in Samuel. While Chronicles mentions elsewhere that David reigned seven years in Hebron (1 Chr 29:27), in this context the Chronicler is emphasizing God's blessing of David in Jerusalem, where he intends to move the ark. Since a reference to Hebron would detract from this emphasis, its omission may be intentional. The list as a whole continues the Chronicler's message about the prosperity and productivity that were signs of Yahweh's blessing of David. In addition, it may be seen as providing a contrast to Saul, whose line, for all practical purposes, ended on Mount Gilboa.

The third kind of blessing received by David is that of military victory leading to enhanced international reputation (14:8-17). Once again, the Chronicler has borrowed texts from Samuel but has radically altered their setting and meaning. In Samuel, the Philistines leave David alone as long as his domain includes only Judah. It is only when he becomes king over Israel and threatens to unite it with Judah, that the Philistines, who would be squeezed between the two, come against him. In Chronicles, this background is lacking, and the Philistines attack as soon as David is made king over "*all* Israel."

There are minor differences between the versions of the first battle in 2 Sam 5:17-21 and 1 Chr 14:8-12 that appear to be mainly changes in style and updates of vocabulary introduced by the Chronicler. The reading "by my hand" in 1 Chr 14:11, where 2 Sam 5:20 has "before me" suggests an attempt to give David more credit as God's instrument. It is also a more exact fulfilment of God's promise in verse 10 to give the Philistines into David's hand. More intriguing are the differences between 1 Chr 14:12, in which David has the Philistine gods burned, and 2 Sam 5:21, where David and his men carry away the Philistine idols. The reference to "gods" in Chronicles is likely more original ("idols" in Samuel was probably introduced by a pious scribe who wanted to avoid recognition of their deity). But the burning of the gods follows the prescription of the law in Deut 7:5. Still, it may not have been the Chronicler who made this change, since it occurs already in an early set of Greek versions of Samuel.

This episode continues themes from previous passages in Chronicles. The verb "to burst forth," plays a role in this account as it did in the narrative about the first attempt to bring up the ark. In 1 Chr 14:11, as in 13:11, there is an etiology for a place name containing this word. A more important theme on display here is that of David's reliance on God, as he inquires about going up against the Philistines (v. 10). This inquiry was originally some kind of mechanical process akin to our flipping a coin, whereby some object was manipulated in order to determine the answer to a "yes" or "no" question. The Chronicler here draws another contrast between David and Saul. Saul inquired of a medium and did not keep Yahweh's command (1 Chr 10:13-14); David inquired of Yahweh and followed his instructions.

The second battle account in 1 Chr 14:13-16 reinforces these themes. David again inquires of God and this time receives detailed instructions about where to position his army and when to attack. He follows these instructions to the letter and wins a great victory, eradicating the Philistine threat from what is essentially Benjaminite territory. Once more, there is an implicit contrast with Saul, the Benjaminite, who not only failed to resolve the Philistine problem but also lost his life to them. The reason for Saul's failure and the difference between him and David is that while Saul sought to fight on his own and with his human army, it is the army of God who fights for David and upon whom David relies. The final verse of this chapter has no parallel in Samuel and is an obvious addition by the Chronicler. It brings together his main themes in this chapter:

The disaster brought about by Saul has been reversed. David has defeated the Philistines and reestablished Israel's independence. His renown as king of Israel is recognized by the nations. This is the result of a symbiotic relationship between David's faithfulness and Yahweh's blessing. David is thereby reassured that the failed attempt to transfer the ark was not occasioned by divine disfavor toward him or his household. Hence another attempt is warranted.

The Successful Transfer of the Ark (1 Chr 15:1-29)

This chapter has two distinct parts. The first twenty-four verses relate David's detailed preparations for the second attempt to transfer the ark, and they are unique to Chronicles. The rest of the chapter and on through 16:3 then tells of the successful installation of the ark in Jerusalem drawing on 2 Sam 6:12*b*-19*a*. The first part of the chapter contains two lists: one of the chiefs of the leading families of the Levites, who were the bearers of the ark (vv. 4-10) and the other of the Levitical musicians and singers (vv. 16-24). Both of these passages are often viewed by commentators as later additions for reasons that will be explained below.

The chapter begins with the recognition that David (his name is not present in the Hebrew of verse 1, but he is obviously the subject) has not forgotten about the ark in the midst of his building activities or even better that preparing a place for the ark remained uppermost among his building projects in Jerusalem. The blessing of Obed-edom and of David himself following the initial failure has led him to deduce that the transfer process was faulty the first time. Specifically, those involved failed to follow the prescriptions in the law for carrying the ark. David corrects this (15:2) by commanding that the Levites and no one else carry the ark. The command seems to presuppose the assembly in verse 3, and verse 2 may be out of place or secondary. But it does articulate the necessary change in procedure. The same idea is present in 2 Sam 6:13, where the ark is carried by men the second time rather than on a cart. But Chronicles elaborates the point. David's statement that the Levites alone should carry the ark because God chose them to carry it and minister to it is based on two verses in Deuteronomy (10:8; 18:5). This makes it clear that in Chronicles, the disastrous first attempt was brought about by a failure to follow the Mosaic law, in which David, as his command shows, is well versed. The scene is reminiscent of the first attempt in chapter 13; as in 13:5 David again gathers "all Israel" (15:3). But this time the focus is on the Levites. Nevertheless, David commands the Levites in the observation of their cultic duties.

The list in verses 4-10 follows a specific pattern. Six divisions or families of Levites are listed: Kohath, Merari, Gershom, Elizaphan, Hebron, and Uzziel. This division is unique; in other genealogies there are typically three sons or clans of Levi: Gershom, Kohath, and Merari. In Exod 6:16-25, for instance, Hebron, Uzziel, and Elizaphan are all in the line of Kohath. This is one of the reasons that the list is often considered secondary, occasioned perhaps by the mention of the Levites in verse 11. For each division, Chronicles names a chief and then gives the number of men in the division. The list may be a doublet to verse 11, where the same names occur without their family affiliations. Other scholars agree about the independence of the list in verses 4-10 but think that the six-part division of the Levites reflects a historical setting earlier than the Chronicler and that he incorporated the list through the technique of narrative resumption in verse 11. The focus on the Levites has led several scholars to conclude that the mentions of the priests in verses 4, 11, 14, and 24 are later additions. The references to gatekeepers in verses 18 and 24 also seem unconnected with their contexts and out of place, all the more so since Obed-edom is described in verse 21 (cf. 16:5) as a musician rather than a gatekeeper.

Verses 12-15 follow a pattern of command and completion. David's speech in verses 12-13 consists of a command to the

Levites to bring up the ark (v. 12) followed by the reason for the command in verse 13. Then verse 14, in language nearly identical to verse 12, reports that the Levites sanctified themselves and brought up the ark, and verse 15 describes in detail how they bore the ark with the poles on their shoulders, in conformity with Mosaic commandment (Num 7:9). The process described here accords with the description of the ark in Exod 25:14 as having poles attached by which it was to be carried, but the language does not match with any particular law in the Pentateuch, so that the statement "as Moses had commanded" is probably to be understood as a reference to a general impression about how the ark was to be handled. Of particular interest in this passage is verse 13, which is elliptical; the verb "carry" is not in the Hebrew. This places more weight on the pronoun, so that the clause might be translated, "Because it was not you the first time...." This accords well with the verses in Deuteronomy (10:8; 18:5) that assign the transport and care of the ark to the Levites. It is curious that the Chronicler nowhere alludes to Num 4:15, which threatens death for anyone who touches sacred objects. But David does not blame Uzzah; instead he uses the first person: "Yahweh our God burst out against us, because we did not give [the ark] proper care" (NRSV). A more literal translation of the latter phrase is "because we did not seek it according to the commandment," the "commandment" referring to the instructions in the law regarding the treatment of the ark as indicated in verse 15. David takes partial responsibility for the offense and sees himself sharing also in the punishment.

According to verse 16, David charged the chiefs of the Levites with appointing the singers and musicians for ministering to the ark. Some scholars see verses 16-24 as an addition, contending that it interrupts the connection between verses 15 and 25 and leaves the Levites standing with the ark on their shoulders (v. 15). Others, while not denying all of these verses to the Chronicler, find evidence of glossing in the references to

Obed-edom as a gatekeeper and to the priests in verses 18, 23-24. The three musical leaders appointed by the Levitical chiefs are Heman, Asaph, and Ethan, and they and their kinsmen represent the "first order" of musicians with the individuals listed in verse 18 representing the "second order." Verses 19-21 then list these same musicians according to the instruments they played: cymbals (v. 19), harps (v. 20), lyres (v. 21). Only the name Azaziah in verse 21 does not occur in verse 18. These appear to be two slightly different versions of the same list. However, verses 22-24, apparently continue the second list, naming Chenaniah as the conductor (v. 22), Berechiah and Elkanah as gatekeepers (v. 23), a list of priests who blew trumpets (v. 24a), and Obed-edom and Jehiah as gatekeepers (v. 24b). A third, briefer version of this list occurs in 16:5-6. The source(s) of this list is unknown. Heman, Asaph, and Ethan all appear in headings of Book III of the Psalms (Pss 73–89). The prominence of Heman and the inclusion of Ethan instead of Jeduthun may reflect shifts in the social status and leadership of the various groups of singers. The genealogy of the three is given in 1 Chr 6:31-47 [Heb. 6:16-32]). The terms "Alamoth" and "Sheminith" in verses 20-21 are musical terms of uncertain meaning that also appear in the psalms. An interesting suggestion for the former is that it be understood as "young women," that is, a choir of female singers (Knoppers 2004). The latter may be related to the number eight—an octave or eight-stringed instrument.

With verse 25, the Chronicler returns to his Samuel source (2 Sam 6:12b-19a), but there are several important differences. To begin, Chronicles expands the subject from David alone to "David and the elders of Israel and the commanders of the thousands," probably in line with his emphasis on all Israel being a part of the enterprise. The first half of verse 26 also betrays the Chronicler's hand and interest. The Samuel version (6:13) refers to the bearers of the ark sacrificing every six paces. For the Chronicler, however, the successful transfer of the ark on this attempt is due not simply to human effort but principally "because God helped the Levites."

The next verse (2 Sam 6:14 // 1 Chr 15:27) varies so much in the two witnesses as to be almost unrecognizable. The Chronicler has obviously added the middle part of 15:27: "as also were all the Levites who were carrying the ark and the singers and Chenaniah the leader of the music of the singers" (NRSV), since this is dependent on the depiction in Chronicles of the music that accompanied the ark. Both versions agree that David was wearing an ephod of fine linen. However, the Chronicler has apparently "toned down" the version in Samuel by omitting the reference to David's dancing and by referring to the ephod as a "robe," both of which occasion Michal's criticism in 2 Sam 6. The reference to a robe may also have been meant to deflect criticism of David for usurping a priestly role by wearing an ephod, which was a garment typically worn by priests. In verse 28 Chronicles has "all Israel" for 2 Sam 6:15's "David and all the house of Israel" and extends the list of instruments to include trumpets, cymbals, harps, and lyres. Both fit the Chronicler's interests, but unintentional expansion is also possible.

Finally, it also seems odd at first glance that the Chronicler has retained the mention of Michal in verse 29 (= 2 Sam 6:16). The verse interrupts the narrative about the progression of the ark, and the Chronicler has deleted the account of the conversation between David and Michal (2 Sam 6:20-23) for which the verse prepares in Samuel. Nevertheless, the verse does further the contrast between Saul and David that has surfaced previously in Chronicles. Michal's despising of David and of the celebration as a whole indicates that she, like her father, lacks an appreciation of the ark's importance.

Installation of the Ark and the Levitical Orders (1 Chr 16:1-43)

The first three verses of this chapter continue the account of the movement of the ark in parallel to 2 Sam 6:17-19a. The

Chronicler divided the Samuel account in the middle of verse 19 and retained verses 19*b*-20*a* as the close of the story (1 Chr 16:43). But between them he inserted the material in 16:4-42, which has no parallel in Samuel. The resulting depiction of the event is significantly different in Chronicles from Samuel. The bulk of the addition in Chronicles relates thanksgiving offered by the Levites in the form of a psalm and shared by the people. Chronicles also tells of further arrangements for the continuation of such worship activities in Jerusalem and in Gibeon.

The differences between 1 Chr 16:1-3 and its Samuel predecessor are slight. The only one worthy of note is in verse 1 where Chronicles uses a plural verb without an expressed subject and thus has the people as a whole rather than David alone offer sacrifices to God. The people, therefore, are not merely present but are active participants in the cultic celebrations.

Verses 4-5 represent a transitional stage in the development of the Levites. Their function as bearers of the ark is near its end, so that their primary role will soon shift to that of providing the music in the temple. Verse 5 is a third, briefer version of the list of singers in 15:17-18, 19-24; the names are identical or very similar, but there are fewer of them. It is difficult to explain the differences if this list was composed from the other two rather than being independent. Asaph alone is mentioned among the three houses of singers. But 16:37-42 explains that the Levitical musicians were divided into two groups; those under Asaph were stationed in Jerusalem with the ark, while those under Heman and Jeduthun went to Gibeon to minister in the tabernacle. In this listing of the singers, then, Asaph is dominant, and Jeduthun's name occurs instead of Ethan's. The reference to priests in verse 6 is sometimes perceived as foreign to the context and taken as a later addition.

Verse 7 bridges the list of musicians and singers in verses 4-6 with their task exemplified in the following psalm. The psalm is one of thanksgiving, and the introit, "O give thanks to Yahweh" occurs in both verses 8 and 34. Verses 8-22 are taken from Ps 105, which is a recitation of the faithful deeds of Yahweh. Certain verses of the psalm already seem quite appropriate to the setting in Chronicles. For instance, the admonition to "seek Yahweh . . . seek his presence continually" in 16:11 fits well with the new presence of the ark in Jerusalem. The psalm has been altered elsewhere in Chronicles so as to fit even more closely with its narrative setting. The Chronicler borrowed only the first fifteen verses of the psalm, halting the historical recitation just before the Joseph episode. This has the effect of emphasizing that the people and activities of David's day represent the fulfillment of the promises to the patriarchs. It is the faithfulness of Yahweh in carrying out those specific promises that provides the reason for giving thanks on this occasion. A minor alteration in verse 15 reinforces this message. Where Ps 105:8 has the perfect form of the verb, "he has remembered," Chronicles reads the plural imperative, telling the people to "remember." God's faithfulness is beyond question; what is needed is for the Israelites to recognize that they are God's covenant people and to learn to trust in his faithfulness. The Chronicler thus adapts the psalm to address the audience of his day, encouraging them to bolster their faith. The psalm's function in this context, then, is both liturgical and theological. It encourages the people to greater faith while illustrating the significance of music in Israel's worship.

With verse 23 the Chronicler changed his source from Ps 105 to Ps 96. As mentioned earlier, this kind of piecing together different psalms to form a new one was a compositional technique attested elsewhere inside and outside of the Bible. There are a few intriguing differences between verses 23-33 and Ps 96. The opening of the psalm (96:1-2) is shorter in Chronicles (v. 23), but the reason for this is not clear. The references in the psalm to Yahweh's "sanctuary" (96:6) and "his courts" (96:8) have been revised in Chronicles, since the temple has not yet been built at this point in the Chronicles narrative. Most of the references to God judging the nations in Ps 96:10-13 have also been removed from Chronicles, probably because they differ from the Chronicler's main concern in this psalm—praise to Yahweh for keeping his ancestral promise. Thus, the next verse in Chronicles (v. 34), taken from Ps 106:1, is eminently appropriate, since it praises Yahweh for his "steadfast love" or "loyalty." The last two verses of the Chronicles psalm are adapted from the end of Ps 106 (vv. 47-48). In particular, the assembly is commanded to speak in Chronicles (v. 35). The Chronicler omits the historical recitation of Ps 106 and has David command the Levites to call upon God for deliverance. The cry, "Gather and rescue us from among the nations," though not entirely appropriate for the setting under David, certainly would have spoken to the audience of the Chronicler's own day. Then the last two lines of the Psalm are turned into narrative as it is reported that the people utter "Amen," and praise Yahweh.

Williamson (1982:185-86) has noted a correspondence between this psalm in verses 8-36 and David's prayer in 29:10-19; following a doxology, each has three sections dealing with three themes: the promise to the sojourning patriarchs, Yahweh's kingship, and a petition. The two passages, thus, provide a framework around 1 Chr 17–29, which has as its primary focus David's preparations for the building of the temple. It is in that direction that the material now turns.

With verse 37 the Chronicler rejoins the narrative at the point where he inserted the psalm. As in verse 7, he refers to David's stationing of Asaph and his kinsmen as ministers before the ark. The Obed-edom of verse 38a is evidently the same as the one is verse 5. Verse 38b, however, may be an interpolation. It lists gatekeepers again. The Obed-edom mentioned here, uniquely, as a son of Jeduthun, is different from the one in verses 5 and 38a. Hosah is also mentioned for the first time with no introduction.

In verse 39 the scene shifts to Gibeon and the description of David's provision for worship in the tabernacle there. The main issue of this passage is its origin and historical reliability. According to Joshua 9 (see also 2 Sam 21) Gibeon was not conquered by the Israelites, but its inhabitants were assimilated as their servants. It would, therefore, not have been an acceptable venue for the tabernacle. The point of this passage, however, is theological rather than historical; it establishes the unbroken continuity of Israelite centralized worship beginning under Moses at the tabernacle and continuing through David until the construction of the temple under Solomon. This was an interest of the Chronicler's and suggests that the passage is his handiwork and not a later Priestly addition, as some have asserted. The Chronicler's "source" for the datum that the tabernacle once resided at Gibeon was probably 1 Kgs 3:3-5. He deduced that since Solomon went to Gibeon to sacrifice, the tabernacle must have been there at the time. The one other feature of note here is the occurrence of "Jeduthun" rather than "Ethan" as in 6:31-48 [Heb 16-33]; 15:16-24 as the third Levitical leader along with Asaph and Heman.

The ending of this episode in 1 Chr 16:43 is taken from 2 Sam 6:19*b*-20*a* and thus serves as part of the framework for the entire section, chapters 13–16, and for the account of the second, successful attempt to transfer the ark in 15:25–16:43. Once again the Chronicler has completely altered the meaning of the borrowed material by changing its setting. In their original setting, 2 Sam 6:19*b* is the conclusion to one episode—the transfer of the ark—and 6:20*a* the introduction to another— the rebuke by Michal. Since the Chronicler has omitted the latter, the one-time introduction now becomes a conclusion, or perhaps better, a "benediction," since it incorporates blessing. It thereby corresponds to the end of the account of the first attempt to bring up the ark, which also incorporates blessing (13:14). At the same time, the reference to David returning to his house sets the stage for the next episode in 1 Chr 17.

Theological Analysis

Because so much of 1 Chr 13–16 consists of lists, and what is not list seems simply taken from Samuel, it is easy to overlook the extraordinary theological richness of this section. To begin with, this section stresses the importance of proper worship and ritual activity. Indeed, the focus of the entire narrative in the rest of 1 Chronicles now becomes preparation for the temple. In the second attempt to transfer the ark, David exemplifies meticulous preparation with the priesthood and the liturgy. It is not liturgy or music for its own sake but in order to please God.

Underlying the Chronicler's stress on correct worship is the sense of the importance of reverence and awe before the divine. This idea helps to address the most immediate theological problem in this unit—the tragedy of Uzzah, which aborted the first attempt to bring the ark into Jerusalem. How could God kill an otherwise innocent man whose intentions were good? It is probably impossible to answer this question in a way that will satisfy modern readers. The message that the story seems intended to convey to the Chronicler's audience is that of the meaning and importance of the holy. The ark was a symbol of Yahweh's holy presence, and holiness is something that cannot be taken lightly. The role of clergy, such as the Levites, is a weighty one because they maintain the sacred. While they will soon no longer have the ark to transport, they will have the more important task of taking care of the temple and its fixtures. The failure, however unintentional, to exercise sufficient care with the holy can have the most serious consequences. The lesson David and the Levites learned from this tragedy was the need to treat the sacred with proper respect and distance. A companion lesson implicit in the story is that the way to ensure the proper treatment of the sacred and the proper observation of ritual and cultic activities in general is by full and careful adherence to the divinely revealed word. The error of David and the Levites lay in their neglect of the regulations for transporting the ark laid out in the law of Moses.

Nevertheless, the Chronicler's view of ritual worship should not be misunderstood. It does not consist simply of following a set of prescriptions. Ritual activities alone are not enough to please God. The Chronicler uses this occasion to introduce the importance of music into the cult. While sacrifices continue in Gibeon, since the temple is not yet built, the Chronicler has David institute the Levitical orders of musicians as a permanent feature of the worship in Jerusalem. In Chronicles, true worship is a joyful expression of the human heart, celebrated in community with music. In the model presented in 1 Chr 13–16, the people come before God not as individuals but as a community —united and in harmonious accord. Moreover, they come "with joy." They praise and give thanks to God not out of obligation but because they are moved by gratitude and by the festivity of the occasion. Thus, worship in Chronicles is reverent and joyful—reverent but not somber, joyful but not frivolous.

Another factor motivating the people to joy is their perception of the fruition of God's plan and the fulfillment of his promises in their day. The narrative thus emphasizes the faithfulness of God to his word. One might well raise the question as to why the Chronicler shows concern with the ark at all. It is, after all, an artefact that no longer exists or is no longer present in his day. But the ark, along with the tabernacle, does provide an important link with the traditions about worship at Sinai. Hence, this episode of the transfer of the ark connects Israel's most ancient and revered traditions—God's fulfillment of promises to Israel's ancestors and the installment of the ark in the tabernacle at Sinai.

On the human side, the story shows that people need to trust in God's faithfulness and promises. This is one of the greatest virtues of David over against Saul in the Chronicler's presentation. David consistently relied on God and sought the divine will. What is more, we see in this section a David who is open and attentive to the divine response to his inquiries. Thus, in the three-month interval between the first and second transfers of the ark David was aware of the blessings experienced by both him and Obed-edom. As a result, he was able to discern the real reason for the tragedy that befell Uzzah and to correct the error on the next attempt. In this episode one finds yet another of the Chronicler's theological messages—that blessing accrues to the faithful, just as retribution to the wicked. The assumption behind these ideas is the omnipotence of God and divine concern for humans. Yahweh not only triumphs over the idols of the Philistines, which are ineffective anyway, but Yahweh is also to be praised as the creator of the universe who has chosen Israel as his people and will bless them supremely if they will but trust and follow him.

A HOUSE FOR YAHWEH—AND FOR DAVID (1 CHRONICLES 17:1-27)

Now that the ark has been brought to Jerusalem, the Chronicler sets his sights on the building of the temple as a place to house it. While he will not actually recount the building of the temple until 2 Chr 3–4, 1 Chr 17 is the first of several texts that prepare for it. This chapter raises the prospect of a temple and identifies David's son as its future builder. David's wars in chapters 18–20 bring about the *pax Israel* that will make it possible for Solomon to build. Chapter 21 explains how the site of the temple was chosen, and 1 Chr 22–29 details the preparation of materials and personnel for the temple's construction and on-going ritual activity. David's prayers in 17:16-27 and 29:10-19 can be seen as marking this section and, indeed, David's primary role in the Chronicler's history.

Literary Analysis

This chapter closely parallels 2 Sam 7, albeit with minor, but significant differences. It consists of three distinct parts, each marked by a change of setting: a report (vv. 1-2) of David's observation in his house about the ark's resting place and Nathan's approval of his apparent intent to build a temple, an oracle (vv. 3-15) received by Nathan that night, presumably in his house, responding to David's intention by promising him a dynasty, and David's prayer (vv. 16-27) before the ark thanking God for the dynastic promise and asking God to fulfill it. The oracle makes use of two introductory messenger formulas ("thus says Yahweh," vv. 4, 7) that distinguish God's response to David's presumed temple proposal (vv. 4-6) from the dynastic promise (vv. 7-15). The latter consists of three elements: a summary of God's favor to David in the past (vv. 7-8*a*), the assurance of God's continued favor in the future (vv. 8*b*-10*a*), and God's promise to build David a house (vv. 10*b*-15). The two sections of the oracle (vv. 4-6, 7-15) are joined by "and now" in verse 7*a*. The oracle (vv. 3-15) and the prayer (vv. 16-27) are essentially the same length, creating a sense of balance in the chapter as a whole. The prayer, moreover, falls into three sections (vv. 16-19, 20-22, 23-27), which correspond to the three elements of the oracle in verses 7-15.

Two pieces of background information are crucial for a proper appreciation of this chapter. The first is the variety of possible meanings of the Hebrew word for "house." When used of a deity, the house refers to a temple. The king's house may, of course, be his residence or "palace." But the "house of David" also refers frequently to his line of descendants, the dynasty of the kingdom of Judah. Both "houses" are important to the Chronicler: the temple represents access to God, but the Davidic king is responsible for safeguarding its proper use. The second background item has to do with the broader, symbiotic relationship of kings and gods in the ancient Near East. Typically, the king understood himself as the appointee of the national god. The king's construction and maintenance of a temple to his god was an act of reciprocity, an expected display of gratitude for the god's favor and a way of ensuring the continuation of that favor for himself and his people. Temple and palace usually stood side by side, exhibiting both the king's piety and the deity's support of him. The fact that the tradition did not credit David, the founder of the dynasty, with building the temple is remarkable. What is unusual is not that David would propose building a temple but that Yahweh would decline such a proposal. This chapter makes it clear that Yahweh does not reject a temple per se but only David as its builder. The reasons for Yahweh's decision will be explained more fully later on in 1 Chronicles. Thus, in this chapter Yahweh makes known the divine intent to have a temple while denying David the privilege of constructing it.

Exegetical Analysis

Chapter 17 takes up precisely where chapter 16 left off—with David thinking about his house, which, as just noted, is a key concept in the chapter. He notices that the house in which he sits or dwells (yāšab) is much nicer than the ark's resting place. (Note that the next scene in the chapter also begins [v. 16] with David *sitting*, this time before the ark.) The thought about the ark dwelling "in tents" strikes David as soon as he returns home. Chapter 17 is obviously a direct sequel to the account of the transfer of the ark in chapter 16. The immediacy of this transition becomes more obvious when one observes that the Chronicler has omitted the statement in 2 Sam 7:1b that Yahweh had given David rest from all his enemies round about. The statement might be taken to imply that a long time passed between the transfer of the ark and David's observation. The Chronicler also thereby removed the reference to rest, which would have stood in tension with his accounts of David's wars in the subsequent chapters and of Solomon's reign as the time of peace (šālôm), the Hebrew word being a play on Solomon's name.

David never actually articulates his desire to build a temple, though his intention to do so seems clear from his observation to Nathan (v. 1) and from Yahweh's response in verses 4-6. Nathan gives tacit approval to David's idea (v. 2). But he does not speak here as Yahweh's prophet. He uses the messenger formula, "thus says Yahweh," only in verse 3. Hence, there is no contradiction between verse 2 and verses 3-6. Yahweh's refusal to allow David to build the temple (v. 4) is emphatic: "*you* shall not build me the temple" or even "it is not *you* [who] will build me the temple." The Chronicler's points are placed in clearer relief through a comparison with his source in Samuel. While the differences between 1 Chr 17 and 2 Sam 7 may often be due to textual variation (with Chronicles generally preserving the superior text), in this verse they seem telling. Where 2 Sam 7:5 raises a question, "Will *you* build me a house for my dwelling?" 1 Chr 17:4 is more emphatic: "It is not *you* who will build me the house to dwell in." Also, "*a* house" in Samuel has become "*the* house" in Chronicles. It is not a hypothetical temple to the Chronicler but the specific temple in Jerusalem that was the center of Judah's worship for centuries. Yahweh's response may appear initially as a rebuke, but his reference to David as "my servant" (v. 4) and to Israel as "my people" (v. 6) shows that it is not occasioned by any dissatisfaction with either David or Israel. As will become clearer in the second part of the oracle (beginning with v. 7), David is simply not the right man at the right time for the job of building the temple.

A second oracle or second part of the oracle is introduced by verse 7. The messenger formula at the beginning of verse 8 makes clear that this oracle originates with Yahweh not with Nathan. The first portion of the oracle rehearses God's direction of David's life from pastoring sheep to shepherding Israel (v. 7) and God's presence with David (v. 8$a\alpha$), removing his adversaries (v. 8$a\beta$). These adversaries likely referred in 2 Sam 7:9 to Saul, Ishbaal, and others in his household rather than to foreign enemies—all the more so in Chronicles, which lacks the mention in verse 1 of Yahweh giving David rest from his enemies round about. To be sure, Chronicles lacks the stories in 1 Samuel about Saul's enmity toward David. But it also lacks the story of David's summons from the flock to be anointed king (2 Sam 16:1-13) to which 17:7 alludes.

The change in verbs in verse 8b marks a shift from the past to the future, from what God has done for David to what God will do for him. The promise in a nutshell is to make Israel under David preeminent among the nations. It therefore foreshadows David's military victories in chapters 18–20. This connection becomes clear in verse 10, where the reference to giving David rest from his enemies in 2 Sam 7:11 is again omitted from Chronicles. Instead, the Chronicler has Yahweh say that he will "subdue" all of David's enemies. Not only is the God-given rest reserved for Solomon, but the same verb, "subdue," occurs in 1 Chr 18:1 (// 2 Sam 8:1) where David's conquests begin with his subduing the Philistines.

With the promise to build David a "house" in verse 10b, the direction of the oracle shifts again. The contrast to Yahweh's earlier prohibition is highlighted: "You will not build the house for me" (v. 4), but "Yahweh will build a house for you" (v. 10). The similarity in language suggests that in Chronicles the promise of a dynasty to David is a reward for his intention to build the temple (2 Sam 7:11 uses the verb "make" instead of "build"). The focus in verses 10b-14, in contrast to the parallel text in 2 Sam 7:11b-16, is less on the Davidic dynasty than it is on his son who succeeds him as the builder of the temple. This focus surfaces in changes made by the Chronicler to his Samuel source for this promise. Thus, 1 Chr 17:13 lacks any reference to the possibility that David's son may commit iniquity and be disciplined (cf. 2 Sam 7:14). This is because the Chronicler idealizes Solomon even more than David; Solomon is the temple builder and does not sin. The statement in verse 13, "I will be his father and he will be my son," is typically observed by commentators as an "adoption formula." Its sense here, however, may be broader, indicating a close relationship between Yahweh and the Davidic heir. Then, in 17:14 the Chronicler has evidently altered the possessive pronouns so that they refer not to David's ("your") house and kingdom but to Yahweh's ("my"). The point is that the dynasty, the kingdom, and even the heir belong to God, and the fate of them all is ultimately subject to God's will. While the house of the deity in the ancient Near East is typically the deity's temple, the parallel of "house" and "kingdom" or "kingship" in the present context leads most commentators to understand the former as referring to the dynasty. In the Chronicler's view, this kingdom also includes the northern tribes that would later secede from the house of David. The verse goes on to say, "*his* throne [instead of "*your* throne" in 2 Sam 7:16] will be sure forever." The dynastic promise is thereby transferred to Solomon in keeping with the Chronicler's view that the reigns of David and Solomon together represent the ideal era of kingship.

David's prayer in verses 16-27 is a response to God's promise of a dynasty in Nathan's oracle. While the prayer is not, strictly speaking, one of thanksgiving, David's attitude in articulating it is clearly one of immense gratitude and humility. The prayer consists of three sections, verses 16-19, 20-22, 23-27, akin to the three sections within verses 7-15 highlighted above. In verses 16-19 David exhibits utter humility and submission to divine will, contrasting Yahweh's benevolence with his own insignificance. As part of his deference to Yahweh, David refers to himself in the third person as Yahweh's servant, recalling Yahweh's earlier honorific designation of David as "my servant." David's initial questions, "Who am I?" and "Who is my house?" allude both to his lowly origins as a shepherd with which Yahweh began the oracle to Nathan (v. 7) and to Yahweh's promise regarding his "house." The second section, verses 20-22, describes the incomparability of Yahweh and of his people Israel. The third section, verses 23-27, then appeals to God to fulfill his promise regarding David's house. This section repeats several terms from the divine oracle, and these are in turn themes of the chapter as a whole: word or promise, bless, house, and forever.

Theological Analysis

While the main topic of this chapter is the Davidic dynasty, its real focus is God. It is Yahweh, not David, who is the builder of the "house." Yahweh is incomparable—unlike the gods of other nations (such do not really exist anyway, cf. v. 20). The chapter shows that God directs history. God has a plan for Israel, and David's proposal to build a temple does not fit God's schedule. But God's promise to David of an enduring dynasty falls in the sequence, along with the exodus and gift of the land (v. 21), of God's acts on behalf of his people.

David's response is a model of proper human behavior before God. He is humbled by Yahweh's promise because he recognizes Yahweh's greatness and his own comparative insignificance. He thankfully confesses that he owes everything to God's grace. In the final section of his prayer David asks that God fulfill the promise God has just made. This is not a lack of faith on David's part but another instance of his model behavior. In the Chronicler's day the Davidic dynasty had not fully been rebuilt, so through David the Chronicler called on his readers as God's people to pray for God to bring this promise to completion.

Solomon's role as temple builder is only hinted at; he is not mentioned by name. But there is every confidence that David's unnamed son will carry out his task to build the temple. That is Solomon's role in the divine plan. His reign goes together with David's as providing the model of kingship. The righteous king has uppermost on his agenda the maintenance of Israel's worship and relationship with Yahweh. The two "houses" of Israel, dynasty and temple, are intimately entwined.

The Chronicler pinned his hopes, then, entirely upon God. The promise of an eternal Davidic dynasty originated with divine grace. The Chronicler believed that the promise remained in effect after the exile. It was "forever." The Hebrew word does not mean "eternity" in the sense of "endless time" (no such concept existed in ancient Israel) but refers to a period of "long duration" for the "most distant future." The promise to David is enduring from Yahweh's perspective, but the exile shows that it is not unconditional. The human recipients are required to be faithful and obedient or they will suffer punishment. Since Israel has survived the exile, the Chronicler trusts in Yahweh's mercy and patience.

DAVID'S WARS (1 CHRONICLES 18:1–20:8)

The next three chapters go together as they contain a series of battle reports and stories about David's military successes. These chapters divide themselves neatly into three subunits with the same introductory formula, "afterwards" (18:1; 19:1; 20:4). Chapter 18, the first subunit, reports David's conquests of the Philistines (v. 1), Moabites (v. 2), Hadadezer king of Zobah (vv. 3-8), and the Edomites (vv. 12-13), as well as his reception of the envoy from Hamath (vv. 9-11) and his cabinet (vv. 14-17). The second subunit in 19:1–20:3 contains the story of David's war with the Ammonite and Aramean coalition. Then, 20:4-8 recounts the exploits of David's "mighty men" in the Philistine wars.

Literary Analysis

The materials in these chapters are borrowed from 2 Samuel with very little, if anything, added by the Chronicler. They provide, however, an excellent illustration of the Chronicler's creativity and inventiveness through careful editing. The Chronicler chose different passages from Samuel and placed them between two texts dealing with the building of the temple and David's role in it (1 Chr 17 and 21–29). The Chronicler even retained the introductory rubric "afterwards" already present in Samuel at the beginning of each of these passages. But since the rubric is otherwise rare in Chronicles, and since it occurs three times in a row at the head of these three subunits, it plays a unifying role for all of 1 Chr 18–20 that is not the case for the occurrences of the rubric in their original Samuel setting. This unity is further reinforced by the repetition of certain key words in Hebrew, particularly in chapter 18: "defeat, smite, strike" (*nkh*); "take" (*lqḥ*); and "capture" (*lkd*). By gathering these materials that are scattered in 2 Samuel, the Chronicler adds emphasis to the portrait of David as a great warrior-king to whom God gave victory at every turn (18:6, 13).

Another facet of the Chronicler's editorial activity relates to the omission of materials from Samuel. The period of David's reign covered by 1 Chr 18–20 is equivalent to that of 2 Sam 8–21. The major differences are the omissions from Chronicles of the accounts of David's adultery with Bathsheba (2 Sam 11–12) and of the revolts of Absalom and Sheba, precipitated by Amnon's rape of Tamar (2 Sam 13–20). The reason for these omissions is obvious; because they describe David's sin and subsequent turmoil within the royal family and the temple they detract from the idealized portrait of David that the Chronicler is trying to paint.

The recounting of David's wars in these three chapters has several aims in the Chronicler's overall work. To begin, the stories in these chapters drive home the point of chapter 17 that David's reign is not the time for temple building. David will later be disqualified from building the temple because he shed so much blood—an allusion to his activities in these chapters. David's role in God's plan is to exercise his military prowess so as to bring about the time of peace in which the temple may be built. As corollaries, this section explains the extent of David's empire and his acquisition of plunder, which will provide part of the wealth used by Solomon in building the temple (18:7-8). To be sure, these chapters enhance upon and idealize David's image primarily through the omission of materials in Samuel that cast David and his household in a less than favorable light. They also depict David, once again in the light of chapter 17, as a king who piously and humbly fulfills the role that God has assigned to him. Thus, the reigns of David and Solomon together are idealized as Israel's "golden age." Solomon completes the task to which David aspires but is unable to undertake. David's military success, furnished by Yahweh of course, brings about a period of peace and thus paves the way for Solomon to build the temple. This relationship will be set in even greater relief in the last major unit of the book, chapters 22–29.

Exegetical Analysis

David Subdues Israel's Neighbors (1 Chr 18:1-17)

The introduction "after this" in 18:1 forges a deliberate *chronological* link in Chronicles with the Nathan oracle (ch. 17). David launches his wars of conquest after his intention to build the temple has been blocked by Yahweh. The expression "toward Hamath" in 18:3 is lacking in Samuel. It creates a parallel with Solomon, who defeats "Hamath-Zobah" in Chronicles (2 Chr 8:3). Chronicles' numbers in 18:4 (1,000 chariots and 7,000 horsemen) are greater than those in 2 Sam 8:4 (1,700 horsemen). But the Chronicler's numbers are shared by a Dead Sea Scroll fragment of Samuel (4QSam[a]). The different names of the Aramean cities in verse 8 are explained as the result of the confusion of letters in the case of Betah/Tibhath and of modernization (i.e., the Chronicler substituting the name of a city in the same area that was better known in his day) for Berothai/Cun. The mention of Solomon's use of the bronze captured by David in 18:8*b* is lacking in the MT of Samuel but does occur in the LXX. Hence it may have been in the version of Samuel used by the Chronicler and was not necessarily added by him. In either case, it fits with the Chronicler's interest in the temple and in depicting the complementary nature of the reigns of David and Solomon as the model of Israelite monarchy. Finally, in 18:17 the Chronicler has most likely changed the statement in 2 Sam 8:18 that David's sons were priests on the grounds that only Levites could be priests. However, the reading in Samuel is syntactically odd and may be textually corrupt (cf. McCarter 1984:254-55; Knoppers 2004).

Aside from these comparative issues, there are a few other matters in this chapter, especially in the account of David's defeat of the Arameans in verses 3-11, which deserve comment. In verse 3, for instance, the reason for David's encounter with Hadadezer is not entirely clear. Just who is on his way to the Euphrates? The Hebrew is as ambiguous as the English. Logically, however, it must be David who is journeying to set up (2 Sam 8:3 has "restore") his monument, apparently thereby laying claim to all of Aram (Syria). Since Israel was southwest of Aram and the Euphates northeast, Hadadezer would not have encountered David or Israel if he were the one travelling. David's disposal of most of the horses in the next verse may indicate a lack of a developed chariot force in Israel during his reign.

A primary theme of this chapter is the wealth accumulated by David through the spoils of war. Just as Yahweh gave David victory wherever he went (vv. 6, 13), so David collected plunder from all those whom he conquered (v. 11). Twice (vv. 2, 6) it is stated that those whom David defeated became his servants and paid him tribute, probably on a yearly basis. What is important about this wealth is what David did with it, dedicating it to Yahweh (v. 11), perhaps in accord with the instructions for holy war given in Josh 6:19. For the Chronicler, this meant that this wealth could later be used in the construction (v. 8b) and maintenance (1 Chr 26:26-27) of the temple.

Verses 14-17 provide a fitting conclusion to this subunit. They press the list of David's cabinet members into theological service. By including this passage, especially verse 14, the Chronicler emphasizes both his "all Israel" motif and his idealization of David. David's rule is over all Israel—North and South alike. He uses the accoutrements of his reign, such as his royal cabinet, to administer justice and equity to all of the citizens of his kingdom. The "Cherethites and Pelethites" were David's bodyguard. Their name, whose two parts resemble Crete and Philistine, suggest that they were of Philistine origin.

On Abiathar as the son of Ahimelek rather than the reverse, see below on 24:3.

The War with the Ammonite-Aramaean Coalition (1 Chr 19:1–20:3)

The beginning of a new unit in 19:1 is signaled by the introductory rubric, "afterwards," as in 18:1. The account of David's war with the Ammonites in this unit falls into four episodes: the insulting treatment of David's emissary that occasions the war (19:1-5); the first battle against the Ammonites and their Aramean mercenaries (19:6-15); the defeat of the Arameans (19:16-19); and the siege and fall of Rabbah (20:1-3). The entire account is again closely parallel to a passage in Samuel (2 Sam 10–12), with the omission of the Bathsheba story in 2 Sam 11:2–12:25.

The first five verses of chapter 19 depict David as a king who deals loyally with his subjects or treaty partners (it is not clear which of these Nahash is). The fact that verse 2 articulates David's thoughts shows the narrative nature of this material, as opposed, for instance, to a report from royal annals. David's sending of messengers to the Ammonite kingdom was an act of diplomacy. Historically, David may have anticipated negotiating new terms with the Ammonite king Hanun that would reflect David's new superiority. But whatever ulterior motives he may have had historically are ignored and indeed denied by the narrative. He is portrayed as following proper royal protocol. The motives of the Ammonites in responding as they do are also ignored by the narrative. Are they trying to test David's resolve, to break free from subjugation, or what? The biblical account simply presents the Ammonite response as unprovoked, belligerent, and the opposite of the hospitality typically afforded visiting dignitaries. Shaving the beards of David's messengers and cutting off their garments at the waist were a symbolic emasculation intended to humiliate them. David reacts with understanding and even compassion toward the messengers.

He allows them to remain in Jericho long enough to regain their dignity. It is also intriguing that the narrative attributes no emotion to David. He does not act out of anger or a sense of revenge toward the Ammonites but with restraint and deliberateness.

In the second episode (vv. 6-15), verses 6-7 vary more widely from their Samuel predecessor (2 Sam 10:5-6) than does the rest of this chapter, but there does not appear to be any ideological reason for this variation, since many of the variations of Chronicles here are shared by a Dead Sea Scroll fragment of Samuel (4QSam^a). "Aram Naharaim" (v. 6) was properly the area around the great bend of the Euphrates in upper Mesopotamia and as such was considerably north of the Aramean city-states. The Chronicler may have substituted it for Beth-rehob (2 Sam 10:6) because the latter was lesser known in his day. This substitution would also enhance David's victory. In verse 7, Medeba (in Moab) seems too far south to have served as a rallying point for the Arameans and Ammonites. Scholars often propose reading "the waters of Rabbah" instead. Rabbah was the capital of the Ammonites, modern Amman, Jordan.

Joab's speech to Abishai in verse 13 introduces a theological element into the battle narrative. As the speech casts matters, the Israelites are not like the Aramean mercenaries but are fighting for their own holdings east of the Jordan and indeed for "the cities of our God." Joab concludes by recognizing that the battle is in Yahweh's hands and thus by implicitly trusting in him for victory. The result is that a seemingly desperate situation—fighting on two fronts—is turned into triumph through the expertise and cooperation of Joab and Abishai, but ultimately because God so wills it. The smaller size of the Israelite army is apparently the reason that Joab breaks off the war at this point rather than pursuing the Arameans.

The account of the second defeat of the Arameans is again quite similar to that of 2 Sam (10:15-19). The differences in Chronicles serve mainly to magnify David and his victory. In

1 Chr 19:18 Aramean casualties are numbered at 7,000 chariots and 40,000 infantry as opposed to 700 chariots and 40,000 cavalry in Samuel. In 19:19 the Arameans surrender to David rather than to Israel as in Samuel. The fact that David marshals "all Israel" in verse 17, though it is in Samuel as well, fits well with the Chronicler's stress on the nation's unity under David. The main point of this episode is the decisiveness of the defeat of the Arameans (v. 19), who became subject to David and did not again come to the aid of the Ammonites.

Following the defeat of the Arameans, David could turn his attention back to the Ammonites, who were the original source of the conflict. In Samuel the account of the siege and fall of Rabbah (2 Sam 11:1; 12:26-31) provides the framework for the story of David's adultery with Bathsheba (2 Sam 11:2–12:25). The Chronicler's omission of this story has led to some tensions in his narrative. In particular, the statement that David stayed in Jerusalem has lost its significance in Chronicles (in Samuel it set the stage for David's seeing Bathsheba). As a result, after Joab takes Rabbah (20:1), David is suddenly described bringing out the spoil (v. 2) as though he were the city's conqueror. An accidental omission may have contributed to this sudden shift (McKenzie 1985:66; Knoppers 2004).

The spoil of Ammon included a gold crown weighing some 75 pounds, the approximate equivalent of a talent (v. 2). The enormous weight indicates that the crown belonged to the Ammonite national god, Milcom, rather than to "their king" (*malkām*), which has the same consonants in Hebrew as the god's name (*milkōm*). The crown was probably taken from the god's idol. It may also have been the stone from the crown that David wore rather than the crown itself, although it is not clear how the stone alone would have been worn. David's treatment of the Ammonite captives in verse 3 has sometimes been understood as torture. The verse is often emended, as in the NRSV, to read with 2 Sam 12:31 not that David "sawed" the people but that he "set" them to work. Another possibility is that the object of the verb is the city rather than the people and that it was the city that David sawed (in the sense of tearing it apart?).

War with the Philistines (1 Chr 20:4-8)

This third subunit begins, as did the other two, with the Hebrew phrase we have translated "afterwards" (see 17:1; 18:1). The material in this subunit is taken from 2 Sam 21:18-22. Between this subunit and the previous one the Chronicler has omitted all of 2 Sam 13–20. The stories associated with Absalom's revolt in this section of Samuel are in tension with the Chronicler's idealization of David's reign, especially as a time of the unification of all Israel. The Chronicler also omitted 2 Sam 21:1-14, which relates David's execution of Saul's heirs and would have been in tension with the claim in 1 Chr 10 that Saul's house came to an end on Mt. Gilboa. Second Samuel 21:15-22 narrates the exploits of individual Israelites against four Philistine warriors descended from Rapha or perhaps devotees of a god Rapha. These narratives were evidently originally independent and are included in Samuel in the appendix of 2 Sam 21–24. The Chronicler, however, has integrated them into his coherent account of David's wars. The Chronicler has also omitted the first of these four accounts (2 Sam 21:15-17) in which David is almost killed. Perhaps he saw it as detracting from David's prestige or as casting doubt on Yahweh's protection of David.

The term "Rephaim" (20:4) is mentioned elsewhere in the Bible (Gen 15:20; Deut 2:11) as a race of giants. The statement in this verse that the Philistines were subdued is also unique to Chronicles and harks back to God's promise to subdue David's enemies in 1 Chr 17:10. The most intriguing verse in this context is verse 5. Its parallel in 2 Sam 21:19 raised a problem for the Chronicler because it attributed the slaying of Goliath to Elhanan the Bethlehemite rather than to David. This was a blatant contradiction to the famous tale of 1 Sam 17 with which the Chronicler was obviously familiar. The Chronicler resolved the contradiction through creative interpretation. He changed the adjective for

Elhanan's city of origin ("Bethlehemite") to a proper name with the Hebrew direct object marker *('et-laḥmî)* and thereby created a brother for Goliath. This change should not be misunderstood as deceit on the Chronicler's part but rather was a pre-critical, interpretive strategy (harmonization) motivated by his conviction that David had killed Goliath.

Theological Analysis

Perhaps the overriding theological theme of this section of 1 Chronicles is the working out of the divine plan in human affairs. In chapter 17 it became clear that God had a timetable for Israel and that David had been assigned a particular role in that schedule. As the ideal king, David accepted God's plan and set about to fulfill his role of bringing about peace with the surrounding nations in order that the temple could be built. David effected this peace through military conquest of those nations. His victories in chapters 18–20 might also be seen as rewards for his faithfulness. At any rate, as chapter 18 repeatedly observes, David's success originated with God. David exemplifies the proper attitude in his victories. He piously and humbly dedicates the plunder that he takes to Yahweh, and it will eventually go into the building and maintenance of the temple. Others of the Chronicler's typical interests surface in this material as well. For instance, David appears leading *all* Israel to victory. The occurrence of the verb "subdue" at several points in these chapters following its use in 17:10 shows the fulfillment of God's promise to David to subdue his enemies and leads the reader to expect the change in focus to the temple that will occur in the final chapters of 1 Chronicles (21–29).

DAVID'S CENSUS (1 CHRONICLES 21:1–22:1)

This story tells of a sin committed by David. Given the Chronicler's idealization of David and his omission of other materials that would taint the image he is creating, the present story stands out. It is rather surprising to find it included in Chronicles at all. The reason for its inclusion lies in the explanation at the end of the story accounting for the location of the temple and its altar of burnt offering (22:1). The uniqueness and unexpectedness of this story in Chronicles may even be a deliberate strategy by the Chronicler to focus the reader's attention upon it.

The story is transitional in several respects. The selection of the temple's future location represents an important step forward toward its construction. More immediately, the story leads readily into the account of David's further preparations for the temple in chapters 22–29. On a literary level, 1 Chr 21:1–22:1 provides a transition between major units in the book. Chapters 10–21, as we have seen, are largely borrowed from 2 Samuel, while chapters 22–29 are unique to Chronicles. While this story is parallel to the one in 2 Sam 24 (albeit with some striking changes), the ending is the Chronicler's own composition. Moreover, throughout his narrative of this story the Chronicler has introduced allusions to a number of other biblical texts.

Literary Analysis

The structure of this passage is variously described by different commentators, but it can be sketched as follows. The first six verses recount the census commanded by David and executed by Joab. Then verses 7-14 describe the punishment chosen by David and sent by God because of the census. Verses 15-17 tell of the staying of the plague before Jerusalem and of David's repentance. In verses 18-27 one finds the angel's command to build an altar, David's negotiation with Ornan for his threshing floor, and the building and dedication of the altar. Finally, the story concludes in 21:28–22:1 with David's designation of this site as the location for the future temple and the altar of burnt offering.

Exegetical Analysis

The first verse—indeed the very first word (in English)—of the chapter raises several difficult interpretive issues. There are striking differences between the beginning of this story in Chronicles ("Satan stood up against Israel, and incited David to count the people of Israel" [NRSV]) and the beginning of its Samuel predecessor ("Again the anger of the Lord was kindled against Israel and he incited David against them saying, 'Go, count the people of Israel and Judah'" [NRSV]). The Chronicler's motive for some of these changes seems clear enough—he wished to remove from God the culpability for inciting David to sin. "Again" in Samuel alludes to the famine in 2 Sam 21, which the Chronicler had omitted, making the word inappropriate in Chronicles. Also, in line with his emphasis on the unity of Israel he removes the distinction between Israel and Judah that is present in the Samuel version. Chronicles reads the simple name "Israel" several times in this chapter where Samuel refers to "the people" or "the land" (21:2, 4, 14//24:2, 4, 15).

But what exactly is the sense of the Hebrew word śāṭān here? The noun occurs commonly in the Old Testament in the sense of a human enemy or adversary (Num 22:22, 32; 1 Sam 29:4; 2 Sam 19:23; 1 Kgs 5:18; 11:14, 23, 25). In other texts where it obviously refers to a superhuman being, the word appears with the article: "*the* satan" (Job 1–2; Zech 3:1-2). The argument has been made, therefore, that 1 Chr 21:1 represents the latest stage in the development of a Satan figure, in which śāṭān is the proper name for the metaphysical representative of evil as a counterpart to God—in short, the devil—and this is the interpretation suggested by the NRSV translation. But this interpretation is far from certain (cf. Day 1988:127-45). Chronicles does not display elsewhere such a developed concept of the origin of evil or, outside of this chapter, the kind of developed understanding of angels that was necessary for the emergence of a Satan figure.

Another view along somewhat similar lines would see śāṭān in this passage, as well as in some of the other texts cited above, as an earlier stage in the development of devil or Satan figure. In this theory, *śāṭān* is a kind of personification of God's anger or projection of the divine wrath (what scholars call a "hypostasis"). While this is a possibility, the context of the 1 Chr 21:1 offers a simpler solution.

David's actions in this verse are entirely within the human context; there is no reference to the divine realm. Moreover, taking *śāṭān* as a common noun—a human enemy—makes perfect sense in the verse and actually helps to make David's subsequent actions more understandable. An enemy or adversary of David's—an unnamed military foe—arose, and this in turn motivated him to take a census of the fighting men under his command (v. 5). Taking a census of men of fighting age was a typical step in preparing for war in the ancient world. If this interpretation is correct, the net theological result of the Chronicler's reading is that David is personally and exclusively culpable for the offense of the census. This perspective seems emphasized throughout the narrative in the Chronicler's consistent reference to David by name rather than by title, "the king."

In short, in 1 Chr 21:1, the term that occurs is not "*the śāṭān*," the title found in Job 1–2 and Zech 3, nor is it the proper name Satan. The notion of the devil and the use of "Satan" as a proper name for such a figure does not occur in the Old Testament but develops in later Judaism and, as a result of that background, is then found in the New Testament. Rather, the simplest explanation and the one that best suits the context is that *śāṭān* here simply refers to an enemy as it commonly does elsewhere in the Old Testament.

The next question raised by 1 Chr 21:1, whatever the meaning of *śāṭān* in the verse, is what was wrong with counting the people or army. Three answers to this question are commonly given: (1) David's sin was not the census per se but an attitude of pride that the census occasioned in David, which in turn led him to trust in numbers rather than in God. (2) Again the census per se was not wrong, but the innovation of redividing Israel for purposes of taxation and conscription was sinful because it ran counter to Israel's oldest traditions. (3) Census taking also required ritual preparation required of the new soldiers who were conscripted in the census, and the sin was probably a failure to carry out that ritual preparation.

While each of these explanations has possibilities, the fact is that the Chronicler simply does not explain the nature of David's sin; it is apparently unimportant to him. What is clear in his account is that Joab recognizes that a census will bring guilt upon Israel and cautions David to that effect (v. 3; contrast 2 Sam 24:3). David, therefore, is warned ahead of time but goes ahead with the sinful deed. It is an important dimension of the Chronicler's narrative and theology that individuals receive adequate warning in advance of their sins. The Chronicler is likewise uninterested in the details of the census (2 Sam 24:4-8), which are summarized in 21:4; his concern, rather, is the result of the census and its theological implications, to which he immediately turns.

The report in verse 5 of the resulting numbers from the census is difficult in two respects. First, the last clause, which reports a separate number for Judah (470,000), seems to contradict the report earlier in the verse of a number for "all Israel." This final clause may be a gloss occasioned by the separate reports for Israel and Judah in 2 Sam 24:9, although the latter gives Judah's number as 500,000 rather than 470,000. The second problem in this verse is the difference in the other numbers between Chronicles and Samuel. The counterpart to the Chronicles 1,100,000 for all Israel in Samuel is 800,000 for Israel and 500,000 for Judah or 1,300,000 total. The Chronicler evidently calculated that the total in Samuel was for thirteen tribes (counting Ephraim and Manasseh separately) at 100,000 per tribe. Hence he reduced his total by 200,000 because of the omission of Benjamin and Levi (21:6). Levi was probably excluded based on Num 1:49, which forbids taking a census of the Levites, whose sacral duties preclude them from military service. But the reason for Benjamin's exclusion is not clear. The Chronicler's combination of the separate figures given in Samuel is another example of his emphasis on Israel's unity.

In verse 7 the Chronicler provides a motivation for David's repentance that is missing in Samuel, where David's regret for the census is simply reported: "But David's heart smote him" (24:10). Chronicles states that God was displeased with what David had done and changes the Samuel text to read that God smote Israel. At least one scholar (Day 1988:136-37) has argued that "this thing" refers not to David's census but to Joab's failure to count Levi and Benjamin. But this view founders on David's confession in the next verse to having sinned by doing "this thing." The Chronicler thus stresses the sinfulness of David's census over against Samuel, where it could be read up to this point as simply a blunder on David's part. The change has come at a price, however, for it causes a problem in the Chronicler's narrative, which now seems to have the people punished twice—here in verse 7 and again by the plague in verse 14. Another possibility would be to take the statement about God striking Israel in verse 7 as a proleptic resumption or summative preview of the subsequent plague story. But then this smiting could not be seen as motivating David's repentance.

Following David's confession of guilt (v. 8), he is offered his choice of three punishments: three years of famine, three months of flight from enemies, or three days of plague (vv. 9-12). (2 Sam 24:13 has seven years of famine, but the Chronicles reading is almost certainly primitive.) The last of these seems portrayed as the most severe. Why, then, does David choose it? This is not entirely clear in Samuel; indeed it is not clear which of the three he actually chooses. But the Chronicles reading clarifies. There is a deliberate contrast in 1 Chr 21:12 between the sword of the enemies and the sword of Yahweh. Hence, when David commits himself into Yahweh's hands (v. 13) it is obvious which of the three options he is choosing. Moreover, his reason for choosing the plague is evident—he is throwing himself on God's mercy, once more exemplifying proper piety.

Verse 15 is problematic in the present narrative, since according to it God stops the plague on Jerusalem before David's entreaty and offering. However, this problem is found already in 2 Samuel, where 24:16a (through "'stay your hand'") is an interpolation. The Chronicles reading in verse 15 ("And God sent the angel") presents the angel as less autonomous and more directly subject to God's command than in Samuel ("And when the angel stretched forth his hand," 24:16). The name Ornan in Chronicles is probably a secondary development from the Samuel version, Araunah (cf. McCarter 1980:512).

Verses 16-17 shift attention to David's efforts to halt the plague. Verse 16 (which has accidentally been lost from the MT of Samuel) borrows a number of motifs from other texts. These include: elders in sackcloth (2 Kgs 19:2), an angel with a sword (Josh 5:13), falling on one's face (Ezek 1:28), and standing between heaven and earth (Zech 5:9). Then in verse 17, Chronicles preserves the consonants of the original reading, "I the shepherd did wrong" (hr'h hr'wty, interpreted in Chronicles as "I indeed did wrong" hr' hr'wty), which has suffered corruption in Samuel. David is the model leader ("shepherd") of Israel, as he takes full responsibility for his sin and pleads that the punishment be leveled against himself and his house rather than his subjects. Two clauses that are additional to Chronicles in verse 17 ("was it not I who gave command to number the people?" and "but let not the plague be upon your people") further emphasize the personal responsibility that David takes for the people of Israel and for bringing the plague to a halt.

The Hebrew verb forms in verses 18-19 make them parenthetical to verse 17 and the activity they report. David is thus acting here on what Gad had previously relayed to him from the angel. Verses 20-21 have suffered corruption but can be restored on the basis of the parallel reading among the Dead

Sea Scroll fragments of Samuel (4QSam[a]; cf. McCarter 1980:507). They simply explain that Ornan saw David and his party approaching but did not recognize them, since their heads were covered, until David arrived at the threshing floor.

The account of the negotiation for the threshing floor in verses 22-25 is reminiscent of Abraham's purchase of a burial cave in Gen 23. The key word in these verses is the Hebrew verb "to give," which occurs five times. David requests that Ornan *give* him the threshing floor so he can build an altar and then elaborates, "*Give* it to me for full price" (v. 22). Ornan uses the verb twice in verse 23 to say that he will *give* David the land and everything he needs for the sacrifice. David insists on buying it all at full price (v. 24) and then *gives* Ornan 600 gold shekels as the price (v. 25). David's piety again shines through in this episode, especially in verse 24 where he articulates his principled refusal against sacrificing to God what belongs to someone else or has cost him nothing. The purchase price in verse 25 reveals the enormous value that the Chronicler attaches to the site in three ways. First, while 2 Sam 24:24 gives the price as 50 shekels, in Chronicles it is 600 shekels. Second, in Samuel they are shekels of silver, but in Chronicles shekels of gold. Third, in Samuel the 50 silver shekels buy both the threshing floor and the oxen; in Chronicles 600 gold shekels suffice only for "the place," the threshing floor. "Place" in Hebrew is a common term for a sanctuary or shrine, which is what Ornan's threshing floor will become, as the Chronicler explains in the following verses.

Beginning with verse 26*b*, the Chronicler makes use of a motif once more borrowed from other biblical stories (Judg 6:21; 1 Kgs 18:38), in which the initiation of an altar and the divine acceptance of its offering are signaled by fire from heaven. A final phrase "and it [the fire] consumed the burnt offering," has been lost from the MT by accidental scribal omission but can be restored based on the testimony of the versions and other biblical texts (Lev 9:24; 1 Kgs 18:38). The Chronicler employs this motif again in his account of the dedication of the temple in 2 Chr 7:1. In Chronicles, the divine response comes only after David has "called upon Yahweh." In addition, the plague is averted as Yahweh commands the angel of death to sheath his sword (v. 27). Again, in Chronicles, it is Yahweh who explicitly controls the angel at every step. God's demonstration of acceptance of the altar is essential to David's declaration in 22:1. Without the divine exhibition of favor, David's establishment of a shrine as a rival to or replacement of the tabernacle would be utter presumption. As it is, he simply articulates the significance of the fire from heaven.

In the final segment of this account (21:28–22:1), verses 28-30 are a parenthetical remark by the Chronicler or a later interpolation. As Japhet put it, "Should [the temple site] be viewed, in the spirit of the narrative context, as a divine choice and act of grace, or should it be regarded, as in the parenthetic passage, as a concession to human limitation and weakness?" (Japhet 1993:390). There is tension between the apologetic nature of these verses and the surrounding story: the site and altar have been divinely initiated and accepted, so the explanation of David's not going to the tabernacle at Gibeon (2 Chr 1:3-6) seems unnecessary and reflects a legalistic interpretation of the doctrine of centralization. In addition, one might ask why David is afraid if the plague has ceased and the angel has sheathed his sword. Indeed, verse 30 seems to regard the angel's sword as an independent element—comparable to the angel's sword in Gen 3:24—detached from the metaphor for the plague. It is also true that 22:1 could follow directly after 21:27 without the intervening verses. On the other hand, the language and style of verses 28-30 are in line with those of the Chronicler elsewhere, as is the borrowing of motifs such as the angel's sword. And the concern to point out that David's actions were not in violation of the stipulation of centralization does not seem unusual for the Chronicler.

Theological Analysis

The Chronicler's emphasis on the importance of the temple is obviously center stage in this unit. The location of the temple is divinely chosen, or at least approved, and its enormous value and importance are confirmed. But there are several other important themes at work as well. David's role in acquiring the land on which the temple is built is crucial. Even though he is not its builder, the temple in a real sense owes its existence to David. For the Chronicler, it is not the temple as a building that is important but the temple as a conduit to God. The Chronicler knows, after all, that the temple will be destroyed. David's interest in preparing for the temple exemplifies his concern for the sacred and also for the communion with God that the temple represents.

Although he sins, David is once again idealized as a person who is willing to recognize his sin when confronted with it. Furthermore, he repents immediately and makes intercession in the form of sacrifices. David shows his wisdom as Israel's ruler, moreover, in that he places himself in God's hands, reliant on divine grace (v. 13). His trust in God is well founded, as Yahweh saves Jerusalem from the plague. The site of the temple and its altar, therefore, is a constant reflection of God's mercy. David's attitude toward sacrifice is also exemplary, as he refuses to offer what belongs to someone else or what he has received for free. It is not that the sacrificer must "give till it hurts," but that offerings are only meaningful when they constitute something of value to the one who makes them. The value of the sacrifice is meaningless if it does not come from the heart of the offerer.

COMMISSIONING SOLOMON (1 CHRONICLES 22:2–29:30)

The overall nature of the material in this section is apparent from an outline of its contents:

22 – David charges Solomon to build the temple
23 – David organizes the Levites
24 – David organizes the priests
25 – David organizes the musicians
26 – David organizes the gatekeepers, treasurers, officers, and judges
27 – David organizes the secular officials
28–29 – David transfers the kingdom to Solomon and charges all Israel to build the temple

Basically, these chapters describe David's accomplishment of two important tasks: his transfer of the kingdom to Solomon and his preparations for building the temple. Two speeches or sets of speeches in chapters 22 and 28–29 surround various lists of personnel associated primarily with the temple and the cult and some smaller lists of building materials. David is clearly the central figure. Like Moses with the tabernacle—and the comparison is all but explicit at points—David is credited with the entire organization of the temple worship. Thus, for all practical purposes, David replaces Moses as the founder of Israel's worship. Also like Moses with Joshua, David transfers succession to Solomon.

The framework provided by David's speeches in chapters 22 and 28–29 furnishes one reason for considering this section of material a unit. There is an intensification or a narrowing of focus in these chapters on the preparations for building the temple that follow directly upon David's decree in 22:1 regarding the location of the temple and its altar. At the same time, the gathering of the people together with the enumeration of the sacred and military personnel for David's designation of Solomon as his successor are reminiscent of and broadly parallel to the enthronement of David and the transfer of the ark in chapters 11–16.

The matters of unity and structure in this section are complicated by the possibility, advocated by many commentators, that most of chapters 22–29 (23:3–27:34) constitute additions to the original work of the Chronicler. The primary reason for this position is the perception of tensions both within this section and with the ideas expressed elsewhere in Chronicles. The evidence, however, is indecisive. Tensions may indicate the presence of divergent source material and/or secondary additions within chapters 23–27 but do not necessarily mean that the section as a whole is later. Several recent commentators are persuaded that if the Chronicler's compositional techniques are properly understood there is no need to see this section as secondary.

DAVID CHARGES SOLOMON TO BUILD THE TEMPLE (1 CHRONICLES 22:2-19)

The rest of chapter 22 details David's immediate follow-up on his decree fixing the location of the temple and its altar (22:1). He begins by assembling workers and provisions for building the temple (vv. 2-5). Then, he addresses Solomon (vv. 6-16), exhorting him to complete the task for which God has chosen him, and the leaders of Israel (vv. 17-19), urging them to support Solomon in his task.

Literary Analysis

The main part of the chapter is the speech to Solomon (vv. 6-16), which itself consists of three parts, not counting the introduction to it in verses 6-7a: verses 7b-10, 11-13, 14-16. The first of these is introduced by a reference to Solomon as "my son" and explains the background to Solomon's designation as temple builder. Verse 11 introduces the second part with another mention of "my son" and encourages Solomon to faithfulness to God and to his task. Verse 14 begins the third part with "Behold" and then focuses on the materials provided by David for the temple.

Exegetical Analysis

The reference in verse 2 to the "aliens" whom David gathered as laborers should be understood against the background of 1 Kgs 5:13-18 (Heb. 5:27-32); 12:4, which describe a compulsory labor force raised by Solomon from among the northern tribes, and 1 Kgs 9:15-22, which insists that the labor force was composed only of non-Israelite residents in the land. Chronicles here seconds the latter perspective. The reference to the Phoenicians from Sidon and Tyre in verse 4 exhibits the idealized condition in which foreign peoples recognize Yahweh's superiority as well as the magnificence of his temple. That magnificence is hinted at already in the measureless quantities of building materials mentioned in verses 3-4. Verse 5 is then explicit about the magnificence of the future temple and the fame that it is to have among the nations. One might say that this description serves as a blueprint for both David and the Chronicler; it furnishes a rationale for the amount of material each of them devotes to the temple. David recognizes that Solomon by himself is inadequate to the task, even with David's help. Nor can David accomplish it by himself. If the temple is to be the structure envisioned by David, the full commitment of both kings and the entire people of Israel is required.

Verses 8-10 rehearse in summary form the historical background to this moment: Why is it that Solomon and not David is to build the temple? As such, they allude to and interpret the oracle in 1 Chr 17 // 2 Sam 7. In fact, this passage as a whole represents the Chronicler's interpretation of Nathan's oracle, and it is a new interpretation. David's statement in verse 7 that he "planned" (NRSV, better: "intended," lit., "it was with my *heart*") to build the temple reminds one of 1 Chr 17:1-2 // 2 Sam 7:1-3, where Nathan tells David to do all that is with his *heart*. Then the mention in 22:8 of the "word of Yahweh" that came concerning David is a direct allusion to the oracle mediated by Nathan. The explanation that follows in verse 8 is unique to Chronicles and appears to draw on 1 Kgs 5:3-4 (Heb. 5:17-18), where Solomon explains to Hiram that David's wars occupied too much of his time to allow him to work on the temple. For the Chronicler, warfare becomes bloodshed, and Yahweh prohibits David from building the temple because of the blood on his hands. David is not condemned for the bloodshed; the wars, after all, were Yahweh's wars in which David fulfilled the role divinely ordained for him. Hence, the prohibition of temple building would appear to be based on ritual considerations rather than ethical or moral ones. This new interpretation on the part of the Chronicler also indicates his dissatisfaction with the explanation, or lack thereof, provided by the Deuteronomistic History for David's not having built the temple.

Solomon's reign, in contrast to David's, is to be one of rest and peace (v. 9). The first two occurrences of "peace" in the NRSV are misleading. The Hebrew word here is "rest," and it is part of a theme developed by the Chronicler from the Deuteronomistic History. "Rest" and "peace" come only under Solomon. The Chronicler here artfully combines an explicit play on Solomon's name, which sounds similar to the Hebrew word *šālôm*, "peace," with the Deuteronomistic theme of rest. The latter originated in Deut 12 and taught that Yahweh would establish the centralized shrine where he would "cause his name to dwell" after he had given Israel rest from surrounding enemies (von Rad 1966). Solomon's name is given to him by God, and it represents the nature of his reign. Verse 10 then alludes to and reinterprets Yahweh's promise through Nathan in 1 Chr 17:12-13.

The next segment of David's speech (vv. 11-13) contains personal encouragement to Solomon in view of the great task before him. Solomon's success in completing the temple is dependent on God being with him (v. 11) and on his obedience to the law and its commandments (vv. 12-13a). He is, therefore, encouraged to be steadfast in his task (v. 13b). These verses contain a number of Deuteronomistic expressions—"Yahweh be with you," "keep the law," "you will succeed/prosper," "be careful to observe the statutes and ordinances," "be strong and courageous," "do not be afraid or dismayed." These are clustered particularly in the account of the transition from Moses to Joshua in Josh 1, making it clear that the Chronicler has patterned his account of the transition from David to Solomon both here and in chapter 28 after that one. This pattern is one of three techniques identified by Braun (1976) in chapters 22 and 28–29 by which the Chronicler presents Solomon as the chosen temple builder. The other two are the play on Solomon's name as a way of highlighting his reign as the period of anticipated rest and peace and the use of the verb "to choose" in chapters 28–29 to designate Solomon as the one chosen specifically for the task of building the temple.

The third part of David's speech, verses 14-16, is considered by some scholars to be a later addition, because verse 13 provides a fitting conclusion and because the figures in these verses are so exaggerated and out of line with those in 2 Chr 29:4, 7. These verses do seem rather loosely connected to what precedes. As noted above, they begin with "behold," rather than "my son" as do the previous two segments of the speech, and their intent seems to be more to list David's preparations than to encourage Solomon. They also contain some internal tensions: verse 14 gives amounts for the gold and silver, while verse 16 says they were beyond counting, although it may be the workers rather than the metals that are beyond counting (Knoppers 2004). The addition may have been motivated by a desire to harmonize this passage with the reference to David's prior contributions in 29:3 as well as to emphasize for theological purposes the incredible quantities of materials and personnel used in the temple's construction. A talent was about 75 pounds, so that the temple is said here to have contained 7,500,000 pounds of gold and 75 million pounds of silver!

Verses 17-19 are also commonly seen as an addition. They are unconnected to David's preceding speech to Solomon, and they have been seen as a doublet of 23:1 and 28:1. More to the point, 22:17-19 seems to presuppose David's public designation of Solomon as his successor (23:1) and his explanation of the choice of Solomon to build the temple (28:1-8). Its placement before these two texts, therefore, is awkward and may indicate its secondary nature. The expression "the land is subdued before Yahweh" in verse 18 is borrowed directly from Num 32:22, but while in Numbers it looks forward to the future conquest, in Chronicles it describes the result of what David has done, bringing peace and rest, and thus setting the stage for Solomon to build the temple. The primary function of the temple according to verse 19 is to house the ark. The reference to a house "for the name of Yahweh" borrows from the "name theology" of Deuteronomy. Once thought to be a safeguard of divine transcendence in the face of the claim that God somehow resided in Jerusalem, recent treatments have found the origin of the name theology in a king's claim to a site by means of an inscribed monument left there (Richter 2002; Schniedewind 1999:85). The occurrence of the expression here is another instance of the anthological nature of verses 18-19.

Theological Analysis

The paramount concern in this chapter, as in chapters 22–29, if not the entire book of Chronicles, is the temple. The temple is to be "exceedingly magnificent, famous and glorified throughout all lands" (v. 5). The temple, thus, is to bring Israel's renown to the nations, and the amounts of materials set aside for its construction are incredible (vv. 2-4, 14). The magnificence of the temple structure is important not as an end in itself but because it attests the grandeur of Israel's God.

David and Solomon are each idealized in their own respective dealings with the temple. David makes all the preparations for the temple, despite knowing that he cannot build it. This reflects his selfless devotion to God and to the task at hand. The blood that David has shed disqualifies him ritually but not on moral grounds, as his wars were part of God's grand scheme. Solomon is chosen as David's successor specifically for the purpose of seeing the construction through. Both are equally important to the enterprise. Ultimately, though, Yahweh is the one upon whom construction of the temple depends. This is the tacit theological assumption behind David's prayer that Yahweh will grant Solomon success (v. 11) and his exhortation of Solomon to obedience of the divine law (vv. 12-13). Everything—the construction of the temple no less than the operation of the world as a whole—depends on Yahweh. Solomon's obedience to Yahweh, therefore, is crucial, for it is only through his obedience that Yahweh will allow the work to prosper.

DAVID ORGANIZES THE LEVITES (1 CHRONICLES 23:1-32)

Having done all that he could to prepare for the construction of the temple, David now turns his attention to organizing the personnel and assignments for the daily ritual activities in the temple. First Chronicles 23:1 can be seen as a heading to all of chapters 23–29 or to chapters 28–29 if the rest of chapters 23–27 is an addition. The lists that follow in chapters 23–27 are of two kinds of personnel—religious and secular—the former consisting of priests and Levites in various roles as described in chapters 23–26 and the latter the focus of chapter 27.

Literary Analysis

Chapter 23 falls into three parts. Verses 1-6 give an overview of the duties assigned to the Levites and thereby provide an outline for the succeeding chapters. The introductory function of 23:1 was mentioned above. Verse 2 with its reference to the leaders, the priests, and the Levites, represents the organization in reverse order of the following chapters. It is worth noting that only the Levites are mentioned here. Verses 7-23 then list the Levitical divisions in the three branches of Gershon,

Kohath, and Merari. Finally, verses 24-32 more specifically describe the duties assigned the Levites by David.

Chapter 23, like all of the material in chapters 23–27, has been the object of a good deal of speculation about secondary reworking. If 23:2 anticipates 28:1, as some have argued, its reference to the priests and leaders was likely the work of a second, priestly redactor. The Chronicler's original introduction would have referred only to David assembling the Levites. As it now stands, chapter 23 presents an overview of the Levites as a whole, including the priests, although the references to the latter (vv. 13b-14, 25-32) may be later additions.

Exegetical Analysis

The total number of Levites—38,000 (v. 3)—is much larger than the total given for them elsewhere in the Bible (7,580 in Num 4:36; 4,600 in 1 Chr 12:27; 733 in Ezra 2:40-58). The inflated number may indicate the greater value placed upon them here. The figure given here for the age at which Levites were to begin their service (30 years old) differs from the age of initiation found later in this chapter (vv. 24 and 27 = 20 years old). The figure varies throughout the Old Testament: Num 4 consistently gives it as thirty; Num 8:24 as twenty-five; while 2 Chr 31:17 and Ezra 3:8 have twenty. The different numbers may reflect historical changes in the age at which Levites were initiated, depending on the need for them and their availability. But the occurrence of different numbers in such close literary proximity suggests the composite nature of this chapter, unless it is an intentional effort by the author to legitimate the revision of the traditional beginning age of service in the tabernacle to that for temple service (Knoppers 2004).

The Levites are divided first in verses 4-5 according to their functions, then in verses 6-23 according to genealogy. The usual groups are Levites, gatekeepers, and singers, as in chapter 9. Here, a fourth group—officers and judges—is added and given prominence, with 6,000 members, over the gatekeepers and singers. The function of the largest group—24,000 strong—is not entirely clear. The verb translated "have charge of" in the NRSV typically means "to direct." It is not clear whether the Levites are envisioned as the supervisors over the construction of the temple or whether this simply means that they are to oversee its daily service. The phrase, "David said," in the NRSV is not in the Hebrew text and is an effort by the translators to prepare for the unexpected first person verb, "I made," in verse 5. But the latter is likely textually corrupt and should probably be emended to the third person.

Verse 6 does double duty as both a conclusion of verses 1-5 and an introduction to verses 7-23. The three Levitical branches are Gershon (vv. 7-11), Kohath (vv. 12-20), and Merari (vv. 21-23). Gershon is usually spelled "Gershom" in Chronicles (see above on 6:1 [Heb. 5:27]), and his firstborn son is always Libni (cf. Exod 6:17; 1 Chr 6:17 [Heb. 6:2]) except for here and in 26:21. These features indicate that the genealogy in 23:7-11 probably came from a different source than others for Gershom in Chronicles. Verses 9-10 contain two genealogies for Shimei, and verse 9 is probably misplaced. The note in verse 11 about the merger of Jeush and Beriah reflects historical circumstances in which these two families or lines dwindled and came to be counted as one.

The first three generations of the line of Kohath in verses 12-20 are matched by 6:1-15, but then the two lists diverge, the latter following Aaron's line, the present passage listing Moses'. Verses 13-14, however, explain that Aaron's line is "set apart" as priests and not reckoned in this genealogy. The special place afforded to the priests in certain parts of this chapter on the Levites is one of the points used to argue for the secondary nature of those parts. Verse 13 makes use of language borrowed from the Priestly source of the Pentateuch (esp. Exod 30:29-30) but also from the Deuteronomistic History (esp. Deut 10:8). The reference to Rehabiah having numerous sons (v. 17) likely reflects an etymological interpretation. The name is related to a word meaning "wide, spacious." A similar etiology occurs in Gen 26:22 where Isaac names the place Rehoboth because "Yahweh has made room for us."

The third branch is that of Merari (vv. 21-23), who, as elsewhere, has two sons, Mahli and Mushi. However, the names here are different from the line of Mushi traced in 6:29-30, 44-47 (Heb. 6:14-15, 29-32). The differences appear to be grounded in different sources, perhaps reflecting the changes in relationships between Levitical groups at various periods. The daughters of Eleazar (v. 22) apparently maintain an independent house despite having no brothers. Their case is reminiscent of that of the daughters of Zelophehad in Num 27, who keep their heritage of land without father or brothers. Verse 24 concludes the foregoing lists of Levites. The last line of the verse (v. 24b) in the Hebrew text is "from twenty years old and upward," which contradicts verse 3. It is probably an addition—even later than verses 25-32—since it interrupts the sequence between verses 24 and 25.

Verses 25-32 are often recognized as being from a different writer than the foregoing verses because they ignore the divisions laid out in verses 4-5 and emphasize the distinction between priests and Levites. These verses are dependent on the account of the census of Israel in Num 1, as is evident from several instances of shared, peculiar vocabulary (Japhet 1993:417-18). The Levites were not to be counted in a military census (Num 1:49), since they were ineligible for military service. They are enrolled in 1 Chr 23, as in Num 3–4, in their capacity of service to the tabernacle/temple. But the enrollment of the Levites is patterned after the military census.

The duties of the Levites laid out in verses 25-32 are explicitly described as the result of a change in historical circumstances. With the establishment of the temple site, there is no longer any need for the Levites to carry the ark, which was their main function according to Num 1:50-54. There is a wordplay in 23:25-26, where it is stated that Yahweh now resides (šākan) in Jerusalem so that the tabernacle (miškān) no longer needs to be carried. Both terms are typical of the Priestly source of the Pentateuch. But the reference to Yahweh giving rest to his people in verse 25*a* is distinctively Deuteronomic/Deuteronomistic, as is the idea that a change in circumstances calls for changes in the cult (Deut 12). Hence, the author of this Chronicles passage combines language and ideas from both the Deuternomistic History and P (the Priestly source). Nevertheless, the statement in verse 25 that Yahweh "has given rest to his people" also seems to contradict the Chronicler's doctrine of rest elsewhere (17:1; 22:9) where rest is seen as coming only in Solomon's reign.

Verse 27 is widely recognized as a gloss intended to smooth the contradiction between verses 3 and 24 concerning the age of enrollment of the Levites. It obviously breaks the continuity between verses 26 and 28.

The Levitical duties in verses 28-32 are amplified beyond those described in the Pentateuch, where they were concerned mostly with the tabernacle (cf. Num 3-4). At the same time, the description of their new functions adapts the older prescriptions of Num 3–4 to the new situation. That new situation is stressed by the phrase "for the service of the house of Yahweh," which is repeated in verses 28 and 32 and thus provides a frame for the duties listed in between. This frame also subordinates the Levites to the priests, the descendants of Aaron. Thus, while the Levites retain various functions within the temple cult, they are clearly subservient to the priests and serve primarily as their assistants. These specific tasks of the Levites include maintenance of temple facilities and cleansing of sacred vessels (v. 28), preparing the shewbread and various offerings (v. 29), and singing (vv. 30-31). These duties correspond to the three suborders of Levites—gatekeepers, Levites, and singers—found elsewhere in 9:14-34 and below in chapters 25–26. Verse 32 summarizes the tasks of Levites drawing on Num 3:5-8; 18:2-7, both of which stress the servitude of the Levites to the priests as a "gift" to the latter. The writer here appropriates the expression, "tent of meeting," in reference not to the tabernacle but now to the temple.

Theological Analysis

Having the proper personnel is crucial to the proper functioning of the worship in the temple. That is the underlying principle of the present chapter. This chapter ascribes the reorganization of the Levites to David. The limitation of priests to descendants of Aaron and the distinction between priests and (other) Levites are traced back to Aaron (vv. 13-14). That did not change. But the need to reorganize the Levites was occasioned by Yahweh's keeping his promise to bring "rest" to Israel. The primary duty of the Levites had been to carry the ark. But now that the ark had come to rest in Jerusalem, the Levites were no longer needed for that purpose. David, therefore, designated their divisions for other duties, maintaining the temple and its supplies. Once again, David's preparation for the temple is meticulous and a sign of his piety and concern for the proper reverence of God. It may be fair to suggest that a reason for this kind of detailed organization of personnel is to avoid a situation of rivalry between Levitical families. Such in-fighting would be highly inappropriate among sacral servants. Such an organization also illustrates the principle that each servant has a proper role to fulfill or perhaps a talent to bring in the service of God.

DAVID ORGANIZES THE PRIESTS (1 CHRONICLES 24:1-31)

This chapter consists of two parts. Verses 1-19 comprise a register of the twenty-four priestly divisions according to their rotation as assigned by lot. Then verses 20-31 contain a list of Levites comparable to the one in 23:6-23. One of the main goals of this chapter is the description and legitimation of the rotational system presented here.

Literary Analysis

Many scholars believe verses 1-19 to be an addition because they seem out of order. Not only do they interrupt the listing of the Levitical orders, but one would expect the priestly divisions to be given the place of primacy, ahead of the Levitical ones. (See Japhet 1993:410 for counterarguments.) Williamson (1982:162-65) believes both parts of the chapter to be the work of the Priestly reviser—verses 1-19 because of their focus on the priests and their attachment to 23:25-32 and verses 20-31 because of their connection with verses 1-19 and because they update the list in 23:6-23. The reviser introduced the division into twenty-four priestly houses that is reflected here, probably in order to legitimate a system that was already in place. It is unknown just how or when this system developed, but it remained in place for most of the Second Temple period.

Exegetical Analysis

The first line of verse 1 (lit., "As for the sons of Aaron, their divisions") is a sort of title to verses 1-19. The "sons of Aaron" in this title refers to the entire priestly order. The information about Aaron's four immediate sons in verses 1b-2 comes from Num 3:2-4. However, the writer in Chronicles has changed the reference to the death of Nadab and Abihu, perhaps to avoid tarnishing the priestly image. "Nadab and Abihu died before Yahweh" in Num 3:4 has become "Nadab and Abihu died before their father." The two priests, Zadok and Ahimelech, who, according to verse 3, help David organize the priestly divisions, represent, respectively, the lines of Eleazar and Ithamar. In giving Ahimelech's name here (and in v. 6) the writer has followed 2 Sam 8:17, which is widely recognized as textually corrupt. Elsewhere throughout Samuel Abiathar is Zadok's contemporary and the son of Ahimelech. However, the Chronicler may have leveled through his work the papponymous identification of Abiathar's son as Ahimelech (papponymy is the practice of naming a son after his grandfather). The Zadokite priesthood was prominent and is, therefore, associated with the main priestly line of Eleazar (v. 4). The statement in this verse that the "father's houses" were formed based on the relative size of the lines of Eleazar and Ithamar is a clear indication that the organizational scheme was the result of social factors rather than actual hereditary relationships.

The divisions of priests were determined, according to verses 5-6, by lot. This contrasts with 23:1-24, where the divisions of the Levites seem to be the result of David's assignment. The divisions of the singers in chapter 25 are also determined by lot, and there may be an effort on the part of the writer to provide a parallel between the ritual activities of sacrifice and music. The titles in verse 5, "officers of the sanctuary" and "officers of God," are unusual and perhaps are adapted from a military analogy. The lottery process described here seems to have involved an alternation between the lines of Eleazar and Ithamar such that the lot would be cast at each round between two divisions, one from each line, up to the sixteenth division. Thereafter, all the divisions would have to be from the house of Eleazar. However, this understanding of the process is somewhat speculative, since the description in the text is not entirely clear, and lines are not specified for the names in verses 7-18.

Of the names in verses 7-18, five (Seorim, Huppah, Jeshebeab, Happizzez, Gamul) are unique, occurring nowhere else in the Old Testament. Jakim, Hezir, and Pethahiah occur only here as priests. Most of the other names are found in the other lists of priests in 1 Chr 9:10-13; Ezra 2:36-38 // Neh 7:39-42; Neh 10:2-8 [Heb. 10:3-9]; 11:10-14; 12:1-7. Eliashib was also the name of a high priest in Nehemiah's time (Neh 3:1, etc.). Jehezkel is another rendering of the name Ezekiel; this may be a reference to the biblical prophet Ezekiel, since he was also a priest. Hakkoz was excluded from the priesthood according to Ezra 2:62 because he could not prove his pedigree; apparently his claim had since been ratified. Jehoiarib was the name of the Maccabees' ancestor (Macc 2:1). It is striking that the name Pashhur, the largest family of priests according to Ezra 2:38 // Neh 7:41; Ezra 10:22; and Neh 10:3 (Heb. 10:4) is not mentioned here. While it is likely that the line had subdivided and that some of the names in the current list are Pashhur's "heirs," the same must also have happened with the lines of Jedaiah, Immer, and Harim, yet those names continue to appear here. Following the list of priests, verse 19 affirms the antiquity of the priestly duties by attributing them to the founding priest, Aaron, and ultimately to Yahweh.

The heading in verse 20 indicates the supplemental nature of verses 20-31. The list that follows presumes and augments 23:7-23. "The *rest* of the Levites," therefore, refers not to those who were not priests, since these have already been listed in 23:7-23, but to the additional names in 24:20-31, which update the list in 23:7-23 by a single name in most cases. Indeed, the purpose of the passage seems to be to update the earlier list. The statement in 24:31 that these *also* cast lots shows that the interpolator was familiar with verses 1-19 and envisioned the organization of these additional Levites in verses 20*b*-30 as analogous to that of the priests in verses 1-19, although this contrasts with 23:7-23, where the organization is by David's decree. In that sense, 24:30 and 24:31 are in some tension with each other concerning the process of organization of the Levites. This is because verse 30 has effectively been copied from 23:23-24, even though it is not entirely appropriate to its new context.

The list in 24:20-31 updates only the lines of Kohath and Merari; perhaps the beginning with Gershon (cf. 23:7-11) had been lost or no updated information was available. The additional names in these verses do not simply represent the latest generation of Levites. The updating, rather, reflects social developments among the Levites. This is clearest in the line of Merari. Obviously, the ancestor Merari could not have had another son between the respective recordings of 23:7-23 and 24:20-31, and it is highly unlikely that there was a son who had simply gone unnoticed in previous genealogies. Rather, the Levitical family of Jaaziah had risen to prominence during the time between the two lists, and his name along with those of his "sons" reflect far-reaching changes within the line of Merari at this period. The other cases in which a "son" succeeds his "father" in the list likewise indicate changes in leadership, albeit with the preservation of traditional affiliations.

Theological Analysis

It is difficult for modern readers to appreciate the lists of names in this chapter. But their presence testifies to the importance of the priestly class in the post-exilic community. In this sacerdotal system, the priests were viewed as the link to God and the key to proper worship in the magnificent temple. Hence, proper credentials in the form of a pedigree were essential. The priests also established continuity with the past, as they went back not only to David but to Aaron. The priestly divisions detailed in this chapter were established by lot, strongly suggesting their divine origin.

DAVID ORGANIZES THE MUSICIANS (1 CHRONICLES 25:1-31)

This chapter contains two lists of the Levitical singers by two different schemes—first by descent and then again by division. Thus, all of the personal names occur twice in the chapter, although there are sometimes minor variations between the occurrences. The singers are the only group of Levites dually listed in this fashion.

Literary Analysis

This chapter consists of two parts, one part for each list. Verses 1-7 contain the names of the singers according to their descent from one of three "fathers"—Asaph (v. 2), Jeduthun (v. 3), and Heman (vv. 4-6a). While it is obscured in translation, verses 1b and 7 begin with the same phrase in Hebrew *(wayhî mispārām,* "their number/roster was"), which serves as a frame for the unit. On the other hand, verse 7 clearly anticipates verses 8-31, so that if the latter are an addition, verse 7 must be later as well. Verses 8-31 describe the organization of the singers as determined by lot into twenty-four divisions. In Williamson's reconstruction (1979a: 255-57), only verses 1-6 are the Chronicler's work. The rest of the chapter is from the priestly reviser, who leveled through the system of twenty-four divisions.

Exegetical Analysis

The chapter is rich with fascinating details and interpretive challenges. Verse 1 credits David with having "set apart" or "separated" the singers for their specific task. This agrees with David's division of the Levites in 23:6 but contrasts with the system of division by lot in 25:8-31. The music that David put in place for the singular event of the transfer of the ark in chapters 15–16 is apparently now institutionalized as a permanent feature of the temple worship.

It is striking that David does not act alone but in congress with the "officers of the army." Despite this translation, these are not to be understood as military commanders. Rather, the author here borrows language from the Pentateuch (cf. esp. Num 4:3, 23, 30, 35, etc.), where the word "army" is used for the service of the Levites. The use of the term in this context may have arisen from the function of the Levites as a security force for the temple precincts.

Among the three families of singers in 25:2-6, the Asaphites are listed first, indicating their priority. But the fact that they are also the smallest of the three families with only four branches suggests that their priority may have been waning at the time of this list. As for the branches of Jeduthun in verse 3, five are listed, but the total given is six. The name Shimei may be restored on the basis of verse 17. The name Jeduthun may actually have originated as a musical annotation to certain psalms (39:1; 62:1; 77:1). The name and line of Jeduthun were later replaced in the lists by those of Ethan—probably indicating that the Ethanites supplanted their Jeduthun counterparts in social prominence. In the line of Heman, Mattaniah and Bukkiah (Bakbukiah) are listed as Asaphites in Neh 11:17, 22; 12:35. This suggests that the Hemanites began as Asaphites but developed enough prominence to be treated as a distinct line. The references in the present list to Heman being the king's seer, to the divine promise to exalt him (see below), and to the number of heirs indicate that this line was growing in importance.

The last nine names in the line of Heman in verse 4 have long been recognized as artificial. The NRSV renders these names as: Hananiah, Hanani, Eliathah, Giddalti, Romamtiezer, Joshbekashah, Mallothi, Hothir, and Mahazioth. But most of these "names" do not fit the patterns used to form Hebrew personal names. With only slight revocalization of the consonants that make up these names, the list can be reconstructed as a short psalm as follows (each line represents a separate name):

Be merciful to me, O Yahweh,
Be merciful to me!
You are my God.
I magnify
and exalt [you], [my] help.
Dwelling in adversity,
I spoke.
Multiply ("give abundantly")
visions.

It has also been proposed that the list represents not a single verse but *incipits,* that is, beginnings of various psalms and even that these *incipits* came to designate groups of singers who characteristically sang the psalms they began. In this case, the "names" are treated in pairs, except for the third one, Eliathah ("you are my God"). However, there are no good precedents in the book of Psalms for psalms beginning with any of the last four words. Yet another possibility is that these final nine names were simply inventions designed to fill out the number of Heman's sons (14) in verse 5.

In addition to Heman's title of "seer," the task of the singers is described in verses 1 and 3 as prophesying. The background to this idea would seem to be texts like 1 Sam 10:5, in which prophets were accompanied by musical instruments, which may have been used in an earlier era to induce prophetic ecstasy (cf. 2 Kgs 3:15). In the present passage, however, the singing or prophecy was a permanent feature of temple worship and neither an isolated phenomenon nor ecstatic experience. The understanding of the singers as prophets may also derive in part from the idea apparently shared by the book of Psalms that composers like Asaph and of course David were divinely inspired (cf. 2 Chr 29:30). At any rate, this understanding certainly imbues the temple music with special significance and elevates its role in divine-human communication. The singing in the temple becomes not only a way in which humans speak to God but also a way for God to speak to people.

The expression translated "to exalt him" in verse 5 literally means "to raise a horn" *(lĕhārîm qeren)*. It is common in Psalms as an idiom for increasing a person's power, standing, or dignity. Here the object is lacking; this may be due to the accidental loss of the suffix "his" and in any case it seems clear that Heman is the referent.

The numerical summary in verse 7 anticipates the lottery list in verses 8-31, where there are twenty-four groups of singers with twelve in each group for a total of 288. Hence, if verses 8-31 are a later addition, the addition actually begins with verse 7.

Verse 8 is linked by subject and syntax to verses 1-7, but it obviously introduces the organization of the singers by lot in verses 9-31. Although the text is difficult and may be corrupt, it seems clear that the casting of lots here is to determine the assignment of duties and not, as with the priests in 24:7-19 for order of rotation. The precise duties, however, are not mentioned. Most of the list follows an obvious pattern: ordinal number, proper name, "his sons and his brother, twelve." Despite the meticulous pattern of the list, its artificiality has long been noted and is evident from the following chart of the order of the lots.

Asaph	Jeduthun	Heman
1. Joseph	2. Gedaliah	
3. Zaccur	4. Izri	
5. Nethaniah		6. Bukkiah
7. Jesharelah	8. Jeshaiah	9. Mattaniah
	10. Shimei	11. Azarel
	12. Hashabiah	13. Shubael
	14. Mattathiah	15. Jeremoth
		16. Hanahiah
		17. Joshbekashah
		18. Hanani
		19. Mallothi
		20. Eliathah
		21. Hothir
		22. Giddalti
		23. Mahazioth
		24. Romamtiezer

It is hardly possible that lot casting would have resulted in such a regular alternation of names from the three lines of singers, and one that basically reproduces the order of names within lines in verses 2-5. Even the last nine names in the line of Heman presuppose the foregoing list and reflect alternation based upon it. The nine names in verse 4b were divided into two groups of four and five respectively and alternated to produce the order of lots. The one divergence in order from verses 2-5 is the listing of Joseph, the second son of Asaph, in first place rather than Zaccur. This may reflect a change in relative status of the two groups between the times of composition of the two lists.

Theological Analysis

In addition to the messages conveyed in previous chapters—that the installment of the proper personnel is essential and that the selection of duties is done by lot, suggesting that it is actually by divine choice—this chapter highlights the theological significance of music. Music and musicians have a special place in the vision of the temple in Chronicles. The present chapter describes music not simply as praise to God but as revelation from God in the form of prophecy. It is not exactly clear just how music was understood as prophecy. It may simply be that for the Chronicler and those of his age, music was seen as having replaced ecstatic prophecy, which had ceased. But perhaps there is a tacit recognition in this equation that music can be profoundly moving to the human spirit and can also express the deepest human feelings—especially when it occurs in a religious setting or conveys a religious message. On such occasions, music can be felt to "speak" to people and perhaps in that sense to be revelatory or prophetic.

DAVID ORGANIZES THE GATEKEEPERS, TREASURERS, OFFICERS, AND JUDGES (1 CHRONICLES 26:1-32)

The lists in this chapter have a double legitimation function. First, they probably represent the divisions and duties followed in the author's day, whether the author was the Chronicler or a later redactor. Thus, the lists make the point, common in 1 Chr 22–29 as a whole, that the divisions and duties represented here go back to the time of David and were established by his command or by lottery, implying divine choice. They also claim Levitical descent for the gatekeepers, a claim made elsewhere in 1 Chronicles (1 Chr 9:17-32) but lacking in Ezra–Nehemiah (Ezra 2:42; Neh 7:45).

Literary Analysis

Chapter 26 consists of two main sections concerning the gatekeepers (vv. 1-19) and other Levitical officials (vv. 20-32). The section dealing with the gatekeepers contains a list of divisions in the form of a genealogy (vv. 1-11) and an explanation of the gatekeepers' duties (vv. 12-19). The second section details the treasurers and their duties (vv. 20-28) and the officers and judges with their duties (vv. 29-32). The account of the line of Obed-edom in verses 4-8 is likely secondary as it interrupts that of Meshelemiah. The Levitical genealogy for the line of Obed-edom, the largest group of gatekeepers, is also not fully developed. In fact, the treatment of Obed-edom as a gatekeeper is itself evidently a feature of the reviser of Chronicles, since for the Chronicler he is a singer (15:21; 16:5).

Exegetical Analysis

As the list in verses 1-11 now stands, there are twenty-four courses of gatekeepers: seven in the line of Meshelemiah, thirteen in the line of Obed-edom, and four in the line of Hosah. This would make the courses of gatekeepers parallel to those of the priests (24:7-19) and singers (25:8-31). However, the line of Obed-edom in verses 4-8 seems to be a secondary addition; it interrupts the tally for Meshelemiah, which concludes in verse 9, and there is no explicit link between Obed-edom and Levi or Korah. Furthermore, the summary in verse 19 mentions only Korahites and Merarites, without recognition of a third line represented by Obed-edom. The total number of gatekeepers in the present passage (93) in comparison to the total in 9:22 (212) seems to indicate a decline in the vocation for unknown reasons. Both of these figures are much smaller than the number of gatekeepers given in 23:5—four thousand. Either that number is an exaggeration and the others are more realistic, or the smaller figures represent the heads of families rather than individual gatekeepers. As for their function, the description in

9:19-32 suggests that the gatekeepers were a sort of security force, charged first and foremost with *guarding* the temple precincts, especially at its access points, but also with the maintenance of the temple furnishings, utensils, and provisions.

The line of Obed-edom in verses 4-8 includes eight sons and six grandsons through Shemaiah. (Since Shemaiah's line is listed, he may not be counted in figuring the number of courses [13] in the line of Obed-edom.) His fecundity is accounted for in verse 5 by the notation that God blessed him, an allusion perhaps to 13:14. The divine blessing was reward for the ark having resided with Obed-edom for three months. This background is reflected also in the names of Obed-edom's sons. Two of them, Sachar and Issachar, bear the Hebrew word *śākār,* "reward," and Peullethai, essentially means "my works." Together, the names recall the statement in 2 Chr 15:7 and Jer 31:16, "there is reward for your work." The sons of Obed-edom and of Shemaiah are referred to three times in verses 6-8 as "able men." The Hebrew expressions differ in each case, but all three use the term *ḥayil,* meaning "strength" or "ability." The expression in verse 6 is often used of warriors and in this context may emphasize their function as a security or police force. Physical strength may also have been an asset for other duties of the gatekeepers. Hosah, whose line is given in verses 10-11, is also mentioned as a gatekeeper with Obed-edom in 16:38.

Verse 12 presupposes the list of gatekeepers in verses 1-11 and introduces the description of their assignments in verses 13-18. It refers to allocation of duties "just as their kindred," an apparent allusion to the organization of the priests and singers, although no ordinal listing of the gatekeepers follows. The expression "small and great alike" may refer to the relative size of the families of gatekeepers. In this context, it is intended to indicate the equitable distribution, by lot, of the gate assignments among the three branches of gatekeepers just listed. What follows is an account of those assignments (vv. 14-16) and then of the daily watches (vv. 17-18). Since there are four sides to be allotted and only three branches, Shelemiah is allotted two gates, one of them going to his son Zechariah. It is difficult to believe that this allotment occurred by chance; not only did this branch (= Meshelemiah) have priority in the list of verses 1-11, but it also was assigned the east gate, which would have been the most important. Thus, these gate assignments were probably the result of social and historical factors.

Obed-edom is allotted the southern gate and the "storehouses" (v. 15 NRSV). The latter word appears to mean something like "vestibule" (cf. Neh 12:25). The name Shuppim in verse 16 is probably a mistaken repetition of this word, especially since no Shuppim occurs in the previous list of gatekeepers. The last phrase of verse 16 refers back to the allotment as a whole. Its exact referent is not clear. It may mean that the guard duties and shifts at the gates corresponded to each other. Or, it may describe the process of the lottery such that the gatekeepers cast lots between sets of guard posts.

Verses 17-18 detail the daily posts. As the text now stands, there appear to be twenty-four such posts: six on the east, four on the north, four on the south, two pair at the vestibule (the same word used in v. 15), four on the west, and two at the "colonade." However, the first word of verse 18 seems to be an accidental repetition of the last word of verse 17. The number "two" is repeated, as is the term *parbār*, a Persian loanword for some kind of outside structure. In this case, there would be twenty-two posts. The addition of the "two" at the end of verse 17, or at least its retention, may have been partly motivated by a desire to have the number of posts correspond to the number of courses of gatekeepers in verses 1-11, not to mention the number of courses of the priests and singers (24). Verse 19 furnishes a good conclusion to verses 1-3 + 9-11, which may represent the Chronicler's original work in this chapter if verses 4-8 and 12-18 are in fact insertions.

The remainder of this chapter is quite composite. In general, it lists other Levites in the roles of treasurers (vv. 20-28) and officers and judges (vv. 29-32). But verses 21-22, 24-28, and 29-32 all seem to comprise originally independent lists, with verse 23 being an interpolated attempt to bring some order to the material. Together, these lists ascribe a great deal of authority to the Levites. The reference to officers and judges as Levites is unique to Chronicles and effectively identifies David's imperial administrative system as Levitical.

The lists of treasurers introduced in verse 20 indicates that there were two treasuries: those of the temple—perhaps containing valuable implements used in worship—and "dedicated gifts," (lit. "holy things")—special items devoted to Yahweh by David and other leaders. The Gershonites in the line of Ladan (Libni) are in charge of the temple treasuries (vv. 21-22). The placement of Levites in charge of temple property may reflect actual practice at the time of the composition of this chapter, but it may also reflect an effort to encroach on the roles of the priests. The Gershonites were not mentioned in verses 1-19, but they may be alluded to by the word "their brothers," in verse 20, which is the preferred reading over the name Ahijah (MT, followed by the NRSV). Verse 21 is likely corrupt as it contains three introductions to the family of Ladan. Zetham and Joel are called sons of Jehieli in verse 22, and this may reflect the social advance of these two families over against the situation indicated by 23:8, where all three are referred to as brothers.

Verse 23 gives the four branches of the Kohathites. It may have been added in an effort to tie together the diverse materials that follow which detail the duties of certain Amramites (vv. 24-28), Izrahites (v. 29), and Hebronites (vv. 30-32). The connection, if any, between these Levitical Hebronites and those of Judah is unclear. There is no further mention, however, of Uzzielites.

The account of the maintenance of the treasuries in verses 21-22 continues in verses 24-28. But the two texts were originally independent, as indicated by the shift from Gershonites to

Amramites. Presumably, "the treasuries" in verse 24 are to be identified with "the treasuries of the temple of Yahweh" in verse 22, though they may originally have been distinct. The reference to his "brothers" in verse 25 should be understood in the broad sense of Shebuel's "kinfolk." The list in this verse may be read as referring to five brothers or to five generations; the latter is more likely in view of 23:17, which states that Rehabiah was Eliezar's only son.

The account of the dedicated gifts in verses 26-28 borrows from Num 31:48-54 and recalls David's dedication to Yahweh of the spoils from his victories as described in 18:8, 10-11. There was, of course, no temple in David's day, much less in that of Samuel and Saul, so the author apparently understands these as items stored in the tabernacle or elsewhere in anticipation of the temple. The list in verse 28 shows that such dedications were shared by other leaders and officers and to that extent represent the initiatives of the people of Israel as a whole. Not surprisingly, there are no references in 1–2 Samuel to Samuel, Saul, or David dedicating booty to Yahweh; the author's point here is theological. It is rather surprising, however, to find Saul cast in a positive light.

The list of officers and judges in verses 29-32 is tied with the reference to them in 23:4. They are Izharites and Hebronites. The Chenaniah who is their leader (v. 29) is not mentioned elsewhere, though a musical director of the same name is mentioned in 15:22, 27. Their "outside duties" (v. 29) are not specified, but they appear from verses 30 and 32 to be both religious and secular. The Hebronites in two families, those of Hashabiah and Jerijah, administer the entire territory west and east of the Jordan, respectively. Jazer in Gilead is east of the Jordan, as are the Reubenites, Gadites, and half tribe of Manasseh. Thus, the author seems here to be placing David's entire administrative system in the hands of the Levites—a theocracy. Hence, while there may be some authentic source behind this list (Braun 1986:254; Japhet 1993:464), the author has transformed it into an entirely different document.

Theological Analysis

The ideal state envisioned by the Chronicler might fairly be called a theocracy. Its constitution is the law given by God. It is ruled by kings such as David and Solomon whose foremost allegiance is to God. The Chronicler focuses his account on the ways in which these kings provide for the temple and the worship of God. The temple is at the heart of the state, and it is administered by Levites, who are appointed to various roles of service for the temple and the government. The temple is financed by the booty collected and donated by leaders from the victories that they win by God's help (vv. 27-28). This state, like the individuals within it, will prosper by divine blessing (v. 5).

DAVID ORGANIZES THE SECULAR OFFICIALS (1 CHRONICLES 27:1-34)

The lists in this chapter are secular (military and economic) in orientation and contrast with the cultic organization in the previous chapters. They might be seen as following naturally upon the recounting of semisecular duties of Levites at the end of chapter 26 in correspondence to the "leaders" mentioned 23:2, which is a kind of reverse outline for the material that follows it.

Literary Analysis

This chapter contains four lists of secular personnel that were likely originally independent: military divisions (vv. 1-15), tribal officers (vv. 16-22), David's stewards (vv. 25-31), and David's advisors (vv. 32-34). These lists seem entirely unrelated to the Levites and the temple, which have been the primary subjects up to this point. In addition, 27:25-34 is in some tension with 26:30-32, where David places two Levites in charge of the king's affairs. For these reasons, this chapter is often considered to be a redactional supplement.

Exegetical Analysis

The list of military divisions in verses 1-15 consists of twelve divisions (one for each month), each containing 24,000 men and each commanded by one of David's military heroes whose names are given in 1 Chr 11 // 2 Sam 23, as the following chart shows.

1 Chr 27:1-15	1 Chr 11:11-31	2 Sam 23:8-30a
Jashobeam	Jashobeam	Josheb-bashebeth
Dodai	Eleazar son of Dodo	Eleazar son of Dodo
		Shammah
	Abishai	Abishai
Benaiah	Benaiah	Benaiah
Asahel	Asahel	Asahel
	Elhanan	Elhanan
Shamhuth	Shammoth	Shammah
		Elika
Ira	Helez	Helez
Helez	Ira	Ira
Sibbecai	Abiezer	Abiezer
Abiezer	Sibbecai	Mebunnai
	Ilai	Zalmon
Maharai	Maharai	Maharai
Benaiah	Heled	Heleb
	Ithai	Ittai
Heldai	Benaiah	Benaiah

The names in 1 Chr 27 are not identical to those in 1 Chr 11 or 2 Sam 23, though they are obviously closer to the former. The names are also in the same basic order, though it too is not identical. The lists in 1 Chr 11 // 2 Sam 23 continue with many more names. Thus, 1 Chr 27:1-15 is selective and based on 1 Chr 11, albeit perhaps indirectly. The criteria for selection remain unknown, but textual corruption may account for some of the differences. The tribal affiliations supplied for some names in chapter 27 are also new; the source or motive behind these is again unknown. The artificiality of 27:1-15 is further indicated by the fact that each division contains the same large number (24,000) of warriors.

A couple of instances of the author's interpretation in the list call for comment. Benaiah son of Jehoiada (vv. 5-6) figures prominently in 1 Chr 11 // 2 Sam 23 and in the story of the beginning of Solomon's reign in 1 Kgs 1–2. His father is uniquely called a priest here (the better reading is probably "the chief priest"), apparently an attempt to connect Benaiah with "Jehoiada, leader of the house of Aaron" in 12:27. Japhet (1993:475) also suggests that this is an interpretation of the expression "powerful man" that is used for Benaiah's father in 2 Sam 23:20, but employed in Chronicles for priests (cf. 1 Chr 12:29; 2 Chr 26:17). The fact that the author here voices no problem with the son of a priest being a military leader lends support to the idea that David's shedding of much blood did not disqualify him in Chronicles from building the temple on moral grounds but only ritually. In verse 7 the reference to Asahel as a division commander in David's army is anachronistic if he died before David became king of Israel (2 Sam 2). The addition of a reference to his son Zebediah not paralleled in 1 Chr 11 // 2 Sam 23 may be an attempt by the author to lessen the tension.

Verses 16-22 present a fairly rigidly structured listing of the tribal leaders. The typical pattern is: "for tribe name, personal name, son of personal name." Aside from the mentions of the Reubenites, Simeonites, and the children of Ephraim, the pattern varies only in three instances: the first entry (v. 16), where Eliezar is referred to as "chief officer"; the notation that the leader of Judah, Elihu, was David's brother (v. 18); and the designation of the second half tribe of Manasseh "in Gilead," that is, the Transjordan (v. 21). "Elihu" may be a mistake for or variant of "Eliab" (1 Chr 2:13; 1 Sam 16:6; 17:13), and this is what the LXX reads. It has also been suggested that Eliab was an eighth brother of David, elsewhere unnamed, though this seems unlikely. Another possibility is that "brother" here means simply "kinsman" or "relative."

The order of tribes given here is unique; it is similar but not identical to those found in 1 Chr 2:1-2 and Num 1:5-15. Again, a chart best illustrates:

1 Chr 27:16-22	1 Chr 2:1-2	Num 1:5-15
Reuben	Reuben	Reuben
Simeon	Simeon	Simeon
Levi	Levi	
Aaron		
Judah	Judah	Judah
Issachar	Issachar	Issachar
Zebulun	Zebulun	Zebulun
Naphtali	Dan	Ephraim
Ephraim	Joseph	Manasseh
½ Manasseh west	Benjamin	Benjamin
½ Manasseh east	Naphtali	Dan
Benjamin	Gad	Asher
Dan	Asher	Gad
		Naphtali

The major differences in 1 Chr 27:16-22 in comparison to the other two lists are: the inclusion of Aaron as a tribe, the exchange of order between Dan and Naphtali, the designation of separate leaders for the two halves of Manasseh, and the absence of Gad and Asher. For three of these oddities there are ready explanations. The listing of Aaron as a tribe of its own is anomalous, since Aaron is elsewhere included as a descendant of Levi. But an obvious motive for it would be to enhance the status of the Aaronid priests. The dual leadership of Manasseh would have a pragmatic rationale given their geographic separation; they are apparently still considered a single tribe. Though accidental omission is possible, the names of Gad and Asher may have been left out in order to retain the total number of tribes at twelve. The transposition of Naphtali and Dan remains unexplained.

It seems clear that verses 23-24 are an addition, probably by the compiler of the chapter. They differ in genre and topic from the tribal list and appear to be tacked on to it. But, they connect the list of tribal leaders in the foregoing verses with David's census in chapter 21. They explain why David did not count those under twenty years of age, a comment perhaps drawn on Num 1:3 and designed to suggest that David's census was in accord with the command to Moses in Numbers. The historical and theological perspectives of verses 23-24 differ entirely from those of the story of David's census. They seem to offer a corrective to 1 Chr 21, attempting to justify David and to blame the catastrophe recounted in that chapter on Joab. There is widespread assent, therefore, that these two verses are not from the Chronicler's hand.

The list of stewards in verses 25-31 includes: officials over the treasuries—those of the king and those of civic administration at several levels (v. 25); officials over agriculture—vineyards and wine stores, olive and sycamore trees and oil stores (vv. 26-28); and officials over livestock—cattle, camels, donkeys, and sheep (vv. 29-31). The names, branches of service, and geographic locations all seem appropriate. The only hint of artificiality is the fact that the name of Obil, the Ishmaelite in charge of the camels, means "camel driver" (v. 30). On the other hand, it would be appropriate to have an Ishmaelite in such a post. This may well be, therefore, an authentic record of royal stewards. The question is, "From whose reign?" While David cannot be ruled out, the degree of administrative sophistication reflected here is greater than one would expect for his reign. Most of the sites mentioned are in the south, so we should most likely look to the kings of Judah. It is intriguing that 2 Chr 26:10 has a similar record of Uzziah's farming and ranching activities and that the name Uzziah is mentioned in 27:25 as the father of the treasurer, Jonathan. Still, the association of this text with King Uzziah remains speculative.

In contrast to verses 25-31, the list of David's advisors in verses 32-34 appears quite artificial. Most of the names in the latter are familiar from other contexts, and the roles of these individuals as advisors or counselors are not well defined. It has been suggested (Japhet 1993:480) that this passage is influenced by the Persian practice of designating seven close counselors for the emperor.

While the name Jonathan (v. 32) is certainly common, no uncle of David's by that name is otherwise known. However, 20:7 mentions a nephew of David's by this name. In addition, the Hebrew word for uncle *(dôd)* can also mean "beloved friend" or the like, so that the reference may be to a nonrelative. (It is also possible that the reference is to Saul's son Jonathan, but this would be a blatant anachronism.) The Jehiel mentioned in verse 32 is also otherwise unknown, though the name is common enough in Chronicles. As the son of Hachmoni he was apparently related to the hero, Jashobeam (11:11). It is also not clear what his duties "with the king's children" entailed. Was he a tutor, caretaker, or in some other capacity? Ahithophel and Hushai are familiar from 2 Sam 15–17. There is debate about the origin and meaning of the title "king's friend," which is borrowed here for Hushai from 2 Samuel; it may be comparable to our "best man." It is unusual to find Jehoiada referred to in verse 32 as Benaiah's son, since elsewhere Benaiah is the son of Jehoiada. This listing may reflect the practice of papponymy (naming a son after his grandfather), common in the author's day but not in David's (Cross 1975). It is also somewhat unusual to find Abiathar and Joab here as counselors. Abiathar was one of David's priests, though he is not so designated here, perhaps because he was not a Zadokite; Joab was David's army commander. Their presence in this list probably derives from the author's determination on the basis of his reading of Samuel that both men had a close enough personal relationship with David to serve him as advisors.

Theological Analysis

There is little of an overtly theological nature in this chapter. It continues the idealized depiction of Israel begun in previous chapters. The numbers and organization of the military divisions and the tribes suggest that Yahweh has caused Israel under David to prosper. And indeed, verse 23 recalls the divine promise to the patriarchs to make Israel more numerous than the stars. The chapter, therefore, shows that Yahweh is faithful to the promises he has made. One might also suggest on the basis of the list of royal stewards in verses 25-31 that the model king's concerns were not limited to the patently theological or political but that he was legitimately to be concerned with caring for creation—lands and animals—at least that part of it that was under his control.

TRANSFER OF THE KINGDOM AND CHARGE TO SOLOMON (1 CHRONICLES 28:1–29:30)

Chapter 28 resumes the setting, theme, and rhetorical genre of chapter 22, and many scholars believe that it resumes the work of the Chronicler following the lengthy interpolation in chapters 23–27. But it is just as possible that the Chronicler here signals his resumption of David's speeches without chapters 23–27 as a whole necessarily being an addition. (See above on the introduction to chapters 22–29.)

Literary Analysis

David here addresses the leaders (vv. 2-8) and then Solomon (vv. 9-10). He entrusts Solomon with the design for the temple (vv. 11-19) and then exhorts him to carry out his task of building the temple (vv. 20-21). Chapter 29 continues the setting of 28, as the reference to David addressing the "whole assembly" in 29:1 indicates. Like chapter 28, chapter 29 is also largely rhetorical. Chapter 29 falls into four parts: (1) an account of the freewill offerings (vv. 1-9), which consists of an address by David (vv. 1-5) followed by the generous response of the people (vv. 6-9); (2) David's prayer of blessing and thanks (vv. 10-20); (3) the enthronement of Solomon (vv. 21-25); and the concluding formula for David's reign (vv. 26-30).

The list of temple vessels in 28:14-18 is often regarded as secondary. Some recent scholars (Mosis 1973:105n; Throntveit 1987:97-107) also consider 29:1-19, or a significant portion of it, to be a later addition. The latter passage contains some unique features and is somewhat repetitive of chapter 22. On the other hand, its main thrust—to report David's request for provisions and the people's generous response—has a place in the Chronicler's overall presentation and theology. The issue is made all the more important by the occurrence in verse 7 of the word "darics," which is a crucial piece of evidence for the date of the book. Since darics were first minted in 515 B.C.E. the book of Chronicles could not be dated earlier (see the introduction). If verse 7 is part of a secondary addition, however, then it is basically irrelevant for dating the Chronicler's own work, which could be earlier than 515.

These final two chapters of 1 Chronicles might be considered a unit relating Solomon's enthronement comparable to that of David's anointing in chapters 11–12. In that sense, they are parallel to 1 Kgs 1–2. But the two texts are entirely different in their outlook on the transition from David to Solomon. Aside from the incorporation of some Deuteronomistic expressions, the only part of the Kings account that the Chronicler has borrowed is in his concluding formula for David in 29:27 (cf. 1 Kgs 2:11). Otherwise, the contrasts are striking. David, not Solomon, takes center stage in Chronicles. David is aged but still vigorous and in full command of his powers. There is no mention of Adonijah, Bathsheba, or Nathan, and no hint of controversy or rivalry for the throne. David's appointment of Solomon is joyfully accepted by all Israel. Nothing is done in secret. Solomon has no one killed; he is, in fact, completely passive, his role—that of the temple builder—is purely theological.

Exegetical Analysis

David Addresses the Elders and Solomon (1 Chr 28:1-21)

The titles in verse 1 seem to draw especially on the previous chapter, yet they do not include the Levites, who are so prominent in chapters 22–27 as a whole. This may indicate that the verse has been secondarily expanded in order to integrate the additions in those chapters.

David's speech in verses 2-10 is essentially identical in theme and structure to 22:6-13 (cf. Braun 1976:267). Some scholars take this as evidence that the present passage is secondary. But the similarity is not surprising since both concern the same topic, and both are dependent on the promise to David in 1 Chr 17 // 2 Sam 7, yet each is addressed to a different setting: 22:6-13 to Solomon alone and in private; 28:2-10 to the assembly of national leaders and to Solomon in front of the assembly. Each speech has the same three main points: (1) David wanted to build the temple but was forbidden from doing so; (2) Solomon has been chosen by God to succeed David and to build the temple; and (3) Solomon is admonished to be faithful and obedient to Yahweh and encouraged to proceed intrepidly with the building activity.

The description of David standing in verse 2 forms a vivid, and perhaps deliberate, contrast with his portrait in 1 Kgs 1, where he is feeble, apparently bedridden, and impotent. The call to listen, "Hear me," is the characteristic mark of a speech in Chronicles. David addresses the people as his extended family: "my brothers, my people." His reference to the temple as a "house of rest" for the ark plays on two senses of the word "rest." The temple is both a resting place where the ark is deposited and a place of rest or quietness from strife. The former sense of rest may draw on Ps 132, which also contains the image of the temple as God's footstool found in this verse (cf. also Ps 99:5; Lam 2:1). As is typical for the Chronicler, this speech is anthological. Part of the background to the latter sense may be the use of the ark in Samuel as a war palladium; now that David has brought peace through his military victories the ark need no longer function this way. Finally in this verse it is intriguing that David states that he began preparing to build the temple before Yahweh forbade him from doing so.

Verse 3 repeats the statement in 22:8, "You shall not build a temple for my name," and is ultimately based on 1 Chr 17:4 // 2 Sam 7:5. The explanation that follows ("because you are a man of wars and have shed blood") is also that of 22:8, though the phrasing differs slightly. The Chronicler thereby supplies a reason for the prohibition where none is clear in Nathan's original oracle. He does so, moreover, most creatively by placing his explanation in David's mouth as a quotation from Yahweh—a technique that adds authority to the explanation even though it is not to be found in Nathan's oracle.

In chapter 22, the Chronicler uses two devices—the pattern of transition of leadership and the play on Solomon's name—to signal Solomon as the chosen temple builder. In chapter 28 he adds a third—election. Verse 10 states explicitly that Solomon was chosen *(bāḥar)* for the express purpose of building the temple, and this use of *bāḥar* is unique to Chronicles in the Old Testament (Braun 1986:270-71). Verses 4-5 expand on this idea but from a slightly different viewpoint and in slightly different language, so that some have perceived them as an addition. They do seem to detour somewhat from the focus of verses 3 and 6 on who will build the temple. Their primary concern is not who will build the temple but who will sit on David's throne. Still, their function is rhetorical and reinforces the point about the choice of Solomon. They describe the choice of Solomon as the latest in, as it were, a set of concentric circles: God chose Judah out of the tribes of Israel, Jesse's household out of the families of Judah, David from among Jesse's sons, and Solomon from among David's sons. The use of the verb "took delight in" for election (v. 4) and of the expression "the throne of the kingdom of Yahweh over Israel" (v. 5) is unique in Chronicles and may support the idea that these verses are later. On the other hand, the ideology expressed here is certainly in agreement with that of the Chronicler elsewhere.

Verses 6-7 are heavily infused with Deuteronomistic language and imagery deriving ultimately from 1 Chr 17:12-13 // 2 Sam 7:12-14, although they are somewhat closer to 1 Chr 22:10. The main difference is that verse 7 makes the establishment of Solomon's kingdom—by which is apparently meant the continuation of the dynasty—conditional upon his obedience to the law (the "commandments and ordinances"). This reference to conditionality then sets up the admonitions to the leaders in verse 8 and to Solomon in verses 9-10. David's mandate to the leaders in verse 8 to keep and seek the commandments of Yahweh suggests that the other leaders as well as the people as a whole also play an important role in assuring the continuation of the dynasty. The possession of the land also depends on the people's obedience. This language is Deuteronomistic in origin, but the Chronicler uses it to forge a new theological point. The possession of the land here is not something that took place once for all under Joshua but depends on the faithfulness of each generation.

In verses 9-10 David turns to Solomon, encouraging him to "know" David's God. The verb refers not to intellectual assent or acquaintance but to the establishment and maintenance of relationship. Solomon is to serve God "with single mind and willing heart" (NRSV). The language is reminiscent of Deuteronomy's command to love God with all one's heart, soul, and mind (Deut 6:5). But the word translated "willing," though by no means unique to Chronicles, conveys the Chronicler's theological outlook. Service to God is to be whole-hearted but also something that one does willingly and even with pleasure rather than a matter of compulsion. The expression translated "every plan and thought" by the NRSV draws from Gen 6:5, "every inclination of the thoughts," again illustrating the anthological nature of the Chronicler's composition. There is a kind of play on ideas here. The verb "to seek" *(dāraš)* is one of the Chronicler's favorites and the importance of seeking God one of his principal theological emphases. Usually in Chronicles God is the one who is to be sought by humans, as in verse 9*b*. In verse 9*a*, however, it is God who does the seeking and who understands "every plan and thought" of humans. God promises to be available to the faithful who truly seek him. But he also "searches" *(dāraš)* the heart to know the real intentions of human beings, and he will spurn those who abandon him. The privileges of election also bring obligations.

David's transfer of the temple plan to Solomon in verses 11-21 draws on the account about the tabernacle in Exod 25:9, 40, as the use of the word "plan" in 28:11, 12*aα*, 19 makes clear. If anything, the temple design is more explicit. For, while Yahweh shows Moses the tabernacle plan in Exod 25, 1 Chr 28:19 describes the plan for the temple as coming to David in written form "from the hand of Yahweh." The Hebrew expression *miyyad* can simply mean "from" or "at the direction of." But given the reference in this verse to a written document, the Chronicler seems to be claiming that the temple plan is not just divinely inspired or even dictated, but is divinely written. This description is in pronounced contrast to that of 1 Kgs 5–7, where there is no mention of a divine plan, and the temple is apparently designed by Solomon and, at least in part, by the craftsman Hiram of Tyre.

Verses 14-18 contain a detailed list of temple furnishings that is grammatically and syntactically difficult and has no real parallel in the Bible; these verses are often considered an addition. The "vestibule" (v. 11) is sometimes used by the Chronicler for the entire temple (cf. 2 Chr 8:12; 15:8). "The room for the mercy seat" is unique to this verse. The "mercy seat" is mentioned elsewhere only in texts by the Priestly writer of the Pentateuch and only in reference to the tabernacle. It was the cover, bearing the cherubim, over the ark of the covenant in this Priestly conception. Its use here again draws on tabernacle imagery and stresses the temple as the new resting place for the ark. The "room" in which the ark resides may refer to the most holy place, if the "vestibule" is used for the entire temple, or to the temple building proper, distinguished from the vestibule, and enclosing the most holy place. It is apparently the mercy seat that is referred to in verse 18 as the chariot for the cherubim. The image of the ark with the cherubim as a chariot is unique to this verse in the Bible, though it was frequently mined in later Jewish interpretation. The image is motivated at least in part in this verse by the wordplay between the Hebrew words for cherubim and chariot.

David's encouragement of Solomon in verse 20 draws upon and is patterned after the transfer of leadership from Moses to Joshua in Josh 1. There one finds the exhortations "be strong and of good courage" and "do not fear" and the promise of the unflagging divine presence. There are also other intriguing similarities: both Moses and David are great leaders of Israel and founders of the national cult; neither one lives to see the completion of his mission; yet each does the bulk of the preparatory work for that mission.

The expression "all the work for the service" in verse 20 and then the reference to volunteers who are skilled in verse 21 are again reminiscent of the tabernacle pericope in Exodus (on the former see Exod 35:24). The expression "volunteer who has skill" is unique but particularly significant in this context. The words translated "volunteer" and "willing" and "wise, skilled" and "wisdom, skill" occur frequently in Exod 35–36 and elsewhere in the tabernacle context. The former brings to mind the willingness of attitude and even joy that the Chronicler depicts among those who worked on the temple. The latter implies not only the skillfulness of the craftsmen involved but also their wisdom in recognizing the importance of the endeavor. The verse describes three groups of participants in building the temple: priests and Levites, volunteer craftsmen, and officers and all the people. The building of the temple, in short, is an enterprise in which all Israel is involved and for which David has made full preparation of materials, personnel, and operation.

Solomon's Enthronement (1 Chr 29:1-30)

David's speech here begins by reiterating an important point of chapters 22 and 28—that Solomon was chosen by God. The expression "young and inexperienced" rehearses 22:5. David's contrast of Solomon's inexperience with the vastness of the work before him is his first argument appealing to the people for assistance. The task is all the more daunting, David points out, because the temple structure is not for humans but for God. The term used for the structure (NRSV: "temple") is late and occurs in reference to the temple only here and in verse 19. The uniqueness of the term is one of the features noted by those who regard verses 1-19 or most of it as an addition.

David's second point in his effort to persuade the people to contribute to the temple is one of personal example. He mentions first the great provisions he has made as king in preparation for construction (v. 2). Then, he describes the contributions from his personal treasury in verses 3-5. As before, the descriptions here (i.e., in vv. 1-9) are modeled on that of the tabernacle in Exodus. In addition to the similarity of their respective lists of materials used for the temple and tabernacle pericope, Braun (1986:279-80) points to their common use of the words "artisan" and "offer willingly" as indications of this modeling. There are minor problems here. The "precious stones" (v. 2) may seem out of place in a list of building materials, but they are used to adorn the temple according to 2 Chr 3:6. It is not clear whether they are envisioned as gems or simply costly building stones (cf. 1 Kgs 5:17 [Heb. 5:31]; 7:9-11). Also, the reference to the gold of Ophir (v. 4) appears anachronistic, since the Chronicler reports its being brought first by Solomon (2 Chr 8:18-19; 9:10). But these difficulties do not detract from the main thrust of David's speech: Despite all that he has given, much more is still needed for a temple that properly reflects

Yahweh's majesty; the cooperation of all the people is required. Hence, David ends his speech by asking, "Who then will offer willingly, consecrating themselves today to Yahweh?" (29:5 NRSV). Once again, the use of the verb "offer willingly" emphasizes the voluntary and even joyful nature of the giving as envisioned by the author. The expression translated "consecrating themselves" is literally "to fill one's hand" and is typically used for priests. Its use here may be intended to depict Israel in a certain sense as a kingdom of priests.

The report of the people's gifts in verses 6-9 stresses the joyfulness and wholeheartedness of the contribution (esp. v. 9). Their generosity is a testimony to this attitude. The amounts of materials are staggering. A talent weighed something over 75 pounds, so that 5,000 talents of gold would be more than 188 tons, 10,000 talents of silver more than 377 tons, etc. The "daric" (v. 7) was a Persian coin first minted under Darius at the end of the sixth century B.C.E. Its mention here in the context of David's reign is clearly anachronistic, but it does serve to establish the earliest possible date for the composition of Chronicles, assuming this passage is the Chronicler's work and not a later addition.

The next part of this chapter is David's prayer in verses 10-20. The similarity between this prayer and the psalm in 16:8-36 has been noted (see above on the latter text). Both consist of a doxology followed by sections dealing with the sojourning of the patriarchs (vv. 10-13), thanksgiving and presentation of the offering (vv. 14-17), and supplication (vv. 18-19). The two passages form a framework for David's preparations for building the temple. The prayer proper is then followed by the people's benediction of Yahweh in verse 20.

The doxology also resembles those found at the ends of the various collections of the book of Psalms (41:13; 72:18; 89:52 [Heb. 89:53]; 106:48), the main difference being that these refer to Yahweh in the third person. It is evident, therefore, that the author drew heavily on Psalms in composing this prayer. At the same time, the prayer also borrows expressions from a variety of other biblical texts, thus illustrating the anthological technique used by the Chronicler elsewhere. Examples of such borrowing are: "wealth and honor" (v. 13; cf. 1 Kgs 3:13); "who am I and what is my people" (v. 14; cf. 1 Chr 17:16 // 2 Sam 7:18); "our days are [like] a shadow" (v. 15 // Job 8:9); "search the heart" (v. 17; cf. Jer 11:20; 12:3; 20:12, in addition to Ps 7:9 [Heb. 7:10]; 17:3); "purposes and thoughts in the hearts" (v. 18 // Gen 6:5. It is perhaps for this reason that David's prayer approaches poetry with its frequent inclusion of parallel lines and expressions. Another literary technique, one that also reflects the Chronicler's theology, is the accumulation in verse 11 of attributes and epithets of Yahweh. The implication is that superfluity is impossible where the description and praise of Yahweh's grandeur is concerned. A further indication of this perspective is the fourfold repetition in verses 10-12 of the Hebrew word for "all, every." The point, which David develops in the second segment of the speech, is that everything belongs to God.

With the presentation of the people's offering to God in verses 14-17 David stresses their utter dependence on God as the owner of everything. The language of verse 15 is rich with meaning. The expressions "aliens and transients" and "our days are like a shadow," as already suggested, convey both the ownership of God and the brevity of human life. Finally, these expressions, along with the statement that "there is no hope" (cf. Ezra 10:2), may express the desperation of people living in the aftermath of the exile, who could identify with their ancestors' struggle to gain a permanent homeland. Despite, or perhaps because of, the recognition that all they have comes from God, the people have given willingly and joyfully (v. 17) and thereby provide a model for all generations.

The supplication that closes the prayer in verses 18-19 is reminiscent of the story of Solomon in 1 Kgs 3 in that David asks not for wealth or honor (cf. 29:13) but for spiritual perfection. This is expressed by the frequent references to the "heart." For the people, David asks that the "thoughts and purposes" of their hearts be directed toward God (v. 18); for Solomon, that he may keep the law with a "whole heart" (NRSV: "single mind") and may build the temple (v. 19). The verb "to establish," which occurs in both verses and hence both parts of the supplication, provides a wordplay that is difficult to capture in English; David asks that God *establish, prepare* the hearts of the people toward him as he has *established, prepared* for the building of the temple. The prayer closes with a benediction (v. 20) as they bless Yahweh and bow down before him in a gesture of submission; the scene may describe actual worship practice in the second temple.

The next section of the chapter, verses 21-25, describes Solomon's enthronement not so much as the occasion for the celebration but as an extension of it. The sacrifices and enthronement take place the same day as David's speech and the contribution. "On the next day" in verse 21 is out of place, coming as it does immediately before "on that day" in the Hebrew text. It was apparently intended to separate the sacrifices from the contribution. The enormous number of sacrifices signals the importance and grandeur of the celebration. The sacrifices are made "for all Israel," and the people act as a unit and "with great joy." It is noteworthy that the people, not a prophet, anoint Solomon as king and Zadok as priest (v. 22). The word "a second time" is another gloss by someone who perceived a tension here with 23:1. Alternatively, the Chronicler has in mind Solomon's anointing in 1 Kgs 1 as the "first time" (Williamson 1982:187). The anointing of Zadok mirrors that of Aaron and sons in Exod 40:15 and Lev 8 and betrays the idea, found in late literature (Jer 33:14-26; Zech 3; 6) of two anointed leaders, one royal, the other priestly. It may come from a later, priestly hand.

The description of Solomon's reign that follows in verses 23-25 is remarkable in several respects. First of all, he sits not on David's throne, as in the parallel in 1 Kgs 2:12, but on "the throne of Yahweh," an expression that fits well with the Chronicler's emphasis elsewhere on the kingdom belonging to

God (1 Chr 17:14; 2 Chr 9:8). Second, it is rather surprising to find the statement that Solomon "had success" at this point when his reign has just begun. The verb is a favorite of the Chronicler's and is used to express the prosperity of kings judged righteous (1 Chr 22:11; 13; 2 Chr 7:11; 14:7 [Heb. 14:6]; 31:21; 32:30). Its use here is clearly anticipatory. Third, the statement that "all Israel obeyed him" (v. 23) and then the elaboration that the leaders, warriors, and king's sons all pledged loyalty to him (v. 24) is in deliberate and perhaps polemical contrast to the story of Solomon's succession in 1 Kgs 1–2. In Chronicles, Solomon's reign is established without rival from the beginning. Then, verse 25 describes the greatness and majesty with which God invested Solomon. The statement that his reign was more majestic than all those that preceded him in Israel is likely formulaic, since only Saul and David would be in view. However, the words "over Israel" at the end of the verse are lacking in the LXX and may represent a gloss. If so, the comparison originally was universal and intended to make Solomon the greatest king of all time.

The concluding formula for David's reign in verses 26-30 serves with 10:14 to frame the story of that reign. As he has so often done in 1 Chronicles, the Chronicler here incorporates the "all Israel" motif (v. 26), which links the reigns of David and Solomon. Just as David reigned over all Israel (v. 26), so all Israel obeyed Solomon (v. 23) and God exalted Solomon in the sight of all Israel (v. 25). Verse 27 somewhat surprisingly mentions David's seven-year reign in Hebron. But even here there is no indication that his kingdom incorporated less than all Israel. The death and succession formula in verse 28 is adapted from the Deuteronomistic History. The statement that David died "in a good old age" evokes comparison especially with Abraham (Gen 25:8) and Isaac (Gen 35:29), but also with Gideon (Judg 8:32) and Job (42:17). His long life, along with "riches and honor," are the rewards that Solomon received without asking (1 Kgs 3:11, 13). Since the manner of a king's death in Chronicles is often a sign of the king's approval or lack thereof,

David's death portrays him as a truly great king in God's eyes.

The source citation in verses 29-30 is also an imitation of those commonly found in the Deuteronomistic History. The three prophets, Samuel, Nathan, and Gad, are mentioned here in order of their respective appearance in 1 Chronicles. Each is given a different title, though this is not reflected in the NRSV, which uses "seer" for both *rōʾeh* and *ḥōzeh,* the former, for Samuel, likely deriving from 1 Sam 9. The source citation is a device that functions to help validate the Chronicler's account; the claim that sources come from prophets invests them with a special authority. These sources, though, are almost certainly fictional, as indicated by the fact that Samuel is reported to have died (1 Sam 25:1) before the Chronicler's narrative of David even begins. However, this source citation could be the Chronicler's way of referring to three parts of 1–2 Samuel where each of the prophets named is active. The translation "kingdoms of the earth" (NRSV) is misleading. The final word in Hebrew is plural and should be translated "kingdoms of the countries" or the like. It is an expression unique to Chronicles and refers to those countries close to Israel.

Theological Analysis

These two chapters are rich with theological themes, several of which correspond to the Chronicler's ideas elsewhere. Some of these we have met before, but there are also some new ideas. In the first category is the presentation of David and Solomon as model kings. Both are chosen by God for a specific purpose. David is chosen to defeat Israel's enemies so that they can possess the land (28:8); Solomon is chosen to build the temple. There is more here about David because Solomon's work lies ahead. Although David wants to build the temple, he bows to the will of God. In fact, the summary of his reign suggests that he was guided constantly by Yahweh's prophets (29:29). In full command of his faculties, David turns the kingdom over to Solomon, and the people are united in support of Solomon.

David also does all he can to prepare for construction by gathering materials; he is the model of generosity for the people.

David encourages Solomon to be courageous and obedient in carrying out the work of building the temple, and he encourages the people to cooperate fully with willing hearts. The temple, after all, is not just a human project; its very design was delivered by God to David (28:19). The temple and the worship conducted there in the Chronicler's day would have been different in many respects from the original institution. But the Chronicler seeks to demonstrate continuity not only with the first temple but also with the traditions about Israel's earliest cultic institutions, the tabernacle and the ark. The Chronicler's stress on the temple may have been intended as a response to other views of his day that downplayed the significance of an earthly shrine (cf. Isa 66:1-2) and to popular lack of support for the temple as expressed by postexilic prophets such as Haggai and Malachi.

In his description of these events, then, the Chronicler provides a model for unanimous, enthusiastic, generous support of the temple on the part of the people and their leaders. The assembly in 28:1 represents all Israel. Just as all Israel was involved in David's anointing, so all Israel celebrates the transfer of the kingdom to Solomon. More important, all Israel participates in the preparations and for the building of the temple and in contributing to it. Moreover, they contribute willingly and even joyfully, gladly volunteering their gifts with generosity. There is a delightful paradox at work in this episode. The more the people give, the more they rely on God for blessing and prosperity, and the more God gives to them in return. The Israel that the Chronicler presents here is a true kingdom of priests—not in the sense that everyone is ordained to officiate, but in the sense that they all exhibit wholehearted willingness to lend service to the temple project according to their individual capabilities.

David's speeches and prayer remind his audience—and the

Chronicler's readers—of the true dimensions of the temple building project. It is much more than a building project; it is a spiritual exercise. Israel is God's chosen people, and with election comes the responsibility of obedience. There is, to be sure, a danger in disobedience, and awareness of its consequences can be a factor motivating Israel to obedience. Thus, David observes that Israel's continued occupation of its land is not guaranteed but depends on the faithfulness of each generation. But David further challenges his hearers to move beyond even simple obedience. Obedience is a starting place, but it is not enough for a God who understands the depths of human hearts and minds and who seeks allegiance at that level. The goal of human beings before God, as David articulates it, is the knowledge of God. Such knowledge is not merely intellectual assent or memorization but personal acquaintance fostered by prayer and contemplation of the divine law and will. It is, in other words, spiritual perfection.

Hence, with all of his focus on the temple and on David and Solomon, the Chronicler does not lose sight of the true center of Israel's theology, which is Israel's God, Yahweh. The temple is to be magnificent because Yahweh is magnificent and the source of all riches, majesty, power, glory, and victory (29:10-13). But no matter how splendorous the temple might be, it could never match Yahweh's greatness. David encourages the people to give generously to the project of building the temple —but not because God needs the gifts. God already owns everything, especially the kingdom. Besides, what Yahweh really wants is not property and wealth but the devotion of his people. The people need to give as a symbol of their devotion to God, as an example to others, and finally for the benefit that it brings them in fostering joy and community. In David's speeches and prayer, therefore, the Chronicler tries to communicate the proper understanding of the temple and even David in Israel's faith and religion. Neither the Davidic dynasty nor the temple can be the ultimate object of Israel's hope and trust. The

Chronicler knows that both will be destroyed. Israel's hope resides, in the final analysis, entirely in Yahweh, and that hope is well placed, for Yahweh faithfully keeps his promises to his people (29:14-16).

COMMENTARY: 2 CHRONICLES

THE REIGN OF SOLOMON (2 CHRONICLES 1–9)

The Chronicler's account of Solomon is really about the temple. Of the nine chapters devoted to Solomon, six concern the temple directly—preparations for its construction (ch. 2 [Heb. 1:18–2:17]), the construction proper (3:1–5:1), and the dedication of the temple (5:2–7:22), including the installation of the ark (5:2-14). These chapters are framed by descriptions of Solomon's wealth, wisdom, and international fame (1:1-17; 8:1–9:31). These traits are not mentioned only for the purpose of glorifying Solomon; they are crucial for Solomon's completion of the project of building the temple. His wealth provides the materials for the temple's construction; his wisdom provides the motivation for him to undertake the project of construction; and his fame provides the skilled workmanship for the design and execution of the project.

Solomon's reign as a whole is the continuation and fulfillment of David's preparatory efforts recounted in 1 Chronicles 17–29, especially chapters 22–29. Solomon does not in any way take a backseat to David in Chronicles. If anything, he is David's superior, since he is the actual builder of the temple. But their reigns are best considered equal parts of what the Chronicler considers Israel's ideal or "golden" age. Each serves a specific purpose. David's military prowess creates the condition of peace and makes plans for building the temple, and Solomon, whose name resembles the Hebrew word for peace (*shalom*), carries the project to completion.

GOD'S APPEARANCE TO SOLOMON IN GIBEON
(2 CHRONICLES 1:1-17)

The opening unit of 2 Chronicles both provides continuity with the material in 1 Chronicles and serves as the first half of a framing device around the account of the building of the temple. As is typical of his writing style, the Chronicler borrows from the Deuteronomistic History (here from 1 Kgs 3:4-15) but also makes significant changes, thus producing a new work of history and theology.

Literary Analysis

Second Chronicles 1:1 is a sophisticated structural device. The mention of David in verse 1 already provides some continuity with the preceding material in 1 Chronicles. The second half of the verse is unique to Chronicles. The affirmation that Yahweh was with Solomon fulfills David's wish for his son in 1 Chr 28:20, while the statement that Yahweh made Solomon exceedingly great is very similar to the opening of 1 Chr 29:25. The Chronicler used this repetition to frame the final regnal formulae for David in 1 Chr 29:26-30. Thus, 2 Chr 1:1 marks both the decisive transition from David to Solomon as well as continuity between the accounts of their reigns. At the same time, the reference to Solomon's kingdom, along with the statement in 1:13 that he became king over Israel, serves as a frame for the account of the divine appearance in Gibeon. As mentioned, that account is adapted, with some significant changes, from 1 Kgs 3:4-15. Verses 2-5 of 1 Chr 1, in particular, are the Chronicler's composition and obviously reflect his interests.

Exegetical Analysis

Second Chronicles begins with an act of worship. As soon as Solomon "established himself" he led the people to Gibeon. In 1 Kgs 3:4, Solomon's pilgrimage to Gibeon is private and serves merely as a prelude to the story of his dream there. Chronicles, in contrast, has the leaders and representatives of all Israel accompany Solomon and join him in worship and sacrifice there. The religious nature of this, Solomon's first act as king, and the involvement of the entire nation furnish a parallel with David's conquest of Jerusalem and transfer of the ark in 1 Chr 11–16. The Chronicler justifies Solomon's journey to Gibeon (vv. 3-5) by explaining that the tabernacle or tent of meeting and bronze altar were there. This explanation presupposes the existence of two tents—the one set up by David in Jerusalem to house the ark and the tabernacle (cf. v. 13). It also seems to presuppose the centralization of Israel's cult. In Chronicles, then, the construction of the temple did not mark the shift to religious centralization, as in the Deuteronomistic History, but the change from a temporary shrine to a permanent one. The verb "sought" in verse 5 (NRSV: "inquired") expresses a key concept for the Chronicler. The suffix here could refer either to Yahweh ("him") or to the ark ("it"). But in either case it is fair to say that Solomon is depicted as seeking Yahweh from the beginning, as the ideal king should.

For the remainder of the chapter, the Chronicler abridges 1 Kgs 3:4b-15. There are some striking changes, but it is not always certain whether they are motivated by theological concerns or are simply the result of abridgment. For instance, Chronicles does not mention a dream as the means by which Solomon received the revelation from God (1 Kgs 3:5, 15; cf. 2 Chr 7:12 // 1 Kgs 9:2). Some scholars find here a polemic against dream revelation motivated by Num 12:6-8, which describes dreams as a lower form of revelation than direct speech, the assumption being that the Chronicler wanted to portray the revelation to Solomon as the highest type. Others are dubious about this explanation. Another example is the omission of 1 Kgs 3:7b from 2 Chr 1:8. Was this done simply to abridge or did the Chronicler omit Solomon's reference to himself as a small child because he wished to present Solomon as a mature, capable ruler? Yet a third example is the omission of 1 Kgs 3:14. Did the Chronicler leave out this verse (cf. 2 Chr 1:12) because it suggested the possibility that Solomon might sin? If so, why did he have David make Solomon's success conditional on his keeping the law (1 Chr 22:13) and encourage him to do just that (1 Chr 28:9; 29:19).

The most significant change in this passage in relation to Kings is a subtle one that shows the effectiveness and sophistication of the Chronicler's editorial or authorial skill. In 2 Chr 1:9, Solomon asks that the promise to David be fulfilled. This can only allude to the promise in 1 Chr 17, an understanding confirmed by the language of verses 8-9 (such as the word translated "steadfast love"), which borrows from that chapter. But, as Solomon goes on to say (v. 9), Yahweh has already made him king, so the promise cannot be that of his succession of David. It must refer, rather, to the statement that David's son and successor would build the temple (1 Chr 17:12). Unlike Kings, where Solomon prays for wisdom to judge the people, in Chronicles his prayer for wisdom is so that he will be able to lead ("go out and come in," v. 10) the people to build the temple. Solomon's fear in 1 Kgs 3:8-9 that the people are so numerous that he will not be able to govern them without divine wisdom, in 2 Chr 1:9-19 becomes an opportunity for leadership to accomplish the task of building the temple. The reference to the people being as numerous as the dust of the earth (v. 9), which is not in the Kings version, obviously alludes to the patriarchal promise (Gen 13:16; 28:14) and shows that Yahweh does fulfill his promises, so that Solomon and the reader can expect that the temple will be built. It is for this reason that Chronicles also omits the story of Solomon's judgment between the two harlots in 1 Kgs 3:16-28. The purpose and demonstration of Solomon's wisdom in Chronicles is not clever legal judgments but the building of the temple. That is also the purpose for Solomon's wealth in Chronicles. Solomon is incomparable in wisdom, wealth, and honor, as 2 Chr 1:11-13 explains. But the structure of 2 Chr 1–9 makes clear that

Solomon's incomparability in these areas serves the temple. The accounts of Solomon's wisdom and wealth encase that of the temple construction; Solomon's wealth and wisdom are both the reward for his obedience and righteous request and the means by which he is able to fulfill the task for which he has been chosen and which he here requests.

In 1:14-17, the Chronicler borrows a passage from the end of the account of Solomon's reign in Kings (1 Kgs 10:26-29). The identities of the locations mentioned in these verses and the precise role claimed for Solomon in these commercial ventures have elicited a great deal of discussion without certain resolution (cf. Dillard 1987:13-14). Such details are not the Chronicler's primary concern. In his work, this passage serves the dual purpose of explaining the source of at least part of Solomon's wealth and thereby illustrating the fulfillment of the divine promise of wealth in verse 12 (also 1 Chr 29:25). A significant portion of the passage is repeated in 2 Chr 9:25-28, in the same place where it occurs in Kings. Some scholars maintain that the repetition indicates that one of the occurrences of the passage is secondary. But the repetition may also be viewed as a structuring device—a bracket or framework for the account of Solomon, whose wealth and international prestige—both gifts from God—allowed him to build the temple.

Theological Analysis

The first chapter of 2 Chronicles makes several powerful statements in line with the Chronicler's overall theology, but it does so subtly. David and Solomon are presented as two sides of the same coin—two dimensions of Israel's "golden age." Solomon's portrait is idealized, as was David's. Like David before him, Solomon's first thought as king is for Israel's worship, specifically to seek God—a key idea in Chronicles—at the tabernacle in Gibeon. Also like David, he convenes all Israel. He thus understands his role as a religious leader of the entire people of Yahweh.

At Gibeon, Solomon asks God for wisdom. This request for

wisdom grows out of Solomon's sense of obedience to the task with which he has been charged. That is, he wants wisdom in order to lead the people in building the temple. God gives Solomon the wisdom he requests and bestows upon him wealth and honor as well. These gifts are a reward to Solomon for his obedience, but they also serve the purpose of equipping Solomon to fulfill his destiny to build the temple.

SOLOMON PREPARES TO BUILD THE TEMPLE (2 CHRONICLES 2:1-18 [HEBREW 1:18–2:17])

This chapter is loosely based on 1 Kgs 5, though again with significant changes. The centerpiece of the chapter is the correspondence between Solomon and Huram, king of Tyre (vv. 3-15), which is framed by the account of the labor force gathered by Solomon (vv. 2 and 17-18). The declaration of Solomon's decision to build a temple in 2:1 marks the beginning of a distinctive section of 2 Chronicles and is part of skeletal frame around which the entire account of the temple is formed.

Literary Analysis

Together with 3:1; 5:1; 7:11; and 8:16, the notice in 2:1 forms a framework for the narrative detailing the construction, dedication, and initiation of the temple. Then 2:1 announces Solomon's intent and 3:1 the start of construction. Then, 5:1; 7:11; and 8:16 announce the completion of different stages: the temple construction, its dedication, and all of Solomon's building projects, respectively. The Chronicler thus places the building of the temple as close as possible to Solomon's enthronement, once more implying that the temple is Solomon's primary task as king and in a real sense the reason for his reign.

Verse 2 details the labor force Solomon used to build the temple. This information is repeated in verse 18. The repetition is probably an intentional structuring device rather than the result of clumsy glossing. The letters between Solomon and Huram (vv. 3-16) are well structured and evince an oratorical style that is obscured in most English translations. Solomon's introductory remarks (2:3-6) lead up to his request initiated by the expression "and now" in Hebrew. Huram's reply also contains an introduction followed by responses to Solomon's requests marked by "and now" (2:13, 15).

Exegetical Analysis

Verse 1*b* has been adapted from 1 Kgs 5:5 [Heb. 5:19]. The Chronicler adopts the Deuteronomistic "name" theology, which describes the temple as the dwelling place of Yahweh's name. The language of the "name" theology probably owes its origin to the practice by which a king in the ancient Near East would lay claim to a site by placing his name there. But it comes to serve a theological purpose in the Bible—making the point that the temple is Yahweh's dwelling in some sense while avoiding the idea that he is physically present or in any way confined to the temple space. Solomon's palace ("house") receives mention in verse 1*b* (cf. 2:12; 7:11), but no detail about its construction is forthcoming; the focus is on the temple. The source of Solomon's workforce (v. 2) is not described, but this will become an issue in verses 17-18.

Unlike the account in Kings, in Chronicles Solomon takes the initiative in contacting Huram (Hiram in Kings) to obtain supplies and expertise for building the temple. The opening of the letter to Huram (v. 3) explicitly parallels Solomon with David. The introductory or explanatory portion of the letter (vv. 4-6) contains a description of the cult (v. 4) drawn on the Priestly regulations for worship in the tabernacle (Exod 30:1-10; Lev 24:1-9). The fact that it is ill-suited to a message to a foreign king is unimportant; the Chronicler's point is the continuity between tabernacle and temple. Solomon's message also contains theology. The magnificence of the temple is a sign of genuine piety, as its grandeur is representative of the greatness of Israel's God (v. 5). But the temple is not to be considered

Yahweh's actual dwelling place; it is merely the place where the transcendent God may be encountered in sacrificial worship (v. 6, based on 1 Kgs 8:27).

Solomon's first request or demand to Huram is for a skilled, master craftsman (lit., "wise man," v. 7). Both here and in verses 13-14, where the craftsman sent by Huram is named, his capabilities are expanded far beyond those of the bronze worker described in 1 Kgs 7:13-14. The Chronicler's craftsman is analogous to and modeled after Bezalel and Oholiab, the two master craftsmen who worked on the tabernacle (Exod 35:30-33). The vocabulary in the letter (such as the words for "purple," which is Aramaic, and for "crimson," which is Persian) indicates the relative lateness of this passage and makes it clear that the letter was composed by the Chronicler, not by Solomon.

The second request is for building materials (vv. 8-9). It is not known exactly what kind of wood "algum" was, but this same name is found also in extrabiblical sources. The Chronicles version of Solomon's letter omits the statement in Kings (1 Kgs 5:6 [Heb. 5:20]) to the effect that the Israelites do not know how to cut timber like the Sidonians. Chronicles does not admit that Solomon is in any way at the mercy of Huram. "Cor" and "bath" were both measures of capacity, equalling about 6.5 bushels and 6 gallons, respectively.

The language and style of Huram's letter is similar to those ascribed to Persian monarchs elsewhere in Chronicles and Ezra (2 Chr 36:23 // Ezra 1:2; Ezra 6:9-10; 7:12, 21, 23). The opening in verse 11 is adapted from the words of the Queen of Sheba in 2 Chr 9:8 // 1 Kgs 10:9 as a speech of a foreign monarch marveling at Solomon's majesty. The letter is in perfect Hebrew, and Huram is quite familiar with Israelite theology; indeed, his confession in verse 12 of Yahweh as maker of heaven and earth makes him appear as something of a convert to Israelite religion. His further words in that verse well express the Chronicler's viewpoint about the purpose of Solomon's wisdom that appears in chapter 1. Solomon has been "endowed with discretion and understanding" in order to build the temple. The language here is identical to 1 Chr 22:12, where David wishes that Yahweh will grant Solomon "discretion and understanding." Solomon's wisdom is manifested in the temple.

Huram then moves to the granting of Solomon's requests or demands. The craftsman he sends is Huram-abi, the offspring of a Tyrian father and Israelite mother. The name is the same as that of the king, and the Chronicler may have added the -abi element to distinguish them. However, another possible source of that element is the name Oholiab (Exod 31:5), the tabernacle artisan. This possibility is buttressed by the fact that Huram-abi's mother is from Dan in Chronicles, in parallel to Oholiab, rather than Naphtali as in Kings. Throughout this correspondence, there are hints that the Chronicler considers King Huram to be Solomon's inferior: Solomon's requests can be read as orders; Solomon takes the initiative and sets the terms for their arrangement; Huram grants both of Solomon's requests. Huram's reference to both David and Solomon as "my lord" (vv. 14-15) removes any remaining doubt about his subordination. The specification of the transportation process from Lebanon through Joppa to Jerusalem (v. 16) is the Chronicler's expansion based on Ezra 3:7.

The final two verses of the chapter serve, together with verse 2, to bracket the account of Solomon's and Huram's correspondence. In contrast to 1 Kgs 7:13, where Solomon raises the labor force out of Israel, the Chronicler insists (v. 17) that only non-Israelites were compelled to serve. Solomon's census is limited to foreigners, a fact that distinguishes it from David's census of Israel in 1 Chr 21:1, which was judged to be sinful. The expression "aliens who were residing in the land" recalls the policy set by David in 1 Chr 22:2. As throughout his reign, Solomon complements and completes what David started.

Theological Analysis

Solomon's decision to build the temple (2:1) is motivated by and a sign of the wisdom bestowed upon him by God in chapter 1. Its magnificence is to serve as a witness to non-Israelites, so that its construction calls for the very best (2:5). The Tyrian king, Huram, acknowledges Yahweh as maker of heaven and earth (2:12), thus illustrating the effect that the temple will have. The temple itself is not sacrosanct. Ultimately, it is only a building, a structure erected by human hands. Its splendor is meaningful only because it reflects the majesty of the God it honors.

Thus, the temple ultimately only represents Yahweh, whose "name" resides there but whose actual presence transcends any building of human manufacture no matter how opulent. The "name" theology is an effort to resolve the tension between the theological ideas of God's simultaneous immanence and transcendence. How can God, whom even heaven cannot contain, be in some sense present in an earthly location? The attempt by the Chronicler and other biblical writers to grapple with this question led to a radically new concept of God as a spiritual being who could not be represented by corporeal images. It is worth noting that the idea of God as spirit was at least latent in the Old Testament and is not unique to the New Testament (cf. John 4:24). To be sure, the Bible speaks of God as having physical characteristics. But it is important to bear in mind that these are but metaphors, attempts to describe in human terms and images what is ultimately beyond human comprehension. Since most of the images for God in the Bible are male (king, father), it is perhaps especially important for modern readers to be aware of their metaphorical nature.

BUILDING THE TEMPLE (2 CHRONICLES 3:1–5:1)

This unit describes the edifice of the temple, especially the inner sanctuary or most holy place (ch. 3) and the furnishings and utensils used in the temple (4:1–5:1). The account emphasizes the lavishness of the temple rather than details about its architecture, size, and the like.

Literary Analysis

The dimensions of this unit are indicated by a framework formed by 3:1 and 5:1. The constituent details of its construction may be outlined as follows:

3:1-17
- introduction (3:1-2)
- temple (3:3-7)
- most holy place, including cherubim and veil (3:8-14)
- pillars in front of the temple (3:15-17)

4:1–5:1:
- bronze and gold items (4:1-10)
  - altar (1)
  - sea (2-5)
  - lavers (6)
  - lampstands (7)
  - tables and basins (8)
  - courts (9-10)
- Huram's work (4:11-18)
- items of gold (4:19-22)
- conclusion (5:1)

Up to 4:11, the description is adapted, with significant abridgment, from 1 Kgs 6:1–7:39. Second Chronicles 4:12–5:1 follows 1 Kgs 7:40-51 rather more closely. It may seem strange at first that the Chronicler with his strong interest in the temple would abbreviate the description of it in Kings. The explanation for this seems to be that the Chronicler is less concerned with matters of architecture and furnishing than he is with showing the lavish decor of the temple. Hence, he summarizes with regard to the former, emphasizing the rich ornamentation and frequent use of gold.

The features of the temple that the Chronicler highlights are frequently those that were original to the tabernacle, including the cherubim (3:10-13; Exod 25:10-21, on top of the ark), curtain (3:14; Exod 26:31), altar (4:1; Exod 30:1-10), lavers (4:6; 30:18-21), lampstands (4:7; Exod 25:31-37), and tables (4:8; Exod 25:23-29). The main difference is that these items are all smaller and fewer in Exodus; they have been enlarged by the Chronicler in accordance with his view that the temple is in continuity with the tabernacle but surpasses it in grandeur and importance. In short, the Chronicler had three sources for his description of the temple: the account in Kings, the description of the tabernacle in Exodus, and the temple of his own day. He structured the account by a series of occurrences of the verb "and he made" with both Solomon and Huram as subjects (3:8, 10, 14, 15, 16 [twice]; 4:1, 2, 6, 7, 8, 9, 11, 19). The structure of this passage is comparable to the structure in Exod 36–40. Correspondence with the tabernacle description in Exodus is also the key to what the Chronicler has included and omitted from Kings. By harmonizing the temple description with that of the tabernacle, the Chronicler creates a continuity between the two institutions and their respective ages (Moses and David–Solomon) that is not present in the Deuteronomistic History.

Exegetical Analysis

The first two verses of this chapter are the Chronicler's composition. In contrast to 1 Kgs 6:1, which contextualizes the temple building temporally "in the four hundred eightieth year after the Israelites came out of the land of Egypt," Chronicles contextualizes it spatially and signals the importance of the temple by the fourfold identification of the site of its construction. The phrase, "in Jerusalem on Mount Moriah" connects the temple mount with the place where Abraham showed his willingness to sacrifice Isaac (Gen 22). The three designations in the rest of the verse ("where Yahweh had appeared to David his father," "at the place David had designated," and "on the threshing floor of Ornan the Jebusite") recall the Chronicler's distinctive ending to the story in 1 Chr 21 (21:26–22:1), in which David, recognizing that Yahweh had "answered" him with fire from heaven designated the site of Ornan's threshing floor as the location of the temple and its altar. The Chronicler (v. 2) dates the beginning of the temple construction not from the date of the exodus, as in 1 Kgs 6:1, but from the start of Solomon's reign (cf. 1 Kgs 6:37), and this is perceived by some scholars as part of a systematic de-emphasis of the exodus as the beginning point of Israel.

Neither the temple's size nor its form is remarkable. The three-part structure described here and in 1 Kgs 6 was typical of temple architecture in ancient Syria and Canaan. There were different standards for the cubit at different times, as verse 3 indicates, but figuring eighteen inches per cubit yields a good approximation. The temple was about 90 feet long and 30 feet wide. The vestibule in front matched its width (20 cubits = about 30 feet) and perhaps its height (the figure of 120 cubits in 3:4 is certainly an error); 1 Kgs 6:3 gives its depth as 10 cubits (= about 15 feet). The Chronicler's emphasis on the temple's ornamentation is apparent from the repeated mentions of gold in verses 4-9. The meaning of "gold from Parvaim" (v. 6) is unknown. Even the nails were made of gold or perhaps gilded with gold (v. 9), since gold would have been too pliable to function as fasteners.

The cherubim (vv. 10-13) are apparently different from those on the lid of the ark. Cherubim were composite creatures, similar to the great Sphinx in Egypt, which were typically represented in ancient Near Eastern iconography as the guardians of entrances to temples and palaces. The veil or curtain (v. 14) likely owes its presence in Chronicles description to Exod 26:31-33, where a similar feature is described for the tabernacle; Kings does not mention a curtain.

The function of the two pillars (vv. 15-17) is unknown, though it does not appear to have been structural. The fact that they are named suggests that they may have had a liturgical or theological purpose that has been lost to us. "Jachin" and "Boaz" might mean "he establishes" and "in strength," respectively. But the precise significance of these terms in the context of the temple structure is unclear. The height of the pillars in Chronicles (35 cubits) varies noticeably from the figure in Kings and is generally explained as sum of the dimensions given in the latter (2 Kgs 7:15-16)—18 cubits high + 12 cubits around + 5 cubits for the height of the capital. The statement that Solomon made the chains for the pillars in the inner sanctuary (v. 16) is problematic. The Hebrew word for "inner sanctuary" *(děbîr)* is similar to one meaning "necklace" *(rābîd)*—the Hebrew letters for *d* and *r* being nearly indistinguishable in some scripts—so that the text might be read, "he made the chains [another word for a different kind of chain] like a necklace." As noted, the way Chronicles now reads, it is Solomon who makes the pillars, rather than Hiram (= Huram-abi) as in 1 Kgs 7:15. The difference is the result of the Chronicler having shifted the introduction of Huram-abi from its place in Kings immediately before the present passage (2 Kgs 7:13-14) to King Huram's letter in 2 Chr 2:13-14. The change causes only a minor inconsistency that is not noticeable until 2 Chr 4:11, where Huram is said to have finished all the work.

The first five verses of 2 Chr 4 are quite similar to 1 Kgs 7:23-26. However, the mention of the bronze altar in 4:1 is completely lacking in Kings. The reason is uncertain. It may have been lost from Kings by accident; since verses 1 and 2 both begin with the same Hebrew word ("and he made") a scribe's eye could have skipped over verse 1 to the start of verse 2. On the other hand, the Chronicler may have added 4:1 in order to stress the temple's role as a place of sacrificial worship. The dimensions of the altar (20 x 20 x 10 cubits = 30 x 30 x 15 feet) are incredibly large and indicate the enormous significance the Chronicler attached to it, assuming they do not actually refer to a platform upon which the altar stood.

The rest of this passage describes the "molten sea." It was a very large basin that was cast of bronze (hence "molten"). Its size and height indicate that its purpose was ritual rather than functional, although exaggeration of dimensions is frequent in Chronicles' description of the temple. Still, the claim that the sea was used for washing (v. 6) seems to reflect the influence of Exod 30:18 and the description there of the basin used for washing in the tabernacle. Extrapolating from ancient Canaanite mythology, the word "sea" suggests that it represented the primeval sea, whom Yahweh defeated at creation. Verse 3 seems confused in Chronicles, and the Kings version (1 Kgs 7:24) is clearer. The latter describes images of gourds under the brim of the sea all around. Chronicles' mention of oxen under the sea has likely been influenced by the subsequent depiction of the oxen upon which the sea rested. The description of the lavers (v. 6) draws on 1 Kgs 7:38-39.

The descriptions of the lampstands, tables, and courts (vv. 7-9) are unparalleled in Kings. The first two have been added based on Exod 25:23-40; 37:10-24, and that of the courts is based on the temple of the Chronicler's day. The description also seems to reflect exaggeration, since there was only one lampstand in the tabernacle, and only one table is mentioned in Kings (1 Kgs 7:48). With verse 10, Chronicles rejoins the account in Kings, such that 4:10–5:1 closely parallel 1 Kgs 7:39b-51 with only minor differences. For instance, 1 Chr 4:16 has "forks," while 1 Kgs 7:45 reads "basins." But the two words are similar sounding in Hebrew, so that the replacement of one for the other was likely accidental.

In verse 18, Chronicles effectively reverses the point of 1 Kgs 7:47, although the difference is obscured in the NRSV. Kings indicates that Solomon did not determine the weight of the bronze used for the vessels he made because they were so many. Chronicles says that Solomon made so many vessels because (*kî*, not "so that") he had so much bronze available to him ("beyond reckoning," NRSV: "was not determined"). The list of golden items in

4:19–5:1 once more indicates the magnificence of the temple, which is a prime interest of the Chronicler's in this section, as we have seen. The reference to the doors to the most holy place (v. 22) is problematic in view of 3:14, which describes the divider between the two parts of the temple as a veil or curtain rather than doors. The tension is accounted for by the recognition that 3:14 has been influenced by the tabernacle description in Exodus.

We have seen the structural role played by 5:1 in framing the Chronicler's description of the temple. The first word of the verse is the verb "was finished," which puns on Solomon's name (both from the root *šlm)*. The verse is transitional; it signals the completion of the temple construction and leads into its dedication (summarized in 7:11) and additional projects (summarized in 8:16).

Theological Analysis

The mention of David and Solomon together in 5:1 highlights the Chronicler's understanding of them as equal partners in the enterprise of building the temple. David provided the blueprint for the temple and dedicated the items for its service. Solomon follows up on his father's preparations just as David encouraged him to do. Solomon shows himself to be faithful and obedient by carrying out his charge to build the temple. His understanding of his role and his efficiency in carrying it to completion further demonstrate the wisdom with which he has been endowed.

The Chronicler emphasizes the luxurious ornamentation of the temple as a way of showing its theological and cultic significance for Israel. His exaggeration of the size of some of the temple furnishings serves the same purpose. The magnificence of the temple is also a tangible demonstration of God's blessing of Israel under its righteous kings. Above all, however, it symbolizes the majesty of Israel's God. In view of the Chronicler's stress on the splendor of the temple, it is somewhat striking that he devotes more attention to its furnishings and decoration than to the actual building. This is due, above all, to his depiction of the temple in images drawn from the tabernacle in order to demonstrate the continuity between the two centers of Israel's worship in the two eras they represent.

THE DEDICATION OF THE TEMPLE (2 CHRONICLES 5:2–7:22)

The temple having been built, the narrative now turns to its dedication. The present narrative relates five relatively distinct episodes:

> the procession of the ark to the temple (5:2–6:2)
> Solomon's convening of the assembly and speech to it (6:3-11)
> Solomon's prayer (6:12-42)
> sacrifices by Solomon and the people (7:1-11)
> divine revelation to Solomon (7:12-22).

Literary Analysis

The episodes just listed do not represent arbitrary divisions but reflect the presence of literary signals within the text. This unit thus continues to evince the same sophistication of organization as that found in earlier units. We have seen that 5:1 is part of a series of texts upon which chapters 2–8 are structured and that it bridges the account of temple construction with that of its dedication. As another text in this series, 7:11 could be regarded as the end of the present unit on the dedication of the temple. But Yahweh's appearance to Solomon in 7:12-22 comes in response to the temple construction and dedication and in a sense is part of them. In addition, 8:1 could be considered one of the structuring texts, as it also mentions Solomon's building of the temple and transitions to his other building projects.

Within the present unit there are other structuring devices.

New units may be signaled by 5:2; 6:3; and 6:12, each of which mentions some action of Solomon vis-à-vis Israel's assembly. In 5:2, he convenes the assembly; in 6:3 he turns and blesses the people; in 6:12 he stands in their presence before the altar in the posture of prayer. Although it does not mention the assembly, 7:1 is also the beginning of a new unit in which Solomon finishes his prayer and divine fire consecrates the altar. Then, 7:11 is summative, and 7:12 begins the account of Yahweh's appearance to Solomon.

Exegetical Analysis

The first subunit in 5:2–6:2 relating Solomon's transfer of the ark to the temple is the sequel to David's transfer of it to Jerusalem in 1 Chr 11–16. Just as David did, so Solomon assembles all Israel for the occasion, and Solomon's innumerable sacrifices (5:6) recall those of David as the ark advanced. Verses 2-11a are closely parallel to 1 Kgs 8:1-10a. In verse 3 (// 1 Kgs 8:2), the Chronicler omits the Canaanite name of the seventh month, Ethanim (cf. 3:2). In verse 4 (// 1 Kgs 8:3), he substitutes "Levites" for priests as the bearers of the ark in accordance with his understanding of the Levites' role (1 Chr 15:2; cf. Deut 10:8). Chronicles has "Levitical priests," in other words, "the priests, the Levites" without the conjunction (v. 5), as opposed to "the priests and the Levites" as in 1 Kgs 8:4 (the NRSV ignores the difference and levels through the reading of Kings). The expression and its apparent sense that the priests carried these items are unusual in Chronicles, which clearly distinguishes the roles of each. Thus, it is the priests alone who may enter the most holy place to deposit the ark (5:7). "Levitical priests" (v. 5) may be an error (many Hebrew manuscripts do contain the conjunction here) or an effort at harmonizing verse 4 with its source (1 Kgs 8:3) in regard to the bearers of the ark. The same expression occurs in 23:18; 30:27. The reference to the tent of meeting (5:5) appears to be another instance of the Chronicler shaping the temple description in terms of the tabernacle. The fact that Kings shares this and other such telltale readings suggests that it may have been secondarily revised in this chapter to accord with Chronicles or Priestly concerns.

Solomon's wealth is once more used in the service of Yahweh (5:6). The Chronicler goes to pains to identify the exact location of the ark (v. 7), describing it in four ways. The verbatim fashion in which the Chronicler here depends on Kings is apparent in verses 8-10. In verse 8 (// 1 Kgs 8:7) the cherubim stand above the ark in the most holy place; there is no mention of cherubim on top of the ark itself as in Priestly descriptions. Also, the poles, now envisioned as a permanent part of the ark are there "to this day" (2 Chr 5:9 // 1 Kgs 8:8), which could not refer to the Chronicler's time, since Solomon's temple had been destroyed by then. Even in verse 10, the Chronicler rehearses the mention of the exodus, which he seems typically to downplay.

The Chronicler has added the description of the Levitical musicians (vv. 11-13). This description is once more reminiscent of the transfer of the ark to Jerusalem under David. All of 5:11-14 is one sentence in Hebrew and represents the climax of this account. As the priests recessed after having deposited the ark in the most holy place, the Levites began their song, and the cloud and glory *(kābôd)* of Yahweh descended on the building. The cloud and *kābôd* signal Yahweh's presence and acceptance of the temple (cf. Exod 13:17-22; Num 9:15-23; Ezek 10:3-4). Contrary to their descriptions by the Priestly writer in the Pentateuch, they seem here to be identified as one and the same phenomenon. Their descent together upon the temple recalls the inauguration of the tabernacle (Exod 40:34-35). The *kābôd* is mentioned again in 7:1-3 and thus serves to frame Solomon's speech and prayer in chapter 6. Solomon's announcement in 6:1-2 concludes the ceremony of the transfer and deposit of the ark. The thick darkness of 6:1 is mentioned also as being present at Sinai/Horeb (Exod 20:21; Deut 4:11; 5:22), reinforcing the idea that Solomon's temple is conceived of here as the inauguration of a new era for Israel.

The remainder of 2 Chr 6 closely parallels 1 Kgs 8:12-50*a*, with minor differences, except for 6:41-42, where the Chronicler draws on Ps 132:8-10. As noted, the chapter may be divided into two subunits consisting of Solomon's address to the people (vv. 3-11) and Solomon's prayer (vv. 12-42). The scene, including Solomon's rhetoric, is reminiscent of David's address and prayer in 1 Chr 28–29. Solomon announces to assembled Israel that in his construction of the temple God has fulfilled his promise to David (vv. 4, 10). While the Chronicler follows his Kings source closely, the speech takes on particular significance in Chronicles in view of its focus on the temple as essentially the purpose for Solomon's reign. Verses 5*b*-6*a* have no parallel in Kings and have been seen as the Chronicler's expansion. But the election of Jerusalem and David is a principal Deuteronomistic doctrine, and 1 Kgs 8:16 is at best elliptical as it now stands, so that the Chronicles reading is best viewed as the preservation of material lost from Kings by accidental omission (keyed by two the occurrences of "so that my name may be there"). Chronicles lacks the mention of the exodus from Egypt found in 1 Kgs 8:21. It may be that the Chronicler suppresses such references, as some scholars contend, but then it is unclear why he retained the one in verse 5. Perhaps his change here was motivated by his concern to avoid the implication that the covenant was only with the exodus generation and to show that it involves all Israel, including his contemporaries.

The rest of the chapter represents the second subunit, which consists of Solomon's prayer. Verse 13 has no parallel in 1 Kings. The fact that it shares the ending of verse 12, "in the presence of the whole assembly of Israel and [he] spread out his hands" makes it ripe for an accidental scribal omission, and Solomon's rise from his knees in 1 Kgs 8:54 seems to presume the posture he adopts here (2 Chr 7:1, in contrast, makes no mention of his having arisen from his knees). However, the presence of the late word for "outer court" in the verse leads most scholars to believe that it has been inserted into this context by the technique of narrative resumption. The themes of verses 14-17 are those shared by 1 Chr 17 // 2 Sam 7 and revolve around Yahweh's faithfulness to his promise to David. Verse 16 emphasizes the need for obedience to the law on the part of David's heirs, as does 1 Kgs 8:25. Verses 18-25 again convey the Deuteronomistic name theology, which militates against the ideas that Yahweh dwells on earth and that anything on earth can contain him.

The series of disasters envisioned in verses 22-39 were all common experiences of people living in the ancient Near East. They are here portrayed as acts of God—including defeat and captivity (vv. 34-39). The operating theology has strong Deuteronomistic roots: sin provokes Yahweh and leads to disaster, but repentance evokes God's mercy and will bring restoration. Even foreigners who turn to Yahweh will be heard, and indeed Yahweh's mercy and great deeds, as well as the temple itself, function as witnesses of Israel's God (vv. 32-33).

The end of Solomon's prayer in Chronicles is entirely different from its ending in Kings. The Chronicler omits 1 Kgs 8:50b-53 perhaps because he downplays the exodus in order to give more prominence to the period of David and Solomon and to the Davidic covenant as the ground for Israel's future hope. After a final request (v. 40) for divine attentiveness to the prayers of the temple that borrows from Neh 1:6, the Chronicler in verses 41-42 cites an adaptation of Ps 132:8-10. The "anointed one" in verse 42 (reading the singular with Ps 132:10 and other witnesses) is now Solomon rather than David. The call for Yahweh to remember (v. 42b) is adapted from Ps 132:1 and Isa 55:3. The NRSV is misleading at this point. The word translated "steadfast love" is plural in Hebrew and is perhaps better translated "faithful deeds." Scholars are divided over the question of whether the genitive here is subjective or objective. That is, are the "faithful deeds" done by David or on David's behalf? Williamson (1978) has made a compelling case for the objective sense (on David's behalf) in Isa 55:3, though his arguments are not necessarily decisive for the Chronicles context. In either case, the allusion to the Davidic covenant is patent, though it is obviously stronger in an objective genitive. The prayer thus ends with an appeal for Yahweh to fulfill his promise to David.

The next subunit in 7:1-10 describes the consecration and initiation of the temple—first in a sense by Yahweh (v. 1) and then by Solomon (v. 7). The description is adopted, with some significant changes, from 1 Kgs 8:54-66. The first two verses are the concluding frame (with 5:13-14) of Solomon's prayer. The fire from heaven is a literary and ideological motif which shows divine acceptance of the new altar. It is not entirely well integrated into its context, since there has been no previous mention of sacrifices. The Chronicler draws on Exod 40:34-38 and especially Lev 9:23-24 and 1 Chr 21:26 in composing this motif. In addition to showing divine approval with the temple, the fire from heaven and descent of the *kābôd* (glory) also demonstrate continuity with the tabernacle. In contrast to the tabernacle event where those who are present run away in fear, when the people in 2 Chr 7:3 witness the divine activity, they are inspired to worship and give thanks.

The enormous number of sacrifices used to initiate the temple provides a feast for the assembly (cf. v. 8) in accord with the grandeur of the occasion. The mention of the Levitical musicians is the Chronicler's way of reminding the reader of David's role in the realization of the temple and in establishing its liturgy. The celebration described in verses 8-10 is twofold. The dedication of the temple lasts seven days and is followed by the celebration of Sukkot, the festival of booths or tabernacles. The Chronicler's timetable for the description of Sukkot is determined by the prescriptions in Lev 23:34-36 and Num 29:12-38 (cf. Deut 16:13-15), which call for Sukkot to begin on the fifteenth day of the seventh month ("Tishri" = mid-September-October) and to continue for seven days followed by a solemn convocation on the eighth day. The Chronicler, therefore, changes the notice in 1 Kgs 8:66 about dismissal on the eighth day to a notice about the convocation, placing the dismissal on the twenty-third day (2 Chr 7:9-10). This timetable causes some tension with the Chronicler's dating of the dedication ceremonies at "the festival" (= Sukkot) in 5:3. Perhaps more problematic, the Chronicler apparently failed to recognize that his dates for the dedication encompass Yom Kippur, the day of atonement, to be observed on the tenth day of the seventh month according to Lev 23:26-32.

The Chronicler's portrait of the joyfulness of the occasion (v. 10) is a model or ideal not only for future celebrations (2 Chr 15:8-15; 30:10-27; 35:1-19) but also for worship in general. The reference to "all Israel" (v. 8) is an integral part of that model, as indicated by the designation of what are for the Chronicler ideal dimensions of the land settled by Israel, "from Lebo-hamath to the Wadi of Egypt." The use of that expression here recalls the assembly at the occasion of David's transfer of the ark in 1 Chr 13:5 and thus presents David and Solomon as parallel equals. The occasion is summarized as a demonstration of Yahweh's goodness to the model kings, David and Solomon, and to his people, Israel (v. 10).

As noted, 7:11 marks the completion of the temple construction and dedication. The first half of the verse is taken from 1 Kgs 9:9; the second half is the Chronicler's composition. The verb "succeed" (NRSV: "successfully accomplished") in verse 11b is one of the Chronicler's favorite ways of characterizing righteous kings. This statement about Solomon's "success" follows upon David's wish for him and the initial prospects for his reign in 1 Chr 22:11; 29:23, respectively.

God's reply to Solomon's prayer in 7:12-22 balances the promise to David in 1 Chr 17. The balance functions both literarily and theologically, as it parallels the Chronicler's two model kings and the accounts about them as well as the two institutions that are key for the Chronicler—the Davidic dynasty and the temple. Verse 12a provides a slightly different setting for God's appearance to Solomon from that of its counterpart in 1 Kgs 9:2. Chronicles does not locate the appearance in Gibeon but does describe it as taking place at night, apparently the very night that the dedication of the temple was completed. Verses 7:12b-15 have no counterpart in 1 Kgs 9. They obviously draw on Solomon's prayer, especially 6:26-31, and transform the emphasis on obedience in the prayer into an invitation to repent of disobedience that seems directed at the Chronicler's audience. The main difference between the prayer and Yahweh's response is that Yahweh himself is described as the source of the envisioned disasters. Thus, the response (v. 14 in particular) lays out the Chronicler's theology of immediate retribution. The temple is here called a "house of sacrifice" (v. 12). "Humble themselves" (v. 14) is typical language of the Chronicler and expresses a key idea of his theology—humility before God. Verse 15 is a direct reply to Solomon's request (6:40) that Yahweh be attentive to the prayers offered in the temple.

In verse 19, the Hebrew verbs shift from the singular, addressing Solomon, to the plural, addressing the people. It is difficult to avoid the impression that the Chronicler here warns those in the Second Temple period by recalling the destruction of the first temple brought on by apostasy. The verbs in verse 20, "pluck" and "cast out" reflect the influence of Deut 29:27, and the image of becoming a proverb and a byword is taken from Deut 28:37 and Jer 24:9. The question by passersby and the answer that follows it (vv. 20-21) are a motif found in Deut 29:24 [Heb. 29:23]; Jer 16:10; 22:8-9 that goes together with the idea of the ruined temple as an object lesson for other peoples.

Theological Analysis

The obvious focus of this unit is the temple. But the Chronicler's abridgment of the construction account in Kings and the length of that account in Chronicles in comparison with the one relating the dedication of the temple furnish clues about the Chronicler's theological understanding of the temple. The temple represents a new beginning. It is not entirely clear whether the Chronicler actually downplays the exodus, as some scholars have contended. But the temple symbolizes God's presence among Israel in a new way. The time of the temple's construction is the era to which the Chronicler appeals as the model for the institutions that are basic to Israel's existence as a people and that he wishes to see restored in his day. At the same time, the Chronicler also tries to demonstrate the temple's continuity with the tabernacle. While the temple is, in one sense, an innovation, it carries forward the oldest and most sacred traditions of the people of Israel. The Chronicler evinces a great respect for the traditions of the past and for the roots that such traditions provide for new generations of Israelites.

While the temple may represent God's presence with Israel in a more permanent and more intimate way, the Chronicler is clear that the temple is not the place where God really lives. The building itself was not sacrosanct but was secondary to what takes place there. Solomon's temple, after all, had been destroyed by the Chronicler's day. The temple was a "house of prayer," the principal, divinely chosen point of contact through prayer, sacrifice, and liturgical activities between humans and the deity. But it was these activities of contact with God that were foremost in the Chronicler's perspective. The acts and attitudes of worship were more important than the place. This concept would eventually allow for the replacement of the temple by synagogues for Jews and churches for Christians (cf. John 4:24). The celebration at the dedication of the temple exemplifies the joyful attitude that ideally accompanies true worship in the Chronicler's model. Other such attitudes for which Solomon calls on the part of the first worshipers in the temple are humility and penitence.

In this section, as in the previous one, the Chronicler emphasizes the equal participation of David and Solomon as his model kings in the temple enterprise. Each has a divinely given role to play, and each fulfills his role to the best of his abilities. Through his conquest of surrounding peoples David is able both to create a state of peace that will allow Solomon to concentrate on building the temple and to stockpile provisions for its construction. Solomon, in particular, is the model of obedience and its attendant rewards. He uses his wisdom, wealth, and fame to carry out the building project. The completion of the temple represents the fulfillment of God's word to David that his son would build the temple he had initially proposed. It is, therefore, a tangible witness to Yahweh's goodness and faithfulness to his promises. What is more, Solomon involves "all Israel" in the building enterprise, so that the project as a whole—specifically the full participation of rulers and people focusing their efforts on the service of God—is a model for what true Israel of all ages should be.

The Davidic covenant, which has already been mentioned in passing, is a special interest of the Chronicler's in this passage (7:17-18). Just how does the Chronicler understand that covenant in his postexilic context? The answer seems to be that he sees it as both conditional and eternal. Thus, it was always predicated on the obedience of Solomon and David's other heirs. Hence, the fact of the exile as punishment for sin does not contradict God's promise. The Chronicler's doctrine of retribution, which will loom large in the rest of 2 Chronicles is expressed in 6:30—God not only recompenses each person according to his/her deeds, but God also knows each person's innermost thoughts and intentions. It is also found in 7:14—potential disasters envisioned for the future are divine judgment for sin. God is, therefore, the source for restoration, and God is unfailingly merciful and ready to forgive those who humbly repent. Thus, the exile was God's judgment, but was certainly not final. It was an experience out of which the Chronicler admonishes his audience to learn, for the exile does not abrogate God's covenant. Indeed, the Chronicler finds in the covenant with David a source of hope for the restoration of the Davidic monarchy, for he understands this "covenant" as a promise (cf. McKenzie 2001).

SOLOMON'S OTHER PROJECTS (2 CHRONICLES 8:1-18)

Most of this chapter is a kind of miscellany of materials loosely related in some way to the construction and operation of the temple and leading to the declaration in 8:16 that the temple was completely finished. The last two verses of the chapter (vv. 17-18) tell of Solomon's acquisition of gold as a transition to the further information about his wealth in the next chapter.

Literary Analysis

This chapter falls into three sections treating other building projects of Solomon (8:1-11), the establishment of the ritual in the temple (8:12-16), and Solomon's procurement of gold from Ophir (8:17-18). As noted, 8:16 is the last of a series of texts (2:1; 3:1; 5:1; 7:11) that provide the framework for the account of Solomon's building projects; it particularly forms an enclosing bracket with 2:1. The occurrence of the word *šālēm*, "completely," in the verse puns on Solomon's name.

Exegetical Analysis

The chapter loosely parallels 1 Kgs 9:10-28; "loosely" because there are significant differences between the two. Some have argued that the best explanation for the wide variation of verses 1-6 from its Kings source is that the Chronicler made the best sense he could of a corrupt text. This may well have been so. However, most scholars also find reasons for the differences in the Chronicler's interests or in the circumstances that pertained in his day. For instance, 2 Chr 8:1-2 contain a completely different version of the episode in 1 Kgs 9:10-14. Rather than Solomon paying Hiram with cities which Hiram finds unsatisfactory, as in Kings, in Chronicles Huram gives cities to Solomon, evidently in acknowledgment of the latter's dominance or superiority, in accord with the Chronicler's view of their relationship. The reference to Solomon's defeat of Hamath-Zobah in 8:3 is unique to Chronicles and sets up a parallel with David, who previously defeated Zobah (1 Chr 18). The name "Hamath-Zobah" reflects the Chronicler's own time when Zobah was part of Persian province of Hamath. Verse 4 is adapted from 1 Kgs 9:18, which, however, reads Tamar, instead of Tadmor, and locates it in the Judean wilderness. Other textual witnesses to Kings read "Tadmor" (Palmyra), so that the Chronicler almost certainly found this reading in the version of Kings that he used. The Chronicler, perhaps aware that Tadmor was not in Judah, separated it from Baalah (Kiriath-jearim), placing its mention instead in the context of Solomon's activities in Hamath.

After the mention of Baalath in verse 6, Chronicles follows Kings fairly closely through 8:11a. These verses locate the source of Solomon's workforce exclusively in the non-Israelite, indigenous Canaanite peoples. Verse 11a agrees with 1 Kgs 9:24 describing Solomon's relocation of Pharaoh's daughter to her own house outside of the city of David. But while this act is apparently a sign of his affection or privileging of her in Kings, the Chronicler interprets it as an act of piety on Solomon's part, moving her away from the sacred ark. The basis for his interpretation is unclear; is it because she is a woman or because she is a foreigner? Ezekiel 44:9 is sometimes cited as the grounds for the latter understanding. Whatever the foundation for this interpretation, it is another instance of the Chronicler's idealization of Solomon.

Verse 13 expands on 1 Kgs 9:25 with a list, drawn from Lev 23 and Num 28–29, of the annual festivals as occasions for sacrifice. The verse also resembles Deut 16:16 and Ezek 45:17. The Mosaic commandment concerning the sacrificial calendar is combined in verses 14-15 with the Davidic ordinance regarding the divisions of temple personnel as detailed in 1 Chr 23–29. Thus, Chronicles attributes the sacrificial system of the temple to Moses in the era of the tabernacle and the organization of the personnel to David's authority. These verses, and sometimes verse 13 as well, have often been considered later additions by scholars because of their concern with Levitical responsibilities. The title "man of God" for David in verse 14 is unusual, as it is typically used for prophets. Its use here is likely connected to the description of the activity of the Levitical singers as prophecy (1 Chr 25:1-3; cf. also 2 Chr 29:25 where David is named with the "seer" Gad and Nathan the prophets as the founders of the Levitical music used in the temple liturgy).

As mentioned, 8:16 is the final verse of an extensive framework, extending back to 2:1, upon which the account of Solomon's construction projects is built. The last two verses of the chapter really introduce the theme of the next chapter—Solomon's great wealth, about which more will be said in the treatment of that chapter. The amount of gold mentioned here, 450 talents or nearly 17 tons (a talent = about 75 lbs.) is extraordinary. Unfortunately for treasure seekers, the location of Ophir is unknown. Despite Huram's assistance, the gold is brought to Solomon, another indication of Huram's subordination.

Theological Analysis

Solomon's continued piety is on display in this chapter in his transfer of Pharaoh's daughter (v. 11). His installation of the liturgy and personnel of the temple in 8:12-15 represents the culmination of David's work in 1 Chr 23–29 and indeed of the entire system of Israelite worship reaching back to Moses. It is another instance of Solomon's obedience to David's orders and to the purpose established for his reign by God. Verse 16 aptly epitomizes Solomon's work and reign as relating specifically to the temple. The final two verses of the chapter begin a demonstration, continued in the next chapter, of the reward in the form of untold wealth that God bestowed upon Solomon for his faithfulness. The idea seems to be that God gave Solomon wealth and wisdom so that he could build the temple for which he was chosen, and those blessings continued after the temple had been built as rewards for Solomon's completion of his task.

THE QUEEN OF SHEBA AND SOLOMON'S WEALTH (2 CHRONICLES 9:1-31)

This chapter contains the account of the famous visit of the queen of Sheba. The point of the account and of the chapter as a whole is to illustrate Solomon's wisdom, wealth, and international reputation. The chapter thus returns to the theme of 2 Chr 1, which tells of the bestowal of these gifts upon Solomon in the first place in preparation of his building of the temple.

Literary Analysis

Chapter 9 consists of three readily identifiable units: the visit of queen of Sheba (vv. 1-12), Solomon's wealth, reputation, and wisdom (vv. 13-28), and the concluding formulae for Solomon's reign (vv. 29-31). The chapter draws from 1 Kgs 10, except for Solomon's concluding formulae, which parallel 1 Kgs 11:41-43. Not surprisingly, the Chronicler omits most of 1 Kgs 11 (vv. 1-40) because it recounts Solomon's sins and ensuing difficulties with adversaries. The Chronicler's chapter focuses only on the positive dimensions of Solomon's reign; his renowned wealth and wisdom continue as rewards for his faithful completion of the task of building the temple in fulfillment of the divine promise made to him (1:11-12).

Exegetical Analysis

The purpose of the tale of the visit of the queen of Sheba in 9:1-12 is to highlight the incomparable greatness of Solomon. This is effectively done through a series of negative superlatives, some articulated by the queen herself: "there was nothing hidden from Solomon that he could not explain to her" (v. 2), "there was no more spirit left in her" (v. 4), "not even half of the greatness of your wisdom had been told to me" (v. 6), "there were no spices such as those that the queen of Sheba gave to King Solomon" (v. 9), "there never was seen the like of them before in the land of Judah" (v. 11). The queen was incredulous about the reports of Solomon that she had heard and came to believe their truthfulness only when she saw his court with her own eyes. The queen's blessing (v. 8) is quite similar to Huram's in 2:11, which was probably modeled after it. Sheba (roughly modern Yemen) was known for its trade in spices, which is the most distinctive feature of her gifts to Solomon (v. 9). The bestowal of gifts by foreign rulers is another mark of Solomon's prestige. However, true to his image as the greatest of kings, Solomon is not to be outdone by his guest, and he gives to the queen much more than she brought to him, namely, "every desire that she expressed well beyond what she had brought to the king" (v. 12). The latter reading represents an obvious change from 1 Kgs 10:13, which reads "every desire that she expressed as well as what he gave her out of Solomon's royal bounty." The word translated "well beyond" in the NRSV translation of the Chronicles text literally means "besides" and is awkward in Hebrew. The awkwardness is the result of direct borrowing from Kings to that point and then altering the text thereafter.

The theme of Solomon's incomparability continues in verses 13-28, where the key word is "gold," which occurs twelve times through verse 21 and once thereafter (v. 24). By "one year" (v. 13) is apparently meant "annually." The quantities are staggering. At 75 pounds per talent, 666 talents would be nearly 25 tons of gold, and this is the income for only one year, not including the amount received from the governors and Arabian kings. This subunit as a whole is very similar to its forerunner in 1 Kgs 10:14-28 with only minor alterations. It has been alleged that in 2 Chr 9:18 the Chronicler changed the reference to a calf's head on the back of the throne (1 Kgs 10:19) to refer to a golden footstool because of the idolatrous overtones of the former. But it is doubtful that a calf's head on the rear of the throne would be perceived as idolatrous, and the two lines are similar in Hebrew, so that textual corruption seems likely. In verse 21, the Chronicler has evidently failed to understand that "ships of Tarshish" (1 Kgs 10:22) referred to a kind of ship and has taken Tarshish as the ships' destination. It is possible that this misunderstanding existed already in the version of Kings used by the Chronicler. But the change from "fleet of Hiram" to "servants of Huram" accords with the Chronicler's interest elsewhere to depict Huram as subordinate to Solomon. So, in this instance, the expedition is not a joint one between Solomon and Huram as appears to be the case in Kings, but Huram is Solomon's assistant. Verses 25 and 27-28 review 2 Chr 1:14-17, providing yet another literary frame around the account of Solomon's deeds and wealth. The reference to 4000 chariot stalls in verse 25 instead of 1400 chariots as in 1 Kgs 10:26; 2 Chr 1:14 comes from 1 Kgs 4:26 [Heb. 5:6], which, however, has 40,000. Then verse 26 borrows from 1 Kgs 4:21 [Heb. 5:1].

The third subsection in this chapter, 9:29-31, is loosely based on the concluding formulae for Solomon in 1 Kgs 11:41-43. "From first to last" is a merism, indicating the entirety of Solomon's deeds as king. The prophetic sources cited for Solomon's name are reminiscent of those cited for David's in 1 Chr 29:29. Here, as there, different titles are used for each prophet. The present verse also uses different words for each of their works ("history," "prophecy," "visions" in the NRSV). In these ways, the parallel between the two kings is maintained. Nathan and Ahijah are both mentioned in Kings, and it is possible, as was suggested in the case of David, that the material in Samuel–Kings is what the Chronicler has in mind. However, there is no mention in either the Kings or the Chronicles accounts of Solomon of an Iddo (but cf. 2 Chr 12:15). His inclusion might be intended to show that much more information about Solomon was available than what the Chronicler included. It also supports the idea that these sources are fictitious and designed to lend credence in the form of prophetic support to the Chronicler's history.

Theological Analysis

The theology that emerges in this section is a kind of review of some major themes that have occurred repeatedly throughout Solomon's reign. Solomon is once again presented in parallel and as an equal to David. Each of them is chosen for a specific purpose. Both are devoted patrons of the temple. As with David, all Israel is behind Solomon in the construction and dedication of the temple. In many ways their reigns together form a unified period representing the ideal age of Israel. If anything, Solomon's reign would have to be considered superior to David's: Solomon does not sin; the temple is built; and Solomon's wealth and wisdom bring enormous prestige to Israel.

If there is a single statement encapsulating the theology of this unit, it is the one from the mouth of the queen of Sheba in 9:5-8. She observes that Solomon's wealth and wisdom are a tangible indication of God's love for Israel. They are at once a reward for Solomon's faithfulness and the means by which he can faithfully execute his charge of building the temple. In Chronicles, faithfulness leads to reward. Solomon carried out the act of supreme faithfulness by building the temple and therefore received the supreme reward in the form of wisdom, wealth, and fame. Therein lies the reason for the different portrayal of Solomon in Chronicles from that of 1 Kings. The Chronicler's regard for the significance of the temple and his theology of reward/retribution prevented him from recounting Solomon's apostasies.

THE DIVIDED KINGDOM (2 CHRONICLES 10–36)

The major interests of the Chronicler—the temple, the Davidic dynasty, and "all Israel"—continue in the final section of his work. Ironically for the last-named interest, the history of the northern kingdom is not systematically recounted but is only touched on when it overlaps with Judah's history. This is because the Chronicler regards the northern kingdom as an illegitimate state that is in rebellion against the house of David and that is apostate because of its rejection of the temple as the only divinely ordained sanctuary. Nevertheless, the Chronicler also views the people of the north as still part of God's chosen people of Israel. In addition to these interests, the distinctively Chronistic doctrine that surfaces in 2 Chronicles is that of individual responsibility and immediate retribution/reward. In stressing this doctrine, the Chronicler may be responding to the idea that the exile was punishment for the sins of previous generations of ancestors, an idea found in the Deuteronomistic History.

THE REIGN OF REHOBOAM (2 CHRONICLES 10:1–12:16)

Solomon was succeeded by his son, Rehoboam, whose reign presented special problems for the Chronicler. The division of the kingdom following Solomon was well known from the book of Kings. But the Deuteronomistic historian attributed the division to Solomon's apostasy, something the Chronicler's view of Solomon did not allow him to do. A partial solution lay at hand in the Chronicler's view that the rebellion of the northern tribes against the house of David was rebellion against Yahweh and apostasy against the temple and its institutions, which Yahweh had ordained. The way in which the Chronicler addressed these problems and formed his materials on Rehoboam into a unified narrative illustrates his skill as an editor and author.

Literary Analysis

The account of Rehoboam's reign in 2 Chr 10–12 is neatly organized and falls nicely into three subunits corresponding to the chapter divisions. The tone of the three subunits is also well balanced, chapters 10 and 12 representing a negative orientation on Rehoboam's reign surrounding chapter 11, which is positively oriented. Each chapter also has its own internal structure. Chapter 10 relates a series of conversations, following the introduction (vv. 1-2), between Rehoboam and the Israelites (vv. 3-5), Rehoboam and the older advisors (vv. 6-7), Rehoboam and his younger advisors (vv. 8-11), and again Rehoboam and the Israelites (vv. 12-15). The chapter concludes with the report of the resultant schism (vv. 16-19). Chapter 11 evinces a tripartite description of Rehoboam's defensive construction (vv. 1-12), the influx of priests and Levites from Israel (vv. 13-17), and Rehoboam's wives and children (vv. 18-23). Chapter 12 reports Shishak's invasion (vv. 1-12) followed by the concluding summary and regnal formula for Rehoboam (vv. 13-16).

This overall structure of these chapters was necessitated for the Chronicler by theological considerations. The division of the kingdom at the beginning of Rehoboam's reign had to be at least partly his fault, since it could not be blamed on Solomon. Similarly, the invasion of Shishak had to be punishment in response to Rehoboam's sin. But the Chronicler had other material at least attributed to Rehoboam's reign that cast him in a better light, and that could only go, therefore, in the middle.

Exegetical Analysis

Following Solomon's death, Rehoboam goes to Shechem to be made king (10:1). The simple statement in this verse contains several striking features. An attentive reader might note that the situation described is the reverse of those for David (1 Chr 11:1) and Solomon (1 Chr 28–29). The people do not come to Rehoboam, but he goes to them. This difference does not bode well for the future of the kingdom. The meeting takes place at Shechem in the north, where "all Israel" has gathered. It is important to note that from this point on in Chronicles "Israel" may refer either to the entire nation, Judah included, or to the northern tribes or nation alone; as we will see later in this chapter, it may also refer to Judah, including emigrants from the north, as "true (in the sense of "faithful") Israel." In 10:1 "all Israel" evidently refers to the people of the north, since it is they who summon Jeroboam and then make the demands of Rehoboam (vv. 3-4). They come to Shechem with every intention, apparently, of making Rehoboam king. It is only his attitude toward them that leads them to secede.

The account of the division in 1 Kgs 12 is notorious for its inconsistencies regarding Jeroboam's role (vv. 1-3, 12, 20). Many scholars believe that the inconsistencies stem from the influence of the Chronicler's deliberately altered text, especially in 10:2-3. It is more likely, however, that the Chronicler corrected a reading in his Kings source that had become corrupt in the course of transmission (McKenzie 1987). In either case, the problem is exclusively in Kings; in Chronicles Jeroboam's involvement from the beginning is unambiguous. The Chronicler's omission of 1 Kgs 11 obscures both the background of Jeroboam and the reason for the people's demand (10:4). But these details are incidental to the Chronicler's main concern, which is to account for the division theologically. Besides, the Chronicler has consistently omitted the references in Kings to Israelites in the royal labor force, and he routinely omits information about the north anyway, except where it intersects with his history of Judah.

There is debate among scholars as to whether the old and young advisors were simply distinguished by age or actually represented two formally constituted houses within the government. The older, wiser advisors recognize the ultimatum behind the people's demand and also realize what is at stake. Their counsel to Rehoboam is phrased slightly differently in Chronicles (10:7) from the way it appears in Kings (12:7) and may reflect the Chronicler's perspective on the figure of the king as someone who should be lenient toward his subjects.

The young advisors do not appreciate the gravity of the situation. In citing the people's demand they leave out the conclusion, "and we will serve you" (v. 9), which implies that the people will refuse to accept Rehoboam as king if he does not ease their burden. The young men respond with aphorisms (vv. 10-11) and treat the occasion as an opportunity for Rehoboam to strut his *machismo*: "My little *finger* is thicker than my father's loins." The Hebrew text does not actually contain the word "finger" and might better be translated "my little member"—a reference to the reproductive organ. As a whole, Rehoboam's tyrannical threat of increased harshness as a response to a request for leniency in these verses recalls the Pharaoh's answer to the Hebrew slaves in Exod 5:7-8. For that reason, it is fair to assume that Yahweh does not condone Rehoboam's response.

God is not mentioned at all in this story until its conclusion (v. 15). This verse is borrowed essentially verbatim from 1 Kgs 12:15, and it causes problems in Chronicles. The verse alludes to Ahijah's oracle in 1 Kgs 11, which the Chronicler has omitted. Perhaps he assumes that his readership knows it or perhaps it is the fact of its fulfillment rather than the specifics that is important to him. A more serious problem is theological. The verse accords with the outlook in Kings that the division of the kingdom was Yahweh's will and that Jeroboam's reign was instituted by prophetic initiative. In Chronicles, however, Jeroboam and the north are in sinful rebellion, not just against the Davidic line and Judah, as in verse 19 (// 1 Kgs 12:19), but against God. The tension between these two explanations is partially assuaged if we adopt the view that the initial schism was divine punishment for Rehoboam's arrogance but that the continued separation of Israel and especially the religious and cultic measures taken to support the separation are sin.

The conclusion to the story in 10:16-19 contains several ironies and returns full circle to its beginning. As we saw, the fact that Rehoboam went to meet Israel rather than Israel coming to him did not bode well. Now all Israel takes its leave of him as their king. Indeed, the man who came to be made king barely escapes with his life (v. 18). The contrast with David and

Solomon is reinforced by the people's cry (v. 16): "What share do we have in David? We have no inheritance in the son of Jesse," which reverses Amasai's rallying cry for David in 1 Chr 12:18: "We are yours, O David; and with you, O son of Jesse." Just as Rehoboam, coached by his young advisors, answered the people with aphorisms, so now the people respond in kind. The version of their cry in Chronicles conflates 1 Kgs 12:16 with 2 Sam 20:1, the influence of the latter appearing in the addition of the word "each." The motivation for this conflation is to imply that, as in 2 Sam 20:1, the people of Israel are in rebellion.

While "all Israel" in the north rebelled against Rehoboam (v. 16) and stoned Hadoram (v. 18), a number of northerners were living in Judah, and it was they, along with the native Judahites, who represented the true people of Israel (v. 17). "The cities of Judah" in this verse is a common way the Chronicler has of designating the full extent of Judah. The people who remain in the north are still part of Yahweh's people, but they are in rebellion (v. 19), and as the Chronicler will make clear, they need to repent of their apostasy and join with their brothers in subjection to the Davidic king.

Rehoboam's foolishness and insensitivity are most clearly manifest in his sending of Hadoram, the head of the forced labor corps, to Israel, presumably to attempt to compel them to submit to Rehoboam. Rather than submit, the Israelites kill Hadoram. The full measure of the stupidity of Rehoboam's act here is obscured in Chronicles because of the omission of texts in Kings that include the Israelites in the royal workforce. Rehoboam sends the leader of the very institution to which the Israelites have so vehemently objected. On the other hand, the omission makes the rebellion of the Israelites that much less founded in substantive issues and all the more the work of Yahweh initially—though not worthwhile perpetuating. At this point, the Chronicler omits 1 Kgs 12:20, which states that the Israelites called for Jeroboam only after the secession. As noted, in Chronicles Jeroboam is involved and culpable from the beginning.

The first four verses of chapter 11 obviously continue the story from chapter 10 as Rehoboam musters his troops in order to force the Israelites to remain in his kingdom. However, these verses also set the stage for the positive information about Rehoboam's reign in chapter 11. In Chronicles, building activity such as that described in 11:5-12 is always a sign of divine blessing. The same is true of large families and numerous offspring as in 11:18-23. Then, in 11:13-17, the emigration of priests and Levites from the north is described as making Rehoboam's kingdom strong and secure. The first four verses of the chapter provide the reason for these blessings: Rehoboam and his men listened to and obeyed the word of Yahweh's prophet. That notice of obedience in the story, borrowed from 1 Kgs 12:21-24, provided the point of departure for the Chronicler's inclusion and organization of the material in this chapter. The Chronicler also made a couple of minor, but significant, changes in the wording of his source. Instead of "to all the house of Judah and Benjamin, and to the rest of the people" (1 Kgs 12:23), 2 Chr 11:3 reads "to all Israel in Judah and Benjamin," since, for the Chronicler, the kingdom of Judah always included people from the north and embodied true Israel.

The list of fortified cities (vv. 5-12) does not fit the narrative circumstances entirely well. These cities by and large were located on the eastern and western sides of the kingdom rather than on the north, as one would expect, since Rehoboam was primarily concerned about defending against Israel. Many scholars suggest that this list, which does not occur elsewhere in the Bible, originated in the reign of Hezekiah (ca. 715–687 B.C.E.). This suggestion finds support in the fact that large storage jars of a distinctive kind that were used in a distribution system of King Hezekiah in eighth-century Judah were found at several of these locations. Gath (v. 8) may not be the well-known Philistine town but a site closer to Adullam and Mareshah.

Zorah and Aijalon were originally within the territory of Dan but were taken over by Judah as shown by their occurrence in other lists of Judahite cities (Josh 15:33; 1 Chr 2:53; 2 Chr 28:18). Hebron is isolated in the list and seems out of place; one would expect to find it mentioned earlier in the list with other southern cities such as Bethzur or Ziph, rather than following Aijalon, the most northern city in the list.

The Chronicler combines his positive regard for the priests and Levites (vv. 13-17) with his polemic against the north's cultic institutions. The priests and Levites leave their homes in the north to resettle in Jerusalem and Judah. Jeroboam prevented the priests and Levites from serving as priests in the north. Of course, Jerusalem was the only place they could legitimately serve anyway, in the Chronicler's view. But his point here is a polemical one—Jeroboam's sin is multifaceted (v. 15). He appointed an illegitimate priesthood to serve at the high places in the worship of satyrs and calves. The word for satyrs or "goat demons" is an allusion to Lev 17:7 and obviously characterizes the northern cult as outright apostasy. "Calves," of course, alludes to Jeroboam's shrines at Dan and Bethel (1 Kgs 12:25-33). The priests and Levites are not the only defectors. Verse 16 spells out the Chronicler's view that the nation of Judah from its beginning included faithful northerners and was therefore true Israel. Verse 17 makes clear that Rehoboam's period of success and prosperity was limited; it would come to an end with his prideful sin.

The final segment of this chapter (vv. 18-23) is remarkable in several respects. In the first place, such a detailed list of names and information for a king is quite unusual; only David and Jehoshaphat boast similar lists in Chronicles. Certain specifics in the list are also very much unexpected. For instance, David's son Jerimoth is not mentioned anywhere else. These verses are unparalleled in Kings, and their source as well as their historical reliability are unknown. The reason for the Chronicler's inclusion of this information, particularly at this point rather than in the regnal summary for Rehoboam at the end of the account about him, is its implication that Rehoboam received God's blessing during this period of his reign.

The repeated mention of Maacah (vv. 20-22) is part of a notorious crux that has yet to be resolved. Here and in 1 Kgs 15:2 she is named as Rehoboam's wife and Abijah's/Abijam's mother, while in 1 Kgs 15:10, 13 she is referred to as Abijam's wife and Asa's mother. Second Chronicles 15:2, the parallel to 1 Kgs 15:2, gives the name of Abijah's mother as Micaiah, daughter of Uriel. There is no clear way to reconcile these conflicting data. The point of the repeated references to Maacah is to explain why Abijah was Rehoboam's favorite son and designated heir to the throne. Rehoboam's wisdom lay in dispersing his other sons and granting them regional authority and luxurious upkeep as a way of preventing them from plotting against his chosen crown prince. The final three Hebrew words of the chapter are corrupt and literally read, "he requested a crowd of women." The problem is resolved relatively easily by redividing the consonants so that they read, "he took wives for them."

The account of Shishak's invasion in 2 Chr 12:1-12 borrows from 1 Kgs 14:25-31 with significant recasting and supplementation. Second Chronicles 12:2 finds a rough parallel in 1 Kgs 14:25, and 2 Chr 12:9-11 is very close to 1 Kgs 14:26-28. But the rest of Chronicles' version is unique to it. The principal reason for the difference is theological. The Chronicler makes explicit what is implied in Kings: Shishak's invasion must have been punishment for sin (2 Chr 12:1, 2*b*, 12). The Chronicler does not detail Rehoboam's sins, as in 1 Kgs 14:21-24, nor does he indicate that they were cultic in nature. The Chronicler seems more interested in the cause: Failing to recognize that the strength of his reign was due to Yahweh's blessing, Rehoboam became proud and was unfaithful to Yahweh (v. 2). Similar descriptions are used for Uzziah (2 Chr 26:16) and Hezekiah (2 Chr 32:25-26), so that the language and theology here are typical of the Chronicler. The punishment, characterized by the prophet Shemaiah according to the principle "measure for measure" (v. 5), was abandonment of Rehoboam by Yahweh. Specifically, Yahweh abandoned Rehoboam to Shishak.

The description of Shishak's invasion proper (vv. 3-8) has been inserted by the Chronicler into the Kings base through the technique of narrative resumption; the phrase "King Shishak of Egypt came up against Jerusalem," is repeated almost verbatim in verses 2a and 9a. The event is also portrayed on the Egyptian king's relief on the temple at Karnak. The Egyptian army was indeed composite, as the Chronicler suggests in verse 3, though his description likely comes less from historical data than from a desire to detail the enormousness of the Egyptian force. The Egyptian record does not mention the fortified cities (v. 4); the Chronicler probably includes them because of his listing of them in 11:5-10, indicating that Shishak would have had to pass them on his way to Jerusalem. In fact, the sites mentioned on the Karnak relief are not, for the most part, in Judah, suggesting that Rehoboam may have paid Shishak off, as might also be inferred from the anecdote about the shields (vv. 9-11). The reference to the king and the princes (of Israel!) "humbling themselves" (vv. 6-7, 12) uses another favorite term and idea of the Chronicler's. This response saves Jerusalem from the destruction that would have been brought on by Yahweh's wrath and gives them instead "some deliverance." Yahweh's action, therefore, in bringing Shishak is didactic and not just punitive.

The concluding formula for Rehoboam in 2 Chr 12:13-16 combines material from both the introduction (1 Kgs 14:21) and the conclusion (1 Kgs 14:29-31) for Rehoboam in Kings. The expression about seeking Yahweh (v. 14) is characteristic of the Chronicler, as is the citation of prophetic sources (v. 15).

Theological Analysis

This section repeats several important points within the Chronicler's theology. The first of these is his view of Israel. While the northern tribes are a part of Israel, they have wandered astray in rebellion against the Davidic ruler and into religious apostasy. True Israel is embodied in Judah, whose residents include the faithful from all tribes. This theme will be developed further in the next chapter.

Another key theme in this section deals with obedience and reward, sin and punishment. Rehoboam's pride and arrogance get him and the nation into trouble. They are part of the cause for the schism. When Rehoboam proves obedient to Yahweh's prophet, his reign propers. When he again becomes proud and abandons Yahweh's law, punishment comes in the form of Shishak's invasion. Rehoboam's repentance saves his reign and his nation. Repentance and obedience go hand in hand in Chronicles. Humility is a prerequisite for both. Despite Rehoboam's repentance, Yahweh's righteousness still exacts some discipline (12:6-8). God's purpose here is less punitive than pedagogical; the point of it is to teach Rehoboam a lesson, not to exact some measure of divine revenge. The account of Shishak's conquest of Rehoboam's recently constructed fortresses suggests that the Chronicler may be making the point that the kingdom's real security lies in faithfulness to God rather than in the works of human hands.

THE REIGN OF ABIJAH
(2 CHRONICLES 13:1–14:1*a* [HEBREW 13:1-23*a*])

Since the division of the kingdom in the Chronicler's view was at least partly the result of Rehoboam's arrogance, he was certainly not a model for future kings of Judah in its relationship to Israel and to God. The Chronicler turned to Rehoboam's successor, Abijah, to provide such a model of proper kingly behavior.

Literary Analysis

The Chronicler's portrait of Abijah as an exemplary figure meant that his account would have to differ substantially from the one in Kings (1 Kgs 15:1-8), where Abijam is evaluated negatively. Hence, only the introduction and conclusion to Abijah's reign in 2 Chr 13:1-2*a* (// 1 Kgs 15:1-2) and 2 Chr 13:22–14:1 [Heb. 13:22-23] (// 1 Kgs 15:7-8) find parallels in Kings; 2 Chr 13:3-21 is unique to Chronicles and is saturated with the Chronicler's language, style, and ideology. These verses have long been recognized as the Chronicler's work, though the extent to which they may be based on older sources has been disputed. However, Klein (1983) has now made a compelling case for the view that the contents of the chapter can all be attributed to canonical sources (Kings and the list of places in Josh 18:21-24) and the Chronicler's theological interests, without the necessity of positing any additional source. Still, some scholars continue to hold that the Chronicler most likely had some basis in other sources for his reversal of the negative assessment of Abijah in Kings.

The bulk of the chapter recounts a single battle. After the introduction to Abijah (vv. 1-2), the battle lines are described (v. 3). Then comes Abijah's speech to Jeroboam and Israel before the battle (vv. 4-12) followed by the report of the specifics of the battle and its results (vv. 13-21).

Exegetical Analysis

Synchronisms of the sort found in verses 1-2*a* are common in Kings, but this is the only such instance in Chronicles, which lacks independent accounts of the northern kingdom. On the problem associated with the name of Abijah's mother, Micaiah or Maacah (1 Kgs 15:2), see above on 2 Chr 11:20-22. In verse 2*b*, the Chronicler has taken the mention of continual war between Abjiah and Jeroboam from 1 Kgs 15:7 and used it as a point of departure or a sort of heading for his account of the single battle (vv. 3-21).

The Chronicler lays out the setting for that battle in verse 3. The Hebrew expression weakly translated "went out to battle" in the NRSV actually means "to initiate" (lit., "bind") the battle.

Thus, Abijah is cast as the aggressor. His aggression seems blatantly to contravene the order of Shemaiah against the people of Judah attacking their brother Israelites (11:4). Yet the Chronicler says nothing about this tension. The large numbers in verse 3 (cf. v. 17) are certainly exaggerated. It is intriguing that the figures resulting from David's census according to 2 Sam 24:9 were 800,000 and 500,000 for Israel and Judah, respectively. The imbalance in the respective sizes of the armies, whatever the origin of the numbers, well represents the literary and theological motif of the righteous minority being vastly outnumbered by evildoers.

The setting of Abijah's speech (vv. 4-12) is unlikely, to say the least. Could Abijah, standing on a hilltop, make himself heard by 800,000 soldiers, not to mention the 400,000 in his own army? And would the opposing force simply listen politely to his entire speech? Obviously, the speech is merely a forum for the Chronicler to express his own theology. The summons, "listen to me" (v. 4), is characteristic of such addresses in Chronicles. The exact location of Mt. Zemaraim is unknown, though it was near the border of Ephraim and Benjamin, to judge from its mention in Josh 18:22-23 in the context of Bethel, Ephron (= Ophrah), and perhaps Jeshanah (see v. 19 below; Klein 1983). This is precisely the territory that is in dispute in the present text. The setting for Abijah's speech recalls Jotham's in Judg 9:7.

The speech falls naturally into two parts that contrast Israel ("you," vv. 5-9) with Judah ("we," vv. 10-12*a*). The point of the speech, in essence, is that God is on "our," in other words, Judah's, side. Hence, it ends with a plea to the Israelites not to fight against God by opposing Judah (v. 12*b*). The first distinction between the two is that Judah is ruled by a descendant of David, to whom God gave kingship over Israel forever by a "covenant of salt" (v. 5). The contrast with Kings could hardly be greater. In 1 Kgs 11:26-40, for instance, the Davidids lose Israel because of sin but retain Judah and Jerusalem because of the divine promise to David. Thus, the house of David retains a fiefdom only because of God's faithfulness to his word. In Chronicles, the Davidids retain entitlement to the entire kingdom and do not possess it because of Israel's rebellion.

"Covenant of salt" is an expression adapted from Num 18:19, where it is used for Yahweh's promise to the Aaronid priests. The image apparently arose from the properties of salt as a preservative and perhaps from its use in ceremonial meals ratifying treaties. It is obviously used to convey the sense of permanence. The subtle parallel between the Davidic and Aaronic lines is quite fitting in this context; both are God's chosen representatives, so that by rejecting them the Israelites have rejected God. Jeroboam, therefore, is a servant in rebellion against David and his sons and hence against God (v. 6). Jeroboam and his conspirators took advantage of a young and vulnerable Rehoboam (v. 7). The expression "young and resolute" here is reminiscent of those used of Solomon in 1 Kgs 3:7 and especially in 1 Chr 22:5; 29:1. In view of the story of the division in Chronicles, this is certainly a charitable description of Rehoboam, as is perhaps fitting in the mouth of his son and designated heir.

Not only are the Israelites in rebellion, but verses 8-9 explain that they are also guilty of apostasy. Their apostasy consists of three facets, all drawn from 1 Kgs 12:25-33; 13:33-34, which are not paralled in Chronicles. The first facet is idolatry: Jeroboam built the golden calves for worship despite the fact that they are "no gods." Then, he drove out the priests and Levites, whom Yahweh had designated as cultic personnel, just as he had designated David and his descendants as kings. Finally, he appointed replacement priests from the people, allowing anyone who wanted to and who could pay the "fee" for consecration to become a priest. In contrast, the people of Judah observe proper worship of Yahweh with the Aaronid priests and the Levites (vv. 10-11).

The description of cultic activities (v. 11) draws more from the tabernacle liturgy than from the temple, as suggested by the reference to only one lampstand. The verse thus alludes to a continuity of divine service going back to Moses. Judah is therefore true Israel, and Yahweh is on their side. The difference is that "we have not abandoned him" (v. 10*a*) while "you have abandoned him" (v. 11*b*); the pronouns in Hebrew make the contrast between "we" and "you" emphatic. The contrast, nevertheless, is not an ethnic or national one. Despite Israel's sins, they remain the people of Yahweh, albeit in apostasy. Thus, Abijah still calls them "Israelites" (v. 12) and warns them against opposing Yahweh "the God of *your* ancestors." The mention of the battle trumpets (v. 12) alludes to Num 10:2-10; they are the means to summons to holy war and thus illustrate that "God is with us at our head." The strongest warning and main point of the speech comes in verse 12—Israel is about to fight against Yahweh himself and of course will not succeed.

While Abijah has been talking, Jeroboam has been scheming, sending an ambush against Judah so as to force them to fight on two fronts (v. 13). Judah's response, though, is a faithful one; they cry out to Yahweh and sound the trumpets (v. 14). Hence, their success, which is made explicit in verses 16, 18: God defeated the Israelites because the people of Judah relied on him. If the battle is not entirely fictional, its details are no longer important to the Chronicler, whose account is more theological than military. The casualties (v. 17) are literally incredible: 500,000, over half of the Israelite army and more than all of Judah's force.

One might expect Abijah, his victory in hand, to force defeated Israel to rejoin his kingdom. The fact that he does not again suggests the fictional or at least extensively elaborated nature of this story, which contrasts with the historical reality. One might also offer a theological explanation: Israel does not rejoin Judah because it has not repented of its apostasy and rebellion. The sites taken over by Judah (v. 19) were all along the Ephraimite/ Benjaminite border (cf. Josh 18:22-23 where Ophrah = Ephron). This might suggest some historical veracity to the story in this chapter in the form of a border skirmish in which Judah was momentarily successful. On the other hand, it is difficult to believe that the royal shrine at Bethel was ever conquered by Judah or worship there interrupted without it being reported elsewhere.

The summary in verse 20 also appears contrary to historical fact. It implies that Jeroboam died before Abijah, a datum not supported by 1 Kgs 15. The verse reflects a theological necessity brought on by the Chronicler's positive portrayal of Abijah. Since he is righteous he must have been blessed with greater longevity than the wicked Jeroboam. While 13:2 mentions that Abijah's reign lasted only three years, Chronicles does not give figures for Jeroboam, so that this verse can leave the impression that he died before Abijah. The description of his death at Yahweh's hand is reminiscent of the one for Saul in 1 Chr 10:14, both instances signaling divine punishment. The further report about Abijah, in contrast, contains signs of divine blessing: strength and a large family. It seems unlikely that Abijah would have taken fourteen wives and fathered thirty-eight children in only three years as king. But the numbers could include wives married and children born before his accession.

The concluding formula for Abijah in Chronicles is tailored to the account about him. Rather than referring to "all he did" as in 1 Kgs 15:7, 2 Chr 13:22 mentions "his behavior and his deeds" (so NRSV, literally, "his ways and his words"). The latter, in particular, alludes to the speech included earlier in the chapter. Also, for the third and final time Iddo is mentioned in a king's concluding formula. This time he is called a prophet rather than a seer as in 9:29 and 12:15. His work is here called a *midrash*. The precise sense of this term is uncertain, but it does not have the same narrow, technical meaning of "interpretation" or "exposition" as in later rabbinic writing. The NRSV translation, "story," may be appropriate.

Theological Analysis

Abijah's speech is a key passage for the Chronicler's theology, because it succinctly expresses the Chronicler's view of the north and its relationship with Judah. Israel is in a state of rebellion and apostasy. Their secession from the Davidic line is revolt against Yahweh, who chose David and his descendants to rule over all Israel. Following Jeroboam's lead, they have exacerbated their crime by worshiping other gods and adopting an illicit priesthood, again in revolt against Yahweh's chosen. Nevertheless, despite all this sinfulness and rebellion, they remain a part of Israel, God's chosen people.

The battle scene in the chapter is also theologically significant. Judah under Abijah responds properly to the crisis of finding themselves essentially surrounded by enemy forces. They cry out to Yahweh and sound the trumpets, invoking the ancient conventions of holy war. Thus, they trust in Yahweh to rescue them—and he does, demonstrating that superior numbers are meaningless in opposition to divine power. Finally, the contrast at the end of the chapter between the failure and ignominious death of Jeroboam and the power and prodigy of Abijah once again illustrates the Chronicler's view that Yahweh rewards those who trust in him with success and punishes those who are unfaithful with defeat and disaster.

THE REIGN OF ASA
(2 CHRONICLES 14:1*b*–16:14 [HEBREW 13:23*b*–16:14])

Judging from the numbers of verses (16 versus 48), Chronicles account of Asa's reign is three times longer than that of Kings (1 Kgs 15:9-24) and illustrates at length some of the Chronicler's theological concepts. In essence, there are two parts to the Chronicler's account, each focusing on a military threat. Asa responds differently to the two threats, and therein lies the point of the lesson that the Chronicler derives from him. Each episode is accompanied by an oracle purportedly delivered by a prophet for the occasion and expressing the

Chronicler's perspective. Indeed, the two are in several ways mirror images or antitheses of one another, as will be shown in the exegesis. The principle illustrated by both episodes together is articulated in 15:2: "Yahweh is with you while you are with him; if you seek him he will be found by you, but if you abandon him he will abandon you."

Literary Analysis

The unit begins by recounting Asa's righteousness and the blessings he received as a reward (14:1b-8). The first military crisis is provided by Zerah the Cushite, whom Yahweh defeats because of Asa's piety (14:9-15). The prophecy of Azariah (15:1-7) impels Asa to further reforms and to covenant making (15:8-15). A second threat by Israel evokes a less pious reaction from Asa in the form of calling on Ben-hadad of Aram for assistance (16:1-6), and another prophet, Hanani, scolds him for this (16:7-10). The conclusion to Asa's reign recounts his death and burial (16:11-14). Most of this material is unique to Chronicles, and those sections that have parallels in 1 Kgs (15:16-18; 16:1-6, 11-14) attest significant elaboration. The Chronicler's style and interests permeate all three chapters, making it clear that the account of Asa's reign is his handiwork rather than a patchwork of source materials.

Exegetical Analysis

The division between the previous unit and the present one at a half verse may seem strange at first. But the statement in 14:1b that the land had rest for ten years under Asa initiates an important subtheme for the Chronicles account of Asa's reign. To begin with, it signals the importance of Asa. Not since Solomon (1 Chr 22:9) has rest been noted as a characteristic of a king's reign. Yet notices to this effect occur repeatedly for the early portion of Asa's reign in chapter 14: the land and kingdom had rest (vv. 1b, 5, 6); Asa had no war in those years for Yahweh gave him peace (v. 5). The contrast comes at the end of his reign when the prophet Hanani promises him wars (16:9). The reason for the change has to do with Asa's contrasting responses to the two military threats during his reign, especially the war that came in his thirty-sixth year (15:19–16:1).

It is because of the divinely bestowed rest that Asa is able to carry out his reforms and building projects, both at the beginning of his reign (14:6) and after the defeat of Zerah (15:15). The implication of Azariah's message to Asa is that he will be rewarded with peace, in contrast to the great disturbances of previous eras, because of his trust in God (15:5-7). Asa is the first of four reforming kings in Chronicles, and his reforms pave the way for Jehoshaphat, Hezekiah, and Josiah. The Chronicler's account of Asa's reforms is impelled by 1 Kgs 15:12, but the Chronicler has completely altered the nature of Asa's reforms to correspond to the prescriptions of Deuteronomy (7:5; 12:3) and to anticipate those of subsequent reformers, especially Hezekiah (2 Chr 31:1) and Josiah (2 Chr 34:3-7). The Chronicler does not explain when the cultic deviations requiring reform were introduced; indeed, as hinted, the list of reform activities seems to have been imported from the accounts of later kings so that the presence of such deviations in Jerusalem at this point is historically questionable. But Asa's religious reforms according to the law are what characterize him as having done "what was good and right in the sight of Yahweh," an adjustment to 1 Kgs 15:11 based on Deut 12:28. The exact nature of the *ḥammānîm* (v. 4) is uncertain; in addition to "incense altars" (so NRSV), they have been interpreted as pillars for sun worship and cultic buildings. Whatever their nature, the mention of their removal here may be drawn from Lev 26:30. Keeping the law, then, is an important element of the command to "seek Yahweh" (v. 4). However, seeking Yahweh, which is another subtheme of the Chronicler's account of Asa's reign (cf. 14:7; 15:2, 4, 12, 13, 15; 16:12), is more comprehensive, entailing a complete, personal commitment to God.

Asa's building program (vv. 6-7) and his army (v. 8) are typical signs of blessing in Chronicles, especially with the statement at the end of verse 7 that they "prospered" or "succeeded," one of the Chronicler's favorite vocabulary items. Here, they come in reward for Asa's religious reforms. In describing Asa's building projects, the Chronicler may be elaborating on the unusual reference to "the cities that he built" in the regnal formula of 1 Kgs 15:23. The double occurrence of the form "we sought" in 2 Chr 14:7 is awkward and should be adjusted with the versions to read, "as we have sought Yahweh our God he has sought us." The emendation continues the theme of seeking Yahweh in the form of a "measure for measure" statement. The military divisions reflected in verse 8 have been equated with those of Hellenistic armies (Welten 1973:110-11).

The remainder of the chapter is devoted to Asa's encounter with Zerah the Cushite. Cush is the name for Nubia or Ethiopia, the region south of Egypt. This account is well structured with narratives about the preparations for war (vv. 9-10) and Judah's victory (vv. 12-14) on either side of Asa's prayer (v. 11), which is central. The historicity of the episode is suspect for several reasons. In addition to the size of the Cushite army—a million men, which is unquestionably an exaggeration—there is no other record of an Ethiopian invasion at this time or of an Ethiopian ruler named Zerah (though some have tried to identify him as Osorkon I). In fact, the name Zerah is not Egyptian at all, but is Semitic in origin. There are several Zerahs in the Hebrew Bible, the most famous of which is Judah's son, the brother of Perez (Gen 38:30; on the others cf. 1 Chr 4:24; 6:21, 41 [Heb. vv. 6, 26]). It is possible, particularly in view of the reference to tents and livestock (v. 15), that these Cushites were not Ethiopians but nomads from Arabia who had settled in southwestern Judah near Gerar (called "Cushan" in Hab 3:7; cf. 2 Chr 21:16, which refers to "the Arabs who are near the Cushites"). In such a case, the story may have some basis in a historical event, though it has been considerably altered. The Chronicler's concern, after all, is theological rather than historical.

The account of the battle in 14:9-15 is quite similar to that of Abijah's battle against Jeroboam (13:13-19), a fact that further indicates the theological nature of both stories. In each case, the king of Judah faces a military crisis; he and his men cry out to Yahweh, who defeats the enemy, allowing the Judahites to effect a great slaughter and conquer several cities. The battle is located near Mareshah (Tell Sandakhanna) in the Judean highlands, about 25 miles southeast of Jerusalem and an outpost fortified by Rehoboam (1 Chr 11:8). The name Zephathah (v. 10) may be an error for the Hebrew word for "north," the reading presupposed by the LXX, such that the battle is envisioned as occurring just north of Mareshah.

Asa's prayer (v. 11) presents two difficulties. First, the sense of the statement, "there is no difference for you between helping the mighty and the weak" (NRSV), is obscure. The best proposed explanation is that it is elliptical and should be understood to mean, "there is none except you to help [in a conflict] between the mighty and the weak."

The narrative supplies no details about the battle or the tactics involved other than stating that Yahweh struck the Cushites. All that is left to Asa's army is to pursue the fleeing enemy and seize the plunder. Verse 13 is emphatic that all (one million!) of the Cushites were killed. The point is surely theological—Yahweh's victory is complete. The decisive victory instills the "fear of Yahweh" upon the defeated cities (14:14), a theme in Chronicles that one finds for other successful kings: David (1 Chr 14:17) and Jehoshaphat (2 Chr 17:10; 20:29).

Azariah's oracle (15:1-7) is apparently motivated by Asa's faithfulness and in turn moves him to even greater reforms in 15:8-15. Azariah is the son of Oded, a name probably borrowed from the prophet in 2 Chr 28:9-15. His oracle is replete with the language and theological concerns of the Chronicler. It is also anthological in nature, borrowing from and alluding to a broad range of prophetic texts. The summons, "hear me" (v. 2), is a typical introduction for addresses in Chronicles. The "measure for measure" principle that Yahweh is with those who seek him but forsakes those who forsake him is also a favorite of the Chronicler's. Similar ideas are expressed in Isa 55:6; 65:1; Jer 29:13. This doctrine, which is the main point of the oracle, epitomizes Asa's reign, the two parts of which—positive and negative—illustrate the principles and consequences of seeking and forsaking Yahweh.

The period of anarchy envisioned in verse 3 is probably a reference to the time of the judges, as indicated by the cyclical pattern of repentance and return described in verse 4. Hosea 3:4 also describes a time of anarchy. But in Hosea both religious and political institutions are lacking, while the missing items in Chronicles are purely religious in nature. The point in Chronicles does not seem to be that the law did not exist during this period, but that it was not being taught or, consequently, followed. The idea of turning to seek Yahweh "in distress" is also found in Hos 5:15–6:1. The description of the period before the monarchy as one of turmoil and internecine conflict (15:5-6) shares language and imagery with several prophetic texts, most notably Isa 19:2; Hag 2:22; Zech 8:10*b*; 11:6; 14:13. The resonance with Zech 8:9-13 is particularly noteworthy, as it describes the time before the rebuilding of the temple as lawless, and Asa is impelled by Azariah's speech to repair the temple and reform its cult. Azariah's charge (v. 7) also borrows from Jer 31:16*b* and Zeph 3:16 and is reminiscent of David's charge to Solomon in 1 Chr 22:13; 28:10.

Azariah's name has accidentally been lost from the Hebrew text of 15:8, which reads "Oded the prophet." But clearly Azariah must be restored, as it is his oracle that inspires Asa to "take courage" (NRSV: lit., "strengthen himself," a favorite expression of the Chronicler's) and undertake further reforms. These include removal of idols, repair of the altar, and especially the making of a covenant, which receives the lion's share of attention (vv. 9-15). The Chronicler's hand is evident throughout these verses in such things as the reference to the unity of Judah and Benjamin (vv. 8-9, cf. v. 2), the statement that Yahweh was with Asa (v. 9), the emphasis on seeking Yahweh (vv. 13, 15), and the description of the occasion as one of rejoicing (vv. 14-15). The ten-to-one proportion of sheep to cattle (v. 11) also suggests artificiality. The mention of Simeon (v. 9) is unusual, since its tribal allotment was south of and in fact incorporated within Judah, whereas Ephraim and Manasseh were both north. Some scholars have proposed that the reference is actually to Tel Simonia, a site in the Jezreel valley.

The date of the assembly in the third month (v. 10) would have placed it around or at the time of "Pentecost," and the occurrences of the words for "oath" and "swearing" (*šb*^{c}, vv. 14-15) may be a wordplay on the Hebrew name of the festival, *šĕbū*^{c}*ôt,* "weeks." The covenant envisioned here is not a mutual agreement but a unilateral commitment of the people to Yahweh, as indicated by their oaths. Verses 12 and 15 are very similar to Deut 4:29 in their language about seeking Yahweh with one's whole heart; they thus highlight the Chronicler's special interest in seeking Yahweh in combination with Deuteronomy's regarding the whole of one's being (cf. Deut 6:5; Jer 29:12-13). The threat of death to anyone who does not seek Yahweh (v. 13) fits with the mandate of the exclusive worship of Yahweh in Deuteronomy and elsewhere and is also reminiscent of Persian period decrees or warnings cited in Ezra (Ezra 7:6; 10:8). The pericope ends with the confirmation of Azariah's prophecy: Yahweh is found by those who seek him, and Asa is again given peace (v. 15).

The final four verses of the chapter are borrowed by and large from 1 Kgs 15:13-15, some scholars think at a secondary level. Asa's removal of his mother from being queen mother because of her idolatry (v. 16) is a further sign of his great piety. The precise duties and function of the position of queen mother are unknown. The Chronicler has evidently added the reference to crushing the image to make Asa's demolition of it comparable to those of Moses (Exod 32:20) and Josiah (2 Kgs 23:6).

The next verse presents two tensions with material elsewhere in the Asa account. The statement that the high places were not removed seems to contradict 14:3 [Heb. 14:2], which claims that he did take away the high places. The solution may lie in the fact that 15:17 states, in contrast to its parallel in 1 Kgs 15:14, that the high places were removed from Israel. The claim in 14:3 would then be implicitly limited to Judah. The Chronicler may also be building a contrast between Asa, on the one hand, and Hezekiah and Josiah, on the other, since the reforms of the latter two do include the north. The second problem of 15:17 lies in the summary that Asa's heart was true "all his days," which seems contradicted by the next chapter. This may simply be a case of the Chronicler repeating his Kings source uncritically; it is difficult to find any other explanation. The last verse of the chapter is present only in Chronicles and accords with the chronological and theological scheme for Asa's later years.

The Chronicler "periodizes" Asa's reign by making it, from the thirty-sixth year on, a story of failure. He was compelled to do this, in a sense, by the account in his Kings source about Asa's disease at the end of his life (1 Kgs 15:23). For the Chronicler, such suffering necessitated a theological cause, which he found in the story of Asa's warfare with Baasha of Israel. Second Chronicles 16 is, in essence, an elaboration of these two data. Thus, the story of Asa's alliance in 2 Chr 16:1-6 draws from 1 Kgs 15:16-22. The speech of Hanani the prophet and Asa's reaction to it in 16:7-10 is the Chronicler's addition. Then, Asa's regnal summary in 16:11-14 is an elaborated version of 1 Kgs 15:23-24a. The entire chapter provides an antithetical counterpart to the "good" period of Asa's reign in 14:9–15:19. In each case, there is a threat of war; Asa's reaction and the results of the war are detailed; a prophet appears with a divine oracle, and Asa's reactions to it are described, followed by the resulting consequences.

The chronological data in 2 Chr 15:19–16:1 are problematic, though the problem is not internal to Chronicles but only in comparison with Kings. According to 1 Kgs 16:8 (cf. 15:33) Baasha died in Asa's twenty-sixty year, while the conflict between Asa and Baasha in 2 Chr 16 is set during Asa's thirty-sixth year. While the origin of the figures thirty-fifth (15:19), thirty-sixth (16:1), and thirty-ninth (16:12) years remains uncertain, the artificiality of the chronological scheme in Chronicles is relatively clear. As noted, the Chronicler placed Asa's misdeeds at the end of his reign in order to account for his disease as punishment. In addition, the description of the conflict in 16:1 as a single event, in contrast to 1 Kgs 15:16, which notes that there was continual warfare between Baasha and Asa, allows the Chronicler to depict Asa's reign heretofore as a time of peace in reward for his faithful response to the threat of Zerah.

Baasha's takeover of Ramah would have been a significant threat against Asa and Judah. The Chronicler's focus, however, is Asa's reaction. He uses funds from the temple treasury to bribe the Aramean, Ben-hadad, into attacking Israel (the sites mentioned in verse 4 are all in northern Israel; Abel-maim is a mistake for Abel-beth-maacah as in 1 Kgs 15:20) so that Baasha is forced to withdraw his offensive against Judah (16:1-5). This appears to be a shrewd and effective solution to Asa's problem, at least in the short term. But the Chronicler's assessment is religious rather than political. He sees this as an act of faithlessness on Asa's part, a failure to rely upon God, as he did in 14:9-11.

This failure to rely on God is the criticism leveled by Hanani's prophecy in 16:7-10 (esp. v. 8). The prophecy is framed by a bracket: the expression "at that time" in verses 7 and 10. The Chronicler has likely gotten the name of Hanani from Jehu's patronym in 1 Kgs 16:1 (cf. 2 Chr 19:2; 20:34) and has assumed that the father was a prophet, like his son. The language of the prophecy is late (cf. Japhet 1993:736), and the ideology is the Chronicler's; it is, in short, his composition. There are two consequences of Asa's unfaithfulness. First, whereas he could have conquered the Arameans, they have now escaped (16:7). This verse brings to mind a number of other passages by comparison and contrast. In addition to Asa's contrasting, faithful response in chapter 14, there was David's conquest of the Arameans in 1 Chr 19. There are also stories about other prophets with similar messages, including 1 Sam 13:13; 1 Kgs 20:35-43; and 2 Kgs 13:14-19. Finally, Isa 10:20-21; 31:1 use similar language about relying or failing to rely on Yahweh instead of foreign rulers. The second consequence is that Asa, whose reign has been peaceful for the most part, will now have wars (16:9). The first part of this verse, "for the eyes of Yahweh range throughout the entire earth," affirms God's sovereignty over human events in terms borrowed from Zech 4:10.

To make matters worse for himself, Asa responds angrily to Hanani's oracle and has the prophet thrown in prison (16:10). Again, the response is reminiscent of other prophetic stories— Ahab's response to Micaiah in 2 Chr 18:26 // 1 Kings 22:27 and Jeremiah's imprisonment, also in stocks, in Jer 20:2-3 (cf. Jer 29:26). Asa does not stop there, but is also accused of oppressing some of his own people. Before, in chapters 14–15, he united with the people and led them in reliance upon God; now he turns against them and compounds his failure to trust in Yahweh's deliverance.

With 16:11, the Chronicler turns to the concluding regnal formula for Asa. While he has been citing works composed by prophets as sources, he here mentions "the Book of the Kings of Judah and Israel" (cf. 1 Chr 9:1). The referent is unknown, but this may be the Chronicler's way of alluding to Samuel–Kings. Asa's disease of the feet (16:12) may be punishment not for turning to Aram, which has already been punished by continual warfare, but for his treatment of the prophet and the people. Just what this disease was is unclear. The term "feet" sometimes occurs in the Hebrew Bible as a euphemism for the genitals; if that is the case here Asa's affliction may have been a venereal disease. The Chronicler is less concerned with the nature of the disease than he is with the theological implications surrounding it. Even with the disease, Asa has the opportunity to trust in God, but he relies instead on human healers or "physicians" (16:12). The details of Asa's burial (v. 14) seem to imply that he was held in high regard by the people of Judah and may suggest the Chronicler's ambivalence about his reign. The spice burning seems to have been a special measure for Asa (but cf. Jer 34:5).

Theological Analysis

The primary theological lesson of Asa's reign is succinctly expressed in 2 Chr 15:2: those who seek Yahweh will be found by him, while those who forsake him will be forsaken by him. Asa's career vividly illustrates both of these principles. For most of his reign he does seek Yahweh and is rewarded with peace. But at the end of his reign, in contrast, when he forsakes Yahweh, he experiences warfare and disease. The main point of the account about Asa in Chronicles, then, seems to be to provide a paradigm for the principle of immediate retribution or reward.

Of equal importance in the Chronicler's account of Asa's reign is its illustration of what it means to seek Yahweh. To be sure, this involves keeping the law and engaging in the proper and exclusive worship of Yahweh, as indicated by Asa's reforms in 14:3-5. More to the point, however, Asa's story as a whole shows that seeking Yahweh means reliance upon him in times of crisis. Thus, in his encounter with Zerah the Cushite, he cries out to Yahweh for help. When he is attacked by Baasha, in contrast, he relies on his own cleverness and the assistance of a foreign king. Nothing is said here about cultic offenses; Asa's shortcoming is a failure to rely on God (cf. 16:12). This, in turn, leads him to resist the prophetic word and to forsake his duties as king by even oppressing his own people (16:10). The story of Asa, then, provides a powerful message for the Chronicler's readership in the postexilic period and beyond to rely not upon themselves or foreign powers but to trust in God during times of crisis and for aid against their enemies.

THE REIGN OF JEHOSHAPHAT (2 CHRONICLES 17:1–20:37)

Jehoshaphat is one of the most righteous kings of Judah in Chronicles, as also in Kings. The length of the section devoted to Jehoshaphat is an indication of his significance for the Chronicler and of the Chronicler's favorable orientation toward him. Nevertheless, it is clear that the Chronicler has some reservations about Jehoshaphat because of his association with Ahab and his heirs in the north and what the Chronicler traces as the enduring, deleterious effects of that association.

Literary Analysis

Except for the story about Micaiah in chapter 18, the account of Jehoshaphat's reign is largely unique to Chronicles. Even the excerpts at the beginning and end that derive from Kings have been changed and/or reordered, yielding an entirely new product. The unit divides into readily indentifiable units. An introduction characterizing Jehoshaphat and his reign (17:1-6) is followed by the account of his campaign to teach the law in Judah (17:7-19). The campaign thus serves to illustrate the extremely positive characterization of Jehoshaphat in verses 1-6. It also provides the rationale for descriptions of the tribute brought to him in 17:10-13a and of his army in 17:13b-19, both of which are typically tokens of divine favor in Chronicles.

The story of Micaiah and the death of Ahab in 18:1–19:3 is borrowed from Kings (1 Kgs 22), except for the prophetic rebuke in 19:1-3, which is only in Chronicles. The rest of chapter 19 describes Jehoshaphat's judicial reforms. Most of chapter 20 recounts Jehoshaphat's rebuff of an incursion of a transjordanian coalition (20:1-30). The unit concludes with a summary of Jehoshaphat's reign (20:31-37), which incorporates the incident about the wreck of his fleet of ships (30:35-37).

Exegetical Analysis

The introduction to Jehoshaphat in 17:1*a* is lifted from the concluding regnal formula for Asa in 1 Kgs 15:24*b*. The second half of the verse is ambiguous. It may be misconstrued as a reference to military preparation as in the NRSV, "[Jehoshaphat] strengthened himself against Israel." This translation is supported by the description of Jehoshaphat's fortifications, some in Ephraimite cities (v. 2). However, the rest of the account of Jehoshaphat's reign indicates anything but an adversarial relationship with Israel. In addition, the same expression occurs in reference to Solomon's accession of power in 2 Chr 1:1, where the NRSV translates "Solomon . . . established himself in his kingdom," implying consolidation of royal authority. But it is unclear what is intended here by "Israel." It can hardly be the northern kingdom, considering the recognition of Ahab as king of Israel in chapter 18.

In verse 2, the term *nĕṣîbîm* could refer either to "officers" or to "garrisons," the latter being preferable following the reference to "forces." The Chronicler does not mention any Ephraimite cities taken by Asa; the allusion here may be to cities taken by Abijah (13:19). A similar problem arises in verse 3, where the Hebrew text actually says "he walked in the earlier ways of David his father." The NRSV's omission of David's name as erroneous (probably an accidental repetition of a similar word) is appropriate. The reference must originally have been to Asa; the Chronicler divides Asa's reign into "good" and "bad" periods, but not David's.

Verses 3-4 reintroduce the theme of seeking Yahweh that was so important for Asa's reign. Indeed, there is considerable similarity between the accounts of Asa's and Jehoshaphat's reigns in Chronicles, and some scholars believe that the Chronicler patterned his account of Jehoshaphat after that of Asa. Both reigns begin with reform, military strength, and prosperity. Both kings are then condemned for making an alliance with a foreign power. Each is credited both with having removed and not removed the high places (14:2-5; 15:17; 17:6; 20:33). The attribution of great riches and honor to Jehoshaphat (v. 5) may be an ominous sign. In Chronicles, such rewards often lead to pride and thence to disobedience. The word for "tribute" in this verse is perhaps better rendered "gift." First Samuel 10:27a also reflects the practice of the people bringing a gift to their new king as a sign of their fealty. The initial verb of verse 6 means "to be high, lifted up," and with the heart as its subject typically refers to pride (cf. 26:16). Here, though, the writer specifies that Jehoshaphat's heart was lifted up "in the ways of Yahweh." Still, one cannot help being struck by the language and wondering whether Yahweh's having established (v. 5; cf. 12:1) Jehoshaphat's kingdom and endowed him with wealth was seen by the Chronicler as at least a temptation to sin. The second half of verse 6 is contradicted by 20:33, according to which Jehoshaphat did not remove the "high places."

As soon as Jehoshaphat has consolidated his reign, he undertakes in his third year a mission of instruction (vv. 7-9). Some scholars propose that this was the first year of Jehoshaphat's sole reign after he had served as coregent during the last two years of his father's life (cf. 16:12-13). The teachers he sends out are in three categories: royal officials, Levites, and priests. This unique set of instructors is surprising for the Chronicler, since such instruction seems elsewhere to be the exclusive domain of the priests (Lev 10:11; Deut 31:9-13; Jer 18:18; Ezek 7:26; Hag 2:11; Neh 8:1-8). The inclusion of officials is especially unusual and finds a parallel only in Ezra 7:25, suggesting that the image of a ruler teaching has its origin with

Ezra–Nehemiah in the Persian period. The notion of itinerant teachers is similar to that of an itinerant judge—like Samuel (1 Sam 7:16). These features indicate that this description for Jehoshaphat's reign has its origin not in history but in the author's imagination of the past. This is further indicated by the assumption that "the book of the law" (v. 9) was in existence in Jehoshaphat's day. The first historically credible mention of such a book (actually a scroll) is in the reign of King Josiah (2 Chr 35:14-15; 2 Kgs 22:8). The name Ben-hail (v. 7) is unusual and perhaps should be interpreted as the expression, "men of worth," further describing the instructors, rather than a proper name.

As we have seen for previous kings, peace, prosperity, building projects, and military strength are all signs of divine favor and blessing in Chronicles. These are the elements of the description of Jehoshaphat's reign (vv. 10-19). Verses 10-11 mention the lack of war, which is evidently due to the fear of Judah under Jehoshaphat on the part of other nations and peoples. Jehoshaphat is the first king since Solomon to receive tribute from foreign nations (v. 11; cf. 9:22-28; subsequently Uzziah [26:8] and Hezekiah [32:23a]). Following the mention of Jehoshaphat's construction projects (vv. 12-13a) the rest of this chapter is devoted to an account of his troops in Jerusalem. These are listed by tribe—Judah (vv. 14b-16) and Benjamin (vv. 17-18). The numbers are intriguing when compared with those for Asa (14:8 [Heb. 14:7]). Asa's army consists of 300,000 men from Judah and 280,000 men from Benjamin. These are the same figures for the first two divisions of Jehoshaphat's army. Then, the remaining three divisions, one from Judah and two from Benjamin, total 580,000. All of this suggests the artificiality of the numbers in these verses. However, the numbers also indicate a greater esteem on the part of the Chronicler for Jehoshaphat over Asa. Verse 16 notes that one of the commanders, Amasia, was a "volunteer." This is one of the Chronicler's favorite words, and in this context it suggests an enthusiasm for Jehoshaphat's reforms on the part of at least some of his subjects.

Second Chronicles 18:1–19:1 is the only extended narrative about the northern kingdom in Kings (1 Kgs 22) that is included by the Chronicler. At least one reason for its inclusion is the prominent role of Jehoshaphat in the story. The chronological setting of the Chronicler's version of the story is keyed to Judah (vv. 1-2) rather than to Israel as in 1 Kgs 22:1-2. The story is also included for what it says about prophecy and the relationship of Israel and Judah. The first three verses of the Chronicles version vary more substantially from their Kings source than the remainder of the story. The opening statement that Jehoshaphat had great riches and honor is similar to 17:5, and as observed there, represents at least a temptation to pride and apostasy. The marriage alliance with Ahab (v. 1b) further suggests impending judgment against Jehoshaphat because of the negative evaluations for Ahab in Chronicles and Kings (2 Chr 21:6; 2 Kgs 8:18). Chronicles depicts Jehoshaphat as the superior king both by the description of him as having great riches and honor (v. 1a) and by what appears to be Ahab's attempt to buy Jehoshaphat's help with a lavish banquet (v. 2). The negative orientation on Ahab and the joint venture he proposes is further indicated by the verb "to entice, incite, induce" (cf. 1 Chr 21:1; Deut 13:6 [Heb. 13:7]). In addition, the Chronicler has omitted 1 Kgs 22:3, which explains that Ahab sought to recover what belonged to Israel. (Ramoth-Gilead was east of the Jordan in territory claimed by both Israel and Aram.) In Chronicles, Ahab's military expedition appears as an act of sheer aggression.

Beginning with verse 4, the Chronicles account is essentially the same as that of Kings. An underlying theme of the story is the discernment of true prophecy. There are several indications that Micaiah is a true prophet. The first of these is that he stands independent of the court prophets, who apparently seek to appease the king (cf. v. 12). Another such indication is that only Micaiah appears clearly as a prophet of Yahweh (v. 6); the origin of the other 400 prophets is ambiguous. Third, Micaiah never prophesies good concerning Ahab (v. 7). Ahab's words imply a fear on his part that Micaiah's pronouncement may affect the outcome of the battle. Fourth and fifth indications of Micaiah's veracity are his affirmation to the messenger (v. 13) that he can speak only what God tells him to say and then his speaking the truth "in the name of Yahweh" (vv. 15-16). Finally, the clearest indication that Micaiah is a true prophet is the fact that his oracle comes true; Ahab does not return but dies in his chariot (vv. 27-34). This final point is clearer in Chronicles than in Kings, where Ahab actually does return to Samaria, albeit dead.

The story is well told and contains several indications of literary crafting. The mention of the kings' robes (v. 9) seems superfluous on first read, but alludes to the role that the robes will play in the story. Ahab's disguise through a change of robes (v. 29) suggests that he believes Micaiah's word enough to take precautions against it. While he fools the Arameans (v. 31), he cannot fool God. The arrow shot "at a venture" (NRSV: "unknowingly") that strikes Ahab (v. 33) is surely to be perceived as guided by Yahweh. The message is clear: Ahab cannot escape the prophetically mediated divine word. As noted, in Chronicles Ahab does not return to Samaria. The expression "return in peace" is a motif that highlights the conflict between Ahab and Micaiah and displays the veracity of the prophetic word: Ahab orders his servants to imprison Micaiah until he (Ahab) returns in peace (v. 26); Micaiah replies that if Ahab does return in peace Yahweh has spoken through him (v. 27). Ahab's failure to return shows Micaiah's genuineness as Yahweh's spokesman. Jehoshaphat, in contrast, does return in peace (19:1).

It is not clear exactly what it is about Micaiah's words that alerts Ahab to the fact that he is not speaking the truth. Perhaps it is simply that Micaiah does not preface his words with "thus says Yahweh." It is intriguing in this regard that the Chronicles version uses the passive, "they will be given" rather than "Yahweh will give," perhaps to disassociate Yahweh's name from the false oracle. Micaiah also uses plural verbs in Chronicles, thus speaking to both kings and not just to Ahab as in Kings. Micaiah's genuine oracle (v. 16) makes use of a common metaphor; the absence of a shepherd for the sheep of Israel means that the king is dead.

Micaiah's vision (vv. 18-22) draws upon the ideology of a prophet as a messenger. Just as messengers were sent out from the king and his advisors, so prophets were envisioned as standing in the presence of Yahweh and the divine council (cf. Isa 6; Jer 23:18-22). The other prophets at court were not privy to that council but have been deceived by a "lying spirit" from Yahweh. This is apparently the same "Spirit of Yahweh" mentioned by Zedekiah (v. 23); he thus claims that the lying spirit moved from him to Micaiah to inspire the latter's oracle. Micaiah's response (v. 24) contains a pun: the expression *hinněkā rō'eh* can mean both "you [shall] see" and "you are a seer." Micaiah's concluding admonition, "Hear, all you peoples" (v. 27b) is generally recognized as a gloss drawn from Mic 1:2 that is intended to identify the two prophets.

Perhaps the most significant change introduced by the Chronicler is in verse 31. In 1 Kgs 22:32-33, it is clear that Jehoshaphat cries out in panic and that the Arameans discern from his cry (his accent?) that he is not the king of Israel. The Chronicler has interpreted Jehoshaphat's cry as a sign of piety. He "cries out" for help to Yahweh, who then turns away the attackers (reading with the Greek text). The episode thus illustrates one of the Chronicler's principal doctrines: Yahweh helps those who call upon him (cf. 20:9b; 32:30-21).

This story, then further contributes to the Chronicler's ambivalent view of Jehoshaphat. On the one hand, Jehoshaphat asks for a true prophet of Yahweh to inquire about the wisdom of attacking Ramoth-Gilead, and he cries out faithfully to Yahweh in time of crisis. On the other hand, he makes an alliance with the wicked king of Israel and seems to ignore the warning of the one true prophet, choosing to go ahead and accompany Ahab to Ramoth. The ambivalence continues in 19:1-3. On the way back to Jerusalem, Jehoshaphat is met by another prophet, Jehu son of Hanani, who condemns him for helping Yahweh's enemies. Jehu threatens punishment but then appears to retract the threat because of Jehoshaphat's good deeds of destroying the Arameans and seeking Yahweh. The word "love" in the expression "you love those who hate Yahweh" connotes political alignment. The expressions "set the heart" and "seek Yahweh" (v. 3) are favorites of the Chronicler, indicating that the oracle, and indeed, the entire scene, is his composition. He has taken the prophet Jehu from 1 Kgs 16:1. His patronymic, "son of Hanani," recalls the encounter of Asa and Hanani in 16:7-10. The present passage attributes no reaction of Jehoshaphat to the prophetic oracle. But this in itself contrasts with Asa's angry maltreatment of Jehu's father.

The rest of chapter 19 describes Jehoshaphat's legal reforms, particularly his appointment of judges first in the cities (vv. 5-7) and then in Jerusalem (vv. 8-11). In each instance, the appointment is followed by a speech by Jehoshaphat. The entire episode might be regarded as an extended play on the meaning of Jehoshaphat's name, "Yahweh judges." Jehoshaphat might also be seen as renewing or reinvigorating the system put in place by David (esp. 1 Chr 26:29-32) or, perhaps better, by Moses (Deut 16:18-20; 17:8-13). Jehoshaphat's speeches attest the influence of Deuteronomy's rhetoric. There is considerable agreement among scholars that this passage is the Chronicler's composition. Therefore, many would consider the events it describes to be his invention. Others, however, continue to assert the possibility that the account is based on a genuine historical source of some kind.

The remarkable picture in verse 4 is that of Jehoshaphat going personally among the people, restoring them to God. He then appoints judges (v. 5), presumably to keep the people in line. No distinction is made in this instance between secular and sacred matters; the judges are to remember that in all cases they judge for Yahweh (v. 6). The situation is different in Jerusalem, where a distinction is drawn between "matters of Yahweh" and "matters of the king" (v. 11). The precise nature of this division is not made clear. It may not have been between "religious" and "secular" as it is conceived in modern society, but between cultic and noncultic, with the latter category including matters that modern people would consider religious. The judges in Jerusalem serve as a kind of supreme court to handle disputed cases from the outlying cities (vv. 8-10). The office of a chief priest, particularly as the highest legal authority, arises in the postexilic period. The designation of the Levites as "officers" is unique to Chronicles (1 Chr 23:4; 26:29; 2 Chr 34:13) and is one indication that this passage originated with the Chronicler. Another such indication is the repeated motif of "doing" in the fear of Yahweh, faithfulness, and with a whole heart (vv. 9-10). This language is reminiscent of Deuteronomy's rhetoric (Deut 17:8-13), and the warning function of the judges is similar to that of Ezekiel as a watchman (Ezek 3:16-21).

The final chapter dealing with Jehoshaphat contains another battle account (20:1-30) followed by the conclusion for Jehoshaphat's reign (vv. 31-37). The battle account furnishes a contrast to the story in chapter 18 in several respects. In chapter 18, Jehoshaphat forms an alliance with a foreign power (Israel) for an unprovoked attack on Ramoth-Gilead, while in the present story Jehoshaphat is in a defensive posture and relies on God for help. Thus, while he is scolded for his impropriety in chapter 18, here he is a model of pious behavior. The episode consists of several parts: the invasion (vv. 1-4), Jehoshaphat's prayer (vv. 5-12), Jahaziel's oracle (vv. 13-19), and the battle (vv. 20-30).

The MT of verse 1 describes the invaders as Moabites,

Ammonites, and "some of the Ammonites." The reading reflects an error of transposition of consonants and is typically corrected on the basis of the LXX to "some of the Meunites." The Meunites, from Ma'an, twelve miles southeast of Petra, are mentioned elsewhere in 1 Chr 4:41; 2 Chr 26:7. In this light, the MT reading in verse 2 should probably also be emended from "from Aram" to "from Edom" as in the NRSV. This verse refers to the invaders as "a great multitude," thus conjuring up the image of a massive hoard. Their numbers as well as the fact that they are already at En-gedi, and therefore fast approaching Jerusalem, strike fear in Jehoshaphat's heart. His reaction is exemplary; he seeks Yahweh (v. 3). Then the people, following his lead, also gather in Jerusalem to seek Yahweh (v. 4).

Jehoshaphat's prayer (vv. 5-12) consists of two parts: a confession of Yahweh's universal rule (vv. 6-9) as the basis for a cry for help from present distress (vv. 10-12). Both parts contain rhetorical questions that anticipate an affirmative answer, leading the reader to expect a positive response to Jehoshaphat's petition for help. The title, "Yahweh, God of our ancestors" (v. 6), is a favorite of the Chronicler's (1 Chr 12:17; 2 Chr 11:16; 13:18; 14:4). The mention of "the descendants of your friend Abraham" (v. 7) is similar to Isa 41:8, and the reference to driving out the inhabitants of the land recalls statements in Deuteronomy (1:8, 21; 4:1, 5, 21-22). Verse 8 moves to the building of the temple, and verse 9 is a loose paraphrase of Solomon's prayer at its dedication. Jehoshaphat is acting out just what Solomon envisioned—standing before the temple in time of crisis and calling on God for salvation. Verses 10-11 recall Deut 2:2-8 and represent a kind of reversal of that episode. Theologically, these verses make a powerful statement. By jeopardizing Israel's existence in the land given to it by Yahweh, the invaders threaten to reverse Yahweh's divine plan and challenge his universal sovereignty. A paradox present in the Chronicler's treatment of righteous kings surfaces in verse 12: a large army is a sign of Yahweh's blessing over a righteous king, yet the king is to rely upon God rather than his army in warfare.

Jahaziel's oracle (vv. 13-17) offers the divine response to Jehoshaphat's prayer. Jahaziel is a Levitical singer (v. 14), not a prophet, so that the delivery of the oracle is a one-time or at least a first-time experience for him. The places named in verses 15-17 have not been located. Jeruel means "God sees" and puns on the roots for "see" *(r'h)* and "fear" *(yr')* used in this context ("do not fear" in vv. 15, 17 and "see the victory of Yahweh" in v. 17). It may also allude, at least in sense, to Gen 22:14. The word "see" in the sense of "provide" stresses God's miraculous intervention, which is also brought into relief by the similarity of verse 17 to Moses' words at the sea in Exod 14:13-14. The response of Jehoshaphat and his people (vv. 18-19) is one of complete trust. They believe the prophetic word without question and begin praising God before the battle is even waged.

Jehoshaphat's exhortation to his army at the start of the battle (v. 20) is most unusual. It does not attempt to inspire courage or valor but encourages belief in Yahweh as the path to victory. It is, in effect, a positive version of Isa 7:9, reflecting the Chronicler's anthological style and his vocabulary (e.g., "Hear me" and "success," which NRSV misleadingly translates "be established"). Jehoshaphat also commends belief in Yahweh's prophets, which is an important theme in Chronicles. Praise follows (v. 21) using one of the Chronicler's favorite liturgical refrains, "Give thanks to Yahweh, for his steadfast love endures forever."

The actual battle account in (vv. 22-23) is brief and quite vague. As the singing starts, Yahweh sets an ambush against the invaders. The nature of the "ambush" is not specified. Some interpreters suggest that a supernatural ambush of some kind is intended, but this is not explicit in the text. The ultimate result is certainly miraculous: the entire enemy army self-destructs. The episode recalls several other biblical stories, among them the fall of Jericho at the sound of trumpets and shouting (Josh 6) and the deliverance of Samaria in 2 Kgs 6:24–7:20. There is more space devoted to the account of taking spoil (vv. 24-26) than to that of the battle itself. The Valley of Berakah ("blessing") in verse 26 is a transparent etiology. Here "blessing" has the nuance of praise, since "they blessed Yahweh." It might just as easily have recalled Yahweh's blessing in the defeat of the invading force. The last two verses of the battle narrative (vv. 29-30) are similar to 17:10 in referring to "the fear of God/ Yahweh upon all the kingdoms of the lands/countries" leading to peace. The two texts form a kind of bracket on either side of the account of Jehoshaphat's reign. The language about God giving Jehoshaphat rest round about is reminiscent of the description of Solomon's reign in 1 Chr 22:9 and of David's in 2 Sam 7:1.

The conclusion of Jehoshaphat's reign (vv. 31-37) is borrowed from 1 Kgs 22:41-49 but with some significant changes. The Chronicler emphasizes the spiritual nature of the people's sin at the high places (v. 33). Rather than detailing the ritual activities that took place there, he observes that they had not yet "set their hearts upon the God of their ancestors." Both expressions—"set the heart" and "God of the ancestors"—are favorites of the Chronicler. The verse is contradicted by 17:6, which states that Jehoshaphat did remove the high places. In verse 34, Chronicles cites a different source for information about Jehoshaphat's reign than that cited in 1 Kgs 22:45. As for previous kings, the Chronicler refers the reader to the work of a prophet active during the king's reign, in this case Jehu son of Hanani. Scholars are generally skeptical that such works ever existed. Jehu's work is said here to have been recorded or "taken up" into the "Book of the Kings of Israel." Comparable to what we have seen previously, this may be the Chronicler's way of referring to Judah as faithful or true Israel.

The Chronicler ends his account of Jehoshaphat's reign by attaching the episode in verses 35-37, which once more displays his ambivalence toward the king. The episode owes its origin to 1 Kgs 22:48-49, but the Chronicler has completely altered it so that it now says precisely the opposite. In Kings, Jehoshaphat's initial expedition ends in disaster, and when he is approached by Ahaziah to enter into a joint venture of the same kind he refuses. In Chronicles, it is a joint venture from the beginning. Indeed, this provides the theological reason for its failure: Ahaziah king of Israel "did wickedly" (v. 35), so that joining with him invokes prophetic condemnation and the failure of the mission (v. 37). The prophet Eliezer son of Dodavahu is otherwise unknown, though 2 Sam 23:9 names Eliezer son of Dodo as one of three greatest warriors. As in 2 Chr 9:21 (// 1 Kgs 10:22) with regard to Solomon, the Chronicler understands Tarshish not as a type or style of ship but as their destination. More significant, in the Chronicler's portrayal, for all of his virtues Jehoshaphat ultimately falls short of living up to Solomon's model.

Theological Analysis

The account of Jehoshaphat's reign is theologically remarkable in several respects. The beginning of his reign illustrates the principle of reward that is so important to the Chronicler. Jehoshaphat has riches and honor and a firm hold on the kingdom because he followed the earlier, righteous ways of his father and removed the trappings of worship of other gods (17:1-6). Jehoshaphat also understood the importance of having his subjects well versed in the law of God, so he saw to it that they were taught (17:7-9). At least partly as a result, he had peace because the surrounding peoples feared him and his God (17:10).

The battle narratives set in Jehoshaphat's reign bring out two primary theological lessons: the danger of foreign alliances and the importance of reliance upon God. Despite his wealth and honor (18:1), the two ventures that Jehoshaphat undertakes in tandem with Israel, the expeditions to Ramoth-Gilead and to

Tarshish, result in disaster. Jehu the prophet accuses him of helping the wicked and loving those who hate Yahweh (19:2). The Chronicler thus casts Jehoshaphat as an object lesson of the danger of affiliating with wicked people. The fact that Jehoshaphat does not receive immediate punishment for his alliance with Ahab does not counter the Chronicler's principle of retribution. Punishment is not forthcoming because of Jehoshaphat's previous righteous deeds and desire to seek God (19:3). The story as a whole, therefore, demonstrates the fairness of God's judgments as well as the beneficial efficacy of righteous deeds. In addition, in this instance, as well as in the later case (20:37) when Jehoshaphat is condemned by Eliezer for another joint venture with an Israelite king, he apparently accepts prophetic rebuke with the right attitude of contrition and, unlike his father (16:10), does not lash out at its bearer.

Perhaps above all, Jehoshaphat exemplifies the right attitude and action in time of crisis. The two times that Jehoshaphat finds himself in military jeopardy, at Ramoth-Gilead (ch. 18) and then facing the coalition of invaders from Transjordan (ch. 20), he responds faithfully by calling upon Yahweh for help. In each case, his trust brings him deliverance. In the second instance, the victory is entirely the work of God. These stories surely contain a message for the Chronicler's contemporaries, as well as later readers—that they should place their trust in God, not in foreign powers.

As a whole, the Chronicler's assessment of Jehoshaphat is extremely positive. But the final episode of his reign, the story of the failed shipbuilding venture with Ahaziah of Israel bodes ill for Judah's future. The full impact of Jehoshaphat's error will only emerge in the days of his successors, so we will explore it in the following unit. It is worth mention at this point that Jehoshaphat serves as an example in Chronicles of the disastrous results that bad choices can have for future generations, even when those choices are made by generally righteous persons.

THE REIGNS OF JEHORAM, AHAZIAH, AND ATHALIAH (2 CHRONICLES 21:1–23:21)

The reigns of Jehoram, Ahaziah, and Athaliah are best understood as a single story in Chronicles that traces the negative results of Jehoshaphat's alliance with Ahab. All three monarchs are related to Ahab, king of Israel, and all three follow his (and Jezebel's) apostate ways. As a result, they lead Judah into idolatry and decline, ultimately endangering the Davidic line. All three die ignominiously and are not buried with their royal predecessors—a sign of the Chronicler's low esteem for them. An additional indication of the Chronicler's contempt for them is that he records no source citations for their reigns, in effect denying them any memorial. The problems caused by these three rulers account for the Chronicler's strong sense of ambiguity in his depiction of Jehoshaphat, who initiated the alliance with Israel that produced Jehoram, Ahaziah, and Athaliah.

Literary Analysis

Chapter 21 recounts Jehoram's reign, 22:1-9 the brief reign of Ahaziah, and 22:10–23:21 the reign of Athaliah, focusing on the revolt against her. As usual, the narratives in Kings provide the basis for the Chronicler's accounts. He supplements and alters his Kings source in typical fashion, except for the story of Jehu's revolt (2 Kgs 9–10), which the Chronicler radically abbreviates in a somewhat unusual and creative way.

Exegetical Analysis

The reign of Jehoram (2 Chr 21:1-20)

The account of Jehoram's reign in chapter 21 may be divided into the following segments: Jehoram's accession and evaluation (vv. 1-7), the rebellion of Edom and Libnah (vv. 8-10), Jehoram's other sins (v. 11), Elijah's letter (vv. 12-15), the invasion of the Philistines and Arabs (vv. 16-17), and Jehoram's disease, death, and burial (vv. 18-20). The order of these segments thus illustrates the Chronicler's most basic theological scheme—sin-punishment-sin-warning-punishment. Verses 5-10 are borrowed from 2 Kgs 8:17-22, albeit with significant changes. The Chronicler added verses 11-19 to them and then framed the entire account by repeating verse 5 in verse 20.

The first verse of the chapter (// 2 Kgs 22:50) serves the dual linking function of concluding Jehoshaphat's reign and introducing Jehoram's. The numerous sons of Jehoshaphat (v. 2) are a sign of divine blessing as for other kings (11:18-22; 13:21; cf. 1 Chr 25:5). It is unclear whether these are all of Jehoshaphat's sons or the firstborns of different wives in the harem (cf. 2 Sam 3:2-5). The latter possibility would account for the occurrence in the list of two sons with the same name, Azariah (although in Hebrew the name occurs in two slightly different forms: Azariah and Azariahu). Jehoshaphat is referred to in this verse as the king of Israel. This may simply be the result of a textual error, since several manuscripts and the versions (LXX, Syriac, Vulgate) have "Judah." However, the reading "Israel" fits the Chronicler's view that Judah is true Israel.

Like Rehoboam (11:22-23), Jehoshaphat disperses his sons among the fortified towns of Judah, perhaps to prevent feuding for the throne. Only in this instance the stratagem does not work. Jehoram murders his brothers in order to ensure his hold on kingship (21:4). The language here is unusual and probably does not mean, as translated in the NRSV that Jehoram "ascended the throne of his father." The expression *qûm ᶜal* typically means "arise against." Hence, Jehoram led an "uprising" against his father's, and in a sense his own, kingdom. His actions are reminiscent of those of the series of heads of royal houses in Israel, who annihilate the males of the previous house in order to secure power (1 Kgs 15:29; 16:11-12; 2 Kgs 9-10). It is one of several ways in which Jehoram takes on the characteristics of his northern counterparts. Verse 4 notes that he also killed some of the princes of Israel. It is unclear whether by

"Israel" the Chronicler means the northern kingdom, in which case Jehoshaphat's harmful affiliation with Israel is reinforced, or Judah, in which case the Chronicler again emphasizes Judah as the faithful core of the whole nation. The ambiguity may, in fact, be deliberate.

With verse 5 the Chronicler finally gives the standard accession formula for Jehoram. Having made it clear already that Jehoram was evil, the Chronicler explains the reason for it in verse 6: Jehoram was married to Ahab's daughter and was thus swayed by their evil influence. This is the third and most detrimental affiliation (besides the battle at Ramoth-Gilead and the ships of Tarshish) made by Jehoshaphat with Israel. The problems described in the rest of this and the next two chapters owe their origin to this relationship established by Jehoshaphat. The Chronicler's main point in these chapters is found in the next verse. All of Jehoram's evil cannot negate Yahweh's promise to David. While 2 Kgs 8:19 states that Yahweh would not destroy Judah, the Chronicler has the statement read that Yahweh would not destroy the house of David. He then adds, "because of the covenant that he had made to David" (2 Chr 21:7). The Chronicler understands the covenant with David as a unilateral promise from Yahweh, and his narrative in chapters 21–23 illustrates the effectiveness of that promise and Yahweh's faithfulness to it despite the threats to it posed by the events in these chapters. The term translated "lamp" is better rendered "fiefdom, domain" (Hanson 1968 and Ben-Zvi 1991); the allusion is not only to 1 Chr 17 // 2 Sam 7 but also to 1 Kgs 11:36.

The account of the revolts of Edom and Libnah (vv. 8-10) is borrowed from 2 Kgs 8:20-22. But the Chronicler furnishes a theological explanation (v. 10b) for what is essentially a historical report in Kings: the success of these revolts was retribution for Jehoram's having abandoned Yahweh. Edom's success against Jehoram contrasts with its failed attempt against Jehoshaphat (20:2, 10), a contrast that reflects their respective religious postures. Verse 9 presents some special difficulties.

The parallel in 2 Kgs 8:21 says that J[eh]oram crossed over to Zair, for which Chronicles has "with his commanders." The two variants suggest that the original reading was "to Seir," although it has been suggested that the Chronicles reading was motivated by the desire to implicate the people and royal officials along with Jehoram in his sin.

Another corruption in the Kings text has caused a tension in both versions. If Jehoram "smote [NRSV: "attacked"] the Edomites" why did his army flee to their tents and why did Edom's revolt succeed? A letter has evidently been lost from the verse in Kings, so that the present reading, "he smote Edom" *(wyk 't-'dwm)* originally said exactly the opposite: "Edom smote him" *(wyk'tw 'dwm)*. The version of Kings used by the Chronicler contained the corruption. He sought to remedy the tension it caused by omitting the statement that Jehoram's army "fled to their tents" (NRSV: "fled home"). In his understanding Jehoram and his commanders escaped on this occasion when they were surrounded but were unable to prevent Edom's revolt. The Edomites, or their heirs, the Idumeans, were especially troublesome to the people living in Judah after the exile, so that this episode may have been of particular importance to the Chronicler and his contemporaries.

Libnah was a city-state in southwestern Judah that originally belonged to the Canaanites and was conquered by Joshua (Josh 10:29-30; 12:15). It was then apportioned by Joshua to Judah (Josh 15:42) and was designated a Levitical city (Josh 21:13; cf. 1 Chr 6:57 [Heb. 6:42]). The story of its revolt suggests that it was never fully incorporated within Israel/Judah.

Jehoram's further sinful deeds contrast with those of Asa and Jehoshaphat, both of whom are credited with removing the high places (14:2-5; 17:6). Even if there is some ambiguity about this (15:17; 20:33) at least they did not build them as did Jehoram. Furthermore, while Jehoshaphat brought the people back to Yahweh (19:4), Jehoram "led the inhabitants of Jerusalem into unfaithfulness and made Judah go astray" (21:11).

The basic meaning of the first verb is "commit harlotry," a common image for the worship of other gods in the Old Testament. The second verb means to push or thrust and is common in Deuteronomy for driving into apostasy.

The letter from Elijah (vv. 12-15) is fascinating in several respects. On the one hand, it fits the Chronicler's practice of relating a prophetic warning following a king's sin. Elijah was the ideal figure to provide such a warning, since he appears in Kings as a great prophet and the unflagging nemesis of Ahab and Jezebel and of Baalism. The Chronicler, therefore, obviously assumes the familiarity of his audience with the Elijah stories in Kings. It is not altogether clear in Kings that Elijah's career overlapped with Jehoram's reign. Elijah's ascension (2 Kgs 2:9-12a) is actually reported before Jehoram's accession (1 Kgs 8:16-19). But since it follows the conclusion of Jehoshaphat's reign (1 Kgs 22:45-46) the assumption of an overlap is reasonable. It is also unclear why the Chronicler chose a letter as the medium for the prophetic warning. This is unique in Chronicles, and while this medium was at home in the postexilic period, it would have been most unlikely in the ninth century. Of course, an anachronism of this sort was unimportant to the Chronicler, whose real concern was the letter's message. The letter is undoubtedly the Chronicler's composition. Its rhetoric is his, and its content matches perfectly with the narratives that precede and follow it. The letter highlights the antithesis already established between Israel and Judah, the house of David and the house of Ahab. Thus, "Yahweh, the God of your father David" condemns Jehoram for failing to walk in the ways of his father, Jehoshaphat, or his grandfather, Asa (v. 12). Instead, he has followed the unfaithful ways of the kings of Israel, especially Ahab, thereby betraying his own family in favor of that of Ahab, even to the extent of murdering his own brothers (v. 13). Jehoram's punishment, therefore, is appropriate to his crimes, as his own family (following Japhet's 1993:814 proposed translation of ʿam, "people") will suffer "a great plague" (v. 14). The punishment is twofold—a blow to Jehoram's near family members and possessions, and then to his person (v. 15).

The fulfillment of the threatened punishments as narrated in the remainder of the chapter follows the sequence of the threat. The "great plague" that resulted in the loss of Jehoram's family and property came in the form of an invasion of Philistines and Arabs (vv. 16-17). These invaders provide yet another contrast between Jehoram and his immediate predecessors. The Philistines and Arabs brought tribute to Jehoshaphat (17:11), and the mention of the Cushites (v. 16) recalls Asa's success against them in 14:13. The narrative paints a picture of this invasion that is strikingly improbable. The raiders are able to target the king's family specifically, apparently without much resistance. The only survivor is Jehoram's youngest son, here called Jehoahaz (a variant of Ahaziah). Some scholars suggest that the different name reflects a distinct source used by the Chronicler for this excerpt, though they also admit that such a source probably told of an isolated raid and that it has been drastically revised by the Chronicler. This episode explains why Jehoram was succeeded by his youngest son (22:1). The fact that a son of Jehoram's survived at all reinforces the main message of these chapters—Yahweh's faithfulness to his promise of a continuing Davidic line.

In verse 18 the Chronicler turns to the punishment inflicted on Jehoram's own body. As prophesied (v. 16), so verse 19 reports that Jehoram's bowels came out "day by day" or "gradually" (NRSV: "in the course of time"). However, the current reading of the verse that this happened over the course of two days contradicts the idea of a protracted illness. The usual solution to this problem is to understand "days" as actually meaning years. But while the indefinite sense of "day" or "days" is well attested, there is no precedent for the word meaning "years," especially when modified by a number. It may be that the word "years" was a gloss on the expression for "days" used indefinitely, and that the former came into the text and was revocalized as "two." In any case, the point of the verse is clear; it happened to Jehoram exactly as foretold by Elijah. The remaining statements (vv. 19-20)—that the people made no fire in Jehoram's honor, that he departed to no one's regret, and that he was not buried in the tombs of the kings—along with the absence of any source citation, are all indications of the contempt of the Chronicler for Jehoram because of his wickedness.

The Reign of Ahaziah (2 Chr 22:1-9)

Like 21:1, 22:1 serves to link the accounts of Jehoram and Ahaziah by concluding the former and introducing the latter. Ahaziah is crowned by default, because all of Jehoram's other sons were slain by raiders as retribution for his sins (21:16-17). The precise identity of the "inhabitants of Jerusalem" who made Ahaziah king is uncertain. Perhaps they were the landed nobles known elsewhere as the "people of the land." The number given in verse 2 as Ahaziah's age at his accession (forty-two) is widely recognized as an error for twenty-two (2 Kgs 8:26), since his father died at age forty (21:20).

Verses 3-5 again point out the disastrous results of Jehoshaphat's affiliation with Ahab. His mother was Athaliah, the daughter of Ahab, according to 21:6. In 22:2 she is called the "daughter of Omri." But like the word for "son" in Hebrew, "daughter" can be used to mean "descendant," so that the NRSV translation, "granddaughter," is a likely interpretation. Both Ahaziah's evil ways and the brevity of his reign ("his ruin," v. 4) are blamed on the bad counsel he received from his mother and the counselors of Ahab. The root "counsel, advise" occurs three times in verses 3-5 in material that has been interspersed by the Chronicler into his Kings source. It was the bad counsel of Ahab's advisors that induced Ahaziah to repeat Jehoshaphat's mistake of accompanying his northern counterpart to Ramoth-Gilead for war.

Verses 6-9 then describe the consequences of following that

counsel. These verses condense the story of Jehu's revolt in 2 Kgs 9–10, albeit with revision and reordering. The main difference, of course, is that the Kings narrative is primarily concerned with the revolt and its effects for Israel, while Chronicles focuses on Ahaziah's death and the resulting crisis for Judah. Other, specific differences concern: (1) the sequence of events, in other words, whether Ahaziah is killed before the officials of Judah as in Kings or after them as in Chronicles; (2) the place of Ahaziah's death (compare 2 Kgs 9:27 with 2 Chr 22:9); and (3) the place of Ahaziah's burial—in Jerusalem (2 Kgs 9:28) or at the site of his execution (2 Chr 22:9). None of these differences is insurmountable, and it may be best to understand the Chronicles version as a theological elaboration of the story in Kings, with which the Chronicler assumed his audience was familiar (so Williamson 1982:312).

Verse 7 begins with the observation that Ahaziah's visit to Jezreel was brought about by Yahweh. The word translated as "downfall" in the NRSV is a unique term in the Old Testament that probably means "trampling." A similar word meaning "turn of affairs" should probably be read instead (cf. 2 Chr 10:15). The Hebrew text identifies Ahaziah's visit as the "turn of affairs" rather than the occasion for it as in the NRSV rendering. The point is that the fact that Ahaziah's visit "coincided" with Jehu's revolt was Yahweh's doing. Verse 7 goes on to say that Yahweh had anointed Jehu to destroy the house of Ahab, implying by the subsequent story that Ahaziah was a member of that house. Verse 8 abbreviates 2 Kgs 10:13-14 with one significant change. Chronicles refers to the "sons of Ahaziah's brothers" rather than to his brothers, because according to 2 Chr 21:16-17 all of Ahaziah's brothers had been killed by raiders.

Verse 9 differs more significantly from the story in Kings. This is because in Chronicles Ahaziah's death is the climax and main point of the story and not the by-product that it is in 2 Kgs 9:27-28. As a result, there are differences in details. In

Kings, Jehu encounters Ahaziah in the field outside of Jezreel and assassinates him. In Chronicles, Ahaziah hides in Samaria—perhaps the Chronicler's attempt to portray him as a coward. Jehu has him sought out and brought back for execution. Ironically, it is only his lineage from Jehoshaphat that affords him burial. As with his father, the fact that he is not buried in the royal tombs of Judah and that there is no citation notice for him are indications of disrespect.

The Reign of Athaliah (2 Chr 22:10–23:21)

A power vacuum followed Ahaziah's demise (22:9b), and his mother Athaliah stepped in to fill it (22:10-12). Neither Kings nor Chronicles gives an accession formula for Athaliah because, as a woman and a nonmember of the Davidic line, she is considered illegitimate. Nor are any details about her seven-year reign offered, for the same reason. The final three verses of chapter 22 tell the tale of two women; Athaliah sets out to destroy the Davidic line, while Jehoshabeath rescues it. The tale of two women is also a tale of two houses. The house of David faces extinction at the hands of Athaliah, who, following Jehu's purge, is the last ruler of the house of Ahab. The heroine, Jehoshabeath, represents both the Davidic line and the priesthood because of her relationships. She is Jehoram's daughter (presumably through a wife other than Athaliah) and Ahaziah's (half-?)sister. Her name resembles that of Jehoshaphat, the last righteous king of Judah. She is also the wife of Jehoiada the priest. Thus, she has commitments to both dynasty and temple, and she uses the latter to protect the former, embodied in the baby Joash.

Chapter 23 details the overthrow of Athaliah and her replacement with Joash. It can be outlined as follows: Jehoiada's preparations for revolt (vv. 1-7), the crowning of Joash (vv. 8-11), the assassination of Athaliah (vv. 12-15), covenant and reform (vv. 16-21). The narrative begins with Jehoiada "strengthening himself" (NRSV: "took courage").

The same verb is used of Solomon establishing his kingdom (2 Chr 1:1) and of Jehoshaphat making military preparations against Israel (17:1). He then brings the commanders whose names follow into a covenant (NRSV: "compact"). The word "covenant" here *(bryt)* may be an error for "house" *(byt)*, the text originally relating that Jehoiada gathered these commanders to the temple. If "covenant" is the correct reading, it is a separate covenant from the one in verse 3 between the people and the king.

The commanders could all enter the temple, because they were all apparently priests and Levites. The names in verse 1 all occur in other lists of priests and Levites in Chronicles (Kalimi 1995:71-72). It is, therefore, unlikely that this list is a genuine artifact from Athaliah's reign. The function of these commanders is to circulate among the towns of Judah and to gather the Levites and heads of families to come to Jerusalem (v. 2). Thus, what is essentially a military coup led by the Carites or royal bodyguard in Kings involves "all Israel" in Chronicles (v. 3, compare David's enthronement in 1 Chr 11:1). That this is an ideological change rather than one based on variant historical information is clear from the unrealistic picture that emerges in verses 3-7. Such a large group of people assembled in Jerusalem and making a public covenant could hardly have escaped Athaliah's notice. Indeed, the assembly (v. 3) seems unnecessary and preemptive of the revolt that follows. In this same verse, there is a second covenant (assuming the mention of a covenant in v. 1). But unlike the covenant in verse 1, which has a counterpart in 2 Kgs 11:4, this one is not just with the guards but between "all the assembly" and the king. As mentioned, it thus preempts and renders superfluous the covenant in 2 Chr 23:16. There has not been a covenant between the king and the people since David, yet suddenly with Joash there are two. The presentation of Joash in verse 3 is also awkward. In 2 Kgs 11:4, Jehoiada shows the king to the conspiring commanders. But since the Chronicler replaces this gathering with an assembly of

Levites and leaders from all Israel, Jehoiada's announcement, "Behold the king's son," is premature because Joash is not brought out until verse 11. Joash's right to the throne, as articulated by Jehoiada in verse 3 ("Let him reign as Yahweh promised concerning the sons of David"), is grounded in the Davidic promise, which the Chronicler evidently still sees as effective and a source of hope in his postexilic setting.

In verses 4-7, the Chronicles version obscures what is a relatively clear process in Kings. In 2 Kgs 11:5-9, Jehoiada tells the one-third of the guard going off duty on the Sabbath to guard the palace and the two-thirds coming on duty to guard the king, killing anyone who approaches them. Thus, the maximum number of troops are deployed at a time and place where Athaliah, who is not a worshiper of Yahweh, is not present. Chronicles confuses this plan because of theological considerations. It assumes that the guards are Levites, since they alone can enter the temple, and changes Jehoiada's instructions to command that anyone who enters the temple, rather than anyone who approaches the troops surrounding the king, should be killed (vv. 6-7). The Chronicler's Jehoiada also seems to give orders concerning the liturgical duties of the Levites (vv. 4-5) in the midst of laying out the plans for the revolt. The theological agenda is obviously more important to the Chronicler than the historical details.

Verse 8 reports that "the Levites and all Judah" (as opposed to "the captains" in 2 Kgs 11:9) followed Jehoiada's instructions. Verse 9 has Jehoiada distribute spears and shields that had belonged to David. While 2 Kgs 11:10 mentions only spears and ("small") shields, Chronicles has "large" shields between these two. This Chronicler likely includes the latter as an allusion to the articles donated by Rehoboam as replacements for Solomon's gifts (2 Chr 12:9-10). He places this item between the other two, because according to 1 Chr 18:7 it was only the "small" shields that came from David. Whatever their origin, all of these items are votive offerings to Yahweh; their use was ritual rather than military, as Lev 27:28 forbids the use of such devoted items. Hence, their mention does not contradict the previous statement (v. 7) that the Levitical guards were already armed. The shields of David also have a symbolic function in Chronicles to the extent that they represent David's protection of his heirs.

In verse 10, it is "all the people," not just the guards as in 2 Kgs 11:11, who guard the king. This fits the Chronicler's portrait of the coronation as involving all Israel. The ʿēdût ("covenant" in NRSV, "testimony" in RSV) is probably best understood as a reference to the Ten Commandments (Exod 25:16, 21; cf. Exod 16:34; 25:22; 26:34; 31:18; 32:15; 34:29; 2 Chr 24:6; Pss 19:8; 78:5; 119:14; 132:12; Isa 8:16, 20), perhaps as representing the law that the king was to copy and read daily according to Deut 17:18-20. The Chronicler makes the subject of the plural verbs in his source (2 Kgs 11:12) explicit—it was Jehoiada and his sons who anointed Joash king—thus making clear the religious foundation that kingship in Judah was supposed to have, especially in Joash's case.

Hearing the commotion, Athaliah comes to the temple to find the king standing by "his pillar" (perhaps the pillar where the king appeared for public announcement, either Jachin or Boaz, cf. 2 Chr 3:15-17) and the people celebrating around him (v. 12). Her cry of "treason, treason" (v. 13) is ironic given the fact that she is a usurper. Athaliah is taken out of the temple and executed (vv. 14-15). Just as there was no accession formula for her, so there is no summary of her reign or burial notice.

For the third time in Chronicles, Jehoiada then makes a covenant, this time between the king, the people, and himself (v. 16). The three-way agreement perhaps represents the ideal theocracy as the Chronicler envisions it. The covenant entails an oath to be Yahweh's people, and swearing the oath may have been the essence of the covenant-making ceremony in this instance. What it means to be Yahweh's people is then set out in the following account of religious reforms: the cult of Baal is removed (v. 17), the priests and Levites (MT has "Levitical priests" but see below) are placed in charge of the temple (v. 18), and the unclean are excluded from the temple (v. 19). The latter two verses are absent from the Kings parallel and have been introduced by the Chronicler to emphasize the significance of the priests and Levites. Second Kings 11:18*b* refers to the posting of guards, but the Chronicler has replaced this with the assignment of cultic duties to the priests and Levites. The text of verse 18 has also suffered an accidental scribal omission; the original reading is preserved in the LXX and a few other witnesses, which have: "Jehoiada assigned the care of Yahweh's temple to the priests and the Levites, *and he assigned the divisions of the priests and the Levites* whom David had organized...." These witnesses read "the priests and the Levites" instead of "the Levitical priests" as in the MT, and they also attest the line in italics, which was lost from the MT by a skip of the eye from the first occurrence of "the priests and the Levites" to the second. With the Levites in their proper roles—the ones assigned to them by David—the cultic restoration is complete. The restoration of the Davidic monarchy is then completed by the enthronement of Joash (vv. 20-21).

Theological Analysis

This portion of Chronicles is theologically rich. Of particular significance is the theme of the enduring dynasty promised to David and Yahweh's faithfulness in keeping this promise. Yahweh would not allow the destruction of the Davidic dynasty because of his promise, even though the representatives of the dynasty were sometimes very sinful (e.g., Jehoram, 21:7). The continuation of the dynasty is threatened more than once in this section, but there is always one Davidic heir who survives to perpetuate the line. The reign of Athaliah is particularly instructive in this regard. That there is no Davidid on the throne for six years is not seen by the Chronicler as negating the promise to David. Rather, it is the promise that accounts for the survival of Joash and his eventual replacement of Athaliah. In the Chronicler's postexilic context this must have been a source of hope for the restoration of the Davidic monarchy. God had promised David an enduring dynasty; like Athaliah's reign, the exile represented a hiatus that did not negate the promise. Moreover, the exile, like Athaliah's reign, was preceded and even occasioned by wicked kings. But human wickedness does not nullify divine promise.

This section also brings the contrast between Israel and Judah into particular relief. The great sin of the north is unfaithfulness to Yahweh through the worship of other gods. Yahweh demands exclusivity, so that the cult of Baal must be eradicated in a Yahwistic reform (23:17). By the same token, unfaithfulness to Yahweh, both in the worship of other gods and in reliance upon foreign powers, leads to disaster in the form of foreign domination and of personal ruin, as with both Jehoram and Ahaziah. Despite these wicked kings, the story of Athaliah demonstrates Yahweh's loyalty to Judah because of his promise to David and, at the same time, his animosity toward apostate Israel. As we have seen before, the Chronicler depicts true Israel as present in Judah. His theme of "all Israel" surfaces in this section more subtly than in previous material. However, the word "people" occurs a dozen times in chapter 23, often in the expression "all the people," emphasizing the role of the entire people in the overthrow of Athaliah and the enthronement of Joash. By "all Israel" the Chronicler means "true Israel," all those who remained faithful to Yahweh whatever their tribal affiliation or origin.

Finally, the Chronicler also emphasizes the role of the priests (especially Jehoiada) and Levites in the revolt and in the stabilization of society that follows. The Chronicler's depiction of that society is an idealization much like that of the Davidic–Solomonic period. Under priestly guidance of the king the people rejoice and there is quiet (23:21). It seems unlikely that the Chronicler is here advocating diarchy as the ideal form of government, since he does not do so elsewhere. Rather, Jehoiada represents the religious influence and instruction that should, ideally, guide the king. Unfortunately, this relationship and the accompanying period of quiet would be short lived.

THE REIGN OF JOASH (2 CHRONICLES 24:1-27)

King Joash is a large disappointment in Chronicles. His reign begins with a great deal of promise. But the promise proves empty because of Joash's shallow character and lack of integrity. His faithfulness to Yahweh lasts only so long as his mentor, Jehoiada, is alive. When left on his own, he quickly becomes one of the worst kings of Judah.

Literary Analysis

The account of Joash's reign in Chronicles divides neatly into two sections. Verses 1-16 are positively oriented toward Joash and describe his good deeds while his mentor, Jehoiada, was alive. In particular, verses 4-14 concentrate on the repair of the temple; verses 1-3 are introductory, and verses 15-16 recount Jehoiada's death and burial. The second section describes Joash's downfall following Jehoiada's death. The organization of pericopes embodies the Chronicler's theological perspective: Joash's acts of apostasy (vv. 17-18) were followed by prophetic warnings, including one from Jehoiada's son Zechariah, all of which were ignored by Joash (vv. 19-22), resulting in punishment in the form of foreign invasion (vv. 23-24) and assassination (vv. 25-27). Following the introduction, the Chronicler signals the two sections of his narrative with the similar introductory formulae, "afterwards."

Except for verses 15-22, the entire account is based on 2 Kgs 11:21–12:21 [Heb. 12:1-22], albeit with significant changes that have led some scholars to believe that the Chronicler used additional or variant sources. However, the main reason for the differences in the Chronicles version is theological. The account in Kings depicts Joash as a good king who, despite restoring the temple, suffered disasters in the form of an Aramean invasion and assassination. The Chronicler's theology would hardly allow him to retain this account unchanged. His view of disaster as the inevitable retribution for sin meant that the calamities that befell Joash were necessarily brought on by sin on his part. Hence, he reorganized and supplemented the Kings narrative in line with his theology, as indicated above, although he may have drawn in part from other sources.

Exegetical Analysis

The information in verse 1 is the same as that in 2 Kgs 11:21–12:1 [Heb. 12:1-2] with the Chronicler's standard omission of the synchronism with the northern kingdom. Verse 2, though, contains a significant change. Instead of the statement that "Joash did what was right in the sight of Yahweh all his days because the priest Jehoiada instructed him," Chronicles explains that Joash did what was right "all the days of the priest Jehoiada," that is, only as long as Jehoiada was alive. This verse, then, furnishes an overview for the Chronicler's division of Joash's reign into positive and negative sections in the narrative that follows. Jehoiada takes on the role of Joash's father in procuring two wives for him (v. 3). The birth of children is an indication of divine blessing. It is especially meaningful in this instance as it replenishes the Davidic line through its sole surviving heir.

The reason for Joash's decision to restore the temple (v. 4) is not explained until verse 7. This is one reason that some scholars regard verses 5-6 (or 5b-6) as secondary. Verse 7 presents a couple of textual problems. The Hebrew refers to Athaliah as "wickedness [personified]," using a word that is unique in the Old Testament and that the NRSV translates, "that wicked woman." With only minor change, the word may be read as "the evildoer." Also in this verse, the word for "her sons" should be revocalized as "her builders," since Athaliah has no living sons. The point is that Athaliah and her builders had broken into the temple and had defiled the holy vessels by using them for the worship of the Baals. The raising of funds for the restoration took place in stages, as the story now stands (vv. 5-6). Initially, Joash simply "gathered" the priests and Levites and sent them out to "gather" funds for the repairs from "all Israel." But the Levites did not hurry as Joash instructed, so he rebuked Jehoiada for failing to keep the command not just of the king but also of Moses. The title, "the head," which is used here for Jehoiada, has also been seen as an indication of a secondary addition. The verse alludes to Exod 30:12-16; 38:25-26, which refer to the collection of a tax supporting the tabernacle, but which the Chronicler, characteristically, interprets as applying to the temple as well (cf. also Neh 10:32-33). The Mosaic injunction also concerned a one-time assessment rather than an annual collection. But the point of Joash's allusion is the invocation of Mosaic authority as a counter to the potential claim that he is inventing a new practice.

Next, Joash comes up with a different method of collection. His placement of a chest at the temple gateway allows the people to contribute directly, without the intervention of the Levites (v. 8). This plan is wildly successful, as the people respond enthusiastically and generously, in a way that is reminiscent of the popular response at the initial construction of the temple (vv. 9-11; 1 Chr 29:9). The repairs are carried out (vv. 12-13), and there is even enough left over to pay for replacement utensils (v. 14).

The Chronicles version of this episode differs in several important respects from its parallel in 2 Kgs 12:5-9 [Heb. 12:6-10], where the reason for the delay in effecting repairs is that the priests pilfer from the collection. Joash complains to Jehoiada but uses the plural, addressing all of the priests rather than Jehoiada alone as in Chronicles. It is Jehoiada then who builds the chest to receive contributions, but apparently locked with a hole bored in it to prevent the pilfering. The gifts in Chronicles are much more magnanimous than in Kings, such that the chest was filled and emptied on a daily basis (v. 11). The mention of replacement utensils (v. 14) is in direct contradiction to 2 Kgs 12:13 [Heb. 12:14]. But replacement of cultic vessels is essential in Chronicles, since the older vessels had been defiled by Athaliah and her builders (v. 7). The historicity of Joash's implementation of some kind of temple tax, incidentally, receives support from a recently published ostracon that mentions a payment of three silver shekels to the temple of Yahweh "as Ashyahu [= Joash] the king commanded" (Bordreuil, Israel, and Pardee 1998).

Verses 15-16 give death and burial formulae for Jehoiada. As the only report of the death and burial of someone other than a king, this passage is remarkable and an indication of the great esteem in which the Chronicler held the priest. Jehoiada's long life (130 years) is a sign of Yahweh's blessing upon him "because he had done good in Israel," Israel here being a reference to Judah as "true [i.e., faithful] Israel." In addition, Jehoiada is buried with the kings of Judah. This is, of course, an extraordinary honor and another sign of the Chronicler's esteem. It may also indicate that the Chronicler thought of Jehoiada as a ruler and the more important element of the partnership with Joash.

The Joash who appears in the second half of chapter 24 contrasts so greatly with the one in the first half as to seem like an entirely different person. The root cause of his problems is the same as for Ahaziah (22:3-5)—he heeded bad advice. After the death of Jehoiada, his true advisor, he listened to the officials of Judah and became apostate (vv. 17-18). The MT of verse 18 says that he abandoned the temple *(byt Yhwh)*; other witnesses (LXX, Syr) have "covenant" *(bryt)* of Yahweh instead of "house" *(byt)*. Some scholars prefer *bryt,* while others suggest that both words represent independent expansions of an original that had Yahweh only as the object. The last option may be the soundest from a text-critical perspective. However, the temple reading fits the context well, as it has been the focus for Joash, and it provides some irony: Joash abandons the temple, which had protected him and which he had refurbished. Still, it is not the temple per se that Joash really abandons by worshiping other gods, but Yahweh himself. The "wrath" mentioned here is unspecified, and may be proleptic. The verb "abandon" is characteristic of the Chronicler (2 Chr 12:1; 15:2; 21:10; 24:20; 28:6; 29:6) and a subtheme in Zechariah's oracle (v. 20).

The element of prophetic warning integral to the Chronicler's presentation surfaces with the mention of multiple prophets sent to Joash (vv. 19-20). Verse 20 moves to greater specificity in the presentation of Zechariah's oracle. Zechariah's "clothing" with the divine spirit, which NRSV blandly translates "took possession of," indicates that he is not a career prophet but was seized by the spirit. His oracle highlights some of the Chronicler's favorite terms: "abandon, forsake" and "prosper, succeed." The structure—a rhetorical question followed by an explanation—is the Chronicler's. The theology of retribution is also characteristic of the Chronicler and uses the technique "measure for measure": "Because you have forsaken Yahweh, he has also forsaken you."

As we might expect, Joash and his counselors refuse to listen even to Zechariah. Indeed, they conspire against him and kill him. The crime is especially egregious: it is murder, of a prophet, who is the son of Jehoiada, and it is carried out in the temple court. The manner of execution—stoning—and its doing "at the command of the king" suggest that the accusation against Zechariah was treason. The place of execution is ironic in view of Jehoiada's refusal to shed Athaliah's blood in the temple (23:14), and it is also a violation of the laws specifying that stoning take place outside of the camp or town (Lev 24:14; Num 15:35; Deut 17:5). Joash breaks the commandments of Yahweh (v. 20) but gives the command to execute Zechariah, in effect substituting his own order for Yahweh's. Jesus' recall of Zechariah's execution (Matt 23:35, though

Matthew calls him "the son of Berechiah"; Luke 11:51) is apparently intended to encompass all martyrs in the canon from Genesis (Abel) to Chronicles. The statement in verse 22 that Joash did not remember *(zkr)* Jehoiada's kindness to him puns on Zechariah's name. Thus, Zechariah's last words are a cry for justice. The word translated "avenge" in the NRSV is another favorite of the Chronicler, but it is usually rendered "seek." It thus brings to mind the importance for the Chronicler of seeking Yahweh. This Joash failed to do, so Yahweh will seek judgment upon him.

The judgment against Joash comes in two stages, corresponding to his sin. First, the Arameans attack Jerusalem and destroy all the officials who advised Joash to abandon Yahweh (v. 23). This is quite different from 2 Kgs 12:17-18, where the Arameans merely threaten Jerusalem and withdraw upon receiving tribute from Joash. The Arameans succeed, even though they are a smaller force, because Yahweh delivers up the larger army of Judah to them (v. 24). The intervention of Yahweh on behalf of the smaller, *foreign* army is unique in Chronicles and highlights Aram's function here as an instrument of punishment, a function that renders unimportant the details from Kings, such as Hazael's name. In the second stage, Joash, who was left badly wounded in the Aramean assault is assassinated by his own servants (v. 25). The Chronicler has transferred the source citation from 2 Kgs 12:19 to the very end of the chapter (2 Chr 24:27) in order to make Joash's death the direct sequel of Aram's invasion and to emphasize the idea that both are part of the divine judgment. The Chronicler makes clear the cause-effect relationship between Joash's sin and his death (v. 25). Joash's assassination is "measure for measure" retribution for his execution of Zechariah. Inexplicably, Chronicles gives feminine forms of the names of the conspirators' forebears (v. 26 // 2 Kgs 12:21) and refers to them as an Ammonitess and a Moabitess. As a further sign of his contempt, he observes that Joash, in contrast to Jehoiada, was not buried in the royal tombs (v. 25*b*). The word *midrash* translated "commentary" in the source citation in verse 27 has received a great deal of attention, with some suggesting that it indicates that the Chronicler used an expanded version of Kings as his source. However, the exact meaning of the term in this context remains obscure, to say nothing of the nature of the literary work to which it refers.

Theological Analysis

Foremost among the Chronicler's theological themes in the story of Joash is that of divine reward/retribution for human behavior. The Chronicler illustrates this theme through "periodization," which is a common technique of his work. Joash's reign has two distinct periods: the period of the righteous Joash, during Jehoiada's lifetime, when he refurbishes the temple and the period of the apostate, murderous Joash, who surfaces after Jehoiada's death. The early Joash is rewarded with peace, progeny, and prosperity, while the later Joash is punished with death.

Another prominent theme is that of the importance of heeding Yahweh's priests and prophets. The crucial difference between the two periods of Joash's reign is the presence or absence of Jehoiada. Without the priest, Joash falls prey to bad advice. To make matters worse, the apostate Joash turns a deaf ear to the prophets sent by God to warn him. This is not to excuse Joash, who must still bear responsibility for his decisions and his actions; he should have cultivated the ability to discern good advice from bad and the strength of character to make right decisions on his own. When it comes to the worship of other gods, there is no grey area; to worship them is to abandon Yahweh. The Chronicler's message here may apply especially to the realm of leadership and politics. As we have seen, it is not likely that the Chronicler is suggesting diarchy or government shared by king and priest as the ideal. But it may be fair to say that for the Chronicler political authority alone is inadequate to the task of leading Israel; there must be strong guidance from religious figures as well. Joash's early concern for the temple is exemplary and must not be ignored. But there may be a warning in the Chronicler's account of how quickly the benefits of the early period of Joash's reign are lost to the detrimental consequences of his sinful behavior.

THE REIGN OF AMAZIAH (2 CHRONICLES 25:1-28)

Amaziah's reign, according to Chronicles, was quite similar to that of Joash. As with Joash, Amaziah's reign is divided between positive (vv. 1-13) and negative (vv. 14-28) halves. Also, Amaziah's reign and life end with conspiracy and assassination as did Joash's.

Literary Analysis

The Chronicles account of Amaziah may be divided into the following parts: introduction, including Amaziah's execution of his father's murderers (vv. 1-4), the victory over Edom (vv. 5-13), Amaziah's apostasy and prophetic denouncement (vv. 14-16), and the defeat by Israel and assassination of Amaziah (vv. 17-28). Second Chronicles 25 for the most part preserves 2 Kgs 14. The greatest difference between the two is the expansion of 2 Kgs 14:7 with 2 Chr 25:5-16, which is the heart of the Chronicles version. As for the account of Joash, the Chronicler's changes are necessitated by theological problems raised for him by the Kings version. In 2 Kgs 14, Amaziah, who is judged righteous (14:3), suffers defeat at the hands of Israel (14:8-14) and then is killed in a palace conspiracy (14:19-20). Such a sequence of events clearly ran counter to the Chronicler's theological outlook of individual responsibility and immediate retribution/reward for one's deeds.

Exegetical Analysis

The introduction of Amaziah (v. 1) is the same as that in 2 Kgs 14:2, but the evaluation in the next verse is different. The

Chronicler omits the comparisons with David and Joash. Amaziah is nowhere close to David, and Joash is not viewed positively in Chronicles. The Chronicler replaces "yet not like his ancestor David" with one of his favorites expressions, "yet not with *a true heart*." Though translated in various ways in the NRSV, the expression "true heart" occurs throughout Chronicles (1 Chr 12:38 [Heb. 12:39]; 28:9; 29:9, 19; 2 Chr 19:9; cf. 2 Chr 15:12). Amaziah's revenge on his father's murderers (25:3) is recounted using a different verb for kill *(hrg)* from the one found in 2 Kgs 14:5 *(nkh)*. The former is used for the murders of Zechariah and Joash in 2 Chr 24, so that its repetition here both recalls those deaths and brings closure to this bloody cycle. Contrary to typical ancient Near Eastern practice, Amaziah does not execute the children of the assassins for religious reasons (v. 4). This verse is found in the Kings source and rehearses a principle articulated in Deut 24:16. But the idea that only the guilty party suffers for sin fits well with the Chronicler's theology of retribution.

Verses 5-16 represent an extensive expansion of 2 Kgs 14:7. As it now stands, the expansion is the work of the Chronicler; the rhetorical portions are certainly his. It seems unnecessary to posit sources for the rest of the narrative, though this possibility is urged by some scholars. Amaziah's army of 300,000 (v. 5) represents a decline from the 1,160,000 troops marshaled by Jehoshaphat (17:14-18). Perhaps for that reason, Amaziah felt compelled to hire the Israelite mercenaries (v. 6). The nameless man of God who cautions Amaziah against taking the Israelites with him does so on two grounds (vv. 7-8): "Yahweh is not with Israel" and "God has power to help or to overthrow." God's absence from battle is a guarantee of military defeat (cf. Num 14:43; Deut 1:42), just as God's presence ensures victory (e.g., Deut 20:4; 31:6). Therefore, as we have seen several times in Chronicles, success on the battlefield is not the result of size or strength of a human army but of trust in God. The syntax of verse 8*a* is difficult; many scholars read as the NRSV but then reconstruct the word "why" after "battle": "Why should God fling you down?" In any case, the main point is clear: the Israelites (also called "Ephraimites," perhaps to clarify that they are northerners) are unnecessary, since victory depends on God and not on numbers, and since God is not with them, they are actually a detriment rather than a help. The man of God responds to Amaziah's concern about the loss of his payment for the mercenaries by saying that Yahweh can give him more than what he has spent. If this statement implies a promise of recovery of the payment, as some contend, the promise is never fulfilled. But this may be because of Amaziah's faithless acts shortly after the battle.

Dismissing the Israelites brings Amaziah victory, as the man of God implied (vv. 10-13). The location of Sela, which means "rock, crag" is uncertain, though some identify it with Petra. Meanwhile, the dismissed Israelites, angered at the loss of their portion of the spoil (v. 10), conduct raids on "the cities of Judah from Samaria to Beth-Horon" (v. 13). "Samaria" seems out of place, since one expects to read that the mercenaries conducted raids on Judah. Hence, the suggestion has been made that "Samaria" is an error for "Migron," which can look similar in Hebrew and which refers to a town in the original territory of Benjamin. Another suggestion is that there were cities of predominately Judean inhabitants or claimed by Judah within the borders of Israel.

With verse 14, the second phase of Amaziah's reign begins. It was not unusual in the ancient Near East to display the gods of a vanquished enemy in the temples of the victors. Amaziah would have done better to destroy the Edomite images, as did David (1 Chr 14:12) in the spirit of Deut 7:5; 12:3. Instead, he begins to worship these gods. The verb translated "worship" is the word "seek," which the Chronicler favors. The point is that Amaziah should seek Yahweh rather than other gods, especially do-nothing gods that could not save their people from defeat at Amaziah's hands. Amaziah's actions are foolish, especially following the victory given to him by Yahweh. From a literary perspective, Amaziah's otherwise inexplicable apostasy sets up his destruction announced by the prophet (v. 16). Amaziah's interruption of the prophet and the latter's response (v. 16) play on the word "counsel, advise." Amaziah asks whether the prophet has been made advisor to the king. The prophet ceases prophesying but then adds, "I know that God has 'deemed it advisable' to destroy you because you did this and did not heed my advice." Verse 17 then begins, "Amaziah sought advice."

In verse 17, the Chronicler rejoins his source at 2 Kgs 14:8. Apparently spurred by his advisors to respond to the raid of the Israelites (v. 13), Amaziah decides to challenge King Joash of Israel in battle. This is the force of the message, "Come, let us look one another in the face" (v. 17; cf. v. 19*b*). Joash responds with a parable (v. 18) that is reminiscent of Judg 9:7-15. At first glance, the content of the parable does not seem entirely appropriate, since Amaziah has not proposed a marriage alliance. But the point Joash makes with the parable is fitting and can be seen most clearly in 2 Kgs 14:10: "You have indeed defeated Edom, and your heart has lifted you up. Be content with your glory, and stay at home." Amaziah's victory over Edom has made him overconfident and presumptuous; the reality is that he is out of his league in trying to challenge Joash.

The Chronicles version in verse 19 differs slightly but significantly. In it Joash quotes Amaziah, "See, I have defeated Edom," and Joash then adds, "Your heart has lifted you up to harden [you] [NRSV: "in boastfulness"]. Now stay at home." Chronicles has a form of the verb that means "harden" rather than the form in Kings that means "be glorified," and Chronicles has it at the end of the sentence rather than the beginning of a new sentence, which in Chronicles is clearly marked with "now." The difference is important because in verse 20, which a comparison with Kings shows to be an interpolation, it turns out that Joash is actually speaking for God. Amaziah's problem is not only his pride but also his refusal to listen and to discern the message of God. A similar scene will take place in 35:22 between Pharaoh Neco and King Josiah. Verse 20 also explains that Amaziah's refusal is the work of God in retribution for his apostasy.

As we might expect, therefore, Amaziah is defeated by Joash (vv. 21-23). The battle takes place at Beth-shemesh, "which belongs to Judah." That is, the battle took place at a site not on the border with Israel but in the interior of Judah, thus indicating Amaziah's existing state of weakness. The reference to Obed-edom (v. 24) is unique to Chronicles and does not make much historical sense, given that Obed-edom was alive at the time of David (1 Chr 15:18, 24; 16:38; 26:4, 15). Some try to explain it as a reference to the family of Obed-edom as gatekeepers, but the mention of Obed-edom is still unexpected. It is best explained as a theological point. "Obed-edom" means "servant of Edom" and thus subtly alludes to Amaziah's apostasy in serving the gods of Edom. Moreover, verse 24 indicates that the temple treasures listed there were under Obed-edom's care, so that Amaziah lost the treasure to Israel because of his service of (the gods of) Edom.

The closing formulae for Amaziah are quite similar to those in Kings, albeit with a few significant changes. In verse 26, Chronicles refers to the Book of the Kings of Judah and Israel as his source rather than the Book of the Chronicles of the Kings of Judah as in 2 Kgs 14:18. This is hardly a different source from the book of Kings. The inclusion of Israel fits the Chronicler's "all Israel" interest, but Judah takes precedence. The beginning of verse 27 is another addition by the Chronicler, who describes the conspiracy against Amaziah as having begun "from the time that Amaziah turned away from Yahweh." In this way the Chronicler makes clear the retributive function of Amaziah's assassination. Finally, verse 28 in the MT of Chronicles says that Amaziah was buried "in a city of Judah" rather than "in the city of David." Given the prevalence of the latter expression, it is difficult to believe that the MT reading is secondary. As he has done with previous kings, the Chronicler may well be using the place of burial, in other words, outside of the royal tombs, as a way of expressing his disdain for Amaziah.

Theological Analysis

The primary theological tenets of this chapter are very similar to those for the account of Joash. Perhaps most distinctive again is the theme of retribution. The Chronicler's belief that disaster does not occur arbitrarily but as the consequence of sin and that sin is inevitably punished has shaped his version of Amaziah's reign. Also, as with previous kings, punishment does not come unexpectedly; those who experience disaster have received warnings, which they have ignored. In Amaziah's case, one of those warnings comes from an unusual source—the king of Israel (25:18-19), yet it is still valid. Perhaps the Chronicler implies here that people must be attentive to messages from God and be able to discern their truthfulness regardless of the medium through which they come.

Amaziah's story, like Joash's, shows just how quickly a person's admirable record can be ruined by sin. Amaziah's sin, like Joash's, is a particularly grievous one—that of forsaking Yahweh for other gods. There may be a special warning from the Chronicler to his postexilic audience to avoid particularly the gods of the Edomites (Idumeans), with whom they came into close contact and for whom the Chronicler, like other authors of his time, attests a special animosity. An additional point of this particular narrative may be that Jerusalem is not invulnerable to foreign attack. This point not only prepares the reader for the Babylonian exile but also serves as a warning to the postexilic inhabitants of the Persian province of Yehud.

THE REIGN OF UZZIAH (2 CHRONICLES 26:1-23)

The next king of Judah is known as Azariah or Uzziah. Chronicles prefers the latter, probably to avoid confusion with

Azariah the priest (26:17, 20), and refers to Azariah the king only in 1 Chr 3:12. The account of Azariah the king in 2 Kgs 15:1-7 is brief and consists mostly of the standard regnal formulae. The Chronicler has significantly expanded this account, primarily for theological reasons. His version of Uzziah's reign follows the same pattern as those of Joash and Amaziah—a positive period for the first portion of his reign, broken by sin, and followed by a negative second half.

Literary Analysis

The Chronicler's account of Uzziah was driven by the need to explain two facets of the Kings version: Uzziah's exceptionally long reign of fifty-two years and the disease that took his life. The Chronicler accomplished this by adding 2 Chr 26:5-20 to the generally pedestrian account in Kings. His addition served to interpret the evaluation that Uzziah did what was right *just as his father Amaziah had done* (26:4 // 2 Kgs 15:3). That is, like Amaziah, Uzziah was righteous for the first part of his reign, but then went astray and was punished. The added material in Chronicles, therefore, goes into detail about Uzziah's righteous deeds and rewards, thus justifying his fifty-two year reign while also accounting in more detail for his disease by describing the sin that led him to contract it. The chapter may be outlined as follows: introduction (vv. 1-4), successes while Uzziah sought Yahweh (vv. 5-15), sin and punishment (vv. 16-21), conclusion (vv. 22-23).

Exegetical Analysis

Verses 1-2 are transitional, as they both close Amaziah's account and open Uzziah's. The implication of these verses that Uzziah was made king before Amaziah's death has led many scholars to posit a coregency of Amaziah and Uzziah, perhaps originating with the former's capture (25:23). From a literary and theological perspective, Uzziah's capture of Elat invites the reader to think of him as a new Solomon (2 Chr 8:17-18).

Historically, Eloth (= Elat) was a key port for international commerce, so that controlling it brought considerable economic advantages. The repetition of Uzziah's age at accession (v. 3) is somewhat awkward but is the result of the Chronicler following the Kings version (2 Kgs 14:21-22; 15:2) closely while omitting its material on the northern king, Jeroboam II (2 Kgs 14:23-29). The evaluation of Uzziah (v. 4) is identical to that of 2 Kgs 15:3. The difference is that in Chronicles, "doing according to all that Amaziah had done" is not a compliment.

Uzziah's reign, divided as it is between periods of righteousness-blessing and sin-disaster, is similar to Amaziah's reign. It is even more similar to Joash's reign, as hinted at in verse 5—as Joash was righteous during Jehoiada's lifetime, so Uzziah sought Yahweh "in the days of Zechariah." The Chronicler may have chosen this name for the prophet precisely because it was the name of Jehoiada's son. Zechariah is called an instructor "in the fear of God." While the MT actually has "vision of God," a reading that may stress Zechariah's prophetic office, "fear" is attested by other manuscripts and the versions and seems more appropriate. It is also characteristic of the Chronicler's vocabulary, as is the idea of seeking God (used twice in this verse), and the verb "prosper."

Verses 6-15 then detail the kinds of success given by God to Uzziah. Verses 6-8 describe his military domination of the Philistines, Arabs, and Meunites (reading with LXX against MT's "Ammonites"; cf. on 20:1 above). Gur-baal (v. 7) is often associated with Gari, mentioned in ancient sources outside of the Bible, which lay east of Beersheba, though some prefer reading "Gerar." The "-baal" element of the name *(bᶜl)* is also likely an error for "and against" *(wᶜl)*; the NRSV conflates the two possibilities. The reference to Uzziah's fame spreading to Egypt, especially in conjunction with his defeat of the Philistines again invites comparison with Israel's "golden age." David defeated the Philistines (1 Chr 14:8-17); Solomon had close ties with Egypt (2 Chr 8:11); and both of them reveled in international fame (1 Chr 14:17; 2 Chr 9).

Verses 7 and 8 both play on the name of Uzziah/Azariah. The verb "help," which begins verse 7, is *ʿāzar* and is part of the name Azariah. The word *ḥāzaq* ("be strong") at the end of verse 8 is synonymous with the verb *ʿāzaz* ("be strong"), which makes up part of Uzziah's name. The reference to Uzziah's fame and strength (v. 8) forms a bracket or frame with the similar statement in verse 15. The intervening material displays themes that are typical indications of divine blessing in Chronicles— building projects, prosperity, and a large army. The construction in verse 9 is, to a large extent, restoration of the ruin brought on by Amaziah, as indicated by the "Corner Gate," mentioned also in 25:23. Uzziah's military strength (vv. 11-14), may also be suggested by an excerpt from the annals of the Assyrian emperor, Tiglath-Pileser III, that mentions "Azrayau of Yaudi" as a member of a western coalition. The "machines invented by skilled workers" (v. 15) have occasioned a good deal of discussion. The reference to shooting stones has led to the suggestion that these are catapults and that they thus indicate a date for Chronicles in the third century or later. However, both the identification of the machines and the late date for the invention of catapults have been called into question. Another well-known proposal is that these devices are raised platforms. Obviously, their exact nature remains unknown. The use of "help" (vv. 13, 15) again plays on "Azariah," and the words for "strength" call to mind "Uzziah." The final statement ("for he was marvelously helped until he became strong," v. 15) is particularly artful, not only for the plays on the king's names but also for the use of the passive, which implies the work of God.

The verb *ḥāzaq* ("be strong") also provides a transition to the story of Uzziah's sin and disease (vv. 16-21). When he became strong, Uzziah failed to recognize that Yahweh had helped him. His pride led him to enter the temple in order to burn incense on the altar—a task at which only priests were to officiate (Num 16:40 [Heb. 17:5]; cf. Exod 30:1-10; Num 18:1-7).

The scene recalls the sins of both Saul (2 Sam 13:2-5) and Jeroboam (1 Kgs 12:33; 13:1). Uzziah's real sin is not burning incense—something he does not actually do—but his pride, which leads him to become angry with the priests who stop him from making the offering (v. 19). There before the priests, his forehead suddenly breaks out with "leprosy." The word translated "leprosy" is a broad term for skin disease and is not necessarily the modern ailment (Hansen's disease) known by that name. The verb $z\bar{a}rah$ ("break out"), usually used of the sun breaking forth, occurs here uniquely for the outbreak of disease, suggesting suddenness and inflammation. The scene is ironic in that Uzziah stands before the priests, who make the determination of cleanness or uncleanness due to skin diseases (Lev 13). In addition, Uzziah's condition means that he can no longer approach the temple and in fact must immediately be escorted from the building (v. 20) to live the rest of his life in isolation. The expression translated "house of separation" occurs also in the Ugaritic texts in the context of a description of the underworld. It may refer to a sanatorium or quarantine facility of some kind. While it is often claimed that Uzziah and Jotham were coregents, verse 21b says only that Jotham was over the king's house and governed (lit., "was judging") the people of the land, and the notice of Jotham's reign comes only after that of Uzziah's death (v. 22).

Despite the citation of Isaiah as a source (v. 22), there is no indication that the Chronicler drew any material about Uzziah's reign from Isaiah. The citation may be based simply on Isaiah's reference to Uzziah as one of the kings whose reign his career spanned (Isa 1:1). Isaiah would not likely have any specific information about Uzziah if he was called to prophesy "in the year that King Uzziah died" (Isa 6:1). Uzziah was not buried "with his ancestors," the kings of Judah, but in a nearby field that they possessed (v. 23). This is a change from 2 Kgs 15:7, which has him buried with his forebears in the city of David. Chronicles provides an expanation: "For they said, 'He is leprous.'" It is difficult not to see the

Chronicler's tendency to express judgment in burial place operating here, especially since there are no laws about the burial of "lepers" in the Bible. The tradition about Uzziah's disease continued long after his death, as indicated by a late second/early first century B.C.E. burial marker bearing the inscription, "Here are the bones of Azariah king of Judah. Do not open."

Theological Analysis

The Chronicler's account of Uzziah obviously shares with those of his predecessors the lessons about retribution and the way in which sin undermines good deeds. In addition, his reign teaches the importance of proper respect for what is holy. Uzziah's great sin lay in his failure to keep the sacred and the profane separate. This is a principle encountered before in Chronicles, specifically in the story of the death of Uzzah during David's first attempt to bring the ark to Jerusalem (1 Chr 13:9-10). One wonders whether the similarity of Uzziah's name to Uzzah's was more than consequence and may have influenced the Chronicler's preference for the name "Uzziah" over "Azariah." Perhaps even more serious than Uzziah's lack of respect for the sacred was his pride. The great danger of pride highlighted by Uzziah's story is that it can lead a person to attribute prosperity and blessing to human accomplishments rather than recognizing them as gifts from God.

THE REIGN OF JOTHAM (2 CHRONICLES 27:1-9)

The account of Jotham's reign is something of a relief to the reader of Chronicles following those of predecessors because it is judged to be righteous throughout with no negative period. The account, nevertheless, is quite brief, partly because its counterpart in 2 Kgs 15:32-38 is brief and partly because the Chronicler apparently had no additional information about Jotham.

Literary Analysis

Chronicles follows the order of its Kings source and rehearses most of the material in it while also adding to it. The Kings account consists of very little outside of the standard regnal formulae for Jotham. Essentially, the Chronicler has inserted additional material (27:3-6) between the introduction (2 Chr 27:1-2) and conclusion (27:7-9), which he lifted from Kings (2 Kgs 15:33-34, 36-38). The repetition of Jotham's accession formula (vv. 1, 8) is probably best viewed as a literary construction—a frame around the account of Jotham's reign—rather than a gloss or textual error. The structure of the Chronicles account is: accession formula and evaluation (vv. 1-2), Jotham's accomplishments: building projects (vv. 3-4), military success (vv. 5-6); concluding formulae (vv. 7-9).

Exegetical Analysis

The sixteen years of Jotham's reign (v. 1) were apparently those independent of any coregency he may have shared with his father, although this is not entirely clear from the text. He is the first king since Abijah to receive an entirely positive evaluation (v. 2). The Chronicler makes two significant changes to the evaluation he has borrowed from Kings. The statement that Jotham did not enter the temple (NRSV's "invade" is interpretive) alludes to the sin of Uzziah, to whom Jotham provides a contrast. The statement that the people "still followed corrupt practices" seems to imply idolatry and thus to suggest the continuing influence of Joash and Amaziah. It also shows that for the Chronicler the deeds and thus the fates of the people and the king are not inextricably bound.

Verses 3-6 are typical of the Chronicler in their depiction of building projects and military victory as God's blessings for righteous behavior. Maintenance of the temple (v. 3a) was of particular importance to the Chronicler. The Ophel ("mound" or "acropolis") was the southern spur of the temple mount. In contrast to Uzziah, Jotham's military success did not lead him to conceit. He apparently recognized that his strength was due to his proper behavior (v. 6).

The Chronicler omits the mention of the Syro-Ephraimitic crisis (2 Kgs 15:17) from his conclusion to Jotham's reign (vv. 7-9). Since Kings is inconclusive about the effects of the invasion of Israel and Aram (Syria) for Judah under Jotham, the Chronicler may not have interpreted the invasion as a judgment against Jotham or felt compelled to account for it as punishment for sin. It was simpler just to put off describing the crisis until his treatment of Ahaz, who was already the focus of the invasion in Kings, and for whom the event was easily interpreted as divine judgment. The Chronicler's reference to Jotham's "wars and ways" in verse 7 (but not in Kings) corresponds to the order of topics in verses 5-6. He was the first king since Jehoshaphat to be buried in the royal tombs (v. 9). It is precisely because Jotham was the first king in a long time to be so buried that the Chronicler omitted the expression from 2 Kgs 15:38 that he was buried "with his fathers."

Theological Analysis

Jotham's story is best understood in contrast to those of his predecessors and his successors. The three kings before him all suffered in the second half of their reigns because of sin. Unlike Joash, Amaziah, and Uzziah, Jotham's evaluation is not mixed. He did not become arrogant in his strength and prosperity but maintained awareness that these were rewards that would accrue only so long as he continued his righteous ways. His son Ahaz, in contrast, would prove thoroughly evil.

In fact, the reigns of Jotham, Ahaz, and Hezekiah in Chronicles together illustrate the principle that each person bears responsibility for his/her own behavior and that it is possible to choose the path of righteousness despite what one's forebears have done. These three kings exemplify the principle found in Ezek 18. In both cases, there is a sequence of individuals—a righteous man, a wicked son, and a righteous grandson. Each is responsible for his own actions. The righteous father cannot save his wicked son; nor can the righteous grandson save his wicked father. By the same token, neither righteous man suffers for the wickedness of the middle generation. The Chronicler strongly endorses the principle of individual responsibility, which Ezekiel describes hypothetically. The Chronicler finds this principle exemplified in the reigns of Jotham, Ahaz, and Hezekiah.

THE REIGN OF AHAZ (2 CHRONICLES 28:1-27)

According to Chronicles, Judah reaches its religious nadir in Ahaz. The Chronicler treats Ahaz as the worst king in the history of Judah, a distinction that in Kings belongs to Manasseh. He does so in part by comparing Ahaz's apostasy to that of the northern kingdom (vv. 1-3; cf. Williamson 1982:343-44).

Literary Analysis

While Ahaz in Kings "did not do what was right in the sight of Yahweh" (2 Kgs 16:2), the Chronicler has made significant changes in his Kings base in order to depict Ahaz's sinfulness and the appropriate divine responses:

(1) The Syro-Ephraimitic crisis (2 Kgs 16:5) is interpreted as two separate defeats at the hands of Aram and Israel respectively (28:5-7).

(2) The story of the captivity and return of the people of Judah is added (28:8-15).

(3) The Edomite capture of Elat (2 Kgs 16:6) is transformed into invasions by the Edomites and Philistines (28:17-19).

(4) Ahaz's successful petition for aid from Tiglath-Pileser III (2 Kgs 16:6-9) is also transformed into an Assyrian invasion (28:16-21).

(5) Ahaz's duplication of the altar from Damascus and his removal of certain temple items to cover his tribute payment (2 Kgs 16:10-18) is turned into utter apostasy and closing of the temple (28:23-25).

Chapter 28, then, may be outlined as follows: introduction (vv. 1-4), defeat by Aram and Israel (vv. 5-7), return of the captives from Judah (vv. 8-15), Assyrian attack (vv. 16-21), Ahaz's apostasy and death (vv. 22-27). The section on the Assyrian attack (vv. 16-21) is demarcated by a framework signaled by the word for "help" in verses 16 and 21.

Exegetical Analysis

The reason for Ahaz's evil was that "he walked in the ways of the kings of Israel" (28:2a). Chronicles agrees with Kings on that point. But the Chronicler goes on to explain what he means by this (vv. 2b-3a): Ahaz worshiped and promoted the worship of other gods. The Valley of Ben Hinnom is not mentioned in the Kings account of Ahaz; the Chronicler has borrowed the reference from the Kings account of Josiah's reform (2 Kgs 23:10) and from Jer 7:31-32; 19:2-6; 32:35. While 2 Kgs 23:10 refers to making children pass through fire, Chronicles uses the verb "burn." The difference may be due to a metathesis of consonants, but it also reflects an understanding of this practice as child sacrifice—an understanding likely derived from Jeremiah. The "Valley [gê '] of [the son of] Hinnom" became the refuse dump for the city of Jerusalem, and hence the metaphor for Hell, to which it lent its name (Greek *Gehenna*) in the New Testament. Both Chronicles and Kings liken Ahaz to the Canaanite nations whom Yahweh dispossessed before Israel. The implication is that Judah is in danger of losing its heritage in the land because of Ahaz.

In verse 5 the Chronicler rephrases 2 Kgs 16:5, using the verb "give" twice ("Yahweh gave" and "he was given") to make it clear that Ahaz's defeats came in retribution for his sins. As noted, the single attack by coalition partners in Kings is made into two distinct defeats in Chronicles. Moreover, 2 Kgs 16:5 states explicitly that Pekah and Rezin "could not conquer him," while Chronicles says that they both defeated Ahaz and Judah. The reason for the change is patently theological: "because they had abandoned Yahweh the God of their ancestors" (v. 6*b*). The number of casualties (120,000 in a single day, v. 6) is an exaggeration. The titles of the slain officials (v. 7) are unusual in Chronicles and may have been drawn from some other source. The title "second to the king" occurs elsewhere in the Bible only in Esth 20:3.

The story of the return of the captives (vv. 8-15), which is unique to Chronicles, is somewhat ill suited to the context in that it is not specifically related to Ahaz. However, if the story is intended to foreshadow the Babylonian captivity and return from it, part of the Chronicler's motive in placing it here may have been to suggest that the fate of captivity was sealed by Ahaz. The main point of the story—the brotherhood of Israel and Judah—fits well with the Chronicler's all-Israel motif. While Israel as a whole, and especially its kings, are in a state of rebellion and apostasy, there are still faithful individuals and even leaders in the north. The fact that a prophet of Yahweh appeals to them in the name of "Yahweh, the God of your ancestors" (v. 9) and on the grounds of kinship and that they heed him shows that they are still part of Yahweh's chosen people. If the episode is based on source material, as some scholars contend, the Chronicler has revised it and tailored it to his purposes. The plot of the story unfolds according to the following structure: the account of the captives (v. 8), Oded's prophecy (vv. 9-11), the speech of the Ephraimite chiefs (vv. 12-13), and the return of the captives (vv. 14-15).

The first word of verse 8 ("they took captive") is one of the key words of the unit. This verb *(šbh)* occurs six times in verses 8-15. It forms a play with the word "return" *(šûb)* in verses 11, 15. The number of captives—200,000—is enormous and surely exaggerated. But the large numbers serve to highlight the magnitude of the crime of their captors and slayers. That is the point of the oracle of the otherwise unknown prophet, Oded (vv. 9-11). Yahweh used Israel to punish Judah, but Israel was excessive in its killing, and this angered God. Now their intent to enslave the captives infuriates Yahweh even more. The mention of their own "sins against Yahweh" (v. 10) alludes to the state of rebellion and apostasy of the north. Yet, Yahweh is still their God and they are still a part of his people. The Ephraimite chiefs pick up on the same idea of sin or guilt in their speech (v. 13), where the same word for "sin" or "guilt" occurs three times. The leaders acknowledge that they are already guilt-laden, presumably as members of the apostate and rebellious northern kingdom, and they order the return of the captives in order to avoid the divine wrath. The fact that there is no mention of the king of Israel may indicate that the story originated after the fall of the northern kingdom at a time entirely unrelated to the Syro-Ephraimitic crisis. But it could also be that this feature reflects the author's viewpoint that it is the Israelite monarchy that is particularly illegitimate and in rebellion, while the people of Israel, at least some of them, maintain a sense of kinship with Judah and of openness to Yahweh and his prophets. These Israelites not only release their captives but also clothe and provide for them with the spoil they have gathered (v. 15). This is an extraordinary gesture—all the more so since the spoil represented the income of fighters. The mention of Jericho in this verse has suggested to some that it emanates from a story about a border skirmish that has subsequently been greatly elaborated.

The theme of verses 16-21 is expressed in its framework: Ahaz "sent to the kings of Assyria for help" (v. 16) "but it did not help him" (v. 21). As noted above, the Chronicler has extensively revised his Kings source. In 2 Kgs 16:5-7, Ahaz sends to Tiglath-Pileser III for aid against Israel and Aram, who are apparently forming a coalition to resist the Assyrians. In Chronicles, Ahaz's appeal to Tilgath-Pilneser (the Chronicler's consistent [mis-]spelling) is separated from the Syro-Ephraimitic crisis and is occasioned instead by defeats at the hands of the Edomites and Philistines (vv. 17-18). The defeats are specifically attributed to Ahaz's wickedness, which has infected Judah (v. 19). Strikingly, Ahaz is referred to here as the "king of Israel," an indication that the claim of the Davidic ruler—even the most sinful one—over all Israel still holds in the Chronicler's view. Contrary to 2 Kgs 16:9, where Tiglath-Pileser does help Ahaz, in Chronicles he brings yet more trouble to Ahaz, oppressing rather than strengthening him (v. 20). Indeed, Ahaz's actions begin a long period of Assyrian oppression. His payment of tribute taken from the royal and temple treasuries (v. 21) seems to abstract the account of Hezekiah's similar actions in 2 Kgs 18:14-17, which the Chronicler omits.

The theme of help continues in the final section about Ahaz (28:22-27). "Distress" can be a motivation for seeking help from Yahweh (Ps 18:6 [MT 7] // 2 Sam 22:7; 107:6, 13, 19, 28). But "this same King Ahaz" (v. 22) is an emphatic that implies disdain. It communicates the point that Ahaz refuses to learn from his mistakes and instead compounds them by turning for help to other gods and other nations. Ahaz's worship of the gods of Damascus (v. 23) interprets 2 Kgs 16:10-16 as idolatry by recalling Amaziah's worship of Edomite gods (25:14). Ahaz goes so far as to close the temple and substitute it with installations for the worship of other gods throughout Judah and Jerusalem (vv. 24-25). It seems unlikely that anyone could have obliterated the worship of Yahweh to such an extent in Judah. These details reflect the Chronicler's antipathy toward Ahaz rather than historical reality. They also illustrate the Chronicler's view that the worship of Yahweh and that of other gods are mutually exclusive activities. Furthermore, the Chronicler may be building a contrast with Hezekiah. A further indication of the Chronicler's disdain is his notice that Ahaz was not buried in the tombs of the kings ("of Israel!"), a technique for expressing disfavor that he has used several times before.

Theological Analysis

In this account of Ahaz's reign, the Chronicler makes three important theological claims (cf. Dillard 1987:224-25). First, he depicts Judah's apostasy under Ahaz as equal to that of Israel. This equality of the two kingdoms in sin prepares the way for their mutual repentance and reunification under Hezekiah in the following chapters. Second, the story of the return of the captives from Judah is the centerpiece of the current chapter. The story emphasizes the kinship of Israel and Judah even after exile. It is one of the most forceful assertions in Chronicles of the "all Israel" theme: It shows that there are northerners who are attentive to the word of God and who are still God's people even though the nation as a whole is in a state of rebellion and apostasy. The story may also hint at the future Babylonian captivity of Judah, but it does not seal Judah's fate. As wicked as Ahaz is, there is still the possibility of repentance and restoration, as the reign of Ahaz's successor will demonstrate. Third, Ahaz's sin and punishment again illustrate the Chronicler's doctrine of individual responsibility and immediate retribution. This theme goes hand-in-hand with the previous one. Ahaz's apostasy is punished by repeated military defeat. He is not rewarded because of the righteousness of his father, Jotham. Nor does Ahaz's punishment fall upon his faithful son, Hezekiah, who leads Judah to repentance. Each king and each person is responsible for his or her own decisions and deeds.

THE REIGN OF HEZEKIAH (2 CHRONICLES 29:1–32:33)

The account of Hezekiah's reign in Chronicles is the longest for any king after David and Solomon. Its length is an indication of the Chronicler's esteem for this king, whom the Chronicler regards as a latter-day David or Solomon—or, better, as incomparable in his own role as the restorer of Israel's religious traditions following the nadir of Ahaz.

Literary Analysis

The Chronicles account of Hezekiah may be divided into four parts corresponding to the current chapters: cleansing and consecration of the temple (29), celebration of Passover

(30), reestablishment of temple personnel (31), and Sennacherib's invasion (32). Of these, chapter 32 alone shows a close affinity to the Kings account of Hezekiah (2 Kgs 18–20). Chapter 32 contains the three major episodes of Kings (Sennacherib's invasion, Hezekiah's illness, and the Babylonian envoy) in the same order but in condensed and revised form. The Chronicler has foregrounded these episodes with material about cultic reforms (chs. 29–31) and has surrounded the whole with the framework borrowed from Kings (2 Chr 29:1-2 // 2 Kgs 18:1-3; 2 Chr 32:32-33 // 2 Kgs 20:20-21). Chronicles thus emphasizes Hezekiah's restoration of temple worship following its demise under Ahaz over the story of the encounter with Sennacherib, which is the focus of the Kings account. Allen (1987:366) has observed that 31:20-21 resumes and expands on 29:1, and thus marks chapters 29–31 as distinct from chapter 32, while references to Hezekiah prospering in 31:21 and 32:30 bracket off the latter chapter. A number of scholars consider portions of chapters 29–31 to be secondary expansions emphasizing and detailing the role of the Levites. At the same time, the unity of these chapters is vigorously defended by others, so that no consensus on the matter has been reached.

Exegetical Analysis

Cleansing and Rededicating the Temple (2 Chr 29:1-36)

As noted above, the introduction of Hezekiah's reign is drawn from 2 Kgs 18:1-3 with the standard omission of the northern synchronism. The statement that Hezekiah did as David had done is extremely high praise in Chronicles; only one other king—Josiah—receives such a positive evaluation. The Chronicler removes it for all other kings so evaluated in Kings. It is precisely the opposite of what is said of Ahaz (28:1) and thus sets the tone for Hezekiah's reign in Chronicles: he corrects the cultic apostasies introduced by his father. The Chronicler favors the longest form of Hezekiah's name *(yĕḥizqîyāhû)*, which typically occurs in Kings as *ḥizqîyāh*. The Chronicler frequently plays on the name by using the verb *ḥāzaq*, "to be strong." Thus in 29:3 this is the word translated "repaired"; its use with this sense is unusual, and its choice was clearly motivated by the pun on Hezekiah's name. This verse highlights Hezekiah's contrast with his father; his first act—in the first month of the first year—as king is to reopen the doors to the temple that Ahaz closed.

Hezekiah's speech (vv. 5-11) is the Chronicler's composition, as indicated in part by the vocative "hear me" (v. 5). It is addressed to the Levites, in the broadest sense, and so includes the priests, who must be the first to sanctify (a key term in these verses) themselves so that they can then sanctify the temple. The latter is a two-stage process that involves first cleansing the temple by removing the idols and cultic paraphernalia of other gods—here referred to with the strong word "filth"—and then ritually preparing the site for sacred use. The two stages are reversed here but appear in order below beginning with verse 16. The detailing of the sins of the "fathers" actually contains several allusions to the one father, Ahaz, the most obvious of which is the closing of the doors (v. 7). There are also several different ways of referring to the temple in these verses—"house of Yahweh," "dwelling [or "tent"] of Yahweh," "vestibule," and "holy place" (or "sanctuary")—so that the focus on the temple is obvious. Turning away their faces from the temple represents a reversal of Solomon's prayer (2 Chr 6) that God would hear the prayers of those who turned toward the temple. The description of the wrath that befell Judah and Jerusalem (vv. 8-9) seems disproportionate to the captivity detailed in the previous chapter and is a foreshadowing of the Babylonian exile. The language and imagery draw particularly on Jer 29:18. Hezekiah's pledge of a new covenant (v. 10) must be understood broadly as a call for renewed commitment, since no actual covenant is forthcoming. His special admonition (v. 11) is undoubtedly also addressed to the Levites in the Chronicler's own day.

Of the seven Levitical families (vv. 12-14), six are expected—the three main Levitical lines (Kohath, Merari, Gershon) and the three families of singers (Asaph, Heman, Jeduthun). Elizaphan, originally a prominent Kohathite clan (Num 3:30), may be included as rounding out the number of families for a total of seven and for its link with the time of David (cf. 1 Chr 15:8). Another unusual feature appears in verse 15, where the king's command is equated with "the words of Yahweh." The cleansing of the temple (v. 16) begins with the removal of "the uncleanness" (NRSV: "unclean things"). The process involves the priests, as the only ones authorized to enter the sanctuary, handing items to the Levites, who then deposit them in the Kidron Valley (15:16; 30:14; 2 Kgs 23:4, 6, 12), where they would be swept away by water. The completion of the process on the sixteenth of the month (v. 17) necessitates the postponement of Passover, which is to be celebrated on the fourteenth, though other reasons will be given (see below).

Verses 20-24 describe the sanctification and rededication of the temple altar. The list of kinds of animals offered seems drawn from the description of the dedication of the tabernacle altar in Num 7:84-88. But the dedication ceremony also entails sin offerings (of the male goats) reminiscent of the Day of Atonement for "all Israel" (v. 24), thus the northern tribes as well as Judah. The sin offerings for the consecration of the sanctuary and the purification of the priests are also similar to the regulations in Ezek 43:18-27; 45:18-23. The "they" who do the slaughtering (v. 22) is best understood as impersonal, since it is typically the offerer and not the priests who slaughter the sacrifices; the priests then handle the blood (Lev 1:4-5). The rest of the chapter describes the resumption of cultic activities at the temple and the celebration of this restoration. Verses 25-30 focus on the reinstatement of the Levitical musicians, according to the pattern established by David, whose name occurs four times here. These verses have been considered secondary by some scholars because of the prominence in them of the Levites.

The reference to Gad and Nathan (v. 25) reaffirms the connection of the musical activity of the temple with prophecy, a connection that occurs elsewhere in Chronicles (1 Chr 25:1; cf. 2 Chr 20:14). The trumpet is distinguished as the priests' instrument, apart from those of the Levites (v. 26).

In verses 31-36 the celebration is described. The peace offerings and thank offerings are eaten, while the burnt offerings and consecrated offerings are not. Hence, there is both festivity and spontaneous expression of devotion (v. 31b). The responsiveness of the people and the number of sacrifices are reminiscent of similar occasions under David and Solomon. The number of sacrifices is so large, in fact, that the priests cannot handle them all, and the Levites assist in the slaughter (v. 34). The comment in this verse that the Levites were more fastidious in sanctifying themselves than the priests may reveal the Chronicler's pro-Levitical tendency, but the main point is that "the thing had come about suddenly" (v. 36). The clause "because of what God had done for the people" in this verse is awkward in Hebrew, and the simple emendation of "for the people" to "their heart" improves the sense: "because God had established their heart."

Celebrating the Passover (2 Chr 30:1-27)

The historicity of Hezekiah's Passover celebration is much debated among scholars. Those who deny it point to the many instances of artificiality in the story and of the Chronicler's particular interests and style in the narrative. Those who endorse the basic historicity of the event note the frank admission of irregularities in the celebration and argue that they indicate genuineness rather than invention.

The Chronicles account of the Passover has two parts, which detail the preparations for the Passover (vv. 1-12) and then its celebration (vv. 13-27). Verses 1 and 5, with their references to Hezekiah's message to all Israel, bracket the "flashback" (vv. 2-4) regarding the decision to keep the Passover in the second month. The dating of the decision to Hezekiah's first month (cf. 29:3) is artificial and reflects the Chronicler's interest in depicting Hezekiah's primary concern with the Passover. It also presupposes the calendar of the postexilic period, with the new year in the spring, rather than in the fall as was likely the case in Hezekiah's day. The depiction of a national, centralized celebration in Jerusalem is also anachronistic and runs counter to the observance of the Passover within individual families (cf. Exod 12). The national celebration, however, allows the Chronicler to voice another one of his main interests—that of "all Israel." Thus in 30:1, Hezekiah sends to "all Israel and Judah" and writes letters (another likely anachronism) to Ephraim and Manasseh, inviting them to celebrate the Passover "to Yahweh God of Israel." Indeed, the presence of people "from Beersheba to Dan" (v. 5) is an idealization by the Chronicler. It is often observed, though, that the fact that Hezekiah named his son Manasseh suggests his genuine interest in the north. The letters may also hint at the Chronicler's awareness that the northern kingdom is no longer in existence as a unified whole. In verses 2-4, the Chronicler uses the insufficient number of ritually clean priests and the attendance in Jerusalem to explain the decision to postpone the Passover celebration, rather than the explanation readily available from 29:17 that the cleansing of the temple occasioned the delay. The reason may be that ritual uncleanness allowed him to draw on Num 9:9-11 for legitimation. The word translated "in great numbers" by the NRSV in the last line of verse 5 might also mean "many times, often," referring to the infrequency of past celebration rather than to the extent of participation.

The letter in verses 6-9 is marked off by a bracket (vv. 6, 9) calling on the people to return to Yahweh so that he may return to them ("measure for measure"). The intervening verses admonish the hearers/readers to eschew the stubbornness and rebelliousness of their forebears. The language and message are anthological—"stiff-necked" (v. 8) is a common expression in Deuteronomy, the measure-for-measure call to return resembles

Mal 3:8, and verse 9 shares language with Mal 1:9. But the letter as a whole is especially similar to Zech 1:2-4 and probably draws from it. The word "return" *(šûb)* is key and again puns with the root *šbh*, "to capture." The entire letter and the subsequent celebration pick up and elaborate on the words and ideas in Solomon's prayer in 2 Chr 7:14: return (vv. 6, 9), humble (11), pray (18), seek (19), hear, and heal (20). The assumption that the northern exile has occurred is now explicit (v. 6). The reference to Yahweh as the God of Abraham, Isaac, and Israel invokes both northern and southern traditions. The great sin shared by both Israel and Judah (under Ahaz) is the abandonment of Yahweh's sanctuary in Jerusalem (v. 8). The response of the northerners (vv. 10-11) confirms the Chronicler's view of them as apostate, though still Yahweh's people; most scoff, but a few humble themselves and accept the invitation. Judah, however, is united in enthusiastic response (v. 12). As in 29:15, the king's command is here equated with the word of Yahweh.

The beginning of the celebration refers to the feast of unleavened bread rather than the Passover (v. 13, also v. 21). As in Deut 16:1-8, the two festivals were combined in conjunction with centralization in Jerusalem. However, following his anthological style, the Chronicler also draws upon the inauguration of Passover in Exod 12:1-20 for his description in 2 Chr 30:15-16. Still, the Chronicler counters those who would regard him as a legalist. In verses 17-20 he treats the special circumstances surrounding the keeping of the Passover on this occasion. Many of the celebrants, especially those from the north, were not ritually clean but ate the Passover meal anyway. Hezekiah's prayer (vv. 18-19) illustrates the Chronicler's viewpoint that the attitude of the heart is more important to God than the letter of the law. The statement that Yahweh "healed" the people (v. 20) is obscure. It does not seem to mean that God had sent some disease among the unclean, but rather that God compensated for or overlooked their ritual uncleanness. The prolonging of the celebration for a second week (v. 23) illustrates the people's exhuberance and is reminiscent of the second week of celebration at the dedication of Solomon's temple (2 Chr 7:9), as are Hezekiah's provision of the offerings (v. 24) and the assembly of all Israel for the occasion (v. 25; cf. 2 Chr 1:3; 6:3, 12-13). The latter might also recall David's coronation (1 Chr 13:2, 4) and the assembly to pass the throne to Solomon (1 Chr 29:1, 10, 20). The comparison of Hezekiah to Solomon is explicit (v. 26). Scholars have debated whether the Chronicler presents Hezekiah more as a "new David" or a "new Solomon." A compromise solution might be to recognize that Hezekiah incorporates elements of both. In another sense, Hezekiah is his own king in Chronicles and might be considered as furnishing a paradigm in his own right—that of the reforming king who restores temple worship, none of which is to deny his comparability with David and Solomon.

Reestablishing the Temple Personnel (2 Chr 31:1-21)

Chapter 31 continues the account of cultic reforms from the previous chapters. Inspired and enthused by the Passover, the people follow Hezekiah's lead; as he cleansed the temple, so they remove the paraphernalia of other gods from the rest of the country, including the north—Benjamin, Ephraim, and Manasseh (31:1). The description in Chronicles uses Deut 7:5 to enlarge upon 2 Kgs 18:4. Hezekiah then turns his attention to the organization of the priests and Levites (31:2). In this respect, he continues the organizational work of David (1 Chr 24) and also of Solomon (2 Chr 8:14). The designation of the temple as "the camp of Yahweh" identifies it with the tabernacle during the wilderness period, as we have seen the Chronicler do before. Hezekiah's provision of the temple sacrifices from his own possessions (31:3) again resembles the activities of David and Solomon (1 Chr 29:1-5; 2 Chr 8:12-13). The people are charged with providing for the Levites through their tithes (v. 4). The Chronicler probably draws from the regulations regarding the tithe in Deut 14:22-29. Malachi 3:8-10 indicates that collection of the tithe may have been a problem in the Chronicler's day, so that his treatment of the issue here is aimed at his contemporaries. The purpose clause, "that they might devote themselves to the law of Yahweh" (v. 4), once more uses the verb *ḥāzaq*, punning on Hezekiah's name.

The response of the people (vv. 5-9) again illustrates the principle of mutuality between divine blessing and human generosity. As the people bring their gifts, God blesses their produce and they bring more. The "tithe of the dedicated things" (v. 6) makes no sense and is otherwise unattested; it is probably the result either of a accidental duplication of "tithe" or the accidental loss of a phrase like "all the produce of the field" as in verse 5. The abundance of produce occasions Hezekiah's order to prepare storage facilities (v. 11), as well as his appointment of Levites to oversee the distribution (vv. 12-15). The scene recalls David's appointment of similar Levitical administrators (1 Chr 26:20-28). The cooperation of the king and the chief priest (v. 10) in this endeavor recalls the collaboration of Jehoiada and Joash. A key word in this context is "faithfully," which expresses the integrity of those in charge of the process. Separate criteria are used to enroll the priests and Levites for distribution: the priests are enrolled according to genealogy, while the Levites are enrolled by office or category of service (v. 17). "In the cities of the priests" (v. 15) is likely corrupt and should be emended to "by the hand of the priests," as indicated by the LXX. As noted, the closing verses of the chapter (vv. 20-21) pick up on 29:1-2 and mark the unity of chapters 29–31. The root *ʿāśāh*, "to do, make," occurs repeatedly in these verses and highlights the theme of Hezekiah's activity. The statement that he "prospered" (v. 21) is also used for Solomon (1 Chr 29:23), once more attesting the exclusive company in which the Chronicler places Hezekiah.

Sennacherib's Invasion (2 Chr 32:1-33)

In this chapter the Chronicler condenses the account of Hezekiah in 2 Kgs 18–20 and its parallel in Isa 36–39, albeit with significant changes. Verses 1-23 focus on Sennacherib's invasion, the rest of the chapter on other episodes of Hezekiah's reign in the Kings/Isaiah account. The reference to "the faithfulness" (v. 1) shows that the invasion is not punishment for sin. In that respect it resembles Zerah's invasion in Asa's day (14:9-15). It also hints at Hezekiah's deliverance as a result of his faithfulness. Some scholars also point out the similarity of the clause "after these things" to Gen 22:1 and suggest that it alludes to a test of Hezekiah's faithfulness. The Chronicler does not mention a revolt on Hezekiah's part against Assyria, although the measures in verses 3-6 suggest that he had been planning one for some time. Chronicles also omits the reference to the payment of tribute in 2 Kgs 18:14-17, since it would hardly square with the Chronicler's stress on relying solely on Yahweh.

Verses 3-6 describe typical measures of siege warfare—blocking off or camouflaging water sources outside of a city to keep them from invaders, fortifying Jerusalem's walls and towers, manufacturing weapons, organizing defenses—and are all concentrated on Jerusalem. Such tactics would be common knowledge and do not indicate access to a separate written source. On the other hand, there is some archaeological evidence that Hezekiah's Jerusalem did have two walls with a reservoir between them (32:5), information that the Chronicler would not have derived from the Jerusalem of his own day. The Chronicler stresses the cooperation of the people in these preparations. The fact that both David and Solomon are said to have built the Millo (1 Chr 11:8; 1 Kgs 11:27) encourages comparison of Hezekiah to them. There is a tension between Hezekiah's preparations and his speech (vv. 7-8). What is the point of such preparation if Yahweh will fight the battles for them? Apparently, for the Chronicler, the one does not preclude the other; perhaps his view is that help comes at God's discretion so that it does not rule out human preparedness. The verb *ḥāzaq* occurs twice in verse 5 ("set to work resolutely" and "strengthened") and is found again in verse 7 ("be strong") in play on Hezekiah's name. His words of encouragement (vv. 7-8) draw on a variety of ideas and language from other texts, especially Deut 31:6; Josh 10:25; 2 Kgs 6:16; Isa 7:14; 8:8-10 (cf. 2 Chr 20:15). Hezekiah's confident attitude in this speech differs markedly from that on display in 2 Kgs 18:14-17.

The reason for Sennacherib's impending defeat is made clear in his message and letters to the people of Jerusalem (vv. 12-19). He completely misunderstands the nature of Yahweh and of Hezekiah's reforms. Ironically, he thinks that Yahweh will be displeased by the very reforms that Hezekiah has carried out to gain Yahweh's favor and to unite the people in devotion to him (v. 12). The examples he cites of the failure of the gods of other nations to protect their people are meaningless, because Sennacherib has never faced the one true God. Indeed, that is his most serious mistake and the ultimate cause of his downfall—he treats Yahweh with contempt (v. 17) and on the same level as the gods of the nations (vv. 17, 19). He questions Yahweh's ability to save, leaving himself wide open for a demonstration of his power. The Chronicler's version of these exchanges omits the titles of the Assyrian officials (cf. 2 Kgs 18:17), probably for conciseness. It also omits the reference to Egypt (2 Kgs 18:21) as an unreliable ally, since this would contradict the portrait of Hezekiah as relying solely on God. Finally, the Chronicler omits 2 Kgs 18:23-32 // Isa 36:8-18*a*, in which the Jerusalem officials ask the Assyrian Rabshakeh to speak in Aramaic rather than Hebrew so as not to terrorize the city's defenders and the Rabshakeh refuses, as terrorizing is exactly what he seeks to do. Chronicles mentions that the Assyrians spoke "in the language of Judah" (32:18), but there is no hint of a lack of confidence on the part of the people of Jerusalem.

The king's response, like that of his subjects, reflects calmness and confidence (32:20) rather than despair (2 Kgs 19:1-4 // Isa 37:1-4). He and Isaiah, who plays virtually no role in the Chronicles story, simply "prayed because of this and cried to heaven" (v. 20), which was the perfect response: they relied on God. As a result, Yahweh annihilated the leaders and commanders of the Assyrian army so that Sennacherib was forced to return in shame (note the wordplay with *wayyāšob,* "he returned," and *běbōšet,* "in shame") to his homeland where he was assassinated by his sons in the temple of his god (32:21). The obvious irony is that he who assumed incorrectly that Yahweh could not protect Israel was not protected by his gods from his own family. Historically, Sennacherib's assassination occurred in 681 B.C.E., twenty years removed from this campaign against Judah. The two events are separate in Kings, but in Chronicles Sennacherib's death appears as the immediate consequence of the deliverance of Jerusalem. The fate of Hezekiah is completely the opposite of Sennacherib's (vv. 22-23). He has rest all around (reflecting a slight emendation in v. 22 for MT's "he led them"), and he receives respect and gifts from the nations all because of his trust in Yahweh. These are clearly blessings from Yahweh and they bring to mind Solomon's international prestige and wealth.

The story of Hezekiah's illness in 2 Kgs 20:1-11 presented another theological problem for the Chronicler. If Hezekiah was righteous, why did he become ill? The Chronicler condensed the story into just one verse (v. 24). He then added verses 25-26, apparently in order to derive a theological point from the episode—one that differs from the point of his Kings source. In addition to showing God's response to Hezekiah's prayer (v. 24), verses 25-26 indicate that Hezekiah was momentarily led astray by pride, a typical cause for the downfall of kings in Chronicles. The rest of the story then makes two points. First, Hezekiah is a model of humility and repentance when the unspecified "wrath" comes upon Judah and Jerusalem. Second, God is faithful in responding to Hezekiah's repentance so that the wrath does not come in the days of Hezekiah. The last statement is ambiguous. It would be highly unusual for the Chronicler, who has stressed individual responsibility, to claim here that Hezekiah's punishment was delayed for the next generation, and he does not say this. At the same time, it is difficult not to see here a hint of the impending exile.

The summary of Hezekiah's reign (vv. 27-30) recalls Solomon in its mention of wealth, especially shields, spices, and the note that he "prospered" (cf. 1 Chr 29:23; 2 Chr 9:9, 15-16, 24). The note about prosperity also resumes 31:21. The final verse before Hezekiah's closing formulae (v. 31) obviously alludes to the visit of the Babylonian envoy in 2 Kgs 20:12-19. But the reason for the visit seems different. In Kings they come having heard of Hezekiah's illness but also to survey Hezekiah's wealth. In Chronicles they come because of Hezekiah's miraculous healing, here called a "sign." The statement that God left Hezekiah to himself in order to test him seems to be a cryptic allusion to the Kings story, but the exact point and results of the test are never made clear. Typically, the Chronicler uses the death and burial formulae (vv. 32-33) for one last assessment of Hezekiah. For "his power" in 2 Kgs 20:20, the Chronicler substitutes "his good deeds." Chronicles also cites the "vision" of Isaiah as a source—perhaps in reference to Isa 36–39. Hezekiah is buried in the royal tombs with full honor from Judah and Jerusalem (v. 33). The "ascent" on which he is buried, in addition to a topographic reference, may reflect one last attempt to distinguish this king, who must be considered in the Chronicler's portrayal the third greatest king of Israel behind David and Solomon.

Theological Analysis

Hezekiah is clearly a very important king in the Chronicler's estimation. In many ways on a par with David and Solomon, he is not a "new" David or Solomon but a model in his own right, a paradigm for the restoration of religious institutions and life. The account of Hezekiah hints at the exile (32:26) but then roundly illustrates how to bounce back from it. Together with Jotham and Ahaz, Hezekiah illustrates the fundamental principle of individual responsibility. His repentance and righteousness turn the nation around after Ahaz; Judah's worst king is succeeded by one of its best.

The focus in chapters 29–31 on Hezekiah's cultic reforms shows the importance of right worship as the foundation of right deeds, the right relationship with God, and divine deliverance and protection. But the Chronicler is no legalist. The attitude of the heart takes precedence over the letter of the law (30:18-19). Hezekiah is paradigmatic not just because of his reforms, but also because of his attitude of faithfulness in calling upon Yahweh for help (32:20) and of penitence when his pride got the best of him (32:25-26). Above all, like David and Solomon, he relies on God, though this reliance does not preclude him from making preparations for Sennacherib's invasion. He not only relies on God to help him but also trusts God's discretion to do so in his own good time. The people's attitude is also exemplary. The Chronicler's portrait of the people is quite positive. He voices no concern about the commitment of the defenders of Jerusalem (contrast 2 Kgs 18:26). Generosity and joyfulness are central elements of the popular support of the temple clergy, a matter that may have had special applicability in the Chronicler's community. The same may be true about the response of some of the residents in the north; the Chronicler appears optimistic that at least some northerners of his day will respond faithfully to the opportunity to return to the worship of Yahweh in the temple.

THE REIGNS OF MANASSEH AND AMON
(2 CHRONICLES 33:1-25)

Of the accounts in Chronicles of the reigns of Manasseh (vv. 1-20) and Amon (vv. 21-25), the former is by far the more interesting. The Chronicler's account of Amon is quite close to its Kings counterpart and consists mainly of the standard regnal formulae. But the Manasseh account differs because the Chronicler did not regard him as the worst king of Judah, as did the author of Kings. That role in Chronicles had been assumed by Ahaz. As for other kings, the Chronicler periodizes Manasseh's reign; but Manasseh is unique in that the positive period of his reign comes after the negative one rather than before it.

Literary Analysis

The content of the section on Manasseh can be outlined as follows: Manasseh's wickedness (vv. 1-10), Manasseh's captivity and repentance (vv. 11-13), Manasseh's reforms (vv. 14-17), closing formulae (vv. 18-20). A different outline emerges from a comparison with Kings. Verses 1-9 are closely parallel to their source in 2 Kgs 21:1-9. The references to "the nations whom Yahweh dispossessed/destroyed before the Israelites" (vv. 2, 9) serve as bookends to the catalog of Manasseh's offenses. Verse 10 might be seen as a significantly abbreviated and altered version of 2 Kgs 21:10-15. The account of Manasseh's repentance in captivity and subsequent reform (vv. 11-17) is unique to Chronicles. This very different version of Manasseh's reign is theologically motivated, as explained below. Then 2 Chr 33:18, 20 parallel 2 Kgs 21:17-18, with 33:19 encapsulating key elements of the reign. The brief account of Amon's reign is very similar to 2 Kgs 21:19-24. The closing formula, including the burial formula, for Amon (2 Kgs 21:25-26) is lacking in Chronicles as a result of either accidental or intentional omission (see below).

Exegetical Analysis

The Reign of Manasseh (2 Chr 33:1-20)

Manasseh's fifty-five-year reign (v. 1), the longest of any king of Judah, is one of the factors fueling the Chronicler's different account of his reign. While the long reign fits the point of Kings that Manasseh had an irreversible, deleterious effect, it was impossible from the Chronicler's theological perspective for a king with such a lengthy reign to have been as evil as the book of Kings describes him. Moreover, the Chronicler's theology of individual responsibility would not allow him to blame the exile on Manasseh, as in Kings. Hence, the first part of Manasseh's reign could be evil, as in Kings, but then something had to change.

As noted above, the description of Manasseh's wickedness is framed by references to the pre-Israelite, Canaanite nations (vv. 2, 9). The implication is that Judah under Manasseh deserved the same fate as the Canaanites. Thus, in formulating the list of sins (vv. 3-6), the Chronicler has borrowed from the description of the "abominations of the Canaanites" in Deut 18:9-13. These sins are also a reversal of the reforms effected by Hezekiah, as verse 3 points out. The term "sacred poles" (NRSV) is Asheroth, the plural of the name Asherah, a leading Canaanite goddess. While it could refer to cult objects, its use with "Baals" indicates that the Chronicler has in mind local "manifestations" of these gods. The "host of heaven" are the luminaries (sun, moon, stars) and the zodiac (Deut 4:19; 17:3). Manasseh is accused of worshiping these only in Chronicles. Manasseh's reinstallation of altars to other gods (vv. 4-5) is another reversal of Hezekiah's cleansing measures (cf. 29:16-17).

The Chronicler's reliance on Deut 18:9-13 is evident in verse 6, where he inserts the term "sorcery" (Deut 18:10) into the list of sins in Kings (2 Kgs 21:6). Consulting a medium is such a great sin in the Chronicler's view because it involves "seeking" someone other than Yahweh, as shown by Saul (1 Chr 10:13). This verse also has Manasseh passing his sons through fire in the valley of the son of Hinnom. The reference is apparently to child sacrifice; the location is derived from 2 Kgs 23:10; Jer 7:31; 19:5-6; 32:35. The verse makes clear that Manasseh is every bit as evil as Ahaz, who is accused of the same crime (28:3). The nadir of Manasseh's sin (v. 4) is his construction of idols to other gods in Yahweh's own temple (vv. 7-8). This is the low point because it, in effect, abrogates the promise to David. More than that, since Israel's occupation of the land is contingent on their obedience to the Law of Moses, this deed of Manasseh's threatens Israel's expulsion. The allusion to the exile is obvious—all the more since Manasseh is not alone in his sins but corrupts Judah and Jerusalem (v. 9). Only his repentance prevents the exile from occurring in his day.

As is typical of the Chronicler's style, verse 10 begins the same way as its counterpart in 2 Kgs 21:20, but then the Chronicler makes changes in accord with his message and theology. Rather than the prophetic announcement of Judah's impending fate in 2 Kgs 21:10-15, 2 Chr 33:10 simply states that Yahweh spoke to Manasseh and the people, who in turn refused to listen. Again, the Chronicler's theology of individual responsibility does not allow the exile to be blamed on Manasseh. Although Chronicles does not mention prophets here, the reference to "seers" (v. 18) indicates that he understands them as the medium through which Yahweh spoke to Manasseh.

The primary issue in the rest of the chapter is that of historicity. In brief, there is no direct evidence in the form of Assyrian records of Manasseh's captivity in Babylon. Manasseh is mentioned in the annals of Esarhaddon and Ashurbanipal as a loyal vassal who aided the Assyrian campaign against Egypt (*ANET*, 291, 294). However, indirect evidence supports the plausibility of the story. "In manacles" (v. 11) should better be translated "with hooks" and refers to rings placed in the noses or mouths of captives with which the Assyrians led them away (*ANEP*, 447). Assyrian annals report the capture (albeit in Nineveh, not Babylon, which is an odd feature of the Manasseh story) and subsequent return of the Egyptian king, Necho (*ANET*, 295). Some scholars have gone so far as to connect Manasseh's imprisonment with the rebellion of Assurbanipal's brother, Shamash-shum-ukin, in 652–648 B.C.E., although this is pure supposition. Another possibility is that Manasseh, as an Assyrian vassal, paid an official visit to his overlord and that the Chronicler transformed this notice into the present story.

The answer to Manasseh's prayer in the form of his return to Jerusalem convinces him that Yahweh alone is God (v. 13) and leads him to embark on a series of reforms (vv. 14-17). Verse 14 describes Manasseh's building projects, which indicate divine favor following his repentance. Again, these are historically plausible, as they reflect a continuation of Hezekiah's efforts to strengthen Jerusalem and to rebuild the network of fortified cities that Sennacherib had weakened, especially in view of the weakening of Assyria's hold on Judah. Verses 15-17 detail the correction of many of Manasseh's apostasies described earlier in the chapter. In Kings it is left to Josiah to correct Manasseh's evils, and even then, as the book now stands, it is too little too late to prevent the exile. Josiah's significance in Chronicles is not as great as in Kings, and Manasseh is not blamed for the exile, so that he reverses many of his own sins. The damage, however, is done, as indicated by the "high places" that are left for Josiah to remove (v. 17).

The summary of Manasseh's reign (vv. 18-20) is clearly based on 2 Kgs 21:17-18, but since the contents of the two accounts are so different, the summaries naturally vary as well. While Kings has a source citation for "all that [Manasseh] did and the sin that he committed," Chronicles offers much more detail, rehearsing the episodes of the Chronicles account—Manasseh's sins (the high places, "sacred poles," and idols) but also his prayer and God's reception of it, the words of the seers who spoke to him, and his humbling of himself. The sources cited by the Chronicler are the annals of the kings of Israel (by which he apparently means Judah, since the kingdom of Israel no longer exists) and the "records of his seers" (reading *dibrê ḥôzāy* in v. 19). The mention of Manasseh's prayer as a written document inspired the composition of the apocryphal/deuterocanonical work of that name. Manasseh is buried "in the garden of his house" (v. 20, supplying "in the garden" on the basis of 2 Kgs 21:18). Given the Chronicler's use of burial notices as expressions of favor or disfavor, the lack of reference to the royal tombs suggests continued ambivalence of the Chronicler toward Manasseh despite his repentance.

The Reign of Amon (2 Chr 33:21-25)

In accord with the doctrine of individual responsibility, Manasseh's repentance is effective only for himself and does not apply to son, Amon, whose reign represents a regression to the days of Ahaz and of Manasseh's early period. The Chronicler's account is essentially the same as 2 Kgs 21:19-26 with some predictable changes. As with all kings starting with Manasseh, the name of the queen mother is absent (cf. 2 Kgs 21:19; 2 Chr 33:21). The reason for this is uncertain. In verse 22b the Chronicler rephrases 2 Kgs 21:21 to refer more specifically to Manasseh's idolatry. The change is necessary because in Chronicles Amon does not walk "in all the way in which his father walked," since he does not repent as did his father, as the Chronicler goes on to explain (v. 23). Instead of repenting, Amon "incurred more and more guilt." His punishment was assassination (v. 24), which may have transpired historically because of political reasons, specifically his pro-Assyrian stance. The "people of the land," probably the landed nobility, then replace Amon with his son Josiah (v. 25). The last two verses of the Kings account (2 Kgs 21:25-26) lack a parallel in Chronicles, and the absence of any burial notice is unusual. It is possible that this is a deliberate omission by the Chronicler, thereby showing his disdain for Amon. But it seems more likely that the Chronicler's version of the notice has been lost accidentally when a scribe's eye skipped from one "Josiah his son in his stead" (2 Kgs 21:24; 2 Chr 33:25) to the other (2 Kgs 21:26).

Theological Analysis

Theology dictates the Chronicler's portrayal of Manasseh. Manasseh's lengthy reign and the Chronicler's stress on individual responsibility preclude agreement with the Kings portrait of

Manasseh as Judah's worst king. Manasseh's experience fore-shadows Judah's exile—a point that would explain the captivity in Babylon rather than Nineveh. As such, Manasseh offers a message of hope to the Chronicler's contemporaries. There is hope of restoration after captivity, but it is dependent on repentance and turning again to God. The story also reinforces other elements of the Chronicler's theology: those who have suffered catastrophe should not blame previous generations but should accept responsibility for their actions and their fates. The right response is not blaming others but humility and calling upon God in prayer (v. 12). Manasseh is the model of such humility and prayer as well as their beneficent results. The negative side of individual responsibility is exemplified by Amon, who does not benefit from Manasseh's repentance. Amon, along with the people of Judah as a whole, fail to remain steady in the reform path launched by Manasseh and thus illustrate the principle that it is easier to be led astray into evil than into doing good.

THE REIGN OF JOSIAH (2 CHRONICLES 34:1–35:27)

Like Hezekiah, Josiah is a reforming king. But unlike Kings, where Josiah's reforms make him the greatest king of Judah, in Chronicles Josiah's reform takes a back seat to Hezekiah's. The main focus of the Chronicler's account of Josiah is his celebration of the Passover, which significantly expands the version of the Josiah's Passover in Kings (compare 2 Kgs 23:22-23 vs. 2 Chr 35:1-19).

Literary Analysis

As with previous kings, the Chronicler found the account of Josiah's reign in Kings to be theologically unsatisfactory and introduced significant changes. In particular, by attributing the initiation of Josiah's reform activity to his eighteenth year, 2 Kgs 22 implies that Josiah tolerated the idolatrous perversions in the temple for seventeen years and that it was the discovery of the book of the law that impelled him to act. The Chronicler altered this portrait in several respects. First, as we have seen, he had Manasseh remove the idolatrous paraphernalia from the temple, so that Josiah's reforms concerned the rest of Jerusalem, Judah, and then the north (34:3, 5-6). These reforms began in Josiah's eighth year, while he was still a boy, and so preceded the discovery of the book of the law. The reforms, therefore, were motivated not by the book and the threats it contained, but by the young king's piety. The discovery of the book might even be seen as a reward for Josiah's pious reforms. A principal reason for the substantially longer account of the Passover in Chronicles is the elaboration of the role of the Levites. The references to Josiah's eighteenth year in 34:8 and 35:19 serve as a framework emphasizing that the Passover celebration follows directly upon the finding of the book of the law.

The account is structured in part by chronological notices and may be outlined as follows:

introduction (34:1-2)
cleansing of the land (34:3-7)
    Judah and Jerusalem (vv. 3-5)
    the rest of Israel (vv. 6-7)
repairing the temple (34:8-13)
the book of the law (34:14-28)
    the discovery of the book (vv. 14-21)
    Huldah's oracle (vv. 22-28)
renewal of the covenant (34:29-33)
celebrating the Passover (35:1-19)
Josiah's death (35:20-27).

Exegetical Analysis

The introduction to Josiah's reign (vv. 1-2) is nearly identical to 2 Kgs 22:1-2 except for the absence of the queen mother's name, standard in Chronicles from Manasseh on. The comparison with David (v. 2) is high praise indeed in Chronicles, as it occurs only for Hezekiah and Josiah. Verse 3 is the Chronicler's addition to the Kings account. The Chronicler locates the motivation for Josiah's reforms in his inclination to seek Yahweh from the early age of eight rather than in the book of the law. Then in his twelfth year, at age 20, which may have been considered the age of manhood (cf. 1 Chr 23:24, 27; 27:23; 2 Chr 31:17), Josiah began his purge of the land. The Chronicler has adapted 2 Kgs 23:6, 16b-20 and shifted them to 34:4-7 in his account, the net effect being that Josiah enlarges on the religious reforms of Manasseh in the temple and extends them to Jerusalem, Judah, and Israel before he effects repairs on the temple. Again, the reforms are motivated by Josiah's character rather than the discovery of the book of the law.

The account of the purge of Judah and Jerusalem (vv. 3b-5) is set apart by the references to that effect at the beginning and end of those verses. The pulverizing of the images (vv. 4, 7) may draw on Moses' treatment of the golden calf in Exod 32:20. The practical consequence is that they cannot be rebuilt from the same materials. Strewing the dust over tombs (v. 4) and burning bones on the altars are the ultimate acts of defilement. In verse 4, the Chronicler changes the language of 2 Kgs 23:6 so that the dust is not scattered on the tombs of the common people but more appropriately from a retributive theological standpoint, on "those who had sacrificed to them." Then, in verse 5, Chronicles conflates the two references to bones being burned on altars in 2 Kgs 23:16, 20, only the second of which mentions priests.

Next, Josiah turns his reforms toward the north (v. 6). Ephraim and Manasseh are commonly used as referring to the northern domain. Naphtali was the northernmost of the tribal allotments and may symbolize the full extent of the northern reforms. Simeon, which was originally south of Judah and was absorbed within Judah at an early date, seems out of place. It may serve as a balance to Naphtali, again representing the full extent of the land of united Israel from south to north. But the immediate context deals with the north apart from Judah. Hence, recent scholars have suggested taking "Simeon" as a reference to a site in the Jezreel Valley (Khirbet Simoniain) rather than to the tribe. Josiah's personal involvement in these reforms is indicated by the note at the end of verse 6 that he returned to Jerusalem.

Verses 8-13 describe the repairs on the temple leading up to the finding of the book of the law. Verses 8-11 draw on 2 Kgs 22:3-6 but report the process as something carried out rather than as a series of commands from the king. The process is well organized but has been obscured somewhat by minor textual corruptions. The king appointed Shaphan, Maaseiah (= Asaiah?), and Joah (v. 8), whose names and titles are well attested elsewhere in Kings (2 Kgs 18:18, 26, 37; 22:12, 14 [Maaseiah = Asaiah?]; 23:8) and may have been accidentally lost from the parallel here (2 Kgs 22:2). These three then came to Hilkiah, the high priest, and together they emptied out (reading *ntk* in v. 9 in place of the MT's *ntn*) the money collected in the temple by the Levites. The Chronicler takes pains to note the role of the Levites in the process and to point out that the "remnant of Israel" in the north contributed along with those from Judah, Benjamin, and Jerusalem. That money is then given to the supervisors (v. 10*a*), who in turn give it to those doing the work, including the carpenters and builders. Evidently, Manasseh and Amon, who must be the ones intended by "the kings of Judah" (v. 11*b*) had not properly maintained the temple complex. Verses 12-13 are unique to Chronicles and again lay out the importance of the Levites in this process. Verse 12*b*, at least, may be secondary, as it seems out of place in the context of this report about building repair to observe the musical skill of the Levites. Curiously, only the Merarites and Kohathites are mentioned here; the Gershonites are absent.

Verse 14 provides a transition from the added material in verses 12-13 back to the Kings narrative. Then verses 15-31 follow 2 Kgs 22:8–23:3 relatively closely. Scholars have long observed that the book of the law in Kings was some form of Deuteronomy. For the Chronicler, however, it was likely understood as the entire Pentateuch, as suggested by the title "the book of the law of Yahweh given through Moses" (v. 14). The book is brought to the king with a sense of foreboding (vv. 15-18a) that is justified when it is read in his presence (vv. 18b-19). The seriousness of the situation is indicated by the high status of the officials whom the king sends to Huldah to inquire about the book (v. 20). The wording of the king's command, "inquire of Yahweh for me and for those who are left in Israel and in Judah" coalesces the prophetic roles of inquirer or diviner and intercessor. Huldah's oracle in response (vv. 22-28) is typically Deuteronomistic and is taken from the Chronicles-Kings source with only minor changes. For instance, in verse 24 the Chronicler changes the verb to the plural, "which they read," to be understood in a passive sense, "was read" (so NRSV) in order to accord more closely with verse 18 where Shaphan read the book before the king.

In line with the doctrine of individual responsibility, the Chronicler's account of the covenant (vv. 29-33) stresses the central role of the king. Verses 29-31 are taken from 2 Kgs 23:1-3 with very few changes. In verse 30 (// 2 Kgs 23:2) the word "Levites" replaces "prophets" in accord with the Chronicler's identification of the Levitical musicians as incorporating a prophetic role. The book of the law in this verse is called "the book of the covenant" in anticipation of the covenant ceremony that follows. The covenant in verse 31 is not a covenant with Yahweh but one between the king and the people pledging themselves to keep the law. It is, therefore, a renewal of the commitment to keep the stipulations of the original covenant between Yahweh and Israel.

The last two verses of the chapter (vv. 32-33) are unique to Chronicles. Verse 32a is an adaptation of 2 Kgs 23:3b. In accord with the latter, "in the covenant" should probably be read in place of "in Benjamin." What is more important is the Chronicler's change of subject from the people to the king. Indeed, these two verses focus on Josiah's role in extending the covenant to all Israel and in compelling the people to worship Yahweh. While this would seem to be a positive thing for Judah, verse 33b is rather disheartening in its note that the people did not turn away from Yahweh "all his [Josiah's] days." The statement suggests that Josiah's reform was only surface-deep and leaves open the possibility that the people would again slip into apostasy after he was gone—apostasy that would bring about destruction at the hands of the Babylonians.

The account of Josiah's Passover in 35:1-19 is a vast expansion of the brief notice in 2 Kgs 23:21-23. The Chronicler takes pains to point out that, in contrast to the Passover celebrated by Hezekiah in which there were several irregularities, Josiah's Passover was properly observed in all details. Thus, the Passover lamb was slaughtered on the fourteenth day of the first month (v. 1) as prescribed in Exod 12:1-6. The extensive involvement of the Levites is stressed throughout the account. Indeed, verse 3 reminds the Levites that their primary responsibility now is the temple liturgy. This extensive role of the Levites as well as their divisions (and those of the laity, v. 5) reflect the situation of the Chronicler's own day. The instruction to the Levites to set the ark in the temple (v. 3) is odd, since this was done already in Solomon's day; many scholars propose reading a passive or impersonal form of the verb "to give, set" rather than the imperative. This verse also refers to the Levites as teachers, a role often ascribed to priests.

The duties of the Levites are detailed in verses 3-6 with appeals to the authority of David and Solomon and the law of Moses. They involve, among other things, the slaughter of the Passover lamb (vv. 6, 11) with the priests sprinkling the blood. Again, this division of responsibilities probably hails from the Chronicler's day. The order to "sanctify yourselves" (v. 6) is out of place, as the Levites would presumably already have done so; the word "holy sacrifices" should probably be read instead. The place of the "bulls" or large cattle *(bāqār)* in the celebration is not entirely clear and may originate from the mention of *bāqār* in Deut 16:2 (harmonized with Exod 12). They are eaten by the celebrants, as are the "burnt offerings" (v. 120), so that they are obviously not whole burnt offerings. In any case, the Chronicler highlights the generosity of the king and his officials in providing the animals for sacrifice.

Verse 13 contains another, well-known example of harmonization of conflicting instructions that the Passover lamb be roasted (Exod 12:8-9) and that it be boiled (Deut 16:7). Using the latter verb in its broadest sense, the Chronicler states that they "cooked" the Passover in fire and then that they "boiled" the holy offerings. The Chronicler ends the account of the Passover with the remark that no such Passover had been kept since Samuel (v. 18). The remark seems initially to contradict the account of Hezekiah's Passover, despite the Chronicler's omission of the mention in 2 Kgs 23:22 of the kings of Judah. Evidently, the Chronicler sees Josiah's Passover as unique either in the extent of participation ("all Judah and Israel") or in the precision with which it adhered to the regulations regarding the Passover, or both.

Josiah's death as recounted in Kings was theologically problematic for the Chronicler. How could he have been killed in battle after all of his righteous deeds, especially in view of Huldah's prophecy that he would die in peace? From the Chronicler's perspective Josiah's death had to be punishment for sin. Hence, the Chronicles version is an elaboration of the notice in Kings with motifs drawn especially from the story of Ahab's death in 2 Chr 18:28-34; 1 Kgs 22:29-40. The addition of Carchemish as Neco's destination and the omission of the reference to him going to fight against the king of Assyria (2 Kgs 22:29) may indicate that the Chronicler also had access to historically reliable information about this event. Neco was on his way to fight on behalf of Assyria against Babylon.

Josiah's sin was his failure to heed the word of God in the mouth of Neco (2 Chr 35:21-22), though it is not clear how Josiah was supposed to recognize that Neco's words were from God. Perhaps we are to understand that it was Josiah's willfulness that kept him from discerning the source of Neco's warning. Josiah's disguise fits ill in this context and is a motif drawn from the Ahab story (2 Kgs 18:28). Other such motifs are the random arrow, which strikes the king, and the king's command to take him out of the battle because he is wounded. Despite his sin and violent death, the concluding formula for Josiah (35:24-27) expresses high esteem. The lament composed by Jeremiah (v. 25) has nothing to do with the biblical book of Lamentations but attests the people's regard for the king. The so-called "Book of the Kings of Israel and Judah" (v. 27) is probably an allusion to the biblical book of Kings. However, scholars debate whether the Chronicler's source for the account of Josiah's death was the book of Kings as we now have it or a more developed version of the story (Begg 1987; Williamson 1982a; 1987).

Theological Analysis

It is somewhat surprising to find Josiah's inquiry and Huldah's oracular response from Kings essentially repeated by the Chronicler, first because they present a theological problem for his principle of individual responsibility and second because Josiah's death in battle seems to contradict Huldah's prediction that he would go to his grave in peace. The two issues are related. While they seem at first glance to undercut the principles of individual responsibility and immediate retribution, a closer look shows that they actually work to reinforce these theological themes. Josiah states that Yahweh's wrath, which is about to be poured out on "us," is great because of the failure of "our ancestors" to heed the book of the law (34:21), and Huldah's gloomy prediction about the fate awaiting Judah seems to confirm the inevitability of punishment. Still, the tension with the doctrine of individual responsibility is not as pronounced as it first appears. Huldah's address to "this place" (a common term for a shrine and its environs) and "its inhabitants" indicates that the present generation is guilty of the apostasies detailed in 34:25. The fact that Josiah is exempted suggests that the principle of individual responsibility still obtains. It may even offer hope that avoidance of punishment is yet possible through repentance. That certainly appears to be Josiah's understanding, as the oracle launches him to further reforms and the celebration of the Passover.

But, what of Josiah's violent death? Ironically, it also confirms the notion of individual responsibility. Many scholars contend that the contradiction between Huldah's prediction and Josiah's actual demise is patent and demonstrates the genuineness of her prophecy. That may be true for the version in Kings, but the situation is different in Chronicles. Huldah's prophecy about Josiah assumes that he will remain attentive to the word of Yahweh. But the Chronicler shows that Josiah died because he failed to heed Yahweh's warning. Huldah's oracle was not false because circumstances changed. If they changed in the case of Josiah's personal fate, they might also change for Judah and Jerusalem. What happened to Judah and Jerusalem depended on the actions of their inhabitants. The principle of individual responsibility holds, and the possibility of forgiveness following repentance remains open.

Other theological themes that pervade Chronicles also receive reinforcement in the account of Josiah. His rule, as the Davidic heir, over "all Israel" and the northern participation in his Passover are mentioned in various ways throughout the account: "Manasseh, Ephraim, and Simeon," and as far as Naphtali (34:6), "all the land of Israel" (34:7), "Manasseh and Ephraim ... all the remnant of Israel ... all Judah and Benjamin" (34:9), "in Israel and in Judah" (34:21), "Israel" (34:33), "the people of Israel" and "all Israel and Judah" (35:17-18). Josiah's celebration of the Passover illustrates again the importance of following proper rituals with proper religious leaders and personnel.

Finally, the divine message through Neco suggests that God may sometimes speak through foreign rulers and that his people need to be perceptive to his word whatever the means he chooses to use (cf. Ben Zvi 1999). This point may have held particular significance for the Chronicler and his audience in the days of the Persian Empire. This principle calls to mind Second Isaiah's treatment of the Persian king Cyrus and Yahweh's shepherd (Isa 44:28) and messiah ("anointed," Isa 45:1) because of his decree allowing the people of Jerusalem to return to their homeland and rebuild the temple (2 Chr 36:22-23). God sometimes uses foreigners as instruments to carry out his designs.

THE END OF JUDAH (2 CHRONICLES 36:1-23)

The last four kings of Judah—Jehoahaz (vv. 1-4), Jehoiakim (vv. 5-8), Jehoiachin (vv. 9-10), and Zedekiah—are treated in summary fashion in the last chapter of Chronicles, leading to the account of the destruction of Jerusalem during Zedekiah's reign (vv. 11-21). But Jerusalem's fall is not the end. The book concludes on a hopeful note, with the edict of Cyrus (vv. 22-23) releasing the people of Judah and Jerusalem.

Literary Analysis

The first half of chapter 36 (vv. 1-12*a*) represents a significant condensation of 2 Kgs 23:31–25:30 to which verses 12*b*-21 + 22-23 have been added, the former from the Chronicler's own hand, the latter probably from Ezra 1:1-2. The accounts of the kings' reigns (vv. 1-12*a*) follow a stereotyped pattern: an account of the kings' accession is followed by an evaluation (except for Jehoahaz) and then by a report about the intervention of a foreign king who removes the king of Judah from the throne and the land. The Cyrus edict (vv. 22-23), which concludes the book, links Chronicles with Ezra–Nehemiah and may or may not be original to the Chronicler's work.

Exegetical Analysis

As with his father, Josiah, it is "the people of the land" who make Jehoahaz king. This is probably a political statement, since Jehoahaz was not Josiah's oldest son (on the order of sons see the commentary on 1 Chr 3:15). Jehoahaz likely favored his father's anti-Egyptian policy, and for that reason, was removed by Neco after only three months. The Chronicler omits the reference to the people anointing Jehoahaz (v. 1; cf. 2 Kgs 23:30*b*), believing this to be an act inappropriate for laypersons to perform. As for all kings of Judah beginning with Manasseh, the name of Jehoahaz's mother is lacking in Chronicles. More surprising is the absence of any evaluation for Jehoahaz (cf. 2 Kgs 23:32), and this may have been accidental; the Chronicler typically includes these evaluations, and there is no obvious reason for its intentional omission this time. Neco replaced Jehoahaz with his brother, Jehoiakim, whose pro-Egyptian position would show itself in his rebellion against Babylon. The phrase "deposed him in Jerusalem" does not make much sense, and we should restore a verb with 2 Kgs 23:33: "deposed him from reigning in Jerusalem." Also, it is unlikely that Neco's tribute consisted of only one talent of gold; a number has apparently fallen out before the second occurrence of the word "talent." However, the omission had already occurred in the Chronicler's source (2 Kgs 23:33).

The Chronicles version of Jehoiakim's reign (vv. 5-8) omits the political details found in the Kings parallel (2 Kgs 23:36–24:7), so that the invasion of Nebuchadnezzar is the direct result of Jehoiakim's evildoing (v. 5*b*). The Chronicler omits the following "just as all his ancestors [lit., "fathers"] had done" since Jehoiakim's father was the righteous Josiah. The Chronicles report about the captivity and exile of Jehoiakim contrasts with 2 Kgs 23:5-12, which implies that Jehoiakim died during the Babylonian siege of Jerusalem in 597 B.C.E. (cf. Jer 22:18-19; 36:30). The Chronicler's version is probably influenced by the stereotyped pattern for these final four kings, which results in each of the kings dying outside of the land of Israel. Jehoiakim alone is mentioned as the object of God's punitive acts. The same will hold true for Jehoiachin (see below). The destination of the temple vessels—the king's palace in Babylon (v. 7)—is a summary and thus may not contradict the information in Ezra 1:7; Dan 1:2 that the vessels were taken into the Babylonian temple.

The account of Jehoiachin (vv. 9-10) borrows piecemeal from 2 Kgs 24:8-17. The main difference, as with Jehoiakim, is the focus on the captivity of the king alone without reference to the people. The effect is to downplay the magnitude of this initial wave of captivity in anticipation of the destruction of Jerusalem and the major Babylonian exile of 586. Jehoiachin's age at accession in Chronicles is corrupt. The number should be "eighteen" as in 2 Kgs 24:8 rather than "eight." A scribe attempting to correct the error mistakenly inserted the missing element at a later point in the verse, leading to the addition of ten days to Jehoiachin's reign.

For Zedekiah's reign in 36:11-12, the Chronicler borrows the accession formula from 2 Kgs 24:18a (36:11), the evaluation from 2 Kgs 24:19a (36:12a), and adapts the notice of Zedekiah's revolt against Babylon from 2 Kgs 24:20b (36:13a). The rest of the passage is peculiar to Chronicles and falls into three parts: sin (vv. 12-14), warning and rejection (vv. 15-16), and destruction (vv. 17-21). As is typical of the Chronicler's style, the passage is anthological in nature. In accord with his theology of individual responsibility and immediate retribution, Chronicles blames the exile on Zedekiah and his generation rather than on Manasseh as in Kings. Hence, in contrast to the accounts for the previous three kings, Chronicles supplies a detailed list of sins. The Chronicler evidently understands this Zedekiah to be the son of Jehoiakim and brother of Jehoiachin, rather than the son of Josiah as in Kings (see on 1 Chr 3:15-16). This identification may reflect an effort on the part of the Chronicler to parallel Jehoiakim and Zedekiah as the two kings with long reigns and Jehoahaz and Jehoiachin as the two with very short reigns.

Zedekiah's main sin is failing to humble himself and not listening to the prophet Jeremiah (v. 12; cf. Jer 37–38), choosing instead to stiffen his neck (e.g., Jer 7:26; 17:23) and harden his heart (Deut 2:30). In rebelling against Babylon he also violated the oath he had sworn by Yahweh (v. 12; cf. Ezek 17:19). But in contrast to previous kings, Zedekiah is not treated in isolation. The princes (reading "princes of Judah and the priests" for MT's "princes of the priests"), priests, and people are guilty of unfaithfulness and polluting the temple with the "abominations of the nations" (v. 14) Significantly, the only group not specifically named as culpable is the Levites. The accusations are broad generalizations, but the language is significant. The word for "unfaithfulness" (*m'l*), which occurs twice here recalls the condemnation of Saul in 1 Chr 10:14 and suggests that the two texts may be a kind of framework for the entire narrative history of Chronicles. Many scholars see Saul in Chronicles as a metaphor for Israel's history. The reference to the pollution of the temple, which Yahweh had consecrated, through "abominations" borrows from Jer 7:30; 32:34; Ezek 5:11; 23:38. More important, it suggests that the temple is ripe for destruction, as it is no longer sanctified.

Yahweh's first response to these grievous sins is compassion, "sending persistently" (e.g., Jer 7:25; 25:3-4; 29:19) messengers, that is, prophets. Until the very end, repentance remains a possibility. The very end is graphically described as the point at which there was "no remedy," no "healing." The expression occurs in 2 Chr 21:18 in regard to Jehoram's incurable bowel disease (cf. also Jer 14:19). Only when every possible means of curing Israel of its sin had been exhausted did Yahweh resort to venting his great wrath.

Verses 17-21 describe the concrete form of Yahweh's wrath against Judah. Yahweh himself is the ultimate cause, as it is he who brings up the Chaldeans to enact punishment. In contrast to the description in Kings, Zedekiah's fate is not specifically detailed. The target is the people as a whole. The renewal of the Davidic dynasty thereby appears to remain open for the future. The Chronicler evinces no interest in those who stayed in the land. The focus is on Jerusalem, and it appears as though all the people were either killed or taken captive, leaving the land to enjoy its "sabbath." This notion reflects a very different perspective on the exile from that found in Kings. The Chronicler notes that the exile lasted "until the establishment of the kingdom of Persia" (v. 20). He does not, therefore, depict it with the same sense of finality as in Kings. There is hope for return; more than this, the Chronicler perceives that the exile is only a stage, a time of sabbath rest (v. 21). The Chronicler draws on Lev 26:33-35 and on Jer 25:12; 29:10 for the notion of the exile as a sabbath for the land. While Jeremiah does not refer to the Babylonian captivity as a sabbath, he does describe it as lasting seventy years. It is doubtful that the Chronicler has specific dates in mind for calculating a seventy-year period. Seventy is a symbolic number that indicates an extended, multigenerational period of time that fully compensates for Judah's sin. Since the sabbath was the seventh day, the duration of seventy years also plays on the metaphor of the exile as a sabbath period.

The final two verses of Chronicles (36:22-23) in effect reproduce Ezra 1:1-3a. Scholars debate whether they were an original part of the Chronicler's work or were added to link it with Ezra (see the introduction). It only makes sense that the exile and destruction imposed by a foreign ruler (Nebuchadnezzar) is reversed by another foreign ruler. The view of Cyrus suggested here accords with that of Second Isaiah. Perhaps most important, the book, and because of its canonical placement, the Hebrew Bible, ends with an exhortation to the exiles to return to Jerusalem and to rebuild Israel's institutions. Perhaps that, in a nutshell, is the Chronicler's message—by returning to Yahweh and to Jerusalem the people can restore Israel to the greatness it experienced under David and Solomon.

Theological Analysis

As the conclusion to the Chronicler's opus, this chapter is a rich source of his theology. The destruction of Jerusalem and the exile are the direct result of sin. But in line with the Chronicler's theme of immediate retribution/reward and individual responsibility, there is no accumulation of sins which the exile punishes, as is the case in Kings. Rather, the exile in Chronicles is retribution for the sin of the last king of Judah and his contemporaries. The destruction comes at the hands of the Babylonians, but it is God who brings them. God is in control. Only the Levites, among the various groups of that society, are not explicitly held culpable. Still, the sins that lead to judgment are the same ones that have plagued Israel's history. Basic among them are rebellion or unfaithfulness and the failure to humble themselves in response to the warnings from prophets. Therefore, the disaster that ultimately comes is in fulfillment of the prophetic word of Jeremiah and others. The other main category of sin is that of the worship of other gods, even on the grounds of the temple, with the result that the temple becomes polluted, and the pollution must be eradicated. Even in the face of all this evil, God is compassionate, seeking repentance right up to the end. But the people only mock his messengers, the prophets. When the end does come, it is not final in the Chronicler's viewpoint. It is simply a hiatus, a sabbath rest that, in fact, the land needed. God is infinitely merciful, and there is ample opportunity to start over. The Davidic line continues as do the cultic offices and the people of "all Israel." The temple can be rebuilt. Israel's institutions can be restored. The Chronicler has provided the model for such restoration.

SELECT BIBLIOGRAPHY

WORKS CITED

Allen, Leslie C. 1974a. *The Greek Chronicles: The Relation of the Septuagint of I and II Chronicles to the Massoretic Text. I: The Translator's Craft.* Leiden: Brill.

———. 1974b. *The Greek Chronicles: The Relation of the Septuagint of I and II Chronicles to the Massoretic Text. II: Textual Criticism.* Leiden: Brill.

Auld, A. Graeme. 1994. *Kings Without Privilege: David and Moses in the Story of the Bible's Kings.* Edinburgh: T & T Clark.

———. 1999. What Was the Main Source of the Books of Chronicles? Pages 91-99 in *The Chronicler as Author: Studies in Text and Texture.* Edited by M. Patrick Graham and Steven L. McKenzie. JSOTSup 263. Sheffield: Sheffield Academic Press.

Begg, Christopher T. 1987. The Death of Josiah in Chronicles: Another View. *VT* 37:1-8.

Ben Zvi, Ehud. 1991. Once the Lamp Has Been Kindled . . . A Reconstruction of the Meaning of the MT *Nir* in 1 Kgs 11.36; 15.4; 2 Kgs 8.19 and 2 Chr 21.7. *Australian Biblical Review* 39:19-30.

———. 1999. When the Foreign Monarch Speaks. Pages 209-28 in *The Chronicler as Author: Studies in Text and Texture.* Edited by M. Patrick Graham and Steven L. McKenzie. JSOTSup 263. Sheffield: Sheffield Academic Press.

Blenkinsopp, Joseph. 1974. Did Saul Make Gibeon His Capital? *VT* 24:1-7.

Bordreuil, Pierre, F. Israel, and Dennis Pardee. 1998. King's Command and Widow's Plea: Two New Hebrew Ostraca of the Biblical Period. *Near Eastern Archaeology* 61:2-13.

Braun, Roddy L. 1976. Solomon, the Chosen Temple Builder: The Significance of 1 Chronicles 22, 28, and 29 for the Theology of Chronicles. *JBL* 95:581-90.

———. 1979. Chronicles, Ezra, and Nehemiah: Theology and Literary History. Pages 52-64 in *Studies in the Historical Books of the Old Testament*. Edited by J. A. Emerton. VTSup 30. Leiden: Brill.

———. 1997. 1 Chronicles 1–9 and the Reconstruction of the History of Israel: Thoughts on the Use of Genealogical Data. Pages 92-105 in *Chronicles in the Reconstruction of the History of Israel*. Edited by Kenneth G. Hoglund and Steven L. McKenzie.

Cross, Frank Moore. 1975. A Reconstruction of the Judean Restoration. *JBL* 94:3-18; *Interp* 29:187-203.

———. 1998. *From Epic to Canon: History and Literature in Ancient Israel*. Baltimore: Johns Hopkins University Press.

Day, Peggy L. 1988. *An Adversary in Heaven: Śāṭān in the Hebrew Bible*. HSM 43. Atlanta: Scholars Press.

Dearman, J. Andrew, and M. Patrick Graham, eds. 2001. *The Land That I Will Show You: Essays on the History and Archaeology of the Ancient Near East in Honour of J. Maxwell Miller*. JSOTSup 343. Sheffield: Sheffield Academic Press.

Edelman, Diana. 1988. The Asherite Genealogy in 1 Chronicles 7:3-40. *Biblical Research* 33:13-23.

———. 2001. Did Saulide-Davidic Rivalry Resurface in Early Persian Yehud? Pages 69-91 in *The Land That I Will Show You: Essays on the History and Archaeology of the Ancient Near East in Honour of J. Maxwell Miller*. Edited by J. Andrew Dearman and M. Patrick Graham. JSOTSup 343. Sheffield: Sheffield Academic Press.

Freedman, David Noel. 1961. The Chronicler's Purpose. *CBQ* 23:436-42.

Gese, Hartmut. 1963. Zur Geschichte der Kultsänger am zweiten Tempel in *Abraham unser Vater: Juden und Christen im Gespräch über die Bibel*. Edited by O. Betz, M. Hengel, and P. Schmidt. Festschrift O. Michel. Leiden: Brill.

Graham, M. Patrick, Kenneth G. Hoglund, and Steven L. McKenzie, eds. 1997. *The Chronicler as Historian.* JSOTSup 238. Sheffield: Sheffield Academic Press.

Graham, M. Patrick, and Steven L. McKenzie, eds. 1998. *The Chronicler as Author: Studies in Text and Texture.* JSOTSup 263. Sheffield: Sheffield Academic Press.

Hanson, Paul D. 1968. The Song of Heshbon and David's *Nir. HTR* 61:297-320.

Hoglund, Kenneth G. 1997. The Chronicler as Historian: A Comparativist Perspective. Pages 19-29 in *The Chronicler as Historian.* Edited by M. Patrick Graham, Kenneth G. Hoglund, and Steven L. McKenzie. JSOTSup 238. Sheffield: Sheffield Academic Press.

Howorth, H. H. 1893. The Real Character and the Importance of the Book of 1 Esdras. *The Academy* 43:13-14, 60, 106, 174-75, 326-27, 524.

Japhet, Sara. 1968. The Supposed Common Authorship of Chronicles and Ezra-Nehemiah Investigated Anew. *VT* 18:332-72.

———. 1979. Conquest and Settlement in Chronicles. *JBL* 98:205-18.

———. 1997. *The Ideology of the Book of Chronicles and Its Place in Biblical Thought.* BEATAJ 9. 2nd edition. New York: Peter Lang.

Kalimi, Isaac. 1995. *Zur Geschichtsschreibung des Chronisten: Literarisch-historiographische Abweichungen der Chronik von ihren Paralleltexten in den Samuel- und Königsbüchern.* BZAW 226. Berlin/New York: Walter de Gruyter.

———. 1997. Was the Chronicler a Historian? Pages 73-89 in *The Chronicler as Historian.* Edited by M. Patrick Graham, Kenneth G. Hoglund, and Steven L. McKenzie. JSOTSup 238. Sheffield: Sheffield Academic Press.

Kegler, Jürgen, and Augustin Matthias. 1984. *Deutsche Synopse zum Chronistischen Geschichtswerk.* BEATAJ 33. Frankfurt am Main: Peter Lang.

Kelly, Brian E. 1996. *Retribution and Eschatology in Chronicles.* JSOTSup 211. Sheffield: Sheffield Academic Press.

Klein, Ralph W. 1966. Studies in the Greek Texts of the Chronicler. Th.D. dissertation, Harvard Divinity School.

———. 1983. Abijah's Campaign against the North (2 Chr 13)—What Were the Chronicler's Sources? *ZAW* 95:210-17.

———. 1992. Chronicles, Book of 1-2. *ABD* I:992-1002.

———. 1997. How Many in a Thousand? Pages 270-82 in *The Chronicler as Historian*. Edited by M. Patrick Graham, Kenneth G. Hoglund, and Steven L. McKenzie. JSOTSup 238. Sheffield: Sheffield Academic Press.

Knoppers, Gary N. 2001. Intermarriage, Social Complexity, and Ethnic Diversity in the Genealogy of Judah. *JBL* 120:15-30.

Knoppers, Gary N., and Paul B. Harvey, Jr. 2002. Omitted and Remaining Matters: On the Names Given to the Book of Chronicles in Antiquity. *JBL* 121:227-43.

———. 2004. Classical Historiography and the Chronicler's History: A Re-examination. *JBL* 122:627-50.

Kooij, Gerrit van der. 1991a. On the Ending of the Book of 1 Esdras. Pages 37-49 in *VII Congress of the International Organization for Septuagint and Cognate Studies: Leuven, 1989*. Edited by Charles E. Cox. SBLSCS 31. Atlanta: Scholars Press.

———. 1991b. Zur Frage des Anfangs des 1. Esrabuches. *ZAW* 103:239-52.

Lefèvre, André. 1950. Note d'exégèse sur les Généalogies des Qehatites. *RSR* 37:287-92.

Lemke, Werner E. 1963. Synoptic Studies in the Chronicler's History. Th.D. dissertation, Harvard Divinity School.

———. 1965. The Synoptic Problem in the Chronicler's History. *HTR* 58:349-63.

Mazar, Benjamin. 1954. Gath and Gittaim. *IEJ* 4:227-38.

———. 1960. Cities of the Priests and the Levites. Pages 193-205 in *Congress Volume. Oxford. 1959*. VTSup 7. Leiden: Brill.

McCarter, P. Kyle. 1980. *I Samuel*. AB 9. Garden City, N.Y.: Doubleday.

———. 1984. *II Samuel*. AB 9. Garden City, N.Y: Doubleday.

McKenzie, Steven L. 1985. *The Chronicler's Use of the Deuteronomistic History*. HSM 33. Atlanta: Scholars Press.

———. 1987. The Source for Jeroboam's Role at Shechem (1 Kgs 11:43–12:3, 12, 20). *JBL* 106:297-304.

———. 1997. *All God's Children: A Biblical Critique of Racism*. Louisville: Westminster/John Knox.

————. 1999. The Chronicler as Redactor. Pages 70-90 in *The Chronicler as Author: Studies in Text and Texture*. Edited by M. Patrick Graham and Steven L. McKenzie. JSOTSup 263. Sheffield: Sheffield Academic Press.

————. 2001. The Typology of the Davidic Covenant. Pages 152-78 in *The Land That I Will Show You: Essays on the History and Archaeology of the Ancient Near East in Honour of J. Maxwell Miller*. Edited by J. Andrew Dearman and M. Patrick Graham. JSOTSup 343. Sheffield: Sheffield Academic Press.

Mosis, Rudolf. 1973. *Untersuchungen zur Theologie des chronistischen Geschichtswerkes*. FTS 92. Freiburg: Herder.

Mowinckel, Sigmund. 1964. *Studien zu dem Buche Ezra-Nehemia I: Die Nachchronische Redaktion des Buches. Die Listen*. Oslo: Universitetsforloget.

Na'aman, Nadav. 1991. Sources and Redaction in the Chronicler's Genealogies of Asher and Benjamin. *JSOT* 49:99-111.

Noth, Martin. 1943. *Überlieferungsgeschichtliche Studien: Die sammelden und bearbeitenden Geschichtswerke im Alten Testament*. Halle: Max Niemeyer.

————. 1987. *The Chronicler's History*. Translation of Part II of Noth 1943 by H. G. M. Williamson. JSOTSup 50. Sheffield: Sheffield Academic Press.

Petersen, David L. 1976. *Late Israelite Prophecy: Studies in Deutero-Prophetic Literature and in Chronicles*. SBLMS 23. Missoula, Mont.: Scholars Press.

Pohlmann. K. -F. 1969. *Studien zum dritten Esra: Ein Beitrag zur Frage nach dem ursprünglichen Schluß des chronistischen Geschichswerkes*. FRLANT 104. Göttingen: Vandenhoeck & Ruprecht.

Polzin, Robert. 1976. *Late Biblical Hebrew: Toward an Historical Typology of Biblical Hebrew Prose*. HSM 12. Missoula, Mont.: Scholars Press.

Rad, Gerhard von. 1930. *Das Geschichtsbild des chronistischen Werkes*. Stuttgart: Kohlhammer.

————. 1966. *The Problem of the Hexateuch and Other Essays*, trans. E.W.T. Dicken. New York: McGraw-Hill.

Richter, Sandra L. 2002. *The Deuteronomistic History and the Name Theology*. BZAW 318. Berlin/New York: Walter de Gruyter.

Riley, William. 1993. *King and Cultus in Chronicles: Worship and the Reinterpretation of History.* JSOTSup 160. Sheffield: Sheffield Academic Press.

Schniedewind, William M. 1999. *Society and the Promise to David: The Reception History of 2 Samuel 7:1-17.* New York: Oxford University Press.

Talshir, David. 1988. A Reinvestigation of the Linguistic Relationship Between Chronicles and Ezra-Nehemiah. *VT* 38:165-93.

Talshir, Zipora. 1999. *I Esdras: From Origin to Translation.* SBLSCS and Cognate Studies 47. Atlanta: Society of Biblical Literature.

Throntveit, Mark A. 1982. Linguistic Analysis and the Question of Authorship in Chronicles, Ezra, and Nehemiah. *VT* 32:201-16.

———. 1987. *When Kings Speak: Royal Speech and Royal Prayer in Chronicles.* SBLDS 93. Atlanta: Scholars Press.

Torrey, C. C. 1910. *Ezra Studies.* Chicago: University of Chicago.

———. 1945. A Revised View of First Esdras. Pages 395-410 in *Louis Ginzberg Jubilee Volume.* New York: The American Academy for Jewish Research.

Trebolle Barrera, Julio C. 1992. Édition préliminaire de 4QChroniques. *RevQ* 15:523-29.

Van Seters, John. 1983. *In Search of History.* New Haven: Yale University Press.

———. 1997. The Chronicler's Account of Solomon's Temple-Building: A Continuity Theme. Pages 283-300 in *The Chronicler as Historian.* Edited by M. Patrick Graham, Kenneth G. Hoglund, and Steven L. McKenzie. JSOTSup 238. Sheffield: Sheffield Academic Press.

Weinberg, Joel. 1992. *The Citizen-Temple Community.* Translated by D. L. Smith-Christopher. JSOTSup 151. Sheffield: Sheffield Academic Press.

Welch, Adam. 1939. *The Work of the Chronicler: Its Purpose and Its Date.* Oxford: Clarendon Press.

Welten, Peter. 1973. *Geschichte und Geschichtsdarstellung in den Chronikbuchern.* WMANT 42. Neukirchener-Verlag.

Willi, Thomas. 1972. *Die Chronik als Auslegung: Untersuchungen zur literarischen Gestaltung der historischen Überlieferung Israels.* FRLANT 106. Göttingen: Vandenhoeck & Ruprecht.

Williamson, H.G.M. 1973. A Note on 1 Chronicles VII 12. *VT* 23:375-79.

———. 1977. *Israel in the Books of Chronicles.* Cambridge: Cambridge University Press.

———. 1978. The Sure Mercies of David: Subjective or Objective Genitive? *JSS* 23:31-49.

———. 1979a. The Origins of the Twenty-four Priestly Courses: A Study of 1 Chronicles xxiii-xxvii. Pages 251-68 in *Studies in the Historical Books of the Old Testament.* Edited by J. A. Emerton. VTSup 30. Leiden: Brill.

———. 1979b. Sources and Redaction in the Chronicler's Genealogy of Judah. *JBL* 98:351-59.

———. 1982a. The Death of Josiah and the Continuing Development of the Deuteronomistic History. *VT* 32:242-48.

———. 1982b. Reliving the Death of Josiah: A Reply to C. T. Begg. *VT* 37:9-15.

———. 1996. The Problem with 1 Esdras. Pages 201-16 in *After the Exile: Essays in Honour of Rex Mason.* Edited by J. Barton and D. J. Reimer. Macon: Mercer University Press.

Wilson, Robert. 1977. *Genealogy and History in the Biblical World.* Yale Near Eastern Researches 7. New Haven: Yale University Press.

COMMENTARIES

Allen, Leslie C. 1987. *1, 2 Chronicles.* The Communicator's Commentary. Waco: Word. —Aimed especially at pulpit ministers; a helpful volume by an evangelical Christian scholar.

Braun, Roddy L. 1986. *1 Chronicles.* WBC 14. Waco: Word. — Especially helpful on the genealogies in chapters 1–9 and the preparations for temple construction in chapters 22–29.

Curtis, Edward Lewis. 1910. *The Books of Chronicles.* ICC. New York: Charles Scribner's Sons. —A long-time staple for English-speaking scholars; the series as a whole focuses on history and philology.

De Vries, Simon J. *1 and 2 Chronicles.* FOTL 11. Grand Rapids: Wm. B. Eerdmans Publishing Company. —Detailed analyses of the different genres employed and produced by the Chronicler.

Dillard, Raymond B. *2 Chronicles.* WBC 15. Waco: Word. —A detailed and balanced work of scholarship; a good companion to Braun.

Hooker, Paul K. 2001. *First and Second Chronicles.* Westminster Bible Companion. Louisville: Westminster/John Knox. —A useful commentary with many perceptive insights about the theology of Chronicles.

Japhet, Sara. *I & II Chronicles: A Commentary*. OTL. Louisville: Westminster/John Knox. —An excellent commentary by one of the leaders in Chronicles research; tends to be conservative on questions of authorship and dating.

Knoppers, Gary N. 2004. *I Chronicles*. AB. Garden City: Doubleday. —The latest and most detailed commentary on 1 Chronicles with meticulous text-critical notes.

Myers, Jacob M. *I Chronicles and II Chronicles*. 1965. AB. Garden City: Doubleday. —A two-volume entry in one of the leading commentary series; now largely replaced by Knoppers's contribution to the same series.

Rothstein, J. Wilhelm, and Johannes Hänel. 1927. *Kommentar zum ersten Buch der Chronik*. KAT 18, Leipzig: D. Werner Scholl. —A classic work for Chronicles scholarship in one of the leading German series.

Rudolph, Wilhelm. 1955. *Chronikbücher*. HAT 21. Tübingen: Mohr. —A groundbreaking work of scholarship on Chronicles in its day that still contains valuable insights.

Tuell, Steven S. 2001. *First and Second Chronicles*. Interpretation: A Bible Commentary for Teaching and Preaching. Louisville: John Knox. —Focuses on the application of Chronicles' teachings for modern Christians.

Williamson, H. G. M. 1982. *1 and 2 Chronicles*. NCB. Grand Rapids: Wm. B. Eerdmans Publishing Company. —A handy, yet thorough work covering both 1 and 2 Chronicles by one of the principal leaders in Chronicles scholarship.

FOR FURTHER STUDY

The following two books are useful for anyone wishing to read Chronicles alongside its parallels to other biblical materials.

Endres, John C., et al., eds. *Chronicles and Its Synoptic Parallels in Samuel, Kings, and Related Biblical Texts*. Collegeville, Minn.: Liturgical.—Incorporates translations of the editors and contributors.

Newsome, James D. Jr., ed. 1986. *A Synoptic Harmony of Samuel, Kings, and Chronicles with Related Passages from Psalms, Isaiah, Jeremiah, and Ezra.* Grand Rapids: Baker. —Based on the Revised Standard Version.